D1191818

DEVELOPING LEADERSHIP SKILLS

DEVELOPING LEADERSHIP SKILLS
A Source Book for Librarians

Rosie L. Albritton

Assistant to the Director of Libraries
University of Missouri-Columbia

and

Thomas W. Shaughnessy

University Librarian
University of Minnesota

1990
LIBRARIES UNLIMITED, INC.
Englewood, Colorado

Copyright © 1990 Libraries Unlimited, Inc.
All Rights Reserved
Printed in the United States of America

LIBRARIES UNLIMITED, INC.
P.O. Box 3988
Englewood, Colorado 80155-3988

Library of Congress Cataloging-in-Publication Data

Albritton, Rosie L.
　　Developing leadership skills : a source book for librarians /
　Rosie L. Albritton and Thomas W. Shaughnessy.
　　xxii, 300 p. 17x25 cm.
　　Includes bibliographical references.
　　ISBN 0-87287-577-6
　　1. Library administrators--Training of.　2. Library
administrators--Psychology.　3. Library personnel management.
4. Library administration.　5. Leadership.　I. Shaughnessy, Thomas
W. (Thomas William)　II. Title.
Z682.4.A34A42　　1989
023'.4--dc20　　　　　　　　　　　　　　　　　　　　89-13529
　　　　　　　　　　　　　　　　　　　　　　　　　　　CIP

In Memory of My Parents

who fostered the achievement motive, instilled the lingering values, and provided the unwaivering encouragement to pursue *positive leadership challenges*.

R.L.A.

Contents

PART I
Leadership in Organizations: Implementing
Theories, Models, and Styles

PART V
Libraries, Technology, and Change: The Leadership Challenge

PART VI
Exercises and Inventories

Foreword

Leadership, or the lack of it, is one of the most discussed topics in the library community today. Turnover in the ranks of library directors is high, and university officers are concerned about the difficulty they have in identifying and recruiting excellent candidates. Simultaneously, library administrators report a similar difficulty in recruiting middle- and upper-level managers who can successfully balance the many demands of the job.

Response to the leadership dilemma varies widely. Some librarians point to the failure of library schools; some educators blame the hierarchical structure and uninteresting jobs in research libraries. The librarians of the University of Missouri-Columbia, however, were not satisfied with pointing fingers. They decided to respond directly and constructively to the need for strengthening library leadership.

This sourcebook grew out of a grant awarded to the University of Missouri-Columbia by the Council on Library Resources (CLR). The Internships for Recent Graduates program was developed to encourage libraries to create opportunities for their newest professional staff members. CLR offered the grant program because of its conviction that libraries have an obligation to continue the professional education of recent graduates of MLS programs who are hired for positions in research libraries. The Council on Library Resources devised the library-based internships after a series of meetings with library directors and library school deans. In these meetings, the deans asserted that the best graduates were being recruited by special libraries. The jobs offered by large academic libraries, they said, were too narrowly focused and lacked appeal for the enterprising students who sought autonomy and creativity in their first professional positions. CLR offered grants to up to five research libraries to test new approaches to internships that would concentrate more on the substantive foundations of library service and information systems, thereby expanding the professional horizons of new members of the research library staff. Libraries were encouraged to develop imaginative programs that would accomplish the following objectives:

1. Introduce participants to the full range of university research activity, with key faculty members describing their work and related information needs. The interns would learn about differences in research methodology and information requirements among the disciplines.

2. Provide an introduction to the management and "politics" of the university, involving key university administrative officers.

3. Develop teaching skills, on the assumption that librarians have teaching obligations.

4. Relate professional education to operating situations, perhaps by developing a series of case studies describing the policy formation process in such areas as pricing library services, installing online catalogs, formulating a remote storage strategy, implementing a preservation program, planning for space, and linking collecting practices to membership in consortia.

5. Stimulate research interests and activity in each individual's own area of specialization.

The University of Missouri-Columbia responded with its proposal for an internship designated as the Intern-Scholar Program, which had a twofold purpose: (1) to enable junior librarians to develop new skills, gain insight into the environment of American higher education, and achieve a broader understanding of research library management and operations; and (2) to provide cooperating middle- and senior-level librarians with opportunities to extend their participation in professional staff development and share library management skills as mentors to the new professionals. The leadership program consisted of in-house seminars and discussion groups on topics relevant to future library leadership, conducted by senior-level librarians, visiting scholars, and practitioners; academic coursework in pertinent disciplines such as human resources management, educational research, statistics, and research methods; and a semester-long internship with one of the university's academic officers.

This sourcebook was assembled as a self-instructional tool for the interns because the project leaders believed personal growth and development must necessarily accompany professional development. The readings, instruments, and exercises contained here contributed significantly to the success of the University of Missouri-Columbia's Intern-Scholar Program. It is gratifying to us at CLR that this revised edition of the "Resource Notebook" is now being offered as a sourcebook to other librarians who are interested in expanding leadership skills in the profession.

This book would not have been approved by Melvil Dewey for use in the first library school. Dewey and most of his colleagues believed that library education should be designed for those who would do the routine work; those who would lead library organizations would be men born to the task. Fortunately, views on leadership have changed dramatically after a century, and most librarians agree that individuals can be trained or, indeed, can train themselves to be better leaders. This sourcebook will help those who want to try.

Deanna Marcum
Vice President
Council on Library Resources

Preface

This book is one result of an innovative staff development program developed at the University of Missouri-Columbia (UMC) Libraries under the sponsorship of the Council on Library Resources. It was in 1984 that the UMC Libraries began to prepare for the change to an online catalog and circulation system, and some very successful staff development in the area of computer literacy was conducted at that time. But following the introduction of the Libraries' online systems, it became clear that a highly structured staff development program should be continued, particularly in the areas of managerial and leadership development. In 1986, funds were sought from CLR to implement a program, which came to be called the CLR Intern-Scholar Program, which would attempt to develop the leadership potential of eight relatively inexperienced librarians.

The program consisted of several important elements: structured internships with various campus administrators, formal course work, seminars with distinguished scholars and nationally known librarians, biweekly seminars with UMC library administrators, interactions with designated mentors, and participation in a variety of small group exercises. The project's coordinators, Rosie L. Albritton, Assistant to the Director of Libraries, and Thomas W. Shaughnessy (at that time, UMC Director of Libraries), quickly saw the Intern-Scholars' need for a workbook of readings and exercises which would be the basis for seminar discussions. The workbook came to be known as the Intern-Scholar "Resource Notebook," and went through several revisions as some articles were found to be more useful than others. However, the basic format or structure of the book remained unchanged.

This volume, therefore, represents one outcome from the UMC Libraries' staff development project. However, the authors hope that the most significant and lasting outcome will be the growth and development which seems to have occurred in the program's participants.

Thomas W. Shaughnessy

Acknowledgments

We wish to thank all of the participants (interns, mentors, campus administrators, and others) in the CLR Intern-Scholar Program. Especially the eight librarians who came to be known as the Intern-Scholars: Nancy Myers, Isabel Rife, Ruth Riley, Paula Roper, Catherine Seago, Martha Shirky, Regina Sinclair, and Shelley Worden. Without your commitment, support, and enthusiasm, the program and this book would not have been realized. We extend our sincere thanks and gratitude.

Special recognition is given to Lori Campbell, Special Assistant and Secretary to the Assistant-to-the-Director of Libraries, who completed her MLS degree here at Missouri during the course of the book project, and who assisted in all stages of the preparation of the manuscript — from locating information on copyright holders and publishers, to organizing and coordinating all phases of the permissions requests, to conducting online database searches, and literature reviews, to photocopying, locating articles and books, and preparing numerous drafts and revisions of several parts of the book. Your patience, assistance, and expertise contributed greatly to this project.

Appreciation is also extended to Kyung Ae Park, Graduate Research Assistant to the Assistant-to-the-Director, and a Doctoral candidate in Educational and Counseling Psychology, who managed the project office, coordinated the workflow between this project and other research projects, and spent many hours retrieving and reviewing articles and books. Your insight, encouragement, and support played an integral role throughout the project, and will always be remembered.

Special thanks are also due to Marilyn Schappert, Administrative Assistant to the Director of Libraries, who prepared several drafts of various sections of this book; and to Lori Turner, an undergraduate student at Missouri, who served as a student-assistant and retrieved articles and performed many other tasks.

We owe a special debt of gratitude to our families for their support, understanding, and many sacrifices during the preparation of this book. We could not have met this challenge without the patience, cooperation and love of our children, Malcolm, Milton "Jody" Jr., and Mark; our spouses, Milton and Marlene; and other supportive relatives, such as Uncle Booker. We extend a grateful and appreciative acknowledgment.

To the staff of the University of Missouri-Columbia Libraries who assisted in any way to making this project a success, a sincere thank you. A special note of thanks is extended to members of the Administrative Offices and the Security Staff.

Finally, to the Council on Library Resources and Deanna Marcum, Vice President of CLR, thank you for your vision of the direction that you believe library leadership development and management training should be moving. Your support of the Intern-Scholar Program over the past three years is gratefully acknowledged.

This book is co-edited and was truly a collaborative effort; we could not have done it without each other; and we could not have done it without everyone mentioned above, and more. They made this book possible.

Introduction

The Authority of Management can be delegated. The responsibility of leadership cannot.

—Ken Schatz
Management Consultant

This book was written for librarians who wish to enhance their leadership potential and skills. Today's library manager manages in open systems, taking on ad hoc and lateral responsibilities that are not listed on the organization chart. Nevertheless, those responsibilities are often as important as the manager's functional responsibilities. At every level of management, complexities abound and opportunities emerge that are not part of a librarian's frame of reference. Thus, we need a frame of reference—a model that describes the new skills needed to deal with the new management realities. This new frame of reference is needed by librarians and managers at every level of the organization. The material presented in this book is addressed to librarians at all levels of management, and it is intended to serve as a self-instructional sourcebook for the individual reader or as a text for leadership training groups and formal courses. The articles and excerpts are from the fields of human resources management, organizational theory and behavior, training and development, organizational development, human relations training, and library and information science.

When a librarian becomes a manager, even though much can be done to enhance his or her leadership abilities through developmental programs, the manager-librarian is generally left to his or her resourcefulness to cultivate leadership qualities. Most libraries, as is true of other organizations, do not have developmental programs for leaders because traits and skills which comprise leadership functions have not been clearly specified and are not adequately understood. The core of effective management is effective leadership. Defining leadership involves an analysis both of what a leader *is* (i.e., personal attributes) and of what a leader *does* under particular circumstances.

Researchers and writers have offered many different definitions of leadership. For the purposes of this book, *leadership* is viewed functionally, as a process, and is associated with a learnable set of behavioral practices. These behaviors usually reinforce the security of a group and help bring about integration of the diverse elements of the group. Leadership always functions in relation to other persons and results in a relationship between the leader and followers.

There is evidence throughout the literature that leadership can be taught, learned, and developed. Leadership is not the private reserve of a few charismatic men and women, but a process, an evolution, that represents a combination of skills, experiences, knowledge, and intuitive understandings. This book will emphasize behavioral aspects as the critical features of leadership and support the position that these behavioral skills can be learned. We will not include informal leadership or political leadership strategies, but will focus on the *leadership functions* and *behavioral parts* of the leadership act as related to the *process of organizational management*; an approach to leadership that we will refer to as the *Functional Model of Managerial Leadership*.

Ideas and concepts for the development of a functional model of managerial leadership were drawn from the following works: *The Leader-Manager*, by William D. Hitt; *The Leadership Challenge*, by James Kouzes and Barry Z. Posner; *Positive Management Practices*, by Arthur C. Beck and Ellis D. Hillmar; and *Leaders: The Strategies for Taking Charge*, by Warren Bennis and Burt Nanus. All of these authors focus on behavioral functions of leadership which they believe can be learned and developed, and on the significance of self-management, the deployment of self, positive self-regard, self-development, and self-actualization as key aspects in developing leadership potential.

The functional approach to leadership as described by Hitt can be applied to leadership development in libraries.[1] The model is based on the premise that every manager has a certain amount of leadership potential and that this potential can be further developed. This approach has four core characteristics: (1) having a *clear vision* of what the organization (or department or group) might become, (2) the ability *to communicate* the vision to others, (3) the ability *to motivate* others to work toward the vision, and (4) the ability to *work the system* to get things done. These four characteristics are operationalized through eight basic functions that focus on what leaders actually do: (1) creating the vision, (2) developing the team, (3) clarifying values, (4) positioning, (5) communicating, (6) empowering, (7) coaching, and (8) measuring. By focusing on a core set of functions, we are able to take a systematic approach to the selection and development of potential library leaders. Leadership, as defined above, requires awareness and skills, something anyone can develop.

In addition to the core characteristics and functions, the leadership framework proposed in this book also includes the essential element of leadership development: *self-understanding skills*. This concept includes introspective skills as well as guidelines with which a leader understands both him or herself and employees. For a leader, self-understanding is critical. Kouzes and Posner explained the connection between leadership development and self-development:

> The mastery of the art of leadership comes with the mastery of self. Ultimately, leadership development is a process of self-development. The quest for leadership is first an inner quest to discover who you are. Through self-development comes the confidence needed to lead. Self-confidence is really awareness of and faith in your own powers. These powers become clear and strong only as you work to identify and develop them.[2]

In his study of ninety corporate and public sector leaders, Warren Bennis found the leaders able to recognize strengths and compensate for weaknesses.[3] They were eager to get feedback on their performance. In fact, Bennis's fourth major mark of leaders was "knowing one's skills and deploying them effectively." Bennis's leaders knew themselves and seemed responsible for their own evolution.

Just as in Bennis's interviews, Noel Tichy found that transformational leaders have an amazing appetite for continuous self-learning and development.[4] To better understand themselves, then, leaders need a frame of reference with which to understand their needs, drives, and judgment.

The design and theme of this book support the self-development position, since it is from a sense of self that leadership behaviors emerge. Self-confidence and assertion — natural partners to effective management—come from both experience and personal development. Personal development can be greatly assisted by developmental programs which nurture the participant's self-awareness and understanding of his or her relationship style to others. The acceptance of one's self, which is at the core of courageous leadership, comes primarily through self-understanding and through developmental programs which are grounded in a sound behavioral framework.

The first five parts of this book are based on the developmental model of leadership training that emphasizes self-development, self-awareness, and the functional characteristics of leadership, as described above. The purpose of the developmental approach is to promote effective interpersonal functioning in managers. The book is organized and designed to enable librarians, regardless of their roles in an organization, to assess where they are with respect to leadership ability, and then to take measures to improve their effectiveness as professionals. Each of the five parts is introduced by a brief essay that discusses the nature of the readings included and the relationship of that part to the overall model of leadership development.

Part I, "Leadership in Organizations," defines leadership, looks at the myths and challenges of leadership, and discusses the theoretical implications of the principles and concepts of various leadership models and their application to library management. Part II, "Self-Awareness," defines self-concept and self-esteem; looks at assertion, intuition, introspection, creativity, innovation and the importance of feedback; and suggests ways to learn what others think, improve self-concept, work to change and learn to accept, and understand oneself as a leader. Part III, "Self-Development," examines communication skills, time management, stress management, goal setting, problem solving, listening, and ethics. Part IV, "Professional Growth and Development," discusses career and life-stages planning, plateaus at mid-career, burnout, mentoring relationships, well-being, motivation, and career development techniques related to leadership development; this part also examines group purposes and behavior, relational needs, why people join groups, advantages and disadvantages of groups, working with groups, managing conflicts, and consensus building. Part V, "Libraries, Technology and Change," examines the complexities and problems that library leaders must face in managing libraries in a rapidly changing era, characterized by an information explosion and advanced technology. Part VI, "Exercises and Inventories," includes ten self-assessment instruments, designated as Appendixes A-J. These questionnaires, checklists, exercises, and inventories were selected to provide readers with information concerning their own level of development. This is in keeping with the central thesis of this book, namely, that leadership development depends upon a deep understanding of one's strengths, weaknesses, abilities, and motivations. At the end of the introduction to each part are lists of additional readings that will add to the study of the topics presented.

This book should prove to be especially useful to those engaged in personnel administration, library education, staff development, and continuing education programs, as well as to students and librarians who aspire to take on leadership responsibility. We hope it will be read by a wide variety of librarians—those who have already assumed leadership roles and those who may never have thought of themselves as leaders. This sourcebook is not only a guide for leaders, but also a call to leadership, a challenge for librarians to use and develop their skills and abilities to serve, lead, and become effective leader-managers.

One final note: in this book, readers may note some inconsistencies in spelling, usage, and referencing styles. These differences are due to the nature of these readings, many taken from previously published articles and written by a variety of authors.

Rosie Albritton

NOTES

[1]William D. Hitt, *The Leader-Manager* (Columbus, Ohio: Battelle, 1988).

[2]James M. Kouzes and Barry Z. Posner, *The Leadership Challenge* (San Francisco: Jossey-Bass, 1988), 298.

[3]Warren Bennis and Burt Nanus, *Leaders: The Strategies for Taking Charge* (New York: Harper & Row, 1985).

[4]Noel Tichy and David Rich, "The Leadership Challenge: A Call for the Transformational Leader," *Sloan Management Review* (Fall 1984): 59-73.

REFERENCES

Beck, Arthur C., and Ellis D. Hillmar. *Positive Management Practices*. San Francisco: Jossey-Bass, 1986.

Contributors

Judith M. Bardwick
Management Consultant
In-Transitions, Inc.
La Jolla, California

Patricia Battin
President, Commission on Preservation
    and Access
1785 Massachusetts Ave., N.W.
Washington, D.C.

Arthur C. Beck
Associate Professor of Organization
    Development
Institute for Business and Community
    Development
University of Richmond
Richmond, Virginia

Orlando C. Behling
Department of Management
Bowling Green State University
Bowling Green, Ohio

Warren Bennis
Professor of Business Administration
University of Southern California
Los Angeles, California

Ellen Bernstein
Managing Partner
The Chicago Consulting Group, Ltd.
Chicago, Illinois

Larry Earl Bone (deceased Spring 1989)
Director of Libraries and Professor
Mercy College
Dobbs Ferry, New York

Charles Bunge
Professor
School of Library and Information
    Studies
University of Wisconsin—Madison

Marsha A. Burruss-Ballard
Associate Director
Marshall Brooks Library
Principia College
Elsah, Illinois

Keith M. Cottam
Director of Libraries
University of Wyoming
Laramie, Wyoming

Richard M. Dougherty
Professor
School of Information and Library
    Studies
University of Michigan
Ann Arbor, Michigan

Robin N. Downes
Director of Libraries
University of Houston, Texas

Miriam A. Drake
Director of Libraries
Georgia Institute of Technology
Atlanta, Georgia

Lee Edson
Freelance Writer and Journalist
    specializing in science and medicine
Stamford, Connecticut

Helen M. Gothberg
Associate Professor
Graduate Library School
University of Arizona, Tucson

Norman Hill
Department of Organizational Behavior
Brigham Young University
Provo, Utah

Ellis D. Hillmar
Associate Professor of Organization
    Development
Institute for Business and Community
    Development
University of Richmond
Richmond, Virginia

Michael J. Kruger
Human Resources Development Specialist
U.S. Government
Washington, D.C.

Judy Labovitz
Manager
Cetus Information Service
Cetus Corporation
Emoryville, California

John J. Leach
President
JL Consulting
Wilmette, Illinois
    and faculty member
Institute of Industrial Relations
Loyola University
Chicago, Illinois

Richard I. Lester
Director, Educational Plans and
    Programs
Leadership and Management
    Development Center
Air University
Maxwell AFB, Alabama

Daniel J. Levinson
Professor of Psychology
Department of Psychiatry
Yale University
New Haven, Connecticut

Gregory D. May
President
Gregory May and Associates
Sacramento, California

Donald E. Riggs
University Librarian
Arizona State University
Tempe, Arizona

Burt K. Scanlan
Professor of Management
College of Business Administration
University of Oklahoma
Norman, Oklahoma

Chester A. Schriesheim
Department of General Business
University of Miami
Coral Gables, Florida

Thomas W. Shaughnessy
Director of Libraries
University of Minnesota
Minneapolis, Minnesota

Meryl Swanigan
Manager
Information Research Center
Atlantic Richfield Co.
Los Angeles, California

James M. Tolliver
Department of Administration
University of New Brunswick
Fredericton, N.B., Canada

Celia Wall
Reference Librarian and Assistant
    Professor
Murray State University Libraries
    Kentucky

Leadership in Organizations
Implementing Theories, Models, and Styles

Introduction

Qualities of leadership, especially in a democracy and in democratic institutions, can and should be developed by as many as possible. They can be taught. Leadership should exist not only at the top, but at all levels if an institution is to thrive. In professions, especially, there should be no hierarchical approach to leadership. All should be leaders.

— Larry Earl Bone
"The Leadership Connection"
Library Journal, 1981

The purpose of part I is to explore definitions, theories, and myths of leadership; and to examine the implication of the principles and concepts of various leadership models and their application to library management. The core characteristics and behavioral functions of the functional model of managerial leadership are described in detail, to demonstrate how leadership potential can be developed and enhanced.

Leadership is often defined as the process of directing the behavior of others toward the accomplishment of some objective. This definition corresponds with the theme that leadership is getting things accomplished through people. However, according to Certo, leading is not the same as managing.[1] Although some managers are leaders and some leaders are managers, leading and managing are not identical activities. Management consists of an assessment of a situation and the systematic selection of goals and purposes; the systematic development of strategies to achieve these goals; acquiring the required resources; the organization, direction, and control of the activities required to attain the selected purposes; and the motivating and rewarding of people to do the work. Leadership, on the other hand, is a subset of management. Management is much broader in scope than leading and focuses on behavioral as well as nonbehavioral issues. Leading emphasizes mainly behavioral issues.

When we talk about leadership we are thus talking about a situation in which a person is inducing another person or a group of persons to produce some output or specific performance. There are three factors, as described by Massie and Douglas, that determine the leadership role: the person, the position, and the situation.[2] Leadership involves persons. Leadership operates from some organizational position. The act of leadership occurs within a specific situation. Leadership takes place when these three factors all interact: person, position, and situation.

There is no magic formula, however, for bringing about this dynamic interaction and becoming an effective leader. Management is no easy job and the leadership function of a manager frequently requires many difficult decisions. Libraries, as well as other complex organizations, would greatly benefit if someone could devise a formula for the early identification of effective leadership and managerial success, but as of this writing, no such formula exists. In a rapidly changing environment, where the future promises an acceleration of this change, there is a great need for leadership at all levels within the organization. For this reason, there is a need to understand the essence of leadership. What is leadership? What are the key attributes of leadership? What is it that leaders actually do? Can leadership be learned? The answers to these questions would be of considerable value in selecting potential leaders, in educating and training managers to become effective leaders, and in designing a self-development program for oneself. Thus, the central theme of this chapter is: What constitutes effective leadership in organizations and how can it be developed?

From a historical viewpoint, there have been four different approaches to the study of leadership: the great man theory, the trait approach, leadership styles, and situational leadership. Each of these four approaches provides valuable information for studying leadership in general, but fails to provide a useful and practicable model of effective leadership. In order to describe what leaders actually do, we need, as Hitt proposes, a generalizable model that will aid us in the selection and development of potential leaders.[3]

Hitt suggests that such a model of leadership would not only describe what leaders actually do, but also satisfy three criteria. First, the model must define leadership in terms of *results achieved*—accomplishment of ends, results, objectives. Second, the model must deal with *how* the results were achieved. Third, the model must explain the *time frame*.[4] Hitt proposes a functional model of leadership based on Bennis and Nanus's definition of leadership: "Leadership is what gives an organization its vision, its ability to translate the vision into reality."[5]

A key ingredient in Hitt's model is the type of leader who is best able to get things done, the *transforming leader*. The principal theme of transforming leadership, for Hitt, is lifting people into their better selves. He cites Bass to explain three ways in which the transforming leader motivates followers: (1) by raising their level of consciousness, (2) by getting them to transcend their self-interests. and (3) by raising their need level on Maslow's hierarchy.[6]

Begin with these core characteristics of leadership, having (1) a clear vision of what the organization might become, (2) the ability to communicate the vision to others, (3) the ability to motivate others to work toward the vision, and (4) the ability to "work the system" to get things done. Hitt developed a functional model of effective leadership with eight basic functions of leadership:

1. *Creating the vision*: constructing a crystal-clear mental picture of what the group should become and then transmitting this vision to the minds of others.

2. *Developing the team*: developing a team of highly qualified people who are jointly responsible for achieving the group's goals.

3. *Clarifying the values*: identifying the organizational values and communicating these values through words and actions.

4. *Positioning*: developing an effective strategy for moving the group from its present position toward the vision.

5. *Communicating*: achieving a common understanding with others by using all modes of communication effectively.

6. *Empowering*: motivating others by raising them to their "better selves."

7. *Coaching*: helping others develop the skills needed for achieving excellence.

8. *Measuring*: identifying the critical success factors associated with the group's operation and gauging progress on the basis of these factors.[7]

With this model we are focusing on what leaders *actually do*. By focusing on the core set of functions described above, we are able to take a systematic approach to the selection and development of potential leaders. While these functions may not account for every aspect of a leader's job, they do account for a large portion of it. According to the model's definition, this means that a person who is effective in carrying out these eight functions is very likely to be an effective leader.

In answer to the question, "Are leaders born or made?" we again turn to Hitt's functional model. Hitt proposes that the functional approach to leadership should be guided by the following principles:

> *Effective leadership should be viewed in terms of a continuum.* If we view effective leadership as following along a 10-point scale, with "10" being high and "1" being low, each one of us would fall someplace along this continuum. But it is important to note that any one of us might be, say, an "8" in one situation but only a "4" in another.[8]

Therefore, if we assume that effective leadership is on a continuum, then we can state that practically everyone has a *certain amount* of leadership potential. This potential can be developed and enhanced. The functional approach to leadership allows us to demonstrate that leadership can be learned.

The selections in this chapter reflect the characteristics of the functional approach to leadership. The readings cover both the historical perspective, by reviewing major approaches to the subject of leadership, and the more contemporary and emerging views of the leader's role as one of a change agent within a functional model.

Schriesheim, Tolliver, and Behling provide an overview of the direction leadership research has taken, and summarize various leadership models and theories found in the literature. The differences between leadership and management are also discussed in order to clarify that leadership is a specific process related to interpersonal interactions. The authors discuss implications for organizations as well as individual managers, along with limitations and shortcomings of certain approaches to leadership.

When perseverance and a willingness to learn are present, leadership skills can be learned. Lester offers support for the theory that leaders can be developed. After defining leadership as the "art of influencing and directing people in a manner that wins their obedience, confidence, respect and enthusiastic cooperation in achieving a common objective," he suggests that people can develop and learn leadership just as they learn any other complex skill. Guidelines are listed for planning leadership training and development. Leadership styles and key characteristics of good leaders are presented to help readers develop the basics of their own leadership style.

After five years of research, Bennis reports how he identified the four competencies cited earlier as key components of Hitt's functional leadership model. His research goal was to determine what makes real leaders (as opposed to effective managers) tick. He interviewed ninety outstanding leaders and their subordinates. After several years of observation and conversation, Bennis defined four competencies evident to some extent in every member of the group: management of attention, management of meaning, management of trust, and management of self. He concluded that empowerment is the collective effect of leadership. In organizations with effective leaders, empowerment is most evident in four themes: people feel significant, learning and competence matter, people are part of a community, and work is exciting.

From the field of library education, Larry Bone ponders the following questions: Is it possible to do something in a professional program to further leadership? Could we help our students see the need and the opportunity for quality leadership in librarianship? Would we rest the case for effective administration on a set of management principles alone, or would we plant the seed from which the capacity for leadership in our students might grow? For Bone, the "Leadership Connection" is leadership plus management. He expresses concern that students, in their pursuit of technical proficiency, could miss the connection between leadership and the possession of management skills, as well as the vacuum created when that connection is absent. Bone further rejects the idea that leaders are only born, or that leadership is reserved for the few, and presents a list of qualities that leaders should possess: vision, integrity, courage, judgment, understanding, persuasion, planning, optimism, and flexibility. In citing each quality, he explains how a library leader would apply it to library issues. Finally, his closing proposition appropriately mirrors the core concepts of our leadership model and the strongest point that we want to communicate in this book: "Qualities of leadership, especially in a democracy and in democratic institutions, can and should be developed by as many as possible. They can be taught. Leadership should exist not only at the top, but at all levels if an institution is to thrive. In professions, especially, there should be no hierarchical approach to leadership. All should be leaders."

Leadership in organizations is essentially "managerial leadership." Effective leaders have managerial skills. Over the past few decades there has been a changing picture of what an effective organizational leader should be. An effective leader is someone who does things *with* people, not alone. This leader is not so much an authority figure or pseudo-father, but rather a change agent. The last reading, by Scanlan, looks at some of the basic ingredients of results-oriented and people-oriented leadership, and suggests that after learning the various frameworks of the leadership function we may tend to lose sight of these elements of effective leadership. He outlines the following basics: let people know what is expected, establish and maintain high performance expectations, let people know where they stand, employ broad-based communication, create a supportive climate, learn how to delegate, and establish viable appraisal and coaching programs.

Appendixes A and B include inventories related to the topics presented in part I. These exercises are designed to assist the reader in assessing leadership potential, skills, and performance, and in planning further development of effective leadership qualities and characteristics. The assessment exercises are the "Leadership Potential" survey, and the "Inventory of Transformational Management Skills". Instructions are provided for completing these instruments, scoring, and making some interpretation of the results.

In this part the first part of the functional model of managerial leadership is explored in detail as we describe the four core characteristics of the functional approach, the eight functions of leadership, and the dynamic interaction of the three determinants of leadership. The selections (readings and inventories) should help readers define effective leadership, determine where they are on the leadership continuum, and make plans for further development of leadership potential.

NOTES

[1]Samuel C. Certo, *Principles of Modern Management: Functions and Systems* (Dubuque, Iowa: Wm. C. Brown Co., 1980).

[2]J. L. Massie and J. Douglas, *Managing: A Contemporary Introduction* (Englewood Cliffs, N.J.: Prentice-Hall, 1973).

[3]William D. Hitt, *The Leader-Manager* (Columbus, Ohio: Battelle, 1988).

[4]Ibid.

[5]Warren Bennis and Burt Nanus, *Leaders: The Strategies for Taking Charge* (New York: Harper & Row, 1985).

[6]Bernard Bass, "Leadership: Good, Better, Best," *Organizational Dynamics* 13 (Winter 1985): 26-40.

[7]Hitt, *The Leader-Manager*, 11-12.

[8]Ibid., 15.

ADDITIONAL READINGS

Allcorn, Seth. "Leadership Styles: The Psychological Picture." *Personnel* 65 (April 1988): 46-54.

Anderson, Dorothy J. "Comparative Career Profiles of Academic Librarians: Are Leaders Different?" *The Journal of Academic Librarianship* 10 (January 1985): 326-32.

Bellavita, Christopher. "The Organization of Leadership." *The Bureaucrat* 15 (Fall 1986): 13-16.

Berlew, David E. "Leadership and Organizational Excitement." *California Management Review* 17 (Winter 1974): 21-30.

Bittel, Lester R. *Leadership: The Key to Management Success.* New York: Franklin Watts, 1984.

Brache, Alan. "Seven Prevailing Myths about Leadership." *Training and Development Journal* 37 (June 1983): 120-26.

Bradford, David L., and Allan R. Cohen. *Managing for Excellence.* New York: John Wiley, 1984.

Cribbin, James J. *Leadership: Strategies for Organizational Effectiveness.* New York: AMACOM, 1981.

Dragon, Andrea C. "Leader Behavior in Changing Libraries." *Library Research* 1 (Spring 1979): 53-66.

Frew, David R. "Leadership and Followership." *Personnel Journal* (February 1977): 90-97.

Gardner, John W. "The Tasks of Leadership, Part I: Getting Things Moving." *Personnel* 63 (October 1986): 20-27.

_____. "The Tasks of Leadership, Part II: Setting an Example." *Personnel* 63 (November 1986): 41-46.

Green, Thad B., Jay T. Knippen, and Joyce P. Vincelette. "The Practice of Management: Knowledge vs. Skills." *Training and Development Journal* 39 (July 1985): 56-58.

Hollander, Edwin P., and Jan Yoder. "Some Issues in Comparing Women and Men as Leaders." *Basic & Applied Social Psychology* 1 (September 1980): 267-80.

Kouzes, James M., and Barry Z. Posner. "The Leadership Challenge." *Success* 35 (April 1988): 68-69.

Lawrie, John. "What Is Effective Leadership?" *Management Solutions* 32 (May 1987): 25-30.

Marcum, Deanna. "Management Training for Research Librarianship." In *Advances in Library Administration and Organization*, Vol. 2, 1-19. Greenwich, Conn.: JAI Press, 1983.

Martell, Charles. "Administration: Which Way — Traditional Practice or Modern Theory." *College & Research Libraries* 33 (March 1972): 104-12.

Plachy, Roger J. "Leading vs. Managing: A Guide to Some Crucial Distinctions." *Management Review* 70 (September 1981): 58-61.

Sashkin, Marshall. "True Vision in Leadership." *Training and Development Journal* 40 (May 1986): 58-61.

Schoonover, Stephen C., and Murray M. Dalziel. "Developing Leadership for Change." *Management Review* (July 1986): 55-60.

Tichy, Noel M., and Mary Anne Devanna. "The Transformational Leader." *Training and Development Journal* 40 (July 1986): 27-32.

Tichy, Noel M., and David O. Ulrich. "SMR Forum: The Leadership Challenge — A Call for the Transformational Leader." *Sloan Management Review* 26 (Fall 1984): 59-73.

Wagel, William H. "Leadership Training for a New Way of Managing." *Personnel* (December 1987): 4-8.

Zaleznik, Abraham. "Managers and Leaders: Are They Different?" *Harvard Business Review* 55 (May/June 1977): 67-78.

CHAPTER 1

Leadership Theory
Some Implications for Managers
Chester A. Schriesheim, James M. Tolliver, and Orlando C. Behling

In the past seventy years more than 3,000 leadership studies have been conducted and dozens of leadership models and theories have been proposed.[1] Yet, a practicing manager who reads this literature seeking an effective solution to supervisory problems will rapidly become disenchanted. Although we have access to an overwhelming volume of leadership theory and research, few guidelines exist which are of use to a practitioner. Nevertheless, interest in leadership—and in those qualities which separate a successful leader from an unsuccessful one—remains unabated. In almost any book dealing with management one will find some discussion of leadership. In any company library there are numerous volumes entitled "Increasing Leadership Effectiveness," "Successful Leadership," or "How to Lead." Typical management development programs conducted within work organizations and universities usually deal with some aspect of leadership. This intensity and duration of writing on the subject and the sums spent annually on leadership training indicate that practicing managers and academicians consider good leadership essential to organizational success.

What is meant by leadership, let alone *good* leadership? Many definitions have been proposed, and it seems that most are careful to separate management from leadership. This distinction sometimes becomes blurred in everyday conversations. The first term, *management*, includes those processes, both mental and physical, which result in other people executing prescribed formal duties for organizational goal attainment. It deals mainly with planning, organizing, and controlling the work of other people to achieve organizational goals.[2] This definition usually includes those aspects of managers' jobs, such as monitoring and controlling resources, which are sometimes ignored in current conceptualizations of leadership. *Leadership*, on the other hand, is a more restricted type of managerial activity, focusing on the interpersonal interactions between a leader and one or more subordinates, with the purpose of increasing organizational effectiveness.[3] In this view, leadership is a social influence process in which the leader seeks the voluntary participation of subordinates in an effort to reach organizational objectives. The key idea highlighted by a number of authors is that the subordinate's participation is voluntary.[4] This implies that the leader has brought about some change in the way subordinates want to behave. Leadership, consequently, is not only a specific process (more so than management), but also is undoubtedly political in nature. The political aspect of leadership has been discussed elsewhere, so at this

Reprinted with permission from *MSU Business Topics* 26:34−40 (Summer 1978).

point it suffices to note that a major implication of leadership's political nature is that such attempts at wielding influence will not necessarily succeed.[5] In fact, other types of managerial tasks may have a stronger influence on organizational effectiveness than those interpersonal tasks usually labeled leadership.[6]

Despite this shortcoming, the examination of leadership as it relates to interpersonal interactions is still worthwhile simply because managers may, in many cases, have more control over how they and their subordinates behave than over nonhuman aspects of their jobs (such as the amount and types of resources they are given). In addition, some information does exist concerning which leadership tactics are of use under various conditions. For this information to be of greatest use, however, practicing managers should have some concept of the direction leadership research has taken. Thus, before attempting to provide guidelines for practitioners, we shall briefly review major approaches to the subject of leadership and point out their weaknesses and limitations.

BASIC APPROACHES TO LEADERSHIP

Thinking concerning leadership has moved through three distinct periods or phases.

The Trait Phase. Early approaches to leadership, from the pre-Christian era to the late 1940s, emphasized the examination of leader characteristics (such as age and degree of gregariousness) in an attempt to identify a set of universal characteristics which would allow a leader to be effective in all situations. At first a few traits seemed to be universally important for successful leaders, but subsequent research yielded inconsistent results concerning these traits; in addition, research investigating a large number of other traits (about one hundred) was generally discouraging. As a result of this accumulation of negative findings and of reviews of this evidence, such as that conducted by R.M. Stogdill, the tide of opinion about the importance of traits for leadership effectiveness began to change.[7] In the late 1940s, leadership researchers began to move away from trait research. Contemporary opinion holds the trait approach in considerable disrepute and views the likelihood of uncovering a set of universal leadership effectiveness traits as essentially impossible.

The Behavioral Phase. With the fall of the trait approach, researchers considered alternative concepts, eventually settling on the examination of relationships between leader behaviors and subordinate satisfaction and performance.[8] During the height of the behavioral phase, dating roughly from the late 1940s to the early 1960s, several large research programs were conducted, including the Ohio State University leadership studies, a program of research which has received considerable publicity over the years.

The Ohio State studies started shortly after World War II and initially concentrated on leadership in military organizations. In one of these studies, a lengthy questionnaire was administered to B-52 bomber crews, and their answers were statistically analyzed to identify the common dimensions underlying the answers.[9] This analysis discovered two dimensions which seemed most important in summarizing the nature of the crews' perceptions about their airplane commanders' behavior toward them.

Consideration was the stronger of the two factors, and it involved leader behaviors indicative of friendship, mutual trust, respect, and warmth.

The second factor was Initiation of Structure, a concept involving leader behaviors indicating that the leader organizes and defines the relationship between self and subordinates.[10]

In subsequent studies using modified versions of the original questionnaire, Consideration and Structure were found to be prime dimensions of leader behavior in situations ranging from combat flights over Korea to assembly line works.[11] In addition, studies were undertaken at Ohio State and elsewhere to compare the effects of these leader behaviors on subordinate performance and satisfaction. A high Consideration-high Structure leadership style was, in many cases, found to lead to high performance and satisfaction. However, in a number of studies dysfunctional consequences, such as high turnover and absenteeism, accompanied these positive outcomes. In yet other situations, different combinations of Consideration and Structure (for example, low Consideration-high Structure) were found to be more effective.[12]

Similar behaviors were identified and similar results obtained in a large number of studies, such as those conducted at the University of Michigan.[13] Although the display of highly Considerate-highly Structuring behavior was sometimes found to result in positive organizational outcomes, this was not true in all of the cases or even in most of them.[14] The research, therefore, clearly indicated that no single leadership style was universally effective, as the relationship of supervisory behavior to organizational performance and employee satisfaction changed from situation to situation. By the early 1960s this had become apparent to even the most ardent supporters of the behavioral approach, and the orientation of leadership researchers began to change toward a situational treatment.

The Situational Phase. Current leadership research is almost entirely situational. This approach examines the interrelationships among leader and subordinate behaviors or characteristics and the situations in which the parties find themselves. This can clearly be seen in the work of researchers such as F.E. Fiedler, who outlined one of the first situational models.[15]

Fiedler claims that leaders are motivated primarily by satisfactions derived from interpersonal relations and task-goal accomplishment. Relationship-motivated leaders display task-oriented behaviors (such as Initiating Structure) in situations which are favorable for them to exert influence over their work group, and they display relationship-oriented behaviors (such as Consideration) in situations which are either moderately favorable or unfavorable. Task-motivated leaders display relationship-oriented behaviors in favorable situations and task-oriented behaviors in both moderately favorable and unfavorable situations. Fiedler's model specifies that relationship-motivated leaders will be more effective in situations which are moderately favorable for the leader to exert influence, and that they will be less effective in favorable or unfavorable situations; the exact opposite is the case for task-motivated leaders. (They are most effective in favorable or unfavorable situations and least effective in moderately favorable ones.) According to Fiedler, the favorableness of the situation for the leader to exert influence over the work group is determined by (1) the quality of leader-group member relations (the warmer and friendlier, the more favorable the situation); (2) the structure of the tasks performed by the leader's subordinates (the more structured, the more favorable); and (3) the power of the leader (the more power, the more favorable the situation).[16]

A number of other authors propose similar types of interactions among the leader, the led, and the situation. We will not review all these other models, but the situational model of Victor Vroom and Phillip Yetton deserves mention.[17] Their model suggests the conditions under which the leader should share decision-making power. Five basic leadership styles are recommended. These range from unilateral decisions by the leader to situations in which the leader gives a great deal of decision power to subordinates and serves as a discussion coordinator who does not attempt to influence the group. Which style is recommended depends upon the leader's "yes" or "no" reponse to seven quality and acceptability questions which are asked sequentially. In those cases where more than a single style is suggested, the leader is expected to choose between recommendations on the basis of the amount of time to be invested. While this model, as is the case with most of the situational models, has not been fully tested, the literature supports the basic notion that a situational view is necessary to portray accurately the complexities of leadership processes.

ORGANIZATIONAL IMPLICATIONS

What does this discussion of leadership theory and research have to do with the practice of management?

Selection does not seem to be the primary answer to the organization's need to increase the pool of effective leaders. The results of the numerous trait studies summarized by Stogdill and others indicate that the search for universal personality characteristics of effective leaders is doomed.[18] This statement requires qualification, however. It should be recognized that the assertion concerns leadership effectiveness, which is only one aspect of managerial effectiveness. A manager may contribute to organizational effectiveness in many ways other than by being an effective leader. The role of selection in picking effective managers, as distinguished from effective leaders, consequently may be much greater. Furthermore, present disappointment with attempts at leader selection is derived from research which has sought to identify universal characteristics of effective leaders in all situations. Summaries such as Stogdill's demonstrate that leadership effectiveness is highly dependent upon the relationship between leader characteristics and the demands of particular situations, and thus universal approaches will not work. Exploration of leader traits as they relate to performance in particular situations may reveal that careful selection has some potential. Unfortunately, given the many situational factors which appear to influence leadership effectiveness, it seems unlikely that selection procedures will be able to follow typical actuarial (statistical) selection procedures.[19] (It appears almost impossible to gather enough individuals in identical jobs to do this.) However, this does not preclude the use of clinical (judgmental) techniques for selection of leaders.

A further limitation on selection procedures as ways of increasing the pool of effective managers and/or leaders within organizations is the dynamic nature of managerial jobs and managers' careers. If, as research seems to indicate, leadership success is situation-specific, then the continual and inevitable shifts in the nature of a manager's assignment and his or her movement from one assignment to another may make the initial selection invalid.

Another implication is that existing forms of leadership training appear to be inappropriate, based on the evidence outlined here. There are two reasons for this. First, the majority of such training programs are based upon the assumption that there exists one best way to manage. Great emphasis usually is placed on an employee-centered (Considerate) approach or one which combines a concern for employees with a concern for high output (Initiating Structure). For example, the Managerial Grid and its associated Grid Organizational Development Program are popular approaches to management and organizational development.[20] Both are based on the premise that a managerial style which shows high concern for people and high concern for production is the soundest way to achieve excellence, and both attempt to develop this style of behavior on the part of all managers.[21] Rensis Likert's "System-Four" approach to managerial and organizational development, although different from the Grid approach, also assumes that one best way to manage exists (employee-centered leadership).[22] Clearly, these ideas are in conflict with the evidence and with contemporary opinion.

The other limitation of leadership training is that it seems ineffective in changing the behavior of participants. Leadership training aimed not directly at leadership behavior itself, but at providing diagnostic skills for the identification of the nature of the situation and the behaviors appropriate to it, appears to offer considerable potential for the improvement of leadership effectiveness. Obviously, however, additional research is needed to identify the dimensions of situations crucial to leadership performance and the styles effective under various circumstances.

Fiedler's suggestion that organizations engineer the job to fit the manager also has potential.[23] However, the idea is impractical, if not utopian. Application of this approach is limited because we have not identified the crucial dimensions of situations which affect leadership performance. Also, while the overall approach may offer theoretical advantages when leadership is treated in isolation, it ignores dysfunctional effects on other aspects of the organization's operations. Leadership effectiveness cannot be the only concern of administrators as they make decisions about job assignments. They must consider other aspects of the organization's operations which may conflict with their attempts to make good use of leadership talent. Some characteristics of the job, task, or organization simply may not be subject to change, at least in the short run. Thus, engineering the job to fit the manager may increase leadership effectiveness, but this approach seems risky, at least for the foreseeable future.

It should also be noted that it is not unusual for work organizations to use traits and trait descriptions in their evaluations of both leadership and managerial performance. A quick glance at a typical performance rating form usually reveals the presence of terms such as *personality* and *attitude* as factors for individual evaluation. Clearly, these terms represent a modern-day version of the traits investigated thirty years ago, and they may or may not be related to actual job performance, depending upon the specifics of the situation involved. Thus, some explicit rationale and, it is hoped, evidence that such traits do affect managerial performance should be provided before they are included in performance evaluations. Just feeling that they are important is not sufficient justification.

INDIVIDUAL IMPLICATIONS

The implications of our discussion of leadership theory and research for individual managers are intertwined with those for the total organization. The fact that leadership effectiveness does not depend on a single set of personal characteristics with which an individual is born or which the individual acquires at an early age should provide a sense of relief to many managers and potential managers. Success in leadership is not limited to an elite, but can be attained by almost any individual, assuming that the situation is proper and that the manager can adjust his or her behavior to fit the situation. The process leading to effective leadership, in other words, is not so much one of changing the characteristics of the individual as it is one of assuring that he or she is placed in an appropriate situation or of teaching the individual how to act to fit the situation.

Thus, a manager's effectiveness can be improved through the development of skills in analyzing the nature of organizational situations — both task and political demands. Although it is difficult to provide guidelines, some recent research points to tentative prescriptions.[24]

Generally speaking, a high Consideration-high Structure style often works best. However, this approach cannot be used in all instances because dysfunctional consequences can result from such behaviors. For example, upper management sometimes gives highly considerate managers poor performance ratings, while in other instances high Structure has been related to employee dissatisfaction, grievances, and turnover. It sometimes will be necessary for a manager to choose between high Consideration and high Structure, and in these cases an individual's diagnostic ability becomes important.

If the diagnostician (manager) has little information, it is probably safe to exhibit high Consideration. Although it does not guarantee subordinate performance, its positive effects on frustration-instigated behavior — such as aggression — are probably enough to warrant its recommendation as a general style. However, in some situations Structure probably should be emphasized, although it may mean a decrease in subordinate perceptions of Consideration. Although the following is not an exhaustive list of these exceptions, it does include those which are known and appear important. The individual manager, from a careful analysis of the situation, must add any additional factors that can be identified.

Emergencies or High-Pressure Situations. When the work involves physical danger, when time is limited, or when little tolerance for error exists, emphasis on Initiating Structure seems desirable. Research has demonstrated that subordinates often expect and prefer high Structure in such instances.

Situations in Which the Manager is the Only Source of Information. When the leader is the only person knowledgeable about the task, subordinates often expect him or her to make specific job assignments, set deadlines, and generally engage in structuring their behavior. This does not mean that the leader cannot be considerate if this is appropriate.

Subordinate Preferences. There is limited evidence that some subordinates prefer high Structure and expect it, while others expect low Consideration and are suspicious of leaders who display high Consideration. Other preference patterns undoubtedly exist, and managers should attempt to tailor their behavior to each individual employee, as the situation dictates.

Preferences of Higher Management. In some instances, higher management has definite preferences for certain leadership styles. Higher management sometimes prefers and expects high Structure and low Consideration, and rewards managers for displaying this behavioral style. The manager should be sensitive to the desires of superiors, in addition to those of subordinates. While it is not possible to specify how these expectations may be reconciled if they diverge, compromise or direct persuasion might be useful.[25] Once again, the success of these methods probably will depend both upon the situation and the manager's skill. This leads to the last point — adaptability.

Leader Ability to Adjust. Some managers will be able to adjust their behavior to fit the situation. For others, attempts to modify behavior may look false and manipulative to subordinates. In these instances, the manager probably would be better off keeping the style with which he or she is most comfortable.

LIMITATIONS AND CONCLUSION

The situational approach avoids the major shortcomings of both the trait and behavioral approaches to leadership. However, the implicit assumption that hierarchical leadership is always important has recently come into question. Steven Kerr, for example, points out that many factors may limit the ability of a hierarchical superior to act as a leader for subordinates.[26] Factors such as technology (for example, the assembly line), training, clear job descriptions, and the like, may provide subordinates with enough guidance so that supervisor Structure may be unnecessary to ensure task performance. Also, jobs which are intrinsically satisfying may negate the need for supervisor Consideration, since Consideration is not needed to offset job dullness.

Another problem with the situational approach and with leadership as a major emphasis in general, is that effective leadership may account for only 10 to 15 percent of the variability in unit performance.[27] While this percentage is certainly not trivial, it is clear that much of what affects performance in organizations is not accounted for by leadership. While studying and emphasizing leadership certainly has its merits, it could be argued that there is much to be gained by treating leadership effectiveness as but one component of managerial effectiveness. As an earlier publication emphasized:

> It is necessary to note that leadership is only one way in which the manager contributes to organizational effectiveness. The manager also performs duties which are *externally oriented* so far as his unit is concerned. For example, he may spend part of his time coordinating the work of his unit with other units. Similarly, not all of the manager's *internally oriented* activities can be labeled leadership acts.

Some of them concern the physical and organizational conditions under which the work unit operates. For example, the manager spends part of his time obtaining resources (materials, equipment, manpower, and so on) necessary for unit operations. This is an essential internally oriented activity but hardly constitutes leadership. Clearly, the manager must perform a mix of internal and external activities if his unit is to perform well. Leadership is only one of the internal activities performed by managers.[28]

Thus, the manager should not overemphasize the importance of leadership activities, especially if this causes other functions to be neglected.

For managers to be effective as leaders, they must attempt to be politically astute and to tailor their behaviors, taking into account differences in subordinates, superiors, and situations. Leadership should be kept in perspective. Clearly, it is important, but it cannot be treated in isolation; the importance of leadership depends upon the situation, and the practicing manager must take this into account.

NOTES

[1]R. M. Stogdill, *Handbook of Leadership* (New York: Free Pr., 1974).

[2]A. C. Filley, R. J. House, and Steven Kerr, *Managerial Process and Organizational Behavior*, 2nd ed., (Glenview, Ill.: Scott, Foresman, 1976). See also R. C. Davis, *Industrial Organization and Management* (New York: Harper & Row, 1957).

[3]C. A. Gibb, "Leadership," in Gardner Lindzey and Elliott Aronson, eds., *The Handbook of Social Psychology* (Reading, Mass.: Addison-Wesley, 1969), vol. 4.

[4]See, for example, R. H. Hall, *Organizations: Structure and Process* (Englewood Cliffs, N.J.: Prentice-Hall, 1972).

[5]C. A. Schriesheim, J. M. Tolliver, and L. D. Dodge, "The Political Nature of the Leadership Process" (unpublished paper, 1978).

[6]For examples of other types of managerial tasks that may have more of an impact on organizations, see J. P. Campbell, M. D. Dunnette, E. E. Lawler, and K. E. Weick, *Managerial Behavior, Performance, and Effectiveness* (New York: McGraw-Hill, 1970).

[7]R. M. Stogdill, "Personal Factors Associated with Leadership: A Survey of the Literature," *Journal of Psychology* 25:35-71 (Jan. 1948).

[8]T. O. Jacobs, *Leadership and Exchange in Formal Organizations* (Alexandria, Va.: Human Resources Research Organization, 1970).

[9]A. W. Halpin and B. J. Winer, "A Factorial Study of the Leader Behavior Descriptions," in R. M. Stogdill and A. E. Coons, eds., *Leader Behavior: Its Description and Measurement* (Columbus: Bureau of Business Research, Ohio State Univ., 1957).

[10]Ibid., p. 42

[11]Stogdill and Coons, *Leader Behavior*.

[12]Steven Kerr, C. A. Schriesheim, C. J. Murphy, and R. M. Stogdill, "Toward a Contingency Theory of Leadership Based upon the Consideration and Initiating Structure Literature," *Organizational Behavior and Human Performance* 12:62-82 (Aug. 1974).

[13]See, for example, Daniel Katz, Nathan Maccoby, and Nancy Morse, *Productivity, Supervision and Morale in an Office Situation* (Ann Arbor: Survey Research Center, Univ. of Michigan, 1951).

[14]Kerr et al., "Contingency Theory."

[15]See F. E. Fiedler, "Engineer the Job to Fit the Manager," *Harvard Business Review* 43:115-22 (Sept.-Oct. 1965).

[16]F. E. Fiedler, *A Theory of Leadership Effectiveness* (New York: McGraw-Hill, 1967).

[17]V. H. Vroom and P. W. Yetton, *Leadership and Decision-Making* (Pittsburgh: Univ. of Pittsburgh Pr., 1973).

[18]Stogdill, "Personal Factors."

[19]Kerr et al., "Contingency Theory."

[20]R. R. Blake and J. S. Mouton, *The Managerial Grid* (Houston: Gulf, 1964) and *Building a Dynamic Corporation through Grid Organizational Development* (Reading, Mass.: Addison-Wesley, 1969).

[21]Ibid., p. 63.

[22]Rensis Likert, *New Patterns of Management* (New York: McGraw-Hill, 1961) and *The Human Organization: Its Management and Value* (New York: McGraw-Hill, 1967).

[23]Fiedler, "Engineer the Job."

[24]Kerr et al., "Contingency Theory."

[25]See Filley, House, and Kerr, *Managerial Process*, especially pp. 162-80; and George Strauss, "Tactics of Lateral Relations," in H. J. Leavitt and L. R. Pondy, eds., *Readings in Managerial Psychology* (Chicago: Univ. of Chicago Pr., 1964), pp. 226-48.

[26]Steven Kerr, "Substitutes for Leadership: Their Definition and Measurement" (unpublished paper, 1978).

[27]O. C. Behling and C. A. Schriesheim, *Organizational Behavior: Theory, Research and Application* (Boston: Allyn & Bacon, 1976).

[28]Ibid., p. 294.

CHAPTER 2

Leadership:
Some Principles and Concepts
Richard I. Lester

A familiar sign of the times in the corporate world is the outcry for creative leadership. Some observers believe that the average employee would be unable to respond if Martian spacepeople were to land on a corporate site and demand, "Take us to your leader." Most businesspeople understand the concept of management, but they have problems in the application of leadership because it is more difficult to comprehend. Theoretical sense, is one of the most discussed and least understood subjects in business.

It can be said that managers are necessary, leaders are essential. Modern business has not given enough attention to this distinction; both business and educational institutions have generally placed more emphasis on management than leadership.

DEFINING LEADERSHIP

Experts generally recognize leadership as the art of influencing and directing people in a manner that wins their obedience, confidence, respect and enthusiastic cooperation in achieving a common objective. Practitioners usually define a leader as a person who applies principles and techniques that insure motivation, discipline and productivity when working with people, tasks and situations in order to accomplish the company's objectives.

Considered in the broadest context, people exercise leadership any time they attempt to change or modify the behavior of an individual or a group of individuals.

To understand the nature of leadership, one must first understand the nature of power, for leadership is a specal form of power involving relationships with people. To develop these relationships, leaders must successfully fuse organizational and personal needs in a way that permits people and organizations to reach peaks of mutual achievement and satisfaction. Thus, leaders get things done and make things work. In this context, leaders are facilitators who help to pave the way toward the achievement of corporate goals.

DEVELOPING NEW LEADERS

Some people believe that leadership can be taught, but others contend that an individual can only be taught *about* leadership. If one perceives education as a change in behavior through experience, and effective leadership as a set of behaviors applicable to given situations, then leadership can indeed be taught. Despite the complexity of the leadership role, it can be learned when there is a definite willingness to expend the required time and resources.

Leaders are not born. People can develop and learn leadership just as they learn any other complex skill, but the learning process requires intensive effort, study and continuing application within the work environment. Thus, leaders can be developed. Business must do a better job of finding employees with latent leadership talents, and then training them, if it expects to develop effective leaders.

THE LEADERSHIP TRAINING PROGRAM

Three basic elements of leadership are the leader, the follower and the situation. Leadership programs should emphasize that in accepting their professional obligations and positions of authority, managers should demonstrate leadership qualities in all aspects of work. They should understand that leadership of a business organization can be a most rewarding and exciting experience. Although the primary challenge is successful accomplishment of goals, human resources professionals and managers should emphasize that successful leaders must never overlook the welfare of their employees. Employees are the most important asset any business has.

Leadership development should also focus on the fact that leaders are judged, for the most part, on the timeliness and soundness of their decisions. Knowledge gained through experience, job-related reading, professional training and specialized education is invaluable. The following may be helpful to remember when developing leadership potential:

Visibility and interaction. People cannot lead effectively from the privacy of their office, regardless of their position. True leaders visit their workers on the job and observe their working conditions firsthand. Highly visible leaders leave their "footprints" everywhere in the organization. An effective manager cannot be a lone wolf and expect to lead the pack.

The attitudes of today's employees underscore the need for leadership skills that insure creativity, efficiency, productivity and vitality in a corporate environment constantly faced with the challenge of doing more with less. To meet this challenge, leaders must know their employees, their problems, interests and needs. And today's leader must understand that employees are more sophisticated, better educated, and more conscious of the limits of corporate discipline. As a rule, these men and women are not motivated by intimidation: they must be lead, rather than driven. The effective leader must instill a sense of responsibility, loyalty and duty for the corporation in each employee if he or she is to succeed.

Caring. Good business leaders are demanding of themselves and their employees. Their style is a blend of caring, discipline and self-confidence rooted in an unshakeable dedication to their employees and the company. There is ample evidence that something so simple as caring for one's employees improves leadership effectiveness.

Quality versus quantity. Effective leaders concentrate on quantitative and qualitative productivity. All too often, people in leadership positions concern themselves with how much work their employees perform and not with what they produce. Effective leaders recognize no substitutes for hard, productive work, intense concentration, and willingness to assume total responsibility for the work of their employees. Leaders must develop and recognize their employees if they expect to excel over an extended period of time.

Delegation. Leaders must delegate tasks and require their employees to make decisions. The true test of leadership is the behavior reflected among their employees. Thus, employees need to be involved as a first step toward commitment to company goals.

LEADERSHIP STYLES

Leadership styles for influencing employees resemble fingerprints in the sense that each is different. Thus, in studying different leadership styles, managers should learn how to sort the good from the bad, the effective from the ineffective. Through this process of sifting and selecting, they can begin to develop the basics of their own leadership style.

Whatever the style, it should be predicated on sensitivity and appropriate consideration for both human relationships and task completion. Managers who wish to practice effective leadership should apply the behavioral science approach to enhance their leadership effectiveness. And they should stress the pluralistic view of motivation to show that employee behavior stems from many different types of needs.

The following are considered key characteristics of good corporate leaders:

Sense of responsibility. People who aspire to high positions must subordinate their personal desires and, at times, even the desires of their families to the company. The leader recognizes responsibility and relishes the opportunity to display leadership skills.

Leaders must also exercise self-control if they expect to control others, and they must maintain self-control in the most trying situations. Furthermore, they should strive to keep their personal lives under control and never allow personal problems to color decisions made at work.

Technical and professional competence. Employees will give a manager a reasonable period of time to get his or her feet on the ground, but they will not respect the manager who continually relies on others in the company to make decisions or provide guidance.

Enthusiasm. A leader must be genuinely enthusiastic in all the tasks that comprise the goals of the company. Employees will automatically give more of themselves and take more pride in their work if they know their leader is involved, committed and enthusiastic. Some managers are reluctant to delve into areas in which they have no prior experience or qualifications. It is important for a leader to seek new directions and to delve into unfamiliar areas.

Communications skills. Effective communications is a key leadership variable. Verbal, written and nonverbal communications are essential in acquiring employee cooperation. Communications is the adhesive that holds an organization together.

A good leader also remembers to listen, but listening involves more than mere hearing. Successful leaders interpret and evaluate what they hear. They do not permit personal ideas, emotions or prejudices to distort what they hear. Disciplined listening is difficult, but it is a key communication skill.

High ethical standards. Ethics play a key role in the leadership function because they are the basis of all group interaction and decision making. Professional ethics require readers to maintain high standards of personal conduct and to adhere to those standards in all situations so that employees can rely on their actions. Constructive leaders have well-established value systems that have been tested in a variety of situations. Leaders demonstrate integrity when their concern for company interests is always greater than their personal pride, and when they hold themselves to the same standards even when their superiors may not.

Flexibility. A leader must understand that no two people or situations are ever exactly alike. Yesterday's approach may or may not be the correct approach for today or tomorrow. Effective leaders adapt their approaches to the particular person, group or problem at hand. Leaders should also devote a great deal of thought to understanding the nature of change. Flexibility also implies that adaptable leaders are more capable of managing stress. Leaders should have the ability to take whatever comes their way and thrive on it.

Vision. Leaders need a visual image of where they see the organization going and how it can get there. Vision is indispensable to organizational progress. Furthermore, effective leaders project ideas and images that excite people and develop choices that are timely and appropriate for the situation at hand. Therefore, leaders with vision inspire their employees to do their best.

The message is clear. Leaders are not given esteem along with their rank or position; they earn esteem by manifesting the characteristics of leadership. They first create a tolerant work environment, develop respect between themselves and their employees, and, consequently, win the esteem of their superiors, peers and employees. It is not an easy task to be an effective leader, but the personal satisfaction and sense of achievement and contribution are great and well worth the effort.

CHAPTER 3

The 4 Competencies of Leadership

Warren Bennis *

For nearly five years I have been researching a book on leadership. During this period, I have traveled around the country spending time with 90 of the most effective, successful leaders in the nation; 60 from corporations and 30 from the public sector.

My goal was to find these leaders' common traits, a task that has required much more probing than I expected. For a while, I sensed much more diversity than commonality among them. The group comprises both left-brain and right-brain thinkers; some who dress for success and some who don't; well-spoken, articulate leaders and laconic, inarticulate ones; some John Wayne types and some who are definitely the opposite. Interestingly, the group includes only a few stereotypically charismatic leaders.

Despite the diversity, which is profound and must not be underestimated, I identified certain areas of competence shared by all 90. Before presenting those findings, though, it is important to place this study in context, to review the mood and events in the United States just before and during the research.

DECLINE AND MALAISE

When I left the University of Cincinnati late in 1977, our country was experiencing what President Carter called "despair" or "malaise." From 1960 to 1980, our institutions' credibility had eroded steadily. In an article about that period entitled "Where Have All the Leaders Gone," I described how difficult the times were for leaders, including university presidents like myself.

I argued that, because of the complexity of the times, leaders felt impotent. The assassinations of several national leaders, the Vietnam war, the Watergate scandal, the Iranian hostage crisis and other events led to a loss of trust in our institutions and leadership.

---

*Warren Bennis interviewed 90 outstanding leaders and their subordinates, with the intention of learning what makes real leaders (as opposed to effective managers) tick. After five years of research and thought, he identified four competencies common to all 90 leaders, and they're presented here, in *Training & Development Journal*'s fortieth anniversary series of articles by major figures in human resource development.

I came across a quotation in a letter Abigail Adams wrote to Thomas Jefferson in 1790: "These are the hard times in which a genius would wish to live." If, as she believed, great necessities summon great leaders, I wanted to get to know the leaders brought forth by the current malaise. In a time when bumper stickers appeared reading "Impeach Someone," I resolved to seek out leaders who were effective under these adverse conditions.

At the same time that America suffered from this leadership gap, it was suffering from a productivity gap. Consider these trends:

- In the 1960s, the average GNP growth was 4.1 percent; in the 1970s, it was 2.9 percent; in 1982, it was negative.

- The U.S. standard of living, the world's highest in 1972, now ranks fifth.

- In 1960, when the economies of Europe and Japan had been rebuilt, the U.S. accounted for 25 percent of the industrial nations' manufacturing exports and supplied 98 percent of its domestic markets. Now, the U.S. has less than a 20 percent share of the world market, and that share is declining.

- In 1960, U.S. automobiles had a 96 percent market share; today we have about 71 percent. The same holds true for consumer electronics; in 1960 it was 94.4 percent, in 1980 only 49 percent. And that was before Sony introduced the Walkman!

In addition to leadership and productivity gaps, a subtler "commitment gap" existed, that is, a reluctance to commit to one's work or employer.

The Public Agenda's recent survey of working Americans shows the following statistics. Less than one out of four jobholders (23 percent) says he or she currently works at full potential. Nearly half say they do not put much effort into their jobs above what is required. The overwhelming majority, 75 percent, say they could be significantly more effective on their jobs than they are now. And nearly 6 in 10 working Americans believe that "most people do not work as hard as they used to."

A number of observers have pointed out the considerable gap between the number of hours people are paid to work and the number of hours they spend on productive labor. Evidence developed recently by the University of Michigan indicates the gap may be widening. They found the difference between paid hours and actual working hours grew by 10 percent between 1970 and 1980.

This increasing commitment gap leads to the central question: How can we empower the work force and reap the harvest of human effort?

If I have learned anything from my research, it is this: The factor that empowers the work force and ultimately determines which organizations succeed or fail is the leadership of those organizations. When strategies, processes or cultures change, the key to improvement remains leadership.

THE SAMPLE: 90 LEADERS

For my study, I wanted 90 effective leaders with proven track records. The final group contains 60 corporate executives, most, but not all, from Fortune 500 companies, and 30 from the public sector. My goal was to find people with leadership ability, in contrast to just "good managers" — true leaders who affect the culture, who are the social architects of their organizations and who create and maintain values.

Leaders are people who do the right thing; managers are people who do things right. Both roles are crucial, and they differ profoundly. I often observe people in top positions doing the wrong thing well.

Given my definition, one of the key problems facing American organizations (and probably those in much of the industrialized world) is that they are underled and overmanaged. They do not pay enough attention to doing the right thing, while they pay too much attention to doing things right. Part of the fault lies with our schools of management; we teach people how to be good technicians and good staff people, but we don't train people for leadership.

The group of 60 corporate leaders was not especially different from any profile of top leadership in America. The median age was 56. Most were white males, with six black men and six women in the group. The only surprising finding was that all the CEOs not only were married to their first spouse, but also seemed enthusiastic about the institution of marriage. Examples of the CEOs are Bill Kieschnick, chairman and CEO of Arco, and the late Ray Kroc of McDonald's restaurants.

Public-sector leaders included Harold Williams, who then chaired the SEC; Neil Armstrong, a genuine all-American hero who happened to be at the University of Cincinnati; three elected officials; two orchestra conductors; and two winning athletics coaches. I wanted conductors and coaches because I mistakenly believed they were the last leaders with complete control over their constituents.

After several years of observation and conversation, I have defined four competencies evident to some extent in every member of the group. They are:

- management of attention;
- management of meaning;
- management of trust;
- management of self.

MANAGEMENT OF ATTENTION

One of the traits most apparent in these leaders is their ability to draw others to them, not because they have a vision, a dream, a set of limitations, an agenda, a frame of reference. They communicate an extraordinary focus of commitment, which attracts people to them. One of these leaders was described as making people want to join in with him; he enrolls them in his vision.

Leaders, then, manage attention through a compelling vision that brings others to a place they have not been before. I came to this understanding in a roundabout way, as this anecdote illustrates.

One of the people I most wanted to interview was one of the few I couldn't seem to reach. He refused to answer my letters or phone calls. I even tried getting in touch with the members of his board. He is Leon Fleischer, a well-known child prodigy who grew up to become a prominent pianist, conductor and musicologist. What I did not know about him was that he had lost the use of his right hand and no longer performed.

When I called him originally to recruit him for the University of Cincinnati faculty, he declined and told me he was working with orthopedic specialists to regain the use of his hand. He did visit the campus and I was impressed with his commitment to staying in Baltimore, near the medical institution where he received therapy.

Fleischer was the only person who kept turning me down for an interview, and finally I gave up. A couple of summers later I was in Aspen, Colorado while Fleischer was conducting the Aspen Music Festival. I tried to reach him again, even leaving a note on his dressing room door, but I got no answer.

One day in downtown Aspen, I saw two perspiring young cellists carrying their instruments and offered them a ride to the music tent. They hopped in the back of my jeep, and, as we rode, I questioned them about Fleischer.

"I'll tell you why he is so great," said one. "He doesn't waste our time."

Fleischer finally agreed not only to be interviewed but to let me watch him rehearse and conduct music classes. I linked the way I saw him work with that simple sentence, "He doesn't waste our time." Every moment Fleischer was before the orchestra, he knew exactly what sound he wanted. He didn't waste time because his intentions were always evident. What united him with the other musicians was their concern with intention and outcome.

When I reflected on my own experience, it struck me that when I was most effective, it was because I knew what I wanted. When I was ineffective, it was because I was unclear about it.

So, the first leadership competency is the management of attention through a set of intentions or a vision, not in a mystical or religious sense, but in the sense of outcome, goal or direction.

MANAGEMENT OF MEANING

To make dreams apparent to others, and to align people with them, leaders must communicate their vision. Communication and alignment work together.

Consider, for example, the contrasting styles of Presidents Reagan and Carter. Ronald Reagan is called "the great communicator"; one of his speech writers said Reagan can read the phone book and make it interesting. The reason is that Reagan uses metaphors with which people can identify.

In his first budget message, for example, Reagan described a trillion dollars by comparing it to piling up dollar bills beside the Empire State Building. Reagan, to use one of Alexander Haig's coinages, "tangibilitated" the idea. Leaders make ideas tangible and real to others, so they can support them. For no matter how marvelous the vision, the effective leader must use a metaphor, a word or a model to make that vision clear to others.

In contrast, President Carter was boring. Carter was one of our best informed presidents; he had more facts at his finger tips than almost any other president. But he never made the meaning come through the facts.

I interviewed an assistant secretary of commerce appointed by Carter who told me that after four years in his administration, she still did not know what Jimmy Carter stood for. She said that working for him was like looking through the wrong side of a tapestry; the scene was blurry and indistinct.

The leader's goal is not mere explanation or clarification but the creation of meaning. My favorite baseball joke is exemplary: In the ninth inning of a key playoff game, with a 3 and 2 count on the batter, the umpire hesitates a split second in calling the pitch. The batter whirls around angrily and says, "Well, what was it?" The umpire barks back, "It ain't *nothing* until *I* call it!"

The more far-flung and complex the organization, the more critical is this ability. Effective leaders can communicate ideas through several organizational layers, across great distances, even through the jamming signals of special interest groups and opponents.

When I was a university president, a group of administrators and I would hatch what we knew was a great idea. Then we would do the right thing: delegate, delegate, delegate. But when the product or policy finally appeared, it scarcely resembled our original idea.

This process occurred so often that I gave it a name: the Pinocchio Effect. (I am sure Geppetto had no idea how Pinocchio would look when he finished carving him.) The Pinocchio Effect leaves us surprised. Because of inadequate communication, results rarely resemble our expectations.

We read and hear so much about information that we tend to overlook the importance of meaning. Actually, the more bombarded a society or organization, the more deluged with facts and images, the greater its thirst for meaning. Leaders integrate facts, concepts and anecdotes into meaning for the public.

Not all the leaders in my group are word masters. They get people to understand and support their goals in a variety of ways.

The ability to manage attention and meaning comes from the whole person. It is not enough to use the right buzz word or a cute technique, or to hire a public relations person to write speeches.

Consider, instead, Frank Dale, publisher of the Los Angeles afternoon newspaper, *The Herald Examiner*. Dale's charge was to cut into the market share of his morning competitor, *The L.A. Times*. When he first joined the newspaper a few years ago, he created a campaign with posters picturing the *Herald Examiner behind and slightly above the Times*. The whole campaign was based on this potent message of how the *Herald Examiner* would overtake the *Times*.

I interviewed Dale at his office, and when he sat down at his desk and fastened around him a safety belt like those on airplanes, I couldn't suppress a smile. He did this to remind me and everybody else of the risks the newspaper entailed. His whole person contributed to the message.

No one is more cynical than a newspaper reporter. You can imagine the reactions that traveled the halls of the *Herald Examiner* building. At the same time, nobody forgot what Frank Dale was trying to communicate. And that is the management of meaning.

MANAGEMENT OF TRUST

Trust is essential to all organizations. The main determinant of trust is reliability, what I call constancy. When I talked to the board members or staffs of these leaders, I heard certain phrases again and again: "She is all of a piece." "Whether you like it or not, you always know where he is coming from, what he stands for."

When John Paul II visited this country, he gave a press conference. One reporter asked how the Pope could account for allocating funds to build a swimming pool at the papal summer palace. He responded quickly: "I like to swim. Next question." He did not rationalize about medical reasons or claim he got the money from a special source.

A recent study showed people would much rather follow individuals they can count on, even when they disagree with their viewpoint, than people they agree with but who shift positions frequently. I cannot overemphasize enough the significance of constancy and focus.

Margaret Thatcher's reelection in Great Britain is another excellent example. When she won office in 1979, observers predicted she quickly would revert to defunct Labor Party policies. She did not. In fact, not long ago a *London Times* article appeared headlined (parodying Christopher Fry's play) "The Lady's Not for Returning." She has not turned; she has been constant, focused and all of a piece.

MANAGEMENT OF SELF

The fourth leadership competency is management of self, knowing one's skills and deploying them effectively. Management of self is critical; without it, leaders and managers can do more harm than good. Like incompetent doctors, incompetent managers can make life worse, make people sicker and less vital. (The term *iatrogenic*, by the way, refers to illness *caused* by doctors and hospitals.) Some managers give themselves heart attacks and nervous breakdowns; still worse, many are "carriers," causing their employees to be ill.

Leaders know themselves; they know their strengths and nurture them. They also have a faculty I think of as the Wallenda Factor.

The Flying Wallendas are perhaps the world's greatest family of aerialists and tightrope walkers. I was fascinated when, in the early 1970s, 71-year old Karl Wallenda said that for him living is walking the tightrope, and everything else is waiting. I was struck with his capacity for concentration on the intention, the task, the decision.

I was even more intrigued when, several months later, Wallenda fell to his death while walking a tightrope between two high-rise buildings in San Juan. Without a safety net, Wallenda fell, still clutching the balancing pole he warned his family never to drop lest it hurt somebody below.

Later, Wallenda's wife said that before her husband fell, for the first time since she had known him he was concentrating on falling, instead of on walking the tightrope. He personally supervised the attachment of the guide wires, which he never had done before.

Like Wallenda before his fall, the leaders in my group seemed unacquainted with the concept of failure. What you or I might call a failure, they referred to as a mistake. I began collecting synonyms for the word failure mentioned in the interviews, and I found more than 20: mistake, error, false start, bloop, flop, loss, miss, foul-up, stumble, botch, bungle ... but not failure.

One CEO told me that if she had a knack for leadership, it was the capacity to make as many mistakes as she could as soon as possible, and thus get them out of the way. Another said that a mistake is simply "another way of doing things." These leaders learn from and use something that doesn't go well; it is not a failure but simply the next step.

When I asked Harold Williams, president of the Getty Foundation, to name the experience that most shaped him as a leader, he said it was being passed over for the presidency of Norton Simon. When it happened, he was furious and demanded reasons, most of which he considered idiotic. Finally, a friend told him that some of the reasons were valid and he should change. He did, and about a year and a half later became president.

Or consider coach Ray Meyer of DePaul University, whose team finally lost at home after winning 29 straight home games. I called him to ask how he felt. He said, "Great. Now we can start to concentrate on winning, not on *not* losing."

Consider Broadway producer Harold Prince, who calls a press conference the morning after his show opens, before reading the reviews, to announce his next play. Or Susan B. Anthony, who said, "Failure is impossible." Or Fletcher Byrum, who, after 22 years as president of Coopers, was asked about his hardest decision. He replied that he did not know what a hard decision was; that he never worried, that he accepted the possibility of being wrong. Byrum said that worry was an obstacle to clear thinking.

The Wallenda Factor is an approach to life; it goes beyond leadership and power in organizations. These leaders all have it.

EMPOWERMENT: THE EFFECTS OF LEADERSHIP

Leadership can be felt throughout an organization. It gives pace and energy to the work and empowers the work force. Empowerment is the collective effect of leadership. In organizations with effective leaders, empowerment is most evident in four themes:

- *People feel significant.* Everyone feels that he or she makes a difference to the success of the organization. The difference may be small — prompt delivery of potato chips to a mom-and-pop grocery store or developing a tiny but essential part for an airplane. But where they are empowered, people feel that what they do has meaning and significance.

- *Learning and competence matter.* Leaders value learning and mastery, and so do people who work for leaders. Leaders make it clear that there is no failure, only mistakes that give us feedback and tell us what to do next.

- *People are part of a community.* Where there is leadership, there is a team, a family, a unity. Even people who do not especially like each other feel the sense of community. When Neil Armstrong talks about the Apollo explorations, he describes how a team carried out an almost unimaginably complex set of interdependent tasks. Until there were women astronauts, the men referred to this as "brotherhood." I suggest they rename it "family."

- *Work is exciting.* Where there are leaders, work is stimulating, challenging, fascinating and fun. An essential ingredient in organizational leadership is pulling rather than pushing people toward a goal. A "pull" style of influence attracts and energizes people to enroll in an exciting vision of the future. It motivates through identification, rather than through rewards and punishments. Leaders articulate and embody the ideals toward which the organization strives.

People cannot be expected to enroll in just any exciting vision. Some visions and concepts have more staying power and are rooted more deeply in our human needs than others. I believe the lack of two such concepts in modern organizational life is largely responsible for the alienation and lack of meaning so many experience in their work.

One of these is the concept of quality. Modern industrial society has been oriented to quantity, providing more goods and services for everyone. Quantity is measured in money; we are a money-oriented society. Quality often is not measured at all, but is appreciated intuitively. Our response to quality is a feeling. Feelings of quality are connected intimately with our experience of meaning, beauty and value in our lives.

Closely linked to the concept of quality is that of dedication, even love, of our work. This dedication is evoked by quality and is the force that energizes high-performing systems. When we love our work, we need not be managed by hopes of reward or fears of punishment. We can create systems that facilitate our work, rather than being preoccupied with checks and controls of people who want to beat or exploit the system.

And that is what the human resources profession should care most about.

CHAPTER 4

The Leadership Connection

Larry Earl Bone

"Are you teaching Quality this quarter? I hope you are teaching Quality to your students!" We remembered that refrain from Sarah, the teaching colleague of the protagonist in Richard Pirsig's *Zen and the Art of Motorcycle Maintenance*. She, and later he, became obsessed with the concern for quality and questions of how to achieve it. Leadership—and what constitutes it—was the preoccupation of the author as he began teaching library administration again, this time in a summer session at the University of Michigan. Like the Pirsig characters, he too was haunted by a concept and by questions surrounding it.

Is it possible to do something in a professional program to further leadership? Could we help our students see the need and the opportunity for quality leadership in librarianship, together with the stark reality of its absence in all types of American institutions? Could we succeed in conveying not only the practical and the pragmatic, but also the need for going beyond that? Would we rest the case for effective administration on a set of management principles alone, or would we plant the seed from which the capacity for leadership in our students might grow? Would our experience help the students as future administrators achieve the leadership ideals more easily? These and other questions pursued us, as we pursued leadership. The answers might never be known with certainty. Like quality, leadership could be elusive unless examined analytically.

LEADERSHIP PLUS MANAGEMENT

Left to much of the library and management literature, students, in their pursuit of technical proficiency, could miss the connection between leadership and the possession of management skills, as well as the vacuum created when that connection is absent. Nor is it clear from the literature that the challenges and problems with which libraries are faced require leadership equal to that needed in other areas of society. The major problems today seem as great as any since the beginning of the modern library movement. Problems requiring leadership in their solution, however, have always been with librarianship. In fact, while it is true, as one writer observed in the pages of *LJ* some months ago that "the functions of library managers have changed" with the new political milieus surrounding them, it is doubtful that there was ever a time when true leaders could, as he suggested, "sit in a quiet office and deal with the internal operations of the establishment attributed to them."[1]

There may have been some such librarians in the past, and there may be some today, but it is doubtful that they can be regarded as leaders. It is unlikely, for example, that John Cotton Dana, pushing through the barriers to sell the public libraries to his constituents, was permitted such quietude. It was not given to William Warner Bishop in his efforts to establish a prototype university library, nor to Louis Round Wilson in his creation of a new environment for library education. Allie Beth Martin's outline of a strategy for public library renewal and survival was not an "internal" document. These achievements were not "internal operations," and these American library leaders were hardly watchers from the sidelines. They were active and socially responsible. Their examples help us define leadership.

Eight years ago McAnally and Downs, in what remains as an important statement, enumerated the pressures which had changed the role of the library director.[2] Paramount among these pressures were the fast rate of change pervading all aspects of society—the information explosion, the expansion of technology, the high rate of inflation, the new theories of management, the growing atmosphere of conflict present in many institutions, and the increasing stress placed on the directors. While the authors focussed on the problems troubling university library directors, all of these issues, and more, are faced in some measure by administrators in all types of libraries and in many other institutions. Though eight years have elapsed, these problems remain with us in some form.

THE PRESSURES

An examination of the pressures cited by McAnally and Downs reveals that each of the pressures is involved in some way with rapid changes taking place around us. "Future shock" has become a way of life in our century and in our institutions. Like the society, libraries have come through an intense period of tumult. The information explosion has had a particular effect on libraries. As potential conveyors of a great amount of this information, libraries are being expected to respond quickly to the challenge. The extent to which they fulfill this mission will be a continuing test for them.

The new theories of management, identified by McAnally and Downs as among the pressures, represent another aspect of change that requires strong leadership. They have been a source of difficulty in many libraries, especially larger ones where bureaucracies have not been receptive to any dramatic changes in management style. Management by objectives, a management approach deemed effective by the business community, still encounters resistance in many libraries. This resistance persists despite the insistence by Peter Drucker and other management experts that public service institutions, as well as profit-making ones have a responsibility for establishing clear goals and objectives. Participatory management has sometimes failed in libraries because of misunderstandings of its purposes and unrealistic expectations. Collective bargaining, similarly, has often polarized the various echelons and created an atmosphere of conflict.

Conflict, as many libraries are learning, is not always negative in its effect. Anyone acquainted with the dynamics of organizations recognizes the value in human interaction and the energy which may emanate from competition between individuals and groups. This energy may often serve creative purposes. In our time, conflict and conflict resolution are frequently a permanent part of the institutional picture and should be recognized and used as vehicles for progress.

McAnally and Downs could hardly have known in 1973 how much the inflation rate would accelerate in the next eight years. The resulting economic difficulties for all types of libraries hardly need documentation. Citizen reaction to economic problems, as manifested in the anti-tax movement, creates compelling issues. If there is a positive element in the current economic situation, it is that library leaders will be forced, with their staffs, to establish clearer goals and objectives for libraries, as mentioned earlier. These leaders will be expected to identify the priority roles of those libraries with more precision. The Council on Library Resources study which this author conducted six years ago,[3] prior to Proposition 13 and all that it has come to symbolize, concluded that until public libraries assume a more aggressive leadership stance by establishing priority roles, they are destined to lose out in times of economic constraint. The author found most of the public libraries in the study were not yet showing that leadership willingness. Lowell Martin's controversial prescription for public library service in Philadelphia, while certainly debatable by even the most avid supporters of the public library's information function, is, nevertheless, a recognition of urban realities in one city, and offers one noted leader's suggestions for dealing with them.

If one looks at each of the pressures identified by McAnally and Downs — change, management styles, conflict, inflation and any others that might be added — there are few that do not require skillful leadership. Yet there has not been leadership in great abundance during this period. We should recognize the effects of the vacuum. The greatest problem is not the dichotomy between the traditional librarian and the skillful manager, as Charles McClure asserted last fall.[4] There is a larger dichotomy, between management and leadership. The concept of leadership should never be regarded as mutually exclusive with the best principles of management. Management efficiency will help prevent waste of human and other resources, and may assist in smooth operation. Efficiency alone, however, does not set a direction for institutions nor mesh their goals with those of society as a whole. Skillful management, however, which incorporates the best leadership qualities, can succeed.

The concept of leadership is neither unfathomable nor nebulous. Most Americans, even if they sometimes do not know how to bring it about, seem to recognize leadership, whether in electing officials, in the "captains" of business, or in those directing or operating the country's institutions, including the educational. Without leadership, the people are restless and are ready to make frequent changes.

WHAT IS LEADERSHIP?

Leadership is *vision* — that clear perception of an institution's mission and potential, both now and in the future. This vision employs the exercise of both intelligence and imagination. Like the President-leader described by Emmet John Hughes, the leader with vision must be able "to magnify the trivial event to serve his distant aim ... to grasp the thorniest issue as if it were the merest nettle ... to spurn the arithmetic of expediency for the act of brave navigation, the sublime gamble with no hope other than the boldness of his vision."[5] The library leader must be prepared to act with similar resolve. He or she must be able to understand the short-term and long-term significance of libraries in society. A leader must perceive the needs of not only immediate, but potential clienteles. The focus and sense of purpose arising from a leader's vision will assist others in identifying their own and their institutions' directions. Melvil Dewey's desire "to provide the best books for the largest number at the least cost," the founding motto of the American Library Association, may, in its simplicity, seem obvious to us today. It is, nevertheless, an example of one individual's vision and guiding purpose.

Leadership is *integrity*, a quality almost always identified as essential when leaders from diverse sectors are questioned. Integrity precludes deception, false compromise, or the misleading of one's followers. In rejecting Machiavellian manipulation, it is assumed that truthfulness and forthrightness are better at winning confidence. In libraries, integrity means addressing forthrightly those issues with which the staff are concerned. It means attempting to show what is and what is not possible from the leader's point of view.

Leadership is *courage*—the adherence to what one perceives to be right, even when one risks disapproval. The courageous leader will take stands and actions which may not be popular, but which may be in the best long-term interests of the society or the institution. Courage may even require the sacrifice of one's position. Courage is required in both broad and narrow areas, in both the long-term and the daily execution of one's responsibilities. Excellent examples of courageous leadership abound in librarianship. Individuals in small and large institutions have taken courageous positions against censorship, against political pressures, and in support of the cause of intellectual freedom and the mission of libraries.

Leadership is wise *judgment*. Such judgment includes the careful consideration of all the facts and the mature conclusions drawn from them. Judgment dictates the perspective, it excludes parochialism. Confronted with an assortment of viewpoints on any problem and a variety of solutions, the leader will bring objectivity and fairness to his decisions.

Leadership is *understanding of others*. "He must see what he sees with the eyes of the multitude upon whose shoulders he stands" asserted Harold Laski in his examination of the American Presidency.[6] The leader must be sensitive and receptive to the point of view of those around him. The true leader has no room for hubris, that sign of arrogance and pride which the Greeks identified as a tragic weakness.

Leadership is *persuasion*. Harry Truman once said that leadership "is the ability to get men to do what they don't want to do and like it." Those who lead should be able, at the very least, to convince others that certain sacrifices are necessary to achieve needed ends. The leader must, therefore, persuade others to identify and to hold to priorities, however difficult. In library leadership, persuasion may involve both one's clientele and one's associates.

Leadership is *planning*. Skillful planning is essential for averting crisis management—the antithesis of both good management and leadership. Although the steps being taken by libraries in the direction of goals and objectives are slow ones, they are evidence of the recognition of this leadership component. The Public Library Association of ALA has developed a new set of tools for planning library service that is responsive to community needs.[7] The test will come in its knowledgeable use by effective leaders.

Leadership is informed *optimism*. It has no ear for the voices of despair and of cynicism. Leaders confront problems positively. Like all professions and all institutions which have their harbingers of doom, librarianship has its share of those who predict the demise of libraries. A leader addresses the problems realistically and without discouragement, but should have some ideas for their solution.

Finally, leadership, especially in our time, is *flexibility* and openness to change. The leader must be personally receptive to new ideas and unthreatened by different but perhaps superior ones. Leaders must be flexible themselves, and they must be able to assist others to accommodate change. It is not a contradiction to expect the leader to recognize when this accommodation is without substance or to eschew gimmicks. As Adlai Stevenson advised us, "change for the sake of change has no absolute merit in itself." The most productive change builds on the best traditions and the significant achievements of the past while embracing the differing needs of today's clienteles.

THE CONNECTION

This list of qualities was presented to our students. We acknowledged that many others could be added. Are such qualities attainable? We believe they are. Must every leader possess all of them? Few probably do, although we believe a leader will possess the majority of the qualities.

We reject the proposition that leaders are only born, or that leadership is reserved for the few. Qualities of leadership, especially in a democracy and in democratic institutions, can and should be developed by as many as possible. They can be taught. Leadership should exist not only at the top, but at all levels if an institution is to thrive. In professions, especially, there should be no hierarchical approach to leadership. All should be leaders.

At a time when the editors of *LJ* are exhorting us "to report to the profession every method, measure, and mechanism which will help libraries improve performance and productivity,"[8] let us not forget leadership as one of those mechanisms. The bureaucrats, technocrats, and politicians in this field must make way for the men and women who can make the leadership connection. With leadership, libraries will go a long way toward solving their immediate problems and improving their performance. They will also assure a steady and focussed course for their continued evolution.

NOTES

[1]Baughman, James, "The Invisible Director: The Emerging Metropolitan Library Executive," *LJ*, June 15, 1980, p. 1361.

[2]McAnally, Arthur M. & Robert B. Downs, "The Changing Role of Directors of University Libraries," *College and Research Libraries*, March 1973, p. 103-125.

[3]Bone, Larry Earl. *The Goals and Objectives Experience: A Report to the Council on Library Resources*. Washington, D.C., Council on Library Resources, 1975. ERIC #ED 105873.

[4]McClure, Charles R., "Library Managers: Can They Manage? Will They Lead?," *LJ*, November 15, 1980, p. 2388-91.

[5]Hughes, Emmet John. *The Living Presidency*. Coward, McCann, 1973. p. 74-75.

[6]Laski, Harold J. *The American Presidency: An Interpretation*. Harper, 1940, p. 34.

[7]Palmour, Vernon E. *A Planning Process for Public Libraries*. ALA, 1980.

[8]Berry, John, "Repair, renew, redesign...." *LJ*, February 1, 1981, p. 283.

CHAPTER 5

Managerial Leadership in Perspective
Getting Back to Basics
Burt K. Scanlan

Over the past several years, a number of frameworks have been developed for examining the leadership function. Emphasis has ranged from those which identify alternative styles of management, with either a direct or indirect suggestion that there is one best style, to those which are clearly contingency theories maintaining that the appropriate style is dependent on any number of variables. All of the various frameworks serve several valuable purposes: 1) they stimulate a degree of serious thought among managers about the dynamics of this important function, 2) they help managers to gain insight into what their own style of management is, 3) they help managers understand why they get the reaction they do either in general or in a given situation, and 4) they suggest alternative styles of leadership.

Unfortunately, while training and developing managers in accordance with these various theories, we have lost sight of some of the basic ingredients of results-oriented leadership and need to return to fundamentals. In addition, to some extent at least, we have created a sort of hesitancy about leadership which can work to the disadvantage of the organization, the individual manager and the employees.

With the above thoughts in mind, let's look at several key elements of effective leadership which have either gotten lost in the shuffle or become obscured. They are not magical, nor do they represent brilliant, new theories, but to the veteran manager, these ideas will probably make good common sense. For the newer supervisor, they may help clear away some of the obscurity surrounding leadership.

LET PEOPLE KNOW WHAT IS EXPECTED

A coach will tell us that every player must know what is expected on a particular play — not just what is expected in terms of blocking the defensive end, but the results to be achieved, e.g., knocking the opponent down or holding him to the outside for a minimum of two seconds. People must know what is expected not only from the standpoint of the typical job description which describes physical responsibilities, but in terms of results to be achieved from those activities. The superior and subordinate must reach mutual agreement in five basic areas, including:

- The work that an employee does or the major activities for which he or she is responsible.

- Where the job fits into the total picture and why it is important.

- The factors upon which performance will be judged, such as quality, quantity, cost, innovation, estimation of accuracy, self-development and service to other people or departments.

- How performance will be measured. It may be through quantitative measures or a series of statements describing the conditions which will exist when that area of the job has been adequately performed.

- Specific minimum results or standards of performance which should be met in each of the above areas of accountability as they apply to the job.

Once these are clearly established and understood, subordinates must know that they will be held accountable for the results achieved.

ESTABLISH AND MAINTAIN HIGH PERFORMANCE EXPECTATION

By and large and within reason, managers get the type and level of job performance they expect or informally accept over a period of time. Low expectations breed low performance and apathy, while high expectations lead to high performance and a more demanding performance tone. Regarding low expectations, it is important to remember that standards can be set by default if one is not careful. Failure to confront lower than desired levels of performance is tantamaount to acknowledging them as acceptable. High expectations means setting challenging but achievable goals. It means pinpointing exactly what you want, communicating it, and holding people accountable. It does not mean playing such games as: "If I as manager say I want this, I am pretty sure I can get that, and if I don't, it won't be too bad." Nor does it mean the subordinate giving all kinds of reasons for a low level of performance and the manager pretty well buying into the conversation, thus, getting the subordinate off the hook, so to speak. The focus of high expectations is not only on results as such, but on results which are challenging, motivating and attainable, results which provide people with a sense of accomplishment. Again, given some matters yet to be discussed, employees will generally perform at the level expected of them, and when performance levels are not what you would like, the reason is often that people are doing what they know will be accepted.

LET PEOPLE KNOW WHERE THEY STAND

There are several dimensions to this aspect of results-oriented leadership. First, people must know where they stand with respect to the performance goals established, so that if those goals are not being met, they know precisely where they are falling short. This serves to reinforce attention to the achievement nature of the work climate. Also, it provides a vehicle for the superior and subordinate to discuss and reaffirm the goals and what needs to be done to achieve them, whether by the subordinate, the supervisor or both.

Just as important is letting people know when a job is being done well. So often in organizations we forget to "accentuate the positive" and can't understand why people are not more enthused. The answer may be that they feel nobody really cares anyway. In a situation like this, over a period of time the motivation to succeed will dwindle, and a concern for one's own interests will prevail. Recognition cannot amount to superficial "pats on the back," and it is the results accomplished which should receive emphasis. Recognition, like other leadership techniques, is another way of fostering mental and emotional involvement in a job, and can contribute significantly to the process by which organizational goals are internalized by employees. In other words, a strong sense of personal identification with organizational goals takes place because it is directly related to benefits for the individual. In this case, psychological reward is the form of recognition.

EMPLOY BROAD-BASED COMMUNICATION

Effective leadership requires a broad-based program of communication that is both organizationwide and manager-centered. An approach to communication which goes beyond basic job information can accomplish several things. It promotes a sense of identification, a feeling of being a more important part of a broader whole. This in turn fosters the interest, commitment and closeness which are so important to the process of internalization mentioned previously. Broad-based communication can foster a "team" atmosphere by promoting cooperation through better understanding on the part of everyone. It can get people thinking and talking about "their" organization instead of falling back on the discouraged comment, "I just do my job. That's what I'm paid for." In short, increased supervisor-employee communication creates a feeling of importance, of being in on things.

CREATE A SUPPORTIVE CLIMATE

This is a common element of just about every framework for studying leadership that has been developed. In spite of this emphasis, "supportive climate" is very often misinterpreted, misapplied or inadequately defined. Among other things, a supportive climate would include the following behavior on the part of the manager.

- Exhibiting confidence and trust by allowing subordinates to pursue goals without undue reporting, constant checking and other exaggerated forms of control

- Taking positive actions to contribute to employees' growth and development

- Discussing possible causes of and solutions to specific problems which are making an employee's job difficult

- Training and helping the subordinate to find better ways of doing the work

- Giving help and assistance in solving problems as opposed to always giving the answer

- Making available to the best of one's ability the physical resources required to do the job

- Seeking out and using employees' ideas on how to do the job rather than always projecting the "my way is the best way" image

- Being totally approachable so as to build something beyond a formal superior-subordinate relationship.

LEARN HOW TO DELEGATE

Regarding managerial delegation, all of the following observations are significant:

- Failure to delegate, according to most subordinates, is a common managerial error

- Sound delegation is a key determinant of the long-term growth and development of subordinates

- The true nature of delegation is not always clearly understood

- In addition to contributing to people's growth and development, delegation is a way of maximizing the use of a person's skill and ability, triggering motivation, and freeing the manager to manage, as opposed to becoming overly involved in details

- Delegation is a means by which we develop active, independent and responsible subordinates

- There are many credible reasons why, given certain circumstances, managers do not always delegate and why subordinates may not accept delegation. The bottom-line issue, however, is that properly paced and managed delegation is a hallmark of consistently effective leadership.

Note that delegation is not dumping activities on people to perform, it is not imposing what are perceived as arbitrary standards on people and then applying pressure to have them met, it is not abdication or avoidance of decisions, and it does not mean that the manager loses control. Delegation does mean knowing how to handle and distribute responsibility, authority and accountability.

Assigning Responsibility:The assigning of responsibility is the phase of delegation which over the years has received the greatest emphasis. Most managers give their people a clear indication of the duties or tasks they are to perform. Similarly, most employees could give a quite adequate description of their job in terms of "operations." In assigning responsibility, however, the manager must go beyond the typical job description and specify what results are expected from the work. It is in this latter area that management has most often been remiss.

In defining results expected, one must consider the following questions: For what do we pay people? Do we pay them for working some number of hours during which time they are expected to perform certain tasks, or are we trying to achieve certain specified results through the performance of these tasks? The latter is much more logical. Accordingly, Hank Jones' job amounts to more than running a drill press or assembling component parts; instead, he is responsible for producing a given quantity of parts, for meeting certain quality requirements, for informing the supervisor when materials are in low supply, and so on. Similarly, the job of the production control manager goes beyond the design and day-to-day administration of a production-control program. The stated responsibility should also include minimizing lost time due to parts shortages, establishing the most economical work flow and equipment utilization, scheduling so that manufacturing occurs in the most economic lot sizes, and working with line managers on a continual basis to identify and overcome material flow problems. Delegation of responsibility requires a clear understanding and agreement between a manager and subordinates as to:

- The activities or tasks they are responsible for performing

- The areas of the job in which they are responsible or accountable for achieving results

- The specific results for which they are accountable in each area

- The way performance will be measured in each area of responsibility.

Granting Authority: A manager cannot grant authority without incurring some personal managerial and leadership obligations at the same time. The process of granting authority can be divided into two phases: preliminary planning and continuing support. Assuming understanding and agreement have been reached concerning the results expected, the planning phase of granting authority involves the following:

- Having the subordinates present their ideas and plans as to how the desired results can best be achieved

- Raising questions, suggesting possible alternatives, and opening discussion in order to help them explore all aspects of the situation

- Helping subordinates identify potential problems that might arise and develop solutions to overcome them

- Reaching mutual agreement on the proposed course of action to be followed.

The continuing support phase of granting authority was summarized by Drucker:

The manager has responsibility downward, to his subordinate managers. He has first to make sure they know and understand what is demanded of them. He has to help them set their own objectives. Then he has to help them reach these objectives. He is, therefore, responsible for their getting the tools, the staff, the information they need. He has to help them to do better.[1]

The granting of authority is a blending of two factors: a subordinate's skills, abilities, knowledge and potential to contribute, and a manager's guidance, counsel and help. According to Nathaniel Cantor:

> The manager is responsible for helping the assistant to discover how he can perform his own objectives more effectively and how to make the best use of his potentialities to carry out his, the subordinate's assigned responsibilities.[2]

Creating Accountability: Accountability on the part of the subordinate is the end production of delegation, and without this accountability, there is no true delegation. If a manager has been careful in assigning responsibility and granting authority, then the recipients must be held accountable for the results (good or bad) of their activities.

ESTABLISH VIABLE APPRAISAL AND COACHING PROGRAMS

Performance Appraisal: Two of the main purposes of a coaching and development program should be to lay the groundwork for future improvement and to stimulate employees' desire for such improvement. The chances are good that these objectives will not be accomplished if performance appraisal dwells too heavily on the negative. People have a maximum tolerance level for the amount of criticism they can accept, whether it is aimed at several areas of performance or just one or two. Once this level is reached, further criticism merely makes employees defensive to the point of rejecting the manager's viewpoint.

Managers undertaking a performance review must especially guard against the tendency to overemphasize the negative aspects of performance in a particular area where they would like to see improvement. Instead, once it has been agreed that the area in question is an important one, the emphasis should be on developing plans for improvement. A second caution: avoid trying to accomplish too much, too soon. If there are several areas of concern, then the one or two most important issues should receive attention first and the rest be left for another time. Finally, remember that the negative effects produced by too much criticism cannot be offset by sandwiching in a few complimentary remarks here and there.

In addition, it should be remembered that like the rest of the management function, performance appraisal works best—i.e., eventually results in improved performance—when specific goals and plans for achieving them are established.[3]

Lastly, intentionally or not, many appraisal systems end up focusing on possible wage/salary action, rather than on improvement of future performance. Certainly, rewarding people on the basis of performance is important and should not be underemphasized. However, as soon as the wage/salary issue comes into play, planning for improvement tends to take a back seat. This would suggest that salary and performance reviews should be separated. Not only is such separation desirable, but the review for improving performance should be held first, thus ensuring that definite plans for improvement will be made, which in turn lays the groundwork for the wage/salary decision itself.

Coaching Program: Effective coaching is a day-to-day, not a once-a-year activity. The more time that managers spend in a supportive role with subordinates, rather than doing the work or telling them how to do it, the better the results will be. Their function should be one of discussing problems, getting agreement on objectives, and helping facilitate accomplishment of results by subordinates. Therefore, the process of coaching is a continuous and informal one which takes place as the need arises. This is not to suggest that a once-a-year formal review is not desirable. Indeed, this type of review has its advantages. Too often, however, it becomes a substitute for the day-to-day interaction between managers and their people.

Another weakness in many coaching systems is that the subordinate's role is a passive rather than a participative one. A successful program requires involvement and commitment on the part of the employee, so that the latter will be truly motivated to improve his or her performance. In this, as in any other area of work, the manager should tell employees what is expected of them; provide assistance and support when needed, as well as feedback on their performance; and reward them on the basis of results.

Leadership Check List

1. Have I made it clear what is expected in terms of results? Do I discuss these results with employees?

2. Have I let the employees know where they stand?

3. Do the employees know how to do the work?

4. Have I done a good job of training and development?

5. Do I give employees all the support I can?

6. What have I done or not done to cultivate positive personal relationships?

7. Do the employees know why their jobs are important, how they fit into the overall company structure, and the ramifications of poor performance?

8. Are employees kept informed on what is going on in the department and the company? Not just "need to know" items, but "nice to know"?

9. Do employees have adequate freedom in which to work?

10. Are employees too often put in a defensive position regarding performance?

11. What have I done to get employees mentally and emotionally involved in their jobs?

12. Have employees been allowed to participate in setting goals and deciding means of achieving them?

13. Have good aspects of performance received adequate and periodic recognition?

14. Do I accentuate the positive instead of the negative?

15. Have I shown adequate concern for employees as individuals? For their personal goals?

16. Am I flexible about listening to employees and giving them a chance to implement ideas and suggestions?

17. Have I ever consciously assessed employees' strengths and weaknesses with the idea of structuring the work to capitalize on the former?

18. Are employees adequately and reasonably challenged?

NOTES

[1]Peter F. Drucker, *The Practice of Management* (New York: Harper Brothers, 1954), p. 143.

[2]Nathaniel Cantor, *The Learning Process for Managers* (New York: Harper Brothers, 1958).

[3]Herbert H. Meyer, Emanual Key, J. R. P. French, Jr., "Split Roles in Performance Appraisal," *Harvard Business Review*, Vol. 43, No. 1, 1965.

Self-Awareness
Assessing Leadership Skills

Introduction

To lead is to grow
To grow is to seek truth
To seek truth is to understand yourself.
— author unknown

No one can get you to feel inferior without your consent.
— Eleanor Roosevelt

For a leader, self-understanding is critical. It is from a sense of self that leadership behaviors emerge. Self-confidence and assertion — natural partners to effective management — come both from experience and personal development.

Before a leader can really understand others, she/he must work toward a clear and realistic understanding of self. How you see yourself as a librarian and library manager affects the message you send to others. Your effectiveness as a communicator/leader depends in no small degree upon your self-image, the extent to which others accept that image, and the interaction of your image of yourself and their image of you. As a leader you must understand how your self-concept affects communication sent to and received from others.

Sanzotta suggests reasons why self-awareness is related to good interpersonal relations: (1) knowing how you are perceived by others is the initial step in evaluating your impact on people, and (2) attempting to understand the strengths and weaknesses of others before you have confronted and accepted your own strengths and weaknesses will thwart your objectivity.[1]

Bennis and Nanus cite the creative deployment of self as a creative factor in effective leadership.[2] They refer to this concept as "positive self-regard," and received information on its meaning from responses to one of their three standard questions: "What are your major strengths and weaknesses?" For the most part, the leaders emphasized their strengths and minimized their weaknesses. Bennis and Nanus concluded that "recognizing strengths and compensating for weaknesses represents the first step in achieving positive self-regard."[3] The second element in positive self-regard is "the nurturing of skills with discipline — that is, to keep working on and developing one's talents."[4] Therefore, it was the capacity to develop and improve their skills that distinguished leaders from followers. They seemed to be responsible for their own evolution.

The third aspect of positive self-regard is the capacity to discern the fit between one's perceived skills and what the job requires, or the fit between personal strengths and organizational requirements. This aspect is explored further in part IV of this book.

Self-esteem is a type of positive self-regard and includes an inner sense of the value one places on oneself and confidence in one's ability to accomplish what one sets out to do. Self-esteem can also be called self-image, self-concept, self-worth, and self-structure; regardless of the term used, the definition remains the same: one's perception of one's self. Our self-concept is the total of the things we feel we know about ourselves through our interaction with others.

Self-concept also affects whether or not we are able to act assertively. Assertiveness can be seriously inhibited by low self-esteem. Being assertive means being able to express one's feelings, stand up for one's rights and those of others, and state one's opinions without abusing or taking advantage of others. It does not mean being selfish, aggressive, or belligerent. Assertive individuals have high self-esteem and positive self-regard, and communicate their feelings and opinions to others, give honest feedback, speak clearly, establish appropriate eye contact, and use facial and body expressions consistent with their verbal messages.

Caputo explained the benefits of assertive behaviors for librarians in the following manner:

> Assertive behaviors are direct actions that allow a librarian to attempt the resolution of interpersonal conflicts in rational and considerate ways. They are characterized by honesty, objectivity, accuracy, respect for self and others, reasonable tolerance, and self-expression. Librarians who are able to give a personal opinion on a controversial issue while at the same time recognizing the rights of others to hold differing opinions, ... are engaging in assertive behavior. The assertive librarian can face conflict with an investigative assurance that problems can be solved and decisions can be made through an appropriate analysis that allows respect for human rights ... One of the most significant payoffs for the assertive librarian is the enhanced self-esteem and improved personal relationships that can result from appropriate assertion.[5]

Leaders must develop confidence, poise, decisiveness, and other characteristics associated with assertiveness. Developing assertiveness means that one thinks, speaks, and acts as if one's ideas and feelings are as important as anyone's.

Agor contends that intuition is an important management skill that can be used to increase personal and organizational productivity.[6] In addition to the usual managerial skills, top leader-managers possess intuitive skills that provide them with different approaches for leading and managing in these turbulent times. Whether called insight, judgment, intuition, executive ESP, wisdom, or a sixth sense, these skills help leaders see things that other people don't see. This quality may be what sets the true leader apart from the manager.

The selections in this part concentrate on how library managers can improve their leadership skills through the process of self-awareness. Managers who are aware of and manage their actions consciously and deliberately choose the most effective behavior in any given situation. Becoming aware and willing to learn about themselves, including the way they think, act, and react helps leader-managers understand that all opinions are valid and that opinions are not facts. Another point of the awareness process is learning how to learn, which consists of going from a state of not knowing to knowing. According to May and Kruger (see pp. 76-86), to command any task, learners typically progress through four stages: (1) unconscious incompetence—they are unaware of their incompetence; (2) conscious incompetence —they are aware of their incompetence; (3) conscious competence—they are aware of their incompetence and take successful steps to correct it; and (4) unconscious competence—the accomplishment of the task is automatic. The key stage in the learning process, as May and Kruger explain, is conscious incompetence. To move through and beyond this stage, leader-managers must be willing to dig for information they don't know about themselves.

The first chapter, "Overcoming Internal Barriers to Success," focuses on managers building their own self-esteem and self-confidence, and overcoming fears and insecurity. The idea conveyed is that in using these positive practices themselves, managers will be more aware of how they can help others in these areas. The authors believe that one of the basic problems keeping a manager from managing well is a sense of insecurity resulting from low self-worth, while on the other hand, high self-worth contributes to a positive attitude and makes people hopeful and confident that they can achieve for themselves while they are achieving for the organization. Several techniques are outlined to help increase awareness of self and why we behave, feel, and think the way we do. We are warned, however, that at times we will discover some things about ourselves that we do not like. Beck and Hillmar point out the significance of these discoveries: "It is important to accept your weaknesses and negatives as well as your strengths and positives so that you can accept yourself as a human being. You may also find that the weaknesses or negatives may really be assets at times."

Norman Hill's chapter suggests that among the several personality factors which characterize effective leadership, self-esteem, the evaluation which a person maintains regarding his or her own abilites, is the most fundamental. He argues that those who have a high degree of self-esteem never feel threatened or insecure. This enables them to display the same confidence toward subordinates with which they regard themselves. Just as self-esteem builds confidence in social interactions, it also allows the setting of high expectations for one's self and others in the organization. The author ends the article by refuting the cliche: what you see is what you get. Instead, he claims that what you expect is what you get.

The chapter by Celia Wall conveys a similar theme. The author surveys writings on self-concept and shows that the literature is in agreement about the importance of self-concept and argues that a positive self-concept is of significant importance to women aspiring to library management positions. Wall further asserts that self-concept can be changed or altered, but first an individual must realize there is a need for a change, decide what that change is to be, and make a conscious commitment to begin working toward developing a more positive self-concept. However, changing self-concept is not easy. The author concludes that a positive self-concept is not only useful in succeeding in leadership or management roles, but will also lead to a fuller, happier life.

Top leader-managers seem to blend their vision of the future with their intuitive skills when they are involved in creative high-risk decision making. Edson's discussion of "Intuition" suggests that understanding how intuitive insights appear is the answer to knowing how creative processes are developed. This chapter gives a historical and philosophical explanation of how the concept of intuition has been defined by scholars over the centuries, including Plato, Descartes, and Kant. In defining contemporary thoughts on intuition, Edson devotes approximately one-third of his discussion to the relationship of intuition to new research findings about the brain and the "split-brain" studies. He gives a warning that the new knowledge of mental processes based on physiology has not dispelled the mythology that surrounds intuition. "There is, for example, the illusion that only specially-endowed people have significant intuitive powers. Actually, psychologists agree that we all have intuitive power, though, like intelligence, it is distributed in varying degrees." However, one myth of intuition that needs changing is that it is inherited in a fixed amount. The author closes this chapter by describing methods of improving intuition in problem solving that have long been sanctioned by psychologists. These methods are based on the descriptions by creative individuals of insights that led to major discoveries. The process is said to have five phases: preparation, frustration, incubation, illumination, and elaboration.

The last chapter in part II, "The Manager Within," discusses an experiential approach to developing leadership skills. This approach requires managers to engage in introspection and to operate from a mindset known as managing from a context of mastery. The authors propose that to operate from this context, managers should adhere to the four principles of empowerment: (1) self-mastery, (2) integrity, (3) effective communication, and (4) partnership. To reach the level of *self-mastery* managers must evaluate their lives on a physical, psychological, and spiritual level. In the physical area, managers must first evaluate their eating, drinking, and exercise habits. Psychologically it refers to instructing the mind to handle mental and emotional reactions. To structure the mind psychologically, managers first must be willing to learn about themselves. The spiritual dimension emerges from the realization that there is a higher purpose to life than merely surviving or getting by. To reach this level the manager must aspire to achieve his or her full potential.

Integrity in this context means to be whole or complete and to exist in an unimpaired state or condition. Once again, managers need to apply this to their physical, psychological, and spiritual dimensions. *Effective communication* involves speaking, listening, asking questions, and articulating one's vision. *Partnership* is an expression of a manager's individual commitment to self through a commitment to others. After explaining these principles of empowerment for managerial mastery, the authors give details of a comprehensive experiential learning course designed to help managers learn to manage themselves and their relationships from a context of *self-mastery*.

The appendixes include two inventories that are related to the topics in part II: Appendix C, "The Assertiveness Inventory," and Appendix D, the "Assertiveness Checklist." "The Assertiveness Inventory" will be helpful in assessing your assertiveness. It is followed by the brief "Assertiveness Checklist." These two inventories will serve as excellent follow-up activity to the assertion and self-confidence material presented in this part.

NOTES

[1]Donald Sanzotta, *The Manager's Guide to Interpersonal Relations* (New York, AMACOM, 1979.

[2]Warren Bennis and Burt Nanus, *Leaders* (New York: Harper and Row, 1985).

[3]Ibid., 58.

[4]Ibid., 59.

[5]Janette S. Caputo, *The Assertive Librarian* (Phoenix, Ariz.: Oryx Press, 1984).

[6]Weston H. Agor, *Intuitive Management* (Englewood Cliffs, N.J.: Prentice-Hall, 1984).

ADDITIONAL READINGS

Agor, Weston H. "Manage Brain Skills to Increase Productivity." *Personnel* 63 (August 1986): 42-46.

Alberti, Robert E. and Michael L. Emmons. *Your Perfect Right*. San Luis Obispo, Calif.: Impact, 1986.

Anderson, A. J. "Do People Change Their Management Styles and Practices as a Result of Taking Courses and Attending Workshops?" *Journal of Library Administration* 6 (Winter 1985/1986): 1-14.

Beck, Arthur C., and Ellis D. Hillmar. "The Power of Positive Management." *Personnel Journal* (February 1983): 126-31.

_____. "Releasing Creativity and Innovation." In *Power of Positive Management*, 139-52. San Francisco: Jossey-Bass, 1986.

Bower, Sharon Anthony, and Gordon H. Bower. *Asserting Yourself*. Reading, Mass.: Addison-Wesley, 1976.

Burley-Allen, Madelyn. *Managing Assertively*. New York: John Wiley, 1983.

Caputo, Janette S. "Self-Esteem and Self-Confidence." In *The Assertive Librarian*, 58-72. Phoenix, Ariz.: Oryx Press, 1984.

Conrath, Jerry. "The Imagination Harvest: Training People to Solve Problems Creatively." *Supervisory Management* 30 (September 1985): 6-10.

Cribbin, James J. "Understanding Human Behavior: How Sharp Is Your Cue Sense." In *Leadership: Strategies for Organizational Effectiveness*, 79-94. New York: AMACOM, 1981.

Curtin, Joseph L. "Putting Self-Esteem First." *Training and Development Journal* 42 (October 1988): 41-44.

Flamholtz, Eric G., and Yvonne Randle. "The Inner Game of Management." *Management Review* 77 (April 1988): 24-30.

_____. *The Inner Game of Management*. New York: AMACOM, 1987.

Friend, William. "Unblock the Roadblock to Innovation: Be a Creative Leader." *Association Management* (March 1982): 54-57.

Harper, Stephen C. "Intuition: What Separates Executives from Managers." *Business Horizons* 31 (September/October 1988): 13-19.

"The Johari Window: A Model for Soliciting and Giving Feedback." In *The 1973 Annual Handbook for Group Facilitators*, 115-19. La Jolla, Calif.: University Associates Publishers, 1973.

Keirsey, David, and Marilyn Bates. *Please Understand Me*. Del Mar, Calif.: Prometheus Nemesis Book Co., 1984.

Mintzberg, Henry. "Planning on the Left Side and Managing on the Right." *Harvard Business Review* 54 (July/August 1976): 49-58.

Myers, Isabel Briggs. *Gifts Differing*. Palo Alto, Calif.: Consulting Psychologists, 1985.

O'Brien, Roger T. "Using Jung More (And Etching Him in Stone Less)." *Training* 22 (May 1985): 53-65.

Phelps, Stanlee, and Nancy Austin. *The Assertive Woman*. Fredericksburg, Va.: Impact Bookcrafters, 1975.

Pugliese, Paul. "The Center for Creative Leadership." *Journal of Library Administration* 7 (Spring 1986): 25-30.

Rinke, Wolf J. "Maximizing Management Potential by Building Self-Esteem." *Management Solutions* 33 (March 1988): 11-16.

Slocum, John W., Jr., and Don Hellriegel. "A Look at How Managers' Minds Work." *Business Horizons* 26 (July/August 1983): 58-68.

Sundel, Sandra Stone, and Martin Sundel. *Be Assertive*. Beverly Hills, Calif.: Sage, 1980.

Wiberg, Lars-Erik. "Should You Change Your Leadership Style?" *Management Solutions* (January 1988): 5-12.

CHAPTER 6

Overcoming Internal Barriers to Success

Arthur C. Beck and Ellis D. Hillmar

We read about a pediatrician telling a young mother, "If you do not take care of your-self, you will not have the energy to take care of your baby." There is only so much energy. If we do not replenish ours, we will not have any to give to others. We must be free to receive and ask for help at all times. Otherwise, we are in danger of eventual burnout. Ask yourself who is the most important person in your life. The answer should be "I am!" If it is spouse, child, parent, mentor, or someone else, you are putting that person ahead of you and, there-fore, probably not taking care of yourself adequately. For some, it will sound selfish to put oneself before loved ones. However, if you look at it from the standpoint that you must have good energy if you are to give to others, it is easier to accept the need to take care of your-self. This is part of empowering yourself to use your potency and energy in problem solving.

It is easy to think of yourself in roles—parent, son, sister, or wife at home and account-ant, manager, salesperson, or programmer at work. When you do that, you do not see your-self as a human being. You are more than your role: you are a person, a human being, first. Acceptance of this gives you permission to be clear about your identity and to constantly work to discover all the good things about yourself that you have covered up or denied over the years.

This chapter will concentrate on how managers can get clear with themselves about their persons. These positive practices are helpful to managers in building their own self-esteem and self-confidence and overcoming fears and insecurity. In using these positive practices themselves, they will be more aware of how they can help others in these areas. By getting clear with themselves, they also will be better able to use the other positive practices offered in this book.

This is a highly personal subject and somewhat difficult to write about, as it works dif-ferently for each of us. The best way we know is to share our own experiences and the exper-iences of others to give you some idea of how to go about changing your attitude about your-self. You, the manager, will have to learn to use whatever works for you. When you make human resources a top priority, you will see the need to deal with personal issues. There will be high emphasis on people growing and developing as human beings as well as managers,

Reprinted with permission from *Positive Management Practices*. San Francisco: Jossey-Bass Inc., 1986.

technicians, and operators. We believe that one of the basic problems keeping a manager from managing well is insecurity from low self-worth. Where there is insecurity, some managers may put up a strong front to mask a low self-image. Others may behave very passively, avoiding evaluation and confrontation. There will probably be defensiveness, blaming, criticizing, avoidance, or other destructive behavior.

BEHAVIORAL ASPECTS OF A CLEAR IDENTITY

When you are clear on your identity as a human being, you will be aware of your needs and wants and be willing to ask to get them satisfied. You can also accept your uniqueness and your values and know the reasons behind your behavior. With this awareness, you are better able to look at the behavioral choices you have in situations. When you are aware that you make choices, consciously or unconsciously, you will take responsibility for yourself and your behavior. No one can make you angry; you choose whether to be angry when someone does something to you. Consequently, you say not "You made me angry" but "When you behave that way, I get angry, and I will appreciate your stopping it." There is no blaming in the latter statement; you are asking for what you want. The other person will usually oblige or move into problem solving to lessen the unwanted behavior. Another statement that is disempowering and denies choices is "I can't do that." When you ask yourself "Who is stopping me?", you discover that, in most instances, the person is yourself. Consequently, the straight, responsible statement is "I won't do that" or "I choose not to do that." Such statements put you in a position to look at your choices and the risks involved. On that basis, you then make a conscious decision on the action to be taken.

Clarity on identity results in a high degree of spontaneity and creativity. When you are sure of yourself and willing to share your ideas and thoughts with others, even though you may not always be able to explain them logically, you are listening to your intuition. Also, when you are clear on your identity, you are able to communicate with others with the minimum of defensiveness and blaming. You are also able and willing to develop intimate relationships with others. The closeness and good feelings result in positive and more productive working relationships. You are able to make contact with others more readily and let go of them when appropriate. Finally, you are aware of your technical and managerial competence and willing to use it freely and productively. You are willing to take risks in your organization and in your personal life to achieve improvement and development. This means that you are willing to explore new ways and new insights and are open to discovery and the ideas, suggestions, and feedback of others without feeling threatened. You are open to your own intuition and not dependent exclusively on external data. There is balance in the way you are managing and living your life.

HOW YOU GOT THE WAY YOU ARE

Psychologists say that we make most of the decision on how we live our lives before we are six years old. We were influenced by the social environment in which we lived and by the authority figures in our lives—parents, grandparents, uncles and aunts, older brothers and sisters, ministers and priests, teachers, and so on. Sometimes we blame our parents and others for the way we are. It is important that we accept the fact that we made the decisions on our lives, some consciously and some unconsciously. We made these decisions in order to survive, and they were probably appropriate at that time; we did the best that we knew how. Some of us decided to be like our parents, and some decided to be different. An example is twin boys who had an alcoholic father. At age twenty-one, one of the twins was an alcoholic and the other was a teetotaler.

We learn how to survive. For instance, we know a person who experienced violence in his family when he was a small child and learned how to withdraw to ignore it. This same behavior is still with him at times today. When there is uncomfortable conflict, his first response is to withdraw and avoid it. Now that he is aware of this pattern, he deliberately changes his behavior and deals with the conflict. He also asks for feedback from colleagues and his family when they see him in his avoidance behavior, which is dysfunctional in his organization and with his family.

These early decisions in life are basically centered around our self-worth or, in transactional-analysis langugage, "my OKness with me." We may decide that we are OK in some ways and not OK in other ways—for example, that we have book sense but not common sense. This decision may result in our making top grades in school but poor decisions in our life situations. Other not-OK decisions might be that we are not creative or not good at mathematics. Living with these decisions will result in a negative attitude about creativity and problem solving and difficulty with mathematics or financial concerns.

When we accept responsibility for the decisions that we have made about how to live our lives, we have taken the first step toward change. We can change any of these decisions at any time. Of course, some will be more difficult and painful to change than others, and we may need a good therapist to help us. We can then start a new pattern of responsive behavior. This change can happen by a conscious, deliberate act of will.

WAYS TO DETERMINE SELF-WORTH

You need both self-analysis and help from others to determine whether your behavior shows evidence of low self-worth in these areas (adapted from Osborne, 1976, pp. 55-66):

1. Being overly sensitive—your response to being confronted and receiving negative feedback from others. Do you become defensive and angry, or do you withdraw?

2. Being excessively argumentative, to prove a point. Do you have a win-lose attitude?

3. Being critical of others. Are you aware that often what you criticize in others is what you dislike in yourself?

4. Being intolerant of others and their ideas. Do you see them as threats, or do you think that only you have good ideas?

5. Being a hostile person. Do you project your anger onto others? Do you fly off the handle at the least provocation?

6. Wanting to punish others. Are you forgiving of others, and do you free yourself from the need to get back at those who have done something to you?

7. Not listening to others. Do you ignore others or think of something else while they are talking?

8. Being overly materialistic. Are you concerned only with materialism and not sensitive to the human and feeling aspects of situations? The opposite of this may also be a problem.

9. Being insecure and fearful. Do you allow your insecurity and fear to block your humanness toward others?

10. Putting undue emphasis on status symbols. Do you allow the desire for titles, degrees, and honors to get in the way of being human?

11. Knowing what to do when you lose. Are you hostile or depressed when you lose or things go against you?

12. Having difficulty receiving compliments. Do you feel that you are not worthy of compliments or that you should have done better, that you never do enough?

This checklist helps you determine your self-worth and whether you are spending your time in the positive OK position. These are areas where you place handicaps on yourself in playing the game of life. You can look at your life as a game of tennis, where your goal is getting the ball over the net as often as possible—not winning but keeping on playing. When you have high self-worth, you are not easily defeated.

THE DISADVANTAGES OF LOW SELF-WORTH

Low self-worth brings with it many disadvantages and barriers to top performance. It is the self-fulfilling prophecy—when you expect and feel the negative, that is usually what will happen. You prove you are correct in your perception and feelings. Low self-worth—not OK life position—results in negative behavior and a negative environment. This gives rise to insecurity, hostility, depression, and many barriers to problem solving and productivity, both individually and organizationally. There are feelings of inferiority and superiority. There are many negative "shoulds" that prevent individuals and groups from being free to use their competency in contributing to organizational achievement.

Those with the insecurity of the "I am not OK" position will wait for someone else to take the lead. They will probably be obsessed with the past and have considerable fear of such things as making a mistake, failure, rejection, the unknown, or not being able to handle the results of their actions. People with such fears are not free to be themselves and have handicaps in being productive. They are constantly trying to prove themselves to others. They are defensive, worrying, and blaming and spend their time and energy in "CYA" ("cover your behind") and survival efforts.

Guilt occurs in the "I am not OK" position. If the inner self is pursuing incompatible goals, there is a vague, gnawing sense of remorse, uneasiness, or anxiety when both goals cannot be achieved. Failure to "do right," be perfect, or complete a project may bring on guilt. Violating a negative "should" is the cause for many of their splits in goals. Fifteen minutes is long enough to feel guilt about anything. Either rectify the error or forgive yourself, or both, and move on. If you continue to feel guilty, this negativity will sap your energy, and there will be little or nothing to give to others and the organization.

THE VALUE OF HIGH SELF-WORTH

High self-worth contributes to a positive attitude and makes people hopeful and confident that they can achieve for themselves while they are achieving for the organization. When people are in this state, they are more spontaneous and responsive to their intuitions. They feel more secure in themselves and are willing to take more risks and feel free to accept help from others without being threatened. They grow, develop, and increase their contributions to their organizations. They are excited and energized by the discovery of their many talents and good points. They take control of their lives, aware of the choices that they have, and deliberately make decisions about their lives.

When all of these characteristics are present, a person is living the "being" values identified by Maslow (1968) in his description of the state of self-actualization: wholeness, perfection, completion, justice, aliveness, richness, simplicity, beauty, goodness, uniqueness, effortlessness, playfulness, truth, and self-sufficiency. When managers and their subordinates feel this way, the organization will have available the whole human resource, and the needs of the organization and the individuals will be satisfied.

HOW TO GET CLEAR ON YOUR IDENTITY

In getting clear about yourself, you will be clear on your identity. You will know who you are, your values, your biases and prejudices, your strengths and weaknesses, and how all of these fit together to make you an "OK" human being. To achieve and maintain this clarity, you have to work constantly to develop the necessary self-discipline. It is well to remember that there are "no free lunches." When you accept yourself as the most important person in your life, you will devote the necessary time, effort, and resources. Some things you can do alone; with others, you will need support from associates, friends, and family. Some of the tools and techniques that you can use are listed here:

1. Use silence to listen to your intuition and draw on your inner power source. You will be pleasantly surprised with the solutions to problems that will come to you at these times.

2. Use affirmations and visualization to program your unconscious for positive experiences and achievement of goals.

3. Develop your own distinctive holistic stress-management program, to meet your individual needs.

4. Start or join a support group with others dedicated to the same goal that you wish to achieve.

5. Attend personal-growth workshops that have objectives that are compatible with yours.

6. Read books such as *Be the Person You Were Meant to Be* (Greenwald, 1974) and others. There are a growing number of good books on the bookshelves today.

7. Use psychological tests designed to help you become aware of your values and personality preferences in making decisions. Ones we have found helpful are "Values for Working" (Flowers, Hughes, Myers, and Myers, 1975) and the Myers-Briggs Type Indicator (Myers and Myers, 1980). When you have this understanding of yourself, you are more aware of the choices you have in the way you behave and can choose to behave differently if what you are now doing is causing problems for others or not producing what you want.

8. Work to change negative norms in the organization to norms that are supportive of your goals.

Use all of these techniques to increase your awareness of yourself and why you behave, feel, and think the way you do. Of course, at times you will discover some things about yourself that you do not like. It is important to accept your weaknesses and negatives as well as your strengths and positives so that you can accept yourself as a human being. You may also find that the weaknesses or negatives may really be assets at times. We find the following "five freedoms" articulated by Satir (1976, p. 15) to be helpful: "to see and hear what is here instead of what should be, was, or will be; ... to say what one feels and thinks instead of what one should; ... to feel what one feels instead of what one ought; ... to ask for what one wants instead of always waiting for permission; ... to take risks in one's own behalf instead of choosing to be 'secure' and to not rock the boat."

DISCIPLINE

To do all of this requires self-discipline. This means that you have to maintain the self-control and orderliness to accomplish your goals. The word *discipline* does not appear very often in management or personality literature, and when it does, it usually refers to disciplining someone else—subordinates or children. Peck (1978), in *The Road Less Traveled*, emphasizes the need for discipline, which he defines as "the means of experiencing the pain of problems constructively." He gives four tools for disciplining yourself: (1) delayed gratification, (2) acceptance of responsibility, (3) dedication to the truth, and (4) balancing.

Delayed Gratification. This is a process of scheduling the painful or disliked tasks first and then experiencing the things you like, the pleasurable things. Some children do this by saving the best part of the cake—the icing—for last. This is applied in time management by doing the distasteful things before doing the things you like to do. This discipline is helpful in scheduling exercise and meditation at the same time each day. It also works well when you have a disagreeable item to discuss with a subordinate. When you perform the painful task first, you will do it expeditiously and well.

Acceptance of Responsibility. You must accept responsibility for a problem before you can solve it. If you have a feeling of self-worth, you are willing to accept responsibility for your decisions on how to live your life. Some of these decisions were made when you were a child and were appropriate for your survival but may not be appropriate today. When you take responsibility for this, you can make a deliberate decision to change your behavior so that you can be more positive and productive in your relationships.

Dedication to the Truth. When you are dedicated to the truth, you will endure the pain of self-examination. You will be open to challenges from others and willing to change your behavior when it is dysfunctional. Lying avoids the pain of challenge and circumvents legitimate suffering. We remember advice from Scott Myers, a management consultant:

"When in doubt, be honest." Recently, a lawyer specializing in equal employment opportunity cases advised his client, "Always be honest with your employees, because if you are not, you will be found out, and then your are in deep trouble." Being truthful does not mean total openness, as it is appropriate at times to limit the revelation.

Balancing. Discipline is a demanding and complex task involving flexibility and judgment. Balancing is the discipline that gives you flexibility. An example of this is deciding whether to express anger. If you express it, you must do it in a nondestructive manner and not attack anyone's self-esteem. If you decide not to express it, you must use another way of diffusing it so that you do not dump it on someone else later or do harm to yourself. When you do not handle such things as anger, you will get out of balance, losing mental and emotional equilibrium.

Peck (1978) states that balancing is a discipline because the act of giving up something is painful. As you move through life, you must continually give up parts of yourself. This is applicable in organizations, as you may have to give up some things you cherish so that the organization is successful. You may even have to accept less achievement in your area in order not to disrupt other units.

We have experienced another example of balancing in our understanding of our personality types through the use of the Myers-Briggs Type Indicator. Now that we are aware of our personality preferences, we find that when we insist on behaving the way we like to behave, we may cause problems. We now know that we are capable of behaving in a different way, a way that is supportive of developing productive relationships and keeping things in balance. For instance, we may have a strong preference for making decisions quickly and sticking to schedules. Sometimes this causes problems, as we may push to make the decision prematurely, without sufficient information. Fortunately, we have some people around us who slow us down, and then we realize that we need to take more time to get more information. The decision is usually a better one.

HAVING A CONFIDANT

When a manager—or any person—embarks on this journey, it is desirable to have a confidant, a person with whom you can be vulnerable, let your hair down, and admit your weaknesses and concerns without fear of your admissions being used against you. Preferably the confidant should be a competent counselor, therapist, or consultant working with the organization; there may be more than one person. To facilitate change, a manager will also need a consultant who will give feedback on all aspects of his or her behavior in the organization as well as help make contracts with subordinates and colleagues. Above all, the manager must receive this feedback and use it. If the manager initially rejects the feedback, he or she should apologize when the damaged ego has healed.

Changes discussed in this chapter do not occur overnight. They require a long journey with many painful moments but many, many joyful and productive ones as well. It becomes easier the more you work at it and use the help that is available to you. The positive practices described in this chapter may be the first that a manager uses in embarking on a change in his or her management style, but they will be useful at any time in a manager's self-development. For further exploration of this topic see Huxley (1963), Osborne (1976), Satir (1978), Schwarz (1977), and Scott (1980).

REFERENCES

Flowers, V. S., Hughes, C. L., Myers, M. S., and Myers, S. S. *Managerial Values for Working*. New York: AMACOM, 1975.

Greenwald, J. A. *Be the Person You Were Meant to Be*. New York: Dell, 1974.

Huxley, L. A. *You Are Not the Target*. Beverly Hills, Calif.: Leighton Printing Company, 1963.

Maslow, A. H. *Toward a Psychology of Being*. New York: D. Van Nostrand, 1968.

Myers, I. B., and Myers, P. B. *Gifts Differing*. Palo Alto, Calif.: Consulting Psychologists Press, 1980.

Osborne, C. G. *The Art of Learning to Love Yourself*. Grand Rapids, Mich.: Zondervan, 1976.

Peck, M. S. *The Road Less Traveled*. New York: Simon & Schuster, 1978.

Satir, V. *Making Contact*. Millbrae, Calif.: Celestial Arts, 1976.

Satir, V. *Your Many Faces*. Millbrae, Calif.: Celestial Arts, 1978.

Schwarz, J. *The Path of Action*. New York: Dutton, 1977.

Scott, D. *How to Put More Time in Your Life*. New York: Rawson Wade, 1980.

CHAPTER 7

Self-Esteem
The Key to Effective Leadership

Norman Hill

Leadership is a process of influence. The process can be seen when people join together to accomplish some common objective through their collective efforts. Leadership refers to a person's ability to guide, modify, and direct the actions of others in such a way as to gain their cooperation in doing a job. It is the ability of a person to direct the problem-solving processes of others.

There are a variety of methods available for managers to exert influence and thereby demonstrate their style of leadership. Three primary views exist in the current management literature regarding the most effective way for leaders to influence those with whom they associate.

- *Effective leaders are characterized by supportive behavior exhibited toward the people who report to them.* That is, they are "considerate and warm," eager to help in personal matters, and often willing to bend the rules for unusual circumstances. Since supportive leaders are willing to do favors for subordinates, they anticipate that such good turns will be reciprocated when they ask subordinates to do things. Accrued debts and returned favors, then, become the basis of their influence.

- *Effective leaders utilize participative decision making as supervision and control mechanisms.* This point of view maintains that by involving everyone in both the problem analysis and the derived solution, better information will be generated and everyone will be more committed to implementing the decision and solving the problem. In this way, influence is a function of commitment and involvement.

- *Effective leaders are flexible enough to consider contingency approaches to problems because they realize that every situation is different.* This is an "if/then" approach to leadership. If certain factors exist in the environment, are characteristic of subordinates, and if they are elements of the task, then a particular type of leadership strategy should be employed to be influential. If conditions change, the leader must be more authoritarian or more consultative, depending upon the nature of these demands.

Each of these positions has advocates and critics. Proponents describe how their preferred methods are effective means by which leaders can influence their subordinates, while opponents attempt to include other factors questioning the utility of such an approach. One factor, though, upon which almost all of those who study leadership are in agreement is: those who influence others possess a significant degree of self-esteem.

A factor which has appeared repeatedly in the findings on all types of productive functioning, writes John Gilmore in "The Productive Personality," is self-esteem. Self-esteem is the evaluation which a person maintains regarding his own abilities: it expresses an attitude of approval or disapproval and indicates the extent to which an individual believes himself capable of doing a job and making a significant contribution to something. It is a valuation determined largely by the degree to which a person's successes approach his expectations in those areas that are important to him. Either too few successes or too high expectations may result in a poor self-evaluation.

Several studies have demonstrated that self-esteem does indeed affect a leader's effectiveness. In 1948 B. B. Gardner wrote a book entitled "What Makes Successful and Unsuccessful Executives?" He answered his question by saying that those who possessed a clear sense of identity and knew what they wanted and how to achieve it were promoted sooner and more often than their colleagues who believed that they were not as admirable as they should be.

Another investigation which established a relationship between self-esteem and personal success began way back in 1922. Approximately 1,400 adolescents between the ages of 10 and 11 years with genius-level IQs, placing them in the top 1 percent of the nation's population, were identified by researchers. In follow-up surveys in 1940 and 1950 (when participants were in their early thirties and forties), three factors were found which distinguished the most successful from the least successful. These were integration toward goals, perseverance, and self-confidence. Apparently those who were the most successful recognized both their abilities and limitations, were reasonable in their aspirations and expectations, and were undaunted in pursuing them.

It seems that the reason those who possess a high degree of self-esteem are able to influence others is that their own sense of personal security is not violated in interpersonal exchanges. They feel neither threat nor insecurity because of their positive self-evaluation. In an organizational setting, such people are effective leaders because they exhibit the same confidence toward subordinates with which they regard themselves.

What leaders believe about themselves influences what they believe about subordinates. If they have confidence in their own ability, they will have high — but realistic — expectations of the people who report to them and help employees to satisfy what emerges as their mutual expectations. What leaders expect of them, and the subsequent way in which they treat the people who report to them, in turn largely determines their performance and development.

The influence of one person's expectations upon another's behavior has been demonstrated in organizational settings as well. David Berlew and Douglas Hall, who were at the time of their study associated with MIT, examined several years ago the career progress of managers employed by American Telephone and Telegraph Company. After observing 49 managers over a five-year period, they concluded that the relative success of managers, as indicated by promotions and estimates of each person's performance and potential, depended largely on their supervisors' expectations of them.

Several conclusions can be drawn about the influence leaders can exert through the expectations which they consistently maintain and demonstrate toward subordinates:

- What leaders expect of their staffs affects their performance.

- A unique characteristic of effective leaders is their ability to create high performance standards for the people who report to them to fulfill.

- Less effective leaders fail to develop such positive expectations and so subordinates accomplish less.

Those who occupy positions of authority in organizations are often more effective in communicating low expectations than they are in expressing high expectations. In fact, supervisors often communicate most when they think they are communicating least. What supervisors actually say matters less than how they behave. Expectations seem to be communicated most frequently by nonverbal cues such as the climate and norms a manager creates and perpetuates.

These unwritten rules, illustrated by the amount of attention and feedback given by a supervisor to subordinates, have the greatest amount of impact. Rewarding initiative, correcting mistakes, asking for input, sharing feelings, and being willing to change personal perceptions are some specific ways to communicate positive expectations.

To exert a meaningful influence, expectations must be more than the power of positive thinking. The popular works of authors such as Maxwell Maltz, Norman Vincent Peale, Dale Carnegie, Clement Stone, and others have all shown that self-image and expectations are important factors in task performance, but they all have over-dramatized their effects.

For instance, Harvard psychologist David McClelland has found that subordinates will not be influenced by a supervisor's expectations unless those expectations are considered reasonable and realistic. Goals that are too high or too low will have little impact on them. Influence seems greatest and motivation highest when subordinates feel that they have about a 50 percent probability — a 50/50 chance — of fulfilling their supervisors' explicit expectations.

Effective leaders seem to exhibit two common characteristics: confidence in their own ability and high expectations of others. The high expectations of effective leaders, moreover, are based primarily on how they feel about themselves. What people believe about themselves subtly influences what they believe about others, what they expect of them, and how they treat them. A leader who possesses a positive self-image will generate high performance standards from subordinates and will treat them with the confidence that these expectations and standards will be met. Expectations, then, become self-fulfilling if they appear reasonable and realistic to subordinates. So instead of saying "what you see is what you get," it could more appropriately be said that "what you expect is what you get."

CHAPTER 8

Self-Concept
An Element of Success
in the Female Library Manager
Celia Wall

Despite a somewhat heartening trend over the past few years, the appointment of women to a number of important library management positions, the stark fact remains that the profession is overwhelmingly populated by females and is predominately managed by males. A number of investigators have documented this phenomenon thoroughly. They and others have written persuasively that societal structures, traditional prejudices, and other factors have caused and contributed to it, and that females have ethical and legal rights to greater opportunities for appointment to library management positions, including directorships.

This paper examines a body of literature not perused in great detail by those exploring the status of women in librarianship. It surveys writings about a single characteristic of the human psyche, that of self-concept. It shows that these writings are in essential agreement about the importance of self-concept and argues that a positive self-concept is of significant importance to women aspiring to library management positions.

SOME COMMON MYTHS

Nearly 22 million women, "civilians 16 years old and over," were employed in the United States work force in 1960. This figure represented 33 percent of the total employment during that year. Of those 22 million, five percent were classified as "managers and administrators." By 1981 the number of women employed in the United States had risen to 43 million, or 43 percent of the total work force. Yet, the number of female "managers and administrators" reported in 1981 was only a little over three million.[1] Expressed differently, only seven percent of the women employed in 1981 were classified by the Bureau of Labor Statistics as "managers and administrators."

Reprinted with permission from the *Journal of Library Administration*, Vol. 6 (4), Winter 1985-1986. Copyright by the The Haworth Press, Inc., New York.

Comparable figures for males show that, in 1960, 67 percent of the total employed were males; 14 percent of those were classified as "managers and administrators." By 1981 male representation in the work force had dropped to 57 percent; yet, 15 percent of those males were still classified as "managers and administrators."[2] This comparison makes it very clear that women's representation in management ranks is not keeping pace with their growing numbers in the work force. The question is, why not?

A review of the literature on women in management very quickly reveals some common myths used to justify keeping women in traditional "women's jobs" and where they have fewer responsibilities, less chance for promotion and advancement, and smaller paychecks:

— A women's place is in the home.

— Women only work for pocket money.

— Women cost more to employ because they are absent more.

— Training costs more and is largely wasted because women don't stay on the job as long or as regularly as men.

— Married women take jobs away from men who are the sole support of families.

— Women don't want responsibility on the job so they refuse promotions or job changes.

— The employment of mothers leads to juvenile delinquency.

— Men don't like to work for women supervisors.[3]

While these myths are troublesome and irritating, facts, figures and logic can be used to dispel these myths for anyone interested enough to consider them carefully:

> *A woman's place is in the home.* Homemaking in itself is no longer a full-time job for most people. Goods and services formerly produced in the home are now commercially available; labor saving devices have lightened or eliminated much work around the home.
>
> Today more than half of all women between 18 and 64 years of age are in the labor force, where they are making a substantial contribution to the nation's economy. Studies show that nine out of ten girls will work outside the home at some time in their lives.[4]
>
> *Women only work for pocket money.* Of the nearly 34 million women in the labor force in March 1973, nearly half were working because of pressing economic need. They were either single, widowed, divorced, or separated or had husbands whose incomes were less than $3,000 a year. Another 4.7 million had husbands with incomes between $3,000 and $7,000.[5]
>
> *Women cost more to employ because they are absent more.* A recent Public Health Service study shows little difference in the absentee rate due to illness or injury: 5.6 days a year for women compared with 5.2 for men.[6]
>
> *Training costs more and is largely wasted because women don't stay on the job as long or as regularly as men.* A declining number of women leave work for marriage and children. But even among those who do leave, a majority return when

their children are in school. Even with a break in employment, the average woman worker has a worklife expectancy of 25 years as compared with 43 years for the average male worker. The single women averages 45 years in the labor force.[7]

Married women take jobs away from men who are the sole support of families. There were 19.8 million married women (husbands present) in the labor force in March 1973; the number of unemployed men was 2.5 million. If all the married women stayed home and unemployed men were placed in their jobs, there would be 17.3 million unfilled jobs.[8]

Women don't want responsibility on the job so they refuse promotions or job changes. Relatively few women have been offered positions of responsibility. But when given these opportunities, women, like men, do cope with job responsibilities in addition to personal or family responsibilities. In 1973, 4.7 million women held professional and technical jobs, another 1.6 million worked as non-farm managers and administrators. Many others held supervisory jobs at all levels in offices and factories.[9]

The employment of mothers leads to juvenile delinquency. Studies show that many factors must be considered when seeking causes of juvenile delinquency. Whether or not a mother is employed does not appear to be a determining factor.

These studies indicate that it is the quality of a mother's care rather than the time consumed in such care which is of major significance.[10]

Men don't like to work for women supervisors. Most men who complain about women supervisors have never worked for a woman.

In one study where at least three-fourths of both the male and female respondents (all executives) had worked with women managers, their evaluation of women in management was favorable. On the other hand, the study showed a traditional/cultural bias among those who reacted unfavorably to women as managers.

In another survey in which 41 percent of the reporting firms indicated that they hired women executives, none rated their performance as unsatisfactory; 50 percent rated them adequate; 42 percent rated them the same as their predecessors; and 8 percent rated them better than their predecessors.[11]

HER OWN WORST ENEMY

The same literature review on women in management also reveals a phenomenon which is a much more serious threat to women with management aspirations than any of these myths. Jean Wellington, an associate professor of education at Tufts University and a therapist in private practice, has counseled many working women. She concluded that,

> ... they (women) themselves are often unwitting party to their employment picture. A woman's own self-concept and her value system in relationship to her roles appear to play a part — perhaps a large part — in her overall inferior position in the work force.[12]

This view is also expressed by Higginson and Quick in *The Ambitious Woman's Guide to a Successful Career*:

> It isn't only male attitudes and biases that constitute obstructions for the upwardly mobile woman. Forces within the woman herself, and within other women, pose threats to her success.[13]

In other words, a woman's own attitudes about herself and other women and her own concept of who she is and what she wants to be are ambiguous. Women run into problems many times because their actions transmit to coworkers ambivalent feelings about themselves and their jobs. These ambivalences fall roughly into four categories, "all concerned with the woman's self concept in relation to the right roles for her."

(1) "I Want Success But It Will Hurt Me"[14] — Little girls are not taught such competence-related traits as ambition, competition, and aggression; "the traditional feminine sex role standard does not endorse" such traits.[15] Yet to survive and advance in the working world today — to be a success — an individual, male or female, must possess such traits. A woman, raised to look upon these as masculine qualities, may equate success with lack of feminity. Another problem is that, particularly at the management level, the individuals against whom she is competing are usually male. This goes against the entire upbringing of most women. Traditionally, little girls are taught to develop those skills and arts needed to compete — against other women — for a man, a husband, someone to take care of her.[16] Competing in a man's world, against men, playing the games by men's rules goes against everything women have been taught. It's no wonder a woman may well appear indecisive about whether she really wants success.

(2) "What Am I?"[17] — The second area of ambivalence involves determining which of her several roles receives top priority. Besides having a full-time job, a woman is often expected to be a wife, a mother, a cook, and a housekeeper, many times without much, if any, help from her spouse or children. And society and her upbringing have taught her that to ask, much less demand, such help shows she is shirking her "traditional duties" to her family. If she puts her job first, she is going against her traditional upbringing which has taught her that her home and family come first. Thus the woman who leaves her eight-month old with a sitter during the day so she can return to her job is torn between her own desire for a career and personal fulfillment through her job and her obligations to her family. The result is often a tremendous amount of guilt as well as ambivalent feelings about what she really wants to do.

(3) "I Pledge Allegiance"[18] — The third area of ambivalence pits "perfect wife and mother" against "the feminist conception of the correct female role." What of the career woman who in her late thirties finds herself wanting, needing a home and family? Or the new mother who suddenly discovers that she doesn't want to go back to work or that she resents the time her job takes away from her family? Yet, by accepting such traditional roles as wife and mother and homemaker she feels she is betraying "the movement." The conflict is quite intense at times.

(4) "Proof by Male"[19] — Women often do not have a great deal of respect for the opinions of other women; they need "to be validated by men."

> It is interesting that women managers often report that some of the most pronounced resistance to their advancement comes from other women who seem to have no similar ambitions, or from women who display the traditional prejudice against working for a woman (presumably, working for a woman carries less status than working for a man).[20]

It is hard to reconcile self-validation versus the need to be validated by a male.

A woman's self-concept is important because "everything we do or say, everything we hear, feel or otherwise perceive, is influenced by how we see ourselves."[21] A woman's perception of herself will be reflected in how she deals with others, how she reacts in and perceives various situations and how well she copes with life in general. Felker views the role of self-concept as threefold: "The self-concept operates as a mechanism for maintaining inner consistency; the self-concept determines how experiences are interpreted; and the self-concept proves a set of expectances.[22] Put simply, self-concept translates into actions in both personal and business relations and situations. These actions are viewed by others (the boss, colleagues, subordinates) who in turn make judgments about that person based upon her actions.

A positive self-concept is important to an individual, male or female, who wants to be successful in management. Therefore it is vital that women be aware of the important role self-concept plays in management success, what exactly self-concept is, how it develops, and how it can be changed.

SELF-CONCEPT AND SUCCESS IN MANAGEMENT

Executive Success: Making It In Management is a collection of articles from *Harvard Business Review.* In the introduction, Eliza G.C. Collins, editor, wrote that success as a business executive requires,

> ... that a person have a special set of qualities and skills with which to exercise good judgement, make wise decisions, get along with and lead others. Some of the skills ... can be learned in a didactic process. Others have to be acquired through less rational means; these are the skills of being an effective human being ... functional skills can take managers far in an organization, but what determines their success at the highest levels is their completeness as people.[23]

The book then goes on to devote 104 pages, or 20 percent of the entire text, to seven articles dealing with various aspects of self-concept. The articles in this section "urge executives to develop their self-concepts because it is worth it."[24] Dealt with in these articles are such issues as how conflicts in an individual's self-concept can affect work performance, how a "self-expandable attitude" can improve communications, how a rich emotional life affects work and home life. "The articles in this section celebrate growth," Collins says, and one's self-concept is at the core of the growth process.

Self-Concept Defined

One encyclopedia of psychology defines self-concept as "The total attitudes, judgements, and values of an individual relating to his behavior, abilities, and qualities. Self-concept embraces the awareness of these variables and their evaluation."[25] Felker sees self-concept as "the sum total of the view which an individual has of himself. Self-concept is an unique set of perceptions, ideas, and attitudes which an individual has about himself."[26] Labenne explains self-concept as "the person's total appraisal of his appearance, background and origins, abilities and resources, attitudes and feelings which culminate as a directing force in behaviors."[27] Samuels, in *Enhancing Self-Concept in Early Childhood*, examines self-concept by breaking it down into four dimensions: (1) body self or body image; (2) social self; (3) cognitive self; and (4) self-esteem.[28]

Body Self

Body self or body image "although wholly a psychological phenomenon, embraces not only our view of ourselves psychologically but also physiologically and sociologically."[29] Body image includes current and past experiences of one's body as well as fantasized experiences.[30] The image an individual has in her mind of what she looks like may or may not actually resemble what the body really looks like. There are four factors that go into making up an individual's body image:

(1) the actual subjective perceptions of the body both as to appearance and ability to function;

(2) the integrated psychological factors arising out of the body-concept expressed as somatic delusions;

(3) the sociological factors, namely how parent and society react to the individual; and

(4) the ideal body image, formulated by the individual's attitudes toward the body derived from his experiences, perceptions, comparisons, and identification with the bodies of other persons.[31]

Studies with adults have shown that people who have negative feelings about their bodies will probably have negative feelings about themselves.[32]

Social Self

Social self includes the racial, ethnic, cultural, and religious self. The society in which an individual lives determines the development of the social self since individuals and groups in that society (family, church, and society as a whole) confer "status and (have) expectations that children internalize and strive to live up to."[33] The social self is internalized. Then as an individual moves from situation to situation her reactions to these new environments are predetermined by the internalized social self. At first parents provide the link between social structure and personality; later teachers and peers serve this function.[34]

Cognitive Self

"Cognition is a process by which individuals become aware of and gain meaning from an object or event in their environment. Children's attitudes toward themselves, as well as their knowledge of themselves, result from their increasing cognitive growth and the attitudes around them."[35]

Self-Esteem

Self-esteem is the "evaluative sector of the self-concept."[36] Hamachek defines self-esteem as "an individual's personal judgment of worthiness or unworthiness, approval or disapproval that are expressed in the attitudes he holds toward himself."[37] An individual who has high self-esteem views herself as "a valuable and important person," "at least as good as others of my age and training," "someone worthy of respect and consideration," "able to exert an influence upon people and events," and having a "fairly good understanding" of the kind of person she is. An individual with low self-esteem sees herself as unimportant and unlikeable, unable to do many of the things she wants to do, unsure of her ideas and abilities, ignored by other people, preferring to stick "to known and safe ground," and unworthy.[38]

The Development of Self-Concept

The individual begins the process of forming and developing a self-concept in infancy. The process continues through childhood and adolescence and into adulthood, although the older one gets the more difficult change is. Five phases are present in self-concept formation:

(1) Exploration[39] — Exploration begins in infancy as the newborn begins to explore her own body and her environment. From the baby's discovery of her own toes to the adolescent's discovery that she has a knack for writing poetry, the exploration phase continues. It even extends into adulthood where a woman discovers that for health reasons she must give up jogging and decides to try her hand at sculpture. In each instance the individual is exloring her world and herself to discover her talents and abilities as well as her limitations.

(2) Self differentiation[40] — In this phase the individual becomes aware of the differences between herself and others in her environment. These include differences in physical characteristics, dress, background, mannerisms, and personality.

(3) Identification[41] — This phase goes on more or less simultaneously with phase two. As the individual begins to become aware of the differences and similarities between herself and others, e.g., her mother, she begins to identify with that person and strive to be more like her.

(4) Role playing[42] — This accompanies or follows identification. The individual identifies with another and then seeks to emulate that person. "Whether the role playing is largely imaginative or overtly participatory it gives some opportunity to try the role on for size..."[43]

(5) Reality testing[44] — Reality testing stems from role playing. A young man who wants to be a musician like his father may decide to learn how to play an instrument and join the school band. "Life offers many opportunities for reality testing, in the form of children's play, ... in school courses, ... in extracurricular activities, ... and in part-time or temporary employment."[45]

As an individual goes through each phase she will be influenced by the "significant others" reactions to her experiences, experimenting, and explorations. "Significant others" are "the people who most intimately administer the 'rewards' and 'punishments' in a person's life."[46] For the young child the "significant others" are the parents; later teachers and peers take on this role. The positive or negative reactions of these others to the individual and the individual's behavior contribute to the formation of self-concept.

Changing Self-Concept

Can self-concept, which is initially formed during infancy and childhood, be altered once an individual reaches adulthood? In recent years dozens of popular "self help" books have appeared on the nation's bookstands and at the top of the bestseller lists. Many of these respond with a resounding "yes" — self-concept can be changed even as an adult. Three such books are Maltz's *Psycho-Cybernetics* (1960), Dyer's *Your Erroneous Zones* (1976), and Ringer's *Winning Through Intimidation* (1973).

In *Psycho-Cybernetics* Maltz uses the term "self-image" and claims that the discovery of self-image was the "most important psychologic discovery of this century ... "[47] He defines self-image as,

> ... our own conception of the "sort of person I am." It has been built up from our own beliefs about ourselves. But most of these beliefs about ourselves have unconsciously been formed from our humiliations, our triumphs, and the way other people have reacted to us, especially in early childhood.[48]

There are two things which make this self-image so important to the individual:

(1) "All of an individual's actions, feelings, behaviors — even (his) abilities — are always consistent with his self-image." Maltz believes that an individual will "act like" the person he conceives himself to be. In fact, Maltz believes an individual has no choice in the matter; he cannot act otherwise.[49]

(2) The self-image can be changed.[50] "Once the concept of self is changed, other things consistent with the new concept of self are accomplished easily and without strain."[51]

A major thesis in Maltz's work is that an individual's nervous system "cannot tell the difference between an imagined experience and a 'real' experience. In either case, it reacts automatically to information which you give it from your forebrain."[52] Thus a person responds to a situation based upon his perception of that situation not necessarily upon the reality of that situation. Therefore, "if our ideas and mental images concerning ourselves are distorted or unrealistic, then our reactions to our environment will likely be inappropriate."[53]

The positive aspect of all this is that if an individual's concept of self is a matter of mental images, those images can be changed through the use of imagination and role playing.

> Expand the self-image and you expand the "area of the possible." The development of an adequate, realistic self-image will seem to imbue the individual with new capabilities, new talent and literally turn failure into success.[54]

In *Your Erroneous Zones* Dyer argues that it is not easy to rid oneself of the self-image developed during childhood. "While it is true that your original self-profiles were learned from the opinion of adults, it is not true that you must carry these around with you forever."[55] The major idea advanced by Dyer is that an individual can take charge of himself by beginning to make choices about his life based upon his own beliefs, wants, and needs, not those of other people. An individual can also choose how he feels since, "Feelings are reactions you choose to have" ... "not just emotions that happen to you."[56] Thus, an individual must not only take charge of his life but his emotions; an individual can choose happiness and success over unhappiness and failure. It all revolves around changing the individual's concepts of self and taking responsibility for one's life.

Ringer, in *Winning Through Intimidation*, chronicles his experiences first as an undergraduate student at "Screw U." and then as an unsuccessful and later successful real estate broker. He attributes his success to several basic "theories" which he developed, the main one being the Theory of Intimidation. This theory states that "the results a person obtains are inversely proportionate to the degree to which he is intimidated."[57] What Ringer actually did to change himself from an unsuccessful, easily intimidated real estate broker to a successful broker who refused to be intimidated by others was to develop positive concepts of who he was and what he wanted out of life. Simply put, he changed his self-concept from negative to positive and, as Maltz predicted, his life changed accordingly.

The older a person gets the harder change is, yet there is plenty of evidence that self-concept can be changed at any point in a person's life, assuming she first of all recognizes a need for the change.

BECAUSE IT'S WORTH IT

A woman wanting or expecting to be successful in a library management position must possess a concrete idea of who she is, where she is going, and what she wants out of life. A positive self-concept is vital.

> Above all, an aspiring woman must place a high value on herself — her intelligence, abilities, and potential — in order to succeed ... She must like herself, have confidence in her ability to do the job, take pride in her accomplishments, and value herself highly in relation of others in the marketplace....[58]

An executive who lacks confidence in her abilities, in her ideas, in herself in general communicates her her feelings of incompetence and lack of self confidence in the way she relates to others in business situations and relationships. This is communicated to others by all sorts of cues, e.g., tone of voice, dress, body language, speech patterns, word choice. A woman who is unsure of herself and ambivalent about her goals, ambitions, and expectations communicates these feelings to colleagues, subordinates, and bosses and will never be successful as manager until she realizes the negative feelings she is communicating to others and does something about it. Self-concept can be changed or altered, but first an individual must realize there is a need for a change, decide what that change is to be, and make a conscious commitment to begin working toward developing a more positive self-concept.

> Changing your self-image does not mean changing your self, or improving your self, but changing your own mental picture, your own estimation, conception, and realization of that self. The amazing results which follow from developing an adequate and realistic self-image, come about, not as a result of self-transformation, but from self-realization, and self-revelation.[59]

Changing self-concept is not easy. It is not accomplished overnight but it is worth it because a healthy, positive self-concept is not only useful in succeeding in management. It will also lead to a fuller, happier life.

NOTES

[1]U.S. Department of Commerce, Bureau of the Census, *Statistical Abstracts of the United States*, 1982-83, (Washington, D.C.: Government Printing Office, 1982), p. 386.

[2]Ibid.

[3]Natalie Jaffe, *Men's Jobs for Women: Toward Occupational Equality* (New York: Public Affairs Committee, Inc., 1982), p. 13-15.

[4]L. Sunny Hansen and Rita Rapoza, *Career Development and Counseling of Women* (Springfield, Ill.: Charles C. Thomas Publishers, 1978), p. 304.

[5]Ibid.

[6]Ibid.

[7]Ibid., p. 305.

[8]Ibid.

[9]Ibid.

[10]Ibid.

[11]Ibid.

[12]Jean Wellington, "The Working Woman and Self-Concept: A Growing Ambivalence," *Counseling and Values* 26, no. 2 (February 1982): 133.

[13]Margaret V. Higginson and Thomas L. Quick, *The Ambitious Woman's Guide to a Successful Career* (New York: AMACOM, 1975), p. 14.

[14]Wellington, "The Working Woman and Self-Concept," p. 134.

[15]Grace K. Baruch, "Feminine Self-Esteem, Self-Ratings of Competence, and Maternal Career Commitment," *Journal of Counseling Psychology* 20, no. 5 (September 1973): 487.

[16]Margaret Henning and Anne Jardim, *The Managerial Woman* (Garden City, N.Y.: Anchor Press/Doubleday, 1977), p. 16.

[17]Wellington, "The Working Woman and Self-Concept," p. 135.

[18]Ibid., p. 136.

[19]Ibid., p. 137.

[20]Higginson, *The Ambitious Woman's Guide*, p. 7.

[21]Eliza G. C. Collins, ed., *Executive Success: Making It In Management* (New York: John Wiley and Sons, Inc., 1983), p. 16.

[22]Donald W. Felker, *Building Positive Self-Concepts* (Minneapolis, Minn.: Burgess Publishing Company, 1974), p. 7.

[23]Collins, *Executive Success*, p. 1.

[24]Ibid., p. 13.

[25]H. J. Eysenck, W. Arnold, and R. Meili, eds., *Encyclopedia of Psychology* (New York: The Seabury Press, 1979), p. 971.

[26]Felker, *Building Positive Self-Concepts*, p. 2.

[27]Wallace D. Labenne and Bert I. Greene, *Educational Implications of Self-Concept Theory* (Pacific Palisades, Calif.: Goodyear Publishing Company, Inc., 1969), p. 10.

[28]Shirley C. Samuels, *Enhancing Self-Concept in Early Childhood: Theory and Practice* (New York: Human Sciences Press, 1977), p. 24.

[29]W. A. Schonfeld, "Body Image in Adolescents: A Psychiatric Concept for the Pediatrician," *Pediatrics* 31, no. 6 (1963): 845.

[30]Samuels, *Enhancing Self-Concept*, p. 24.

[31]Schonfeld, "Body Image," p. 846.

[32]Samuels, *Enhancing Self-Concept*, p. 25.

[33]Ibid., p. 27.

[34]Ibid.

[35]Ibid., p. 28.

[36]Ibid., p. 33.

[37]Don E. Hamachek, *Encounters with the Self* (New York: Holt, Rinehart and Winston, Inc., 1971), p. 164.

[38]Ibid., p. 164-65.

[39]Donald E. Super, "Self-Concepts in Vocational Development," *Career Development: Self-Concept Theory* (New York: College Entrance Examinations Board, 1963), p. 11-12.

[40]Ibid., p. 12.

[41]Ibid., p. 12.

[42]Ibid., p. 12-13.

[43]Ibid., p. 13.

[44]Ibid., p. 13.

[45]Ibid., p. 13.

[46]LaBenne, *Educational Implications*, p. 14.

[47]Maxwell Maltz, *Psycho-Cybernetics* (New York: Pocket Books, 1960), p. 2.

[48]Ibid.

[49]Ibid.

[50]Ibid., p. 3.

[51]Ibid., p. 4.

[52]Ibid., p. 32.

[53]Ibid., p. 34.

[54]Ibid., p. 4.

[55]Wayne W. Dyer, *Your Erroneous Zones* (New York: Avon Books, 1977), p. 42.

[56]Ibid., p. 20.

[57]Robert J. Ringer, *Winning Through Intimidation* (New York: Fawcett Crest, 1973), p. 123.

[58]Higginson, *The Ambitious Woman's Guide*, p. 26.

[59]Maltz, *Psycho-Cybernetics*, p. 124.

CHAPTER 9

Intuition

Lee Edson

It was a great chemical mystery of the time, and the 19th-century German chemist August von Stradonitz Kekulé struggled mightily with it. The problem was the molecular structure of organic substances, and it had puzzled chemists for years. They knew that many organic molecules consisted of oxygen, carbon and hydrogen atoms. But how were they arranged? In a square? A circle? A chain?

Kekulé, it's said, carried the problem with him for months. Then, while sitting before the fire one evening, he fell into a reverie. In his half-asleep state, he experienced a strange fantasy — he saw atoms dancing, whirling about like snakes. Then he saw one snake forming a loop and eating its own tail. Kekulé awoke with a start. In that instant, his imagination conjured up a hexagonal ring, each corner taken up by a carbon atom — six atoms in all. He had literally dreamed up the benzene ring, a design that provides the basis for our understanding of the nature of the major compounds of organic chemistry.

Not all invention or understanding arises full-blown from a fireside reverie. Some scientists, as well as artists and businessmen, find sudden answers to problems in an equally mysterious, subconscious process that occurs in the waking state. The process is called intuition. It may come as a sharp, sudden insight or overwhelming hunch. It may arrive as the lightning flash of understanding. It may be a kind of revelation resulting from forgotten experience. It may also be the refined logic of Sherlock Holmes, who could sniff a wet raincoat, glance at a roughened cuff and tarstained finger, and deduce the age, height and educational background of an unknown visitor to Baker Street.

Do such insights arise purely by chance? Or can they be pursued and encouraged to appear at will? The answer to these questions is at the heart of the creative process.

One of the earliest attempts to clarify the nature of intuition comes from Plato, who thought all knowledge was intuitive and from a previous existence (that familiar feeling of déjà vu).

Descartes refined the concept by calling it "rational intuition," meaning the grasp of axioms of logic and mathematics — the "rightness" of such ideas as two times two equals four.

Kant later narrowed down the foundation of all knowledge to two basic intuitive forms, of space and time, which he called "sensible intuition."

Subsequently, language and moral law were also regarded as intuitive and inherited.

Reprinted with permission from the author and *Across the Board*, June 1982, published by the Conference Board, New York.

These ideas dominated philosophy for about a century until the brilliant American philosopher, Charles Sanders Peirce, insisted there was no such thing as intuition. To Peirce, the so-called intuitive flash was merely the rational result of prior thought. We might not always know what those thoughts were, but they were there, ready to use when needed.

Peirce invented the introspective model of mental activity—logical, ordered, each thought following from past thoughts. This was a good model for a world then beginning to track the progress of science and technology. Intuition had no part in it.

Today, however, intuition is an equal partner with logic. Judging character, calling a turn on Wall Street, daring to follow a hunch in business—decisions like these, which often have to be made quickly and without benefit of sufficient data, lift intuition to an important role in everyday affairs.

Dr. Robert Ornstein, a California psychologist, notes that "many different occupations and disciplines involve a concentration in one of the major modes of consciousness. Science and law are heavily involved in verbal logic. Crafts and music are more present-oriented or intuitive. A complete human consciousness involves the polarity of the two modes, as a complete day includes the daylight and the sundown."

This granting of equal mental rights to intuition stems from new findings about the brain, due largely to the "split-brain" studies of psychologists Roger Sperry (who won a Nobel Prize in 1981) and Michael Gazzaniga at Caltech in the 1960s. The subjects of these studies were epileptic patients who had undergone surgery in which the corpus callosum, the fiber pack bridging the cerebral hemispheres, was severed. Disconnecting the hemispheres weakened the electric discharges across the brain that were responsible for the convulsions and thus reduced their severity and frequency. Would it also send each half of the brain into its own private world and destroy the patient's unity of identity and personality?

"Nothing like that happened," recalls Dr. Gazzaniga, now director of cognitive neurosciences at Cornell University Medical College in New York, "but the split-brain work did yield a rich harvest of knowledge of the subtle operations of the brain."

One major discovery was that the right hemisphere, long neglected by psychologists because it didn't possess the gift of speech, did have a "mind" of its own. It could, for instance, communicate after a fashion; it could use symbols and make decisions based on non-verbal processes. On occasion, the decision of the right hemisphere ran counter to that of the left, so that an individual with a split brain might find himself unbuttoning his coat with one hand while buttoning it with the other.

Further split-brain studies, along with data from stroke victims, show that the right hemisphere also appears to have its own consciousness, its own set of values, even its own intuitions. However, this knowledge occurs in emotional and visual forms, rather than in words. Individuals whose right hemisphere is damaged, for example, show emotional flatness. Such people have been described as a "language vehicle without emotional wheels."

Because of these findings, some people have simplistically decided that the right hemisphere of the brain is the sole home of intuition. In California, some cultists have tried to influence educational authorities to promote "right-brain" studies for artistry and meditation in order to free the important "intuitive values of the personality." These values, they argue, have been enfeebled by the coldhearted digital scientific megamachine of the Western industrial states.

The use of the right brain/left brain division has also become the stuff of fads. An artist claims success in teaching art by exercising the "intuitive" side of the brain. A group offers a retreat for right-brain meditation. A bestselling self-help book offers ways to use the right brain. Some academic psychologists have also given their blessing. Julian Jaynes of Princeton, in a moment of poetic license, goes so far as to say, "The gods speak through the right half of the brain."

Dr. Gazzaniga is impatient with such goings-on. "What is important about our work," he says, "is not whether the cold verbal scientist resides in one half of the brain while the warm emotional artist resides in the other, but the insight it gives us into the processes of conscious awareness as well as the workings of the subconscious."

Just what is it that fires the intuitive spark somewhere beneath the level of consciousness? In one revealing experiment, Gazzaniga presented a snow scene to the right hemisphere of a patient's brain and a chicken claw to the left. (This is done by flashing the pictures on the screen, first to one eye and then to the other.) The patient was presented with cards and asked to match the pictures on them with the pictures on the screen. He picked the card showing a chicken with the right hand and the picture of a shovel with the left hand. Then he was asked to reveal what he saw.

"I saw a claw and picked the chicken," he replied.

"And why did you pick the shovel?" Gazzaniga asked.

"Well," the patient said, "you have to clean out the chicken shed."

At first, Gazzaniga thought the response was a gag, but test after test showed that the patient was serious about his choice and was, in effect, revealing how the human brain worked.

As Gazzaniga explains it: "The behavior of the right side of the brain is perceived but not understood by the left side. Undaunted, it feels compelled to explain what its right side had done; so it makes up an answer, just as the patient did with the chicken shed. It builds a story out of the patterns available to its verbal self, hoping it will sell. Whether it does or not depends on the ingenuity and needs of the entire brain.

"We think this is a universal mechanism that underlies all mental processes, including intuition."

In any case, Gazzaniga adds, the brain always acts as an integrated whole, synthesizing the disparate experiences from both sides to become "aware." Thus, intuition, along with other mental processes, appears to be as much a product of the left side and its logical capacities as of the right and its imagery and spatial awareness. Poincaré's mathematical intuitions, as he described them in a memorable essay, were sudden, logical perceptions; Einstein's intuitions were always visual.

Dreaming is a special kind of mental synthesis similar to intuition. According to Allan Hobson of Harvard, the current dean of dream theory, a dream is made up of random events presented to the sleeping brain. Again, both hemispheres seem to be involved. The right half may be satisfied with the images that leap forth unfettered, but the left half, not content to conduct a lonely rearguard action, has to turn these random events into a tale, with an attempt (not always successful) to provide a beginning, middle and end.

Kekulé's fantasy of the snake eating its tail can now be understood in these right/left terms. It is an image looking for a story — the story in this case tying into the worrisome open problem of determining the structure of the building blocks of organic chemistry. The openness requires closure, a satisfying end. So the image crosses the right/left brain barrier, finds its meaning in the left side and, presto, an intuition is born.

The new knowledge of mental processes based on physiology has not dispelled the mythology that surrounds intuition. There is, for example, the illusion that only specially-endowed people have significant intuitive powers. Actually, psychologists agree that we all have intuitive power, though, like intelligence, it is distributed in varying degrees.

One myth of intuition worthy of being shattered is that it is inherited in a fixed amount. Not so. Intuition can grow on you. Listen to Wall Street trader Fred Macaskill, who claims considerable success in investing: "I deliberately try to evoke an intuitive feeling for the market. Whilst browsing in a bookshop, watching the ticker, having a cup of tea, updating my charts, or taking a bath, I deliberately put my mind in neutral and 'feel' which way the market will move."

"To use my emotions, I simply act in the opposite way. If my intuition tells me to buy land and I then experience fear, I know I've done the right thing. If I experience hope or greed, I've probably done the wrong thing."

Macaskill doesn't presume that this method will work for others, but there are methods of improving intuition in problem-solving that have long been sanctioned by psychologists. These methods are based on the descriptions by creative individuals of insights that led to major discoveries. The process is said to have five phases: preparation, frustration, incubation, illumination and elaboration.

In the preparation stage, we scan our own minds and environment for information. We begin to put together a number of mental elements, such as symbols, images, abstract concepts. What we're aiming for is a tentative solution that fits the demands of the problem.

If these early skirmishes are usually frustrating, that's all to the good, say psychologists. They believe it fuels the mental engine and drives it to the next stage of creation.

As Arthur Koestler puts it in *The Act of Creation*, "When all hopeful attempts at solving the problem by traditional methods have been exhausted, thoughts run around in circles in the blocked matrix like rats in a cage. Next, the matrix of organized purposeful behavior itself seems to go to pieces, and random trails make their appearance, accompanied by tantrums and attacks of despair."

Now, according to experts, is the time to relax. This is the incubation period. At some barely conscious level, the mind is grappling with the problem. In Koestler's words, a link to "a quite different matrix of the mind" is being forged. Psychologists now believe that the left brain is listening in on whatever motivation for action and symbolism is occurring in the right brain.

At this point, if nature has taken its course, there is illumination, the sudden appearance of an answer and the emotional satisfaction of "knowing" it is right. In that instant, who wouldn't run like Archimedes down the streets of Syracuse shouting "Eureka!"? In some way, a force has created a synthesis of elements, an intense creative spark. Some philosophers liken the condition to a magnetic field, where scattered iron filings are drawn into a harmonious and symmetrical relationship. Others, more mystical, suggest that intuition is the product of an outside principle, a divine one, perhaps, or a form of ESP that works only on receptive individuals.

The experts don't say if you follow these steps, you will inevitably trigger an intuition—particularly the kind needed to resolve a critical problem. But they do feel that such steps are often necessary preludes to success in problem-solving.

The final stage in the intuitive process, of course, is the logical one of putting the idea to work. Once that is done and proves to be successful, the two sides of the brain join forces and go forth together toward a new problem, a new search and, it may be hoped, a new insight.

CHAPTER 10

The Manager Within

Gregory D. May and Michael J. Kruger

The rapidly changing nature of work presents an unprecedented challenge for today's managers to create conditions that will release the power of a work force. For too long this group has been constrained by stress associated with change, uncertainty and insecurity. To release this stress, managers must learn to free their employees from such inhibiting forces.

In the search for the right managerial prescription, behavioral scientists have conceptualized, applied and evaluated a multitude of theories during the past decades. Yet, despite many insights and successes, the search for the ideal managerial formula continues. Ironically, the formula sought for managerial mastery is closer than realized: Managers need only look within themselves.

The necessary formula is a way of thinking, the unseen or unrecognized frame of reference that determines the meaning managers assign to an event. Events have no meaning in and of themselves. Meaning comes from how the event is viewed.

A manager's mindset before the event assigns meaning and generates behavior, which implies that to be optimally effective, managers must view events from a context that produces inspired action from themselves as well as from others. This mindset, known as managing from a context of mastery, results in a commitment from both managers and employees to meet their highest level of performance.

A management style, for example, that views rapid change as problematic and uncertainty as an adversary will not produce effective responses. The same results if managers consider that viewpoints always must be reduced to the correct one. A more inclusive perspective, one that reflects an evolved way of thinking, must prevail.

A manager working from a context of mastery views all events and circumstances as opportunities to experience peak performance. In this sense events are neither good nor bad. And because the events already happened, managers must decide how to use them and proceed to accomplish preset goals.

Approaching life in this manner allows managers to grow from all work experiences. Doing so, however, requires a continued commitment to view all events as opportunities or possibilities that did not exist before their occurrence.

Managers must approach work with the goal of mastering every situation, each of which provides the opportunity to reach higher levels of awareness, thinking and performance. When dealing in such a manner, life at work becomes an evolution of expanding possibilities.

The managers who operate from this context see themselves as able to engage in all tasks, and recognize that this sufficiency often depends upon asking the right question of the right person. Managers are not supposed to know all the answers. Yet they need to know what question to ask of whom to get the answer that leads to effective decision making.

To acquire this mastery managers must work through a set of questions rather than a set of answers. If there is a commitment to discover the right question, all problems are resolvable. When managing from this context, managers search to discover what is missing or unknown; their behavior is like that of an artist or scientist seeking to determine the next breakthrough.

To achieve maximum value, the context of mastery must become the manager's normal frame of reference. He or she continuously should engage in introspective questions, such as, "From what context am I operating?", "Is it working?" and "Am I thinking from a context of mastery or insufficiency?"

When asking these questions managers can align their thinking and behavior with their commitment to mastery. Any breakdowns in commitment should be viewed as opportunities to correct and expand their course of action.

To operate from this context, managers should adhere to the four principles of empowerment:

- Self-mastery

- Integrity

- Effective communication

- Partnership

Self-mastery. To reach this level managers must evaluate their lives on a physical, psychological and spiritual level. These states then are compared to the optimum state so managers can identify and correct areas that need improvement.

In the physical dimension, managers must first evaluate their eating, drinking and exercise habits. Because the shape of the body reflects how it has been treated, managers must understand that they should train their bodies to standards for well-being. This not only increases the years in their life, but the life in their years. The ability to sustain work efforts with a minimal diminishment of energy, particularly in stressful times, increases if the body is trained.

Psychologically it refers to instructing the mind to handle mental and emotional reactions. It also means reorienting the way a person relates to life.

To structure the mind psychologically, managers first must be willing to learn about themselves, which includes the way they think, act and react. They must be open to distinctions between fact and opinion.

At this point they become aware that a main source of arguments often is the difference between what they believe to be true versus what others believe to be true. This awareness helps managers understand that all opinions are valid and that opinions are not facts. Therefore, the value of sticking to the facts becomes evident.

Another part of the process is learning how to learn, which consists of going from a state of not knowing to knowing. Managers are shown that, to command any task, they typically progress through four stages:

- Unconscious incompetence—they are unaware of their incompetence

- Conscious incompetence—they are aware of their incompetence

- Conscious competence—they are aware of their incompetence and take successful steps to correct it

- Unconscious competence—the accomplishment of the task is automatic.

The key stage in the learning process is conscious incompetence. To move through and beyond this stage, managers must be willing to dig for information they don't know about themselves.

Reactions to events can manipulate us, or we can learn to manage those reactions. When managers permit their reactions to dominate their thoughts and to govern their behavior, they are reaction managed. In this condition they blame, or place responsibility for the cause of their responses, on someone or something other than themselves. They see themselves as victims.

What managers fail to realize, however, is that they let someone or something push their reaction buttons and take control of their feelings and actions. They unknowingly gave up their freedom to choose.

Managers who are aware of and manage their actions consciously and deliberately choose the most effective behavior in any given situation. They are able to effectively respond to life's events because they monitor and take responsibility for the duration and intensity of their reaction, and because they can distinguish between fact and fiction. This also becomes an effective form of stress management, which is conducive to good mental health.

Problems are part of life. Managers can elect to view them as events that drain them physically and psychologically by complicating their lives and causing them difficulty or as opportunities to demonstrate that they can measure up to any challenge.

When managers view problems as opportunities they see a potential that allows them and others to grow from the experience. They realize that, had the problem not appeared, they might not have had the opportunity to see its teaching points.

These managers can make the distinction between the role they have versus who they are. To do this they must not allow their egos to get in the way of expressing the truth. Yet to accomplish this managers must be willing to accept feedback about themselves as valid, and use it to expand their self-awareness and strengthen their relationships with others.

When managers are automatic they operate from a pre-established pattern constructed to preserve their self-image. Their reactions are typically predetermined by past events bearing a similarity to the present. If managers are more concerned about looking good than looking closely at themselves, a major portion of their energy is devoted to protecting their ego and, as a result, the true self becomes hidden. In this mode, managers view feedback as a threat and react emotionally.

The spiritual dimension emerges from the realization that there is a higher purpose to life than merely surviving or getting by. To reach this level the manager must aspire to achieve his or her full potential.

Integrity. To be whole or complete and to exist in an unimpaired state or condition is to have integrity. Once again, managers need to apply this to their physical, psychological and spiritual dimensions.

Physical integrity means completing tasks or projects, putting possessions and papers in their proper place and having all physical objects in good working order. It also includes using all resources efficiently and effectively.

A manager with psychological integrity has sound and meaningful relationships with others, takes responsibility for managing emotional reactions and fully expresses him- or herself without impairing others.

Incomplete conversations cause both parties to spend time thinking about what was left incomplete and unsaid, and that produces mental weariness. Psychological integrity allows managers to structure interactions with a beginning, middle and an end.

Spiritual integrity requires a commitment to commitments. Managers can have either results or reasons why they don't. It's a matter of being committed, not succumbing to rationalizations, justifications or excuses.

Effective communication. Speaking, listening, asking questions and articulating one's vision are integral parts of effective communication.

If managers speak with distinctions, listeners can visualize or comprehend what is being said because it is distinct from everything else. Unlike poetry, which is open to and invites interpretation, there is a specificity and accountability on the manager's part; any misinterpretation comes from the manager.

Listening with intention involves actually hearing the public, external conversation rather than the private, internal dialogue. The listener must subordinate individual thoughts so they are not distracted by internal dialogues of judgments, evaluations and comparisons. Doing so also eliminates the chance of drifting during the conversation.

To ask questions for knowledge, managers must ask questions that elicit information about another's direct experiences. These interactions are more meaningful because they cause the listener to think and reflect upon his or her experiences.

Managers must also articulate a vision by clearly saying where they are going and their commitment to getting there. This is accomplished through metaphors or word pictures that can be grasped and re-created by others. A manager needs to express what he or she will do, and in what time frame, which allows others to understand and to see the intended results.

Partnership. This is an expression of a manager's individual commitment to self through a commitment to others. To achieve this principle he or she must learn to create an environment of contribution, be committed to others' greatness, structure a system of accountability that includes clear requests and commitments, and be committed to others' commitments.

Managers in partnership with others accept all behaviors and actions as a contribution to their learning. Such a partnership is created through a commitment to each co-worker's greatness, and their own greatness is directly related to the greatness of those around them. The star player shifts to team player, which translates into the genuine expression of the entire team's willingness to contribute to the whole.

True partnership is expressed as unity, support, energy, strength and achievement. It empowers the individual as well as the group, which enables a performance level above each individual's previous personal bests. Partnership empowers others by viewing and treating individuals as full partners, by listening, monitoring and managing their individual reactions and verbally acknowledging them for their contributions.

One way managers can understand and accept the validity of managerial mastery is to attend a comprehensive, experiential learning course. Experiential learning refers to individual and group interactions through which principles, concepts and techniques evolve and become self-evident. The experience becomes the learning; the learning becomes the experience.

The major purposes of experiential learning are to experience self-awareness for self-management, and to acquire the ability to make distinctions and commitments. Managers also learn to take personal responsibility for the consequences of their actions. For many, this transformation is accompanied by a dramatic and instantaneous behavioral change.

This is not just conceptual; hundreds of managers have participated in such a learning process and have provided data on its impact on their effectiveness. The end result is that managers can learn to manage themselves and their relationships from a context of mastery.

The results are achieved through in-depth self-awareness and introspection, which leads to inspiration and a commitment to achieve optimum effectiveness. Managers who realize their ability to manage others is contingent upon their ability to manage themselves are concerned with increasing their self-awareness. They also recognize, on the conscious incompetence level, they first must be aware of who they are (distinct from their role) before they can effectively manage themselves or others.

Managers must be willing to discover what they don't know about themselves as they move through the first stages of learning and the steps that occur during the learning process, as illustrated in Figure 1.

LEARNING STAGES   PROCESS STEPS

MASTERY
4. Unconscious Competence
- Managing from a context of sufficiency
- Managing self and relationships effectively

COMMITMENT
3. Conscious Competence
- Following the principles of empowerment
- Committing oneself to being effective and response-able

TRANSFORMATION
- Being inspired to act upon the truth and realize one's potential
- Shifting perspective from reaction to self mastery

2. Conscious Incompetence

AWARENESS
- Understanding truth relative to opinions and beliefs
- Processing feedback from self, instructor, peers, subordinates and bosses

MEDIOCRITY
1. Unconscious Incompetence
- Being satisfied with status quo
- Operating from opinions and beliefs

Fig. 1. A Process Paradigm for Learning Managerial Mastery.

The transformation step represents a critical juncture. It signifies a shift in perspective that takes place for many managers as they progress through the second level of the four stages of learning.

The learning experience focuses on expanding each manager's self-awareness so managing effectively becomes natural. To facilitate this level of awareness, information is collected from questionnaires on each manager approximately six weeks before the course begins. The results are gathered from answers about health habits and from inventories of management practices completed by the managers, their subordinates and bosses.

The impetus for change comes from several sources. Processing the data obtained through the pre-course questionnaires is one such source. Also, the impetus comes from using feedback provided by peers during the training and viewing videotaped segments, as well as gaining competency through rigorous interactions with the class and a facilitator.

To establish a climate conducive to the learning process, managers are provided with statements outlining both the context for learning and the operating rules during the training. The questionnaires and the context for learning are sent to managers six weeks before the class convenes. The context for learning is based on the following conditions:

- The training provides opportunities for change.

- Individual participation enhances the value of the learning experience.

- Learning requires alternating periods of participation and reflection.

- Throughout the training, the course represents a real organization in which individual behavior is representative of behavior in the workplace.

- Adults are responsible for their own learning.

- Learning usually occurs when there is challenge, some stress and discomfort.

- Personal opinions can be safely shared during training.

- Each participant is a valuable resource who brings significant, pertinent experiences to training.

- The course provides an opportunity to form supportive relationships with individuals and groups.

The context statement represents the frame of reference for the learning experience, which is based in part on principles of adult learning. When the course begins, managers are given the opportunity to analyze the statement of context and offer revisions. In addition, the following operating rules are distributed and each participant agrees to:

- Be on time for all sessions

- Be responsible for creating value in each session

- Take responsibility for his or her feelings

- Ask for support and assistance as needed

- Fully engage, self-express and interact in each session requiring active participation

- Only discuss individual experiences outside the group

- Redirect individuals who have complaints.

Establishing the context for learning and agreeing to the operating rules creates the learning climate for everything that follows.

The experiential learning process is guided by a facilitator who uses the Socratic method of teaching. Such a process consists of rigorous inquiry through constant analysis, self-examination and questioning of beliefs, axioms, theories and explanations.

Managers subject their beliefs, many of which were formed when they were not in a position to question or analyze them, to extensive inquiry. This process typically results in some discomfort as they experience insights and begin the process of discarding illusionary and ineffective notions of how the world works.

During the course, managers are introduced to several key metaphors that are presented in a sequence that parallels the four stages of learning. Each concept or metaphor is critically examined and validated by the managers. In addition, the concepts are applied immediately during training because they are linked directly to other aspects of the learning experience. The immediate applications of the concepts are in harmony with the spirit and intent of experiential learning.

Metaphors are used to make distinctions and illustrate different perspectives. An understanding of distinctions is critical to make decisions for which they can take full responsibility, as illustrated in Figure 2.

A Manager's II vv	When Managing from a Context of Insufficiency II vv	When Managing from a Context of Mastery II vv
State of Awareness	Low	High
View of Problems	As problems that lead to more problems	As opportunities to achieve
Perception of feedback	As a threat	As valid
Commitment	Uncertain	Unwavering, absolute
Stage of learning	Unconscious incompetence	Unconscious competence
Management of reactions	Reaction managed	Self-managed
Orientation to listening	Listens through a filter of reactions	Listens with intention
Integrity	Seldom achieves closure	Always achieves closure
Orientation to diet/exercise	Life degenerating	Life enhancing
Interactions with others	Disempowering—causes others to "contract"	Empowering—helps others to "expand"
Mode of communication	Seeks to be right	Seeks to be effective
Nature of relationships	Entangled	Empowering
Orientation to life	Committed to comfort and convenience	Committed to a commitment to mastery

Fig. 2.

The learning that occurs during the course is powerful. Shifts in perspective result in new insights for achieving an optimum level of effectiveness. Accordingly, the general tendency for many managers is to feel euphoric and to have a renewed sense of commitment to their jobs.

To maximize this level of enthusiasm and to strengthen the transfer of learning after the course, two reinforcement strategies are set in motion during the course. The first is writing management journals, and the second is forming support groups.

During the course managers write a journal entry approximately every two days to capture insights, revelations, concepts, emotions, distinctions, metaphors and perceptions. Each manager has an opportunity to publicly read one journal entry during the course.

At the conclusion, participants take the journals home for revision before they are returned to the coordinator. Upon receipt of the journals, the course coordinator mails one set of journals to each manager weekly until all sets have been distributed. Thus, each week for a six-month period, every manager is given the opportunity to re-access the learning experience as it was perceived by his or her peers.

Support groups composed of participants who agree to remain in contact by telephone for four months after the conclusion of the course become the vehicles for networking with those who learned the same principles, behaviors, skills and language. The basic goals of the support groups are to strengthen individual change efforts and provide a structure for feedback and accountability.

To achieve accountability, a team leader is appointed from each group to keep track of each member's progress in meeting his or her change goals. Team leaders report their group's results to the course coordinator, who then summarizes each group's results and periodically includes them with the management journals.

The reporting system brings visible accountability into the process, which allows managers to see how their group is performing relative to others. In addition, this system makes it easy to pinpoint those groups that are having difficulty producing the intended results. In such cases, the course coordinator offers assistance to the team leader to promote improved group performance.

The program's impact has been demonstrated by the number and nature of the actual commitments to mastery that are made by participants during the course. Commitments typically focus on the areas of health and relationships, such as smoking and alcohol use, and re-establishing relationships that have been left unattended because of a lack of communication.

In addition to the individual commitments that qualitatively illustrate the favorable outcomes of the training, three separate evaluative studies of the program were conducted: two during fiscal year 1983 and one in 1985. The studies examined the results of 11 management courses: five courses were conducted in 1983 and six in 1985.

The first 1983 study consisted of an analysis of the stress management questionnaires that were administered before and after the five courses; the pre-course questionnaires were completed six weeks before the class; the post-course questionnaires were completed six months following training.

The data show that 60% of those who returned their post-course questionnaires improved their stress management by 10 or more points. Managers reported the most improvement on such items as exercise, weight control, relaxation and taking responsibility for removing causes of stress whenever possible.

The second 1983 study assessed the impact of the five courses on managerial effectiveness as perceived by the managers themselves, their bosses and their subordinates. The design of the study required respondents to recall information about their managerial behaviors before and after the training.

Data were collected using a questionnaire, which was pretested on a small group of managers similar to those trained. The questionnaire consisted of 26 items that were designed from the course content and objectives, and was sent to all managers, their supervisors and subordinate managers who had been on the job before the training process.

A useable return rate of 77% was received from the managers, 46% from supervisors and 31% from subordinate managers. Questionnaire data were supplemented by telephone interviews conducted with three managers per class and selected at random.

Managers perceived a positive improvement on all question items as a result of the training. Although their bosses and subordinate managers reported improvement on the same items, the magnitude was not always as great.

The areas in which participants reported the most change were in managing stress, helping subordinate managers to manage stress and managing their reactions to events in the workplace. The bosses concurred with the participants on the the first two areas of change reported. Opinions from subordinate managers differed—they felt the principal areas of change were that the managers now welcomed subordinate managers' opinions, promoted a partnership climate and helped co-workers manage stress.

According to the evaluator, many of the perceived changes afer training were found to be statistically significant. Data obtained from the telephone interviews supported the questionnaire results.

A third study, conducted in 1985, also looked at the impact of the training on the managerial effectiveness of the participants. This evaluation analyzed the difference between pre- and post-course data obtained on an instrument referred to as the Management Practices Inventory (MPI).

This inventory consists of 33 items clustered in seven scales that represent the major content areas of the training course: managing stress; giving information to subordinates; receiving information from subordinates; group dynamics, managing change; developing subordinate managers; and modeling good leader behavior.

Inventory data were obtained from the course participants, their subordinates and bosses six weeks before and two months after the training. The data were used to provide feedback for the self-awareness portion of the training and as a pre- and post-course evaluation tool.

The data were analyzed by an independent contractor who reported the following differences between pre- and post-course ratings on the seven scales:

1) For subordinates, the differences were all positive, fairly uniform across the scales and statistically significant.

2) For bosses, the differences were variable and statistically significant on two scales.

3) For the participant managers, the differences were variable and statistically significant on one scale.

The evaluator attributed the lack of any large difference between the participant pre- and post-self-ratings to a cognitive restructuring that occurred during the training. This shift resulted from the participants' awareness that their own pre-course ratings were substantially higher than their subordinates' ratings.

Likewise, critical feedback from peers during participative exercises was likely to reinforce the way managers viewed their behavior. Back on the job, they were likely to be more cautious in rating their behavior as improved, whereas their bosses and subordinates evaluated attempts to improve as positive gains.

According to the evaluator, training achieved the desired effect, particularly in the eyes of subordinates whose ratings showed significant improvement across all scales.

As technology continues to alter and depersonalize the world, people will experience a need to interact more frequently and effectively with each other, particularly in the workplace. As a result, it will be increasingly important for managers to develop and sustain effective working relationships with employees.

The challenges facing managers who are part of the high-tech work force are paradoxical in nature. Managers are expected to do more with less. They are also expected to be more competent in dealing with people in an age in which technology puts distance and time between people.

The times mandate that managers acquire an interpersonal ability that promotes an effective balance between technical capability and people competence. The tools managers were taught to gain employee cooperation, dedication and responsiveness are outdated. Traditional theories of motivation fall short of providing managers with the insights and strategies needed to evoke the kind of employee inspiration that will result in the achievement of maximum potential.

Participation in an experiential learning program allows managers to acquire an understanding of, and a strategy for applying, this potential.

Don't look to the Far East to find a prescription for managerial excellence. The formula quite simply is a commitment to manage from a context demanded by the era in which we live. The context of managerial mastery is the framework for creating the conditions that empower managers and those around them to be the best they can be.

REFERENCES

Adams, John D., "Health, Stress and Your Lifestyle" (Stress, Strain and Nutrition Questionnaire), National Training Laboratories Institute, Arlington, Va., 1980.

Bach, Richard, *Illusions: The Adventures of a Reluctant Messiah*. New York: Dell Publishing Company, Inc., 1977.

Bennis, Warren, "The Four Competencies of Leadership," *Training and Development Journal*. August 1984.

Davis, Stanley M., "Transforming Organizations: The Key to Strategy Is Context," *Organizational Dynamics*, **AMACOM. Winter 1982.**

Davis, Stanley M., "The Curious Case of the Missing Management Model," *The Review*. January/February 1982.

Haley, Jay, *Problem Solving Therapy*. San Francisco: Jossey-Bass, Inc., 1976.

JWK International Corp., Annandale, Va., IRS MDP-II Evaluation Report, Office of Personnel Management Contract 42-83. August 31, 1984.

Kiefer, Charles and Stroh, Peter, "A New Paradigm for Organizational Development," *Training and Development Journal*. April 1983.

Knowles, Malcolm, *Modern Theory and Practice of Adult Education*. Chicago: Follett Publishing Co., 1980.

Kruger, Michael J. and May, Gregory D., "Two Techniques to Ensure that Training Programs Remain Effective," *Personnel Journal.* October 1985, pp. 70-75.

Livingston, J. Sterling, "New Trends in Applied Management Development," *Training and Development Journal.* July 1984.

Luthans, Fred, *Organizational Behavior.* New York: McGraw-Hill, Inc., 1973.

Naisbitt, John, *Megatrends.* New York: Warner Books, Inc., 1982.

Peters, Thomas and Waterman, Robert, *In Search of Excellence.* New York: Harper and Row, 1982.

Quigley, Eleanor F. and Kruger, Michael J., "Setting the Context for Learning," *Performance and Instruction Journal.* Vol. 25, Number 10, December 1986.

Robinson, W. Lewis, "Conscious Competence: The Mark of a Competent Instructor," *Personnel Journal.* July 1974, pp. 538-39.

Smith, Kay H., "Analysis of Management Practices Inventory Scores for All Students in MDP-11 Core Courses During FY-85," IRS Contract 86-02533. March 1986.

Watzlawick, Paul, Weakland, John, and Fisch, Richard, *Change: Principles of Problem Formation and Problem Resolution.* New York: W. W. Norton and Company, Inc., 1974.

III

Self-Development
Improving Interpersonal Skills

Introduction

To lead is to communicate
To communicate is to relate
To relate is to share ourselves with others.
— author unknown

Leadership *is* communication. This section demonstrates how communication skills, time management, stress management, listening, and ethics are related to the leadership function. Leaders direct, inform, guide, counsel, persuade, argue, cajole, reason, inspire, plan, talk, listen, and order. The leader-manager maintains control through communication. Followers respond to the oral and written directions of the leader. Leaders are able to transmit information so that people can understand it, and they are able to observe and listen in order to receive communications from those they supervise.

The act of communicating and the associated problems and opportunities can be viewed in a number of ways. The perspective offered here concentrates on interpersonal communication. Interpersonal effectiveness is the ability to manage relationships and to manage one's own feelings and actions as well. The effective leader-manager must think about communicating, just as he or she thinks about leadership style. The road to increased interpersonal communications effectiveness leads us deeper into ourselves, to a point at which we know ourselves better, are able to be congruent, are able to accept the risks of having others know us for what we are, and are open to the possibility of change.

The first chapter, "Techniques for Producing Positive Personal Change," introduces the concepts of affirmation, visualization, and meditation as tools to help leader-managers use their inner resources to the fullest. The authors propose that these methods are helpful in calming mind and body, relieving stress, improving concentration, increasing energy, listening to intuition, and programming oneself to accomplish desired goals. These techniques are briefly reviewed, with references for exploring them in greater depth. Other concepts discussed include relaxation, centering, and grounding.

Hitt suggests the following actions for the leader/communicator:

> To be an effective communicator, the leader-manager must make a commitment to authentic dialogue. This commitment should be manifested in four different forms of communication: interpersonal communication, written communication, oral presentations, and meetings. These four forms of communication should be used to bring about effective organizational communication.[1]

Communication skills can be improved if communication is viewed as a process rather than a series of isolated events. Nonverbal communication carries even more impact than verbal. It includes posture, gestures, voice tone, and facial expressions, as well as clothing, grooming, and the way one uses space and establishes territory.

Most verbal messages are given orally rather than in writing. In addition to using basic skills in communicating assertively, clearly, and tactfully, the library leader-manager needs to develop skill in getting and giving feedback. Getting feedback is necessary for the manager to know what is going on. Some ways of getting good feedback are by (1) asking for data with a clear purpose, (2) helping people bring their ideas into focus, and (3) accepting criticism without resentment. Giving feedback that clarifies and builds relationships helps people understand what the manager is doing.

The ability to determine when it is best to just listen and when it is best to become actively involved in a situation is important to the leader-manager. So are listening skills. Developing active listening skills involves restating the content of the speaker's message, noticing feelings and examining them, listening for behavior patterns, and looking for deeper insight.

The chapter on "Interpersonal Communication Skills" was used as a handout for an Association of Research Libraries' Office of Management Studies workshop attended by the authors. The focus of the reading is "active listening." Active listening is defined as an attempt to understand the speaker from the speaker's point of view. A key factor in poor communication is the tendency to critically judge and evaluate the speaker's person and expressions. Four activities are listed as contributing to active listening: (1) anticipating where the conversation is leading, (2) objectively weighing the evidence being presented, (3) periodically reviewing and summarizing what is being said, and (4) paying attention to non-verbal behavior as well as verbal.

Paraphrasing is also discussed as a way of checking with the other person to be sure of understanding an idea or suggestion as it was intended. Another basic skill for understanding another person is checking with that individual to make sure of understanding his or her feelings. The importance of giving and receiving feedback is also explained in this chapter. Eight guidelines are listed for giving feedback.

The leader-manager role is a demanding one. It requires a high level of health and well-being. Managing stress is essential for maintaining the high level of health and stamina needed to successfully manage today's complex libraries. There is little doubt that rapid change and growing complexity have placed leader-managers under increasing amounts of stress. The management of stress becomes essential in developing leadership potential and to the continuing maturation and long-term viability of the organization.

"Stress" as used here refers to significant disruptions in an individual's environment, whether the disruptions come from within (from unresolved hurts and fears) or from without (from pressures of work, family, or social world). Becoming aware of life events that tend to cause disruption, and therefore stress, can help you anticipate them, make plans for handling them, adjust to them, and learn how to pace yourself when they occur. Reducing the number of problem situations that contribute to stress is the first step in stress management because preventing is certainly less stressful than coping and curing.

Bunge examines "Stress in the Library" by reporting the responses of participants in his stress management workshops during the early 1980s. He reports that some 850 staff members participated in twenty-one locations in Illinois, Minnesota, New York, Tennessee, Texas, and Wisconsin. In some of the workshops all the participants were reference librarians at various types of libraries. In others, there were participants with positions of different types in a variety of libraries. Several sessions were for staff in a single library. During the session participants were asked to name things about their jobs that are stressful or frustrating and that seem to block their fulfillment, and to name things about their jobs that give them satisfaction, joy and fulfillment. The statements made by the participants were grouped into categories. Sources of stress categories were patrons, workload, supervisors and management, schedule and workday, lack of positive feedback, other staff members, lack of information and training, feeling pulled and tugged, technology and equipment, physical facilities, change, and lack of budget and resources. After analyzing the differences among the responses of public service, technical service, all participants, and support staff, Bunge concludes that with the current and projected economic situation and the increasing complexity of libraries, sources of stress are not going to decrease for library staff. He suggests that effectively and happily managing stress starts with self-knowledge that will help to prevent or manage specific stresses that are problems, be they skills at reaching out to others for support, skills at asking for our rights assertively, relaxation skills, better nutrition habits, or a clearer sense of our values and priorities.

One way of preventing stress is managing time well. Leader-managers are busy people. The more you take on responsibility, the more you invite people to give you responsibility. This means that if you wish to handle complex leadership roles, you must learn to manage your time.

Time management is based on periodically listing major objectives and ranking them in order of priority. It also involves keeping a daily "To Do" list that is categorized and numbered according to priorities, delegating, and arranging "quiet times" for uninterrupted work. Using time productively is intertwined with other good management practices.

In "Time Management and the Woman Library Manager," Helen Gothberg asserts that new women managers or women seeking management positions need to recognize the value of ETM—efficient time management. Topics discussed include call management, meetings, office visitors, goals and objectives planning, and the nine basic steps necessary to achieve greater time efficiency. Time wasters are divided into two groups: external time wasters and internal time wasters. External time wasters are designated as follows: telephone calls, meetings, drop-in visitors, a lack of objectives and policies, handling emergencies, dealing with personal problems of employees, and confused responsibility and lines of authority. Internal wasters include unclear communication with others, indecision and procrastination, attempting to do too much at once, the inability to say no, personal disorganization, lack of self-discipline, and failure to delegate responsibility appropriately.

Leader-managers must also give some thought to ethics. They must evaluate and refine the ideals and principles on which their actions are based. They must question their motivations and methods and consciously establish those beliefs to which they will hold. A person without a clearcut, conscious ethical position is like a ship with neither sail nor anchor.

The word *ethics* is derived from the Greek word *ethos*, which refers to character. The dictionary defines ethics as "the discipline dealing with that which is good and bad and with moral duty and obligation." From the standpoint of the organizational leader, ethics may be seen as the rules or standards governing the moral conduct of the members of organizations. Ethical discussions are an attempt to consolidate, understand, and give intellectual coherence to the motives and impulses that characterize our actions. Ethical problems and discussions are among the most difficult and time-consuming activities of the manager. It is the task of the leadership to bring consensus and unity out of the diversity of members.

Ethics is particularly vital to effective leadership, because we evaluate leaders not only on their accomplishments, but on their values. Interpersonal communication is ethical to the extent that it facilitates the individual's freedom of choice by presenting the other person with accurate bases for choice. Communication is unethical to the extent that it interferes with the individual's freedom of choice by preventing the other person from getting information relevant to choice. When there is a question of ethics, you must decide if you believe that the ends justify the means. These decisions will affect your leadership style, and the direction in which you lead others.

The last chapter, "Ethics and Values in the Workplace" was originally a paper presented at the American Library Association 1988 annual conference in New Orleans, as part of a panel presentation on Ethics in Librarianship. The author covers three areas: the librarian's responsibility to library users, his or her responsibility to the organization, and the librarian's responsibility to himself or herself. The theme of this reading is based on John Kultgen's definition of ethics in *Ethics and Professionalism*: ideals, aspirations, and rules of conduct. To the extent that ideals and aspirations can be seen as the basis for ethical conduct, the reading also explores the question, Where does the librarian get his or her ideals? It is important to note that this article was written to address the ethics and values of all librarians at all levels of an organization, and not just for managers: "It shouldn't be just managers who need to be concerned about workplace ethics. This should be of concern to all staff, regardless of level." In answer to the question, How might the typical librarian become more sensitive and responsive?, Shaughnessy suggests reflection and self-assessment as a means of getting back in touch with the values and ideals that led us into the field of librarianship, and of identifying sources of personal energy.

Inventories related to the topics covered in part III are included in appendixes E, F, G, and H. Appendix E, *Interpersonal Communication Inventory*, offers an opportunity to make an objective study of the degree and patterns of communication in your interpersonal relationships. It will enable you to better understand how you present and use yourself in communicating with persons in your daily contacts and activities. A Scoring Key with norms and instructions is also included at the end of the inventory.

To help determine your stress pattern, see appendixes F and G, "Testing Your Knowledge of Stress" and "Determining Your Stress Pattern." As discussed earlier in this chapter, not everyone reacts stressfully to the same things. What kinds of stressors bother you? If you can be aware of situations that cause you to respond stressfully, you may be able to develop strategies for lessening the stress associated with them or for avoiding them. Appendix H, the "NASA Exercise," is designed to compare the results of individual decision making with the results of group decision making, and to help improve the interpersonal skills involved in consensus building. This is a group activity with instructions and worksheets.

NOTES

[1]William D. Hitt, *The Leader-Manager* (Columbus, Ohio: Battelle, 1988), 148.

ADDITIONAL READINGS

Adair, John. *Effective Leadership*. Aldershot, England: Gower, 1983.

_____. *The Skills of Leadership*. Aldershot, England: Gower, 1984.

Allen, Robert F., and Charlotte Kraft. "Organizational Ethics: A Cultural View." In *The Organizational Unconscious*, 105-18. Englewood Cliffs, N.J.: Prentice-Hall, 1982.

Anderson, James G. "When Leaders Develop Themselves." *Training and Development Journal* (June 1984): 18-22.

Beck, Arthur C., and Ellis D. Hillmar. "The Power of Positive Management." *Personnel Journal* 62 (February 1983): 126-31.

Caruth, Don, et al. "How to Communicate to Be Understood." *Supervisory Management* 27 (February 1982): 31-37.

Chusmir, Leonard H., and Victoria Franks. "Stress and the Woman Manager." *Training and Development Journal* 42 (October 1988): 66-70.

Cribbin, James J. "Communicating with Impact: Do You Build Bridges or Chasms?" In *Leadership: Strategies for Organizational Effectiveness*, 173-89. New York: AMACOM, 1981.

_____. "Stress Management: Are You Master or Victim?" In *Leadership: Strategies for Organizational Effectiveness*, 241-55. New York: AMACOM, 1981.

_____. "Your Leadership Values: Do You Stand for Something or Fall for Anything?" In *Leadership: Strategies for Organizational Effectiveness*, 256-72. New York: AMACOM, 1981.

Daniels, Madeline M. *Realistic Leadership*. Englewood Cliffs, N.J.: Prentice-Hall, 1983.

Dyer, William G. "Forms of Interpersonal Feedback." *Training and Development Journal* 35 (June 1981): 103-9.

Gmelch, Walter H. *Beyond Stress to Effective Management*. New York: John Wiley, 1982.

Loden, Marilyn. *Feminine Leadership*. New York: Time Books/Random House, 1985.

Matteson, Michael T., and John M. Ivanavich. "Your Personal Coping Program — It's Up to You." In *Managing Job Stress and Health: The Intelligent Person's Guide*, 261-77. New York: Free Press, 1982.

Nanus, Burt. "Forum-Leadership: Doing the Right Thing." *The Bureaucrat* (Fall 1986): 9-12.

Odiorne, George S. "Goals: The Building Block for Integration and Self-Control." In *The Human Side of Management: Management by Integration and Self-Control*, 55-62. Lexington, Mass.: Lexington Books/D.C. Heath, 1987.

Peterson, Kenneth G. "Ethics in Academic Librarianship: The Need for Values." *The Journal of Academic Librarianship* 9 (July 1983): 132-37.

Ruben, Brent D. "Stress, Communication, and Assertiveness: A Framework for Interpersonal Problem Solving." In *The 1983 Annual for Facilitators, Trainers, and Consultants*, 170-74. University Associates, LaJolla, Calif.: 1983.

Stech, Ernest L. *Leadership Communication*. Chicago: Nelson-Hall, 1983.

Steil, Lyman K., Larry L. Barker, and Kittie W. Watson. "Identifying Your Personal Listening Strengths and Weaknesses." In *Effective Listening: Key to Your Success*, 55-77. Reading, Mass.: Addison-Wesley, 1983.

_____. "What's Your Ear-Q?" In *Effective Listening: Key to Your Success*, 45-53. Reading, Mass.: Addison-Wesley, 1983.

Strong, Graham. "Taking the Helm of Leadership." *Training and Development Journal* (June 1986): 43-45.

Thomas, Joe G. "Communication: New Thought on an Old Subject." *Supervisory Management* 27 (February 1982): 31-37.

Veninga, Robert L. *The Work Stress Connection*. New York: Ballantine Books/Random House, 1983.

Warshaw, Leon J. *Managing Stress*. Reading, Mass.: Addison-Wesley, 1984.

CHAPTER 11

Techniques for Producing Positive Personal Change

Arthur C. Beck and Ellis D. Hillmar

Affirmations, visualization, and meditation are tools to help managers use their inner resources to the fullest potential. These are ways to tap into your spiritual dimension and produce positive results that you cannot always explain. Your spirituality is the part of your being that is often ignored, because it cannot always be explained logically or scientifically. If you are using only your physical and mental parts, you are not drawing on your full resources. These tools are helpful in calming your mind and body, relieving stress, improving your concentration, increasing your energy, listening to your intuition, and programming yourself to accomplish desired goals. When you are using your internal resources fully, you become aware of the enormous power that you possess to make things happen and change yourself.

We will give an overview of these techniques, with references for exploring them in greater depth. We would like you to "taste" these ideas and suggestions and swallow those that fit for you. To effectively evaluate these tools, we recommend practicing them for a minimum of thirty days before evaluating how they are working for you. None of these concepts is new. They have been around for hundreds of years, but only recently have they received widespread attention and been used in many personal- and management-development workshops.

RELAXATION AND CENTERING

To effectively use affirmation, visualization, and meditation, you must first achieve a relaxed state. It is important that your mind is calm and not cluttered with thoughts. When you do a relaxation exercise, you become aware of the multitude of thoughts that flow through your mind, much of the time, making it difficult to concentrate on one subject or activity. When you are relaxed and centered, you are able to use affirmation and visualization techniques to program yourself to accomplish desired goals and to use meditation effectively.

When your body and mind are deeply relaxed, your brain-wave patterns actually change and become slower. This deeper, slower level is called the alpha level. It is contrasted with

Reprinted with permission from *Positive Management Practices*. San Francisco: Jossey-Bass Inc., 1986.

the beta level, the state of being fully awake and conscious; the theta level, the state of dreaming; and the delta level, the state of deep sleep. You are fully aware in the alpha state. The alpha level has been found to be far more effective than the more active beta level for creating real changes in the so-called objective world through the use of affirmations and visualization. This means that you are able to make more effective changes in your work and your life when you are in a relaxed state (Gawain, 1978).

Learning to keep yourself centered enables you to maintain a feeling of balance, a feeling of more strength, a solid integration of mind and body. In *The Centering Book* (Hendricks and Wills, 1975), children describe this centering experience as being lined up right, feeling solid, not thinking but just feeling, being "right on," and being balanced. Many teachers use these centering techniques to calm students and get them in a centered state for taking tests. The same works for adults getting ready for a difficult problem-solving meeting. When in a centered state, you are more in control of yourself and have self-assurance that all your skills and competencies are available to you when you need them. Thus, you perform at your full potential or close to it. A simple centering exercise (Hendricks and Wills, 1975) is presented here:

Find a comfortable position for yourself: sitting upright in a (straight) chair, sitting cross-legged on the floor, or lying on the floor.

Instructions (to be read to others or recorded for yourself):

"Close your eyes and let your [body] relax. Shift around a little until you find a spot where your body rests comfortably. Let a few soothing breaths flow into your body and let yourself go."

Pause (thirty seconds).

"Now feel a little spot of energy at the bottom of your stomach, in the center of your body. You may imagine it as a light, or a warm spot, or just a spot of energy. Relax your body and feel the spot of energy in the center of your body, deep within you."

Pause (fifteen seconds).

"Breathe in slowly through your nose, and, as you do, let each breath make your spot of energy larger. Breathing in on this spot makes it grow. Relax, and breathe smoothly, letting each breath make the spot a little larger. Let it expand to fill your stomach, breathing slowly and deeply."

Pause (one minute).

"Now your stomach is filled, and you may continue breathing on your stomach full of energy as it slowly expands upward to fill your chest."

Pause (one minute).

"Now feel your stomach and chest filled with energy, and, as you breathe, feel your energy expand. Now let the energy flow up through your neck into your head. Breathe slowly, and feel each breath expanding the energy into your head."

Pause (one minute).

"Let the energy circulate freely from the bottom of your stomach, up through your chest, up to the top of your head. Relax, and feel the energy flow throughout your body, and, as you do, feel those parts of your body as one. Feel the flow of energy circulate through your body."

Pause (one minute).

"Now it's time to become alert again. Begin to move your fingers and toes a little. Let your legs feel lively and full of energy. Let your eyes open slowly. When your eyes are fully open, stand up. Feel refreshed and relaxed."

There are many techniques for relaxing and getting centered. In addition to *The Centering Book*, there are *The Second Centering Book* (Hendricks and Roberts, 1977) and *The Relaxation Response* (Benson, 1975). Choose one technique or a combination of several that are comfortable for you, use it for thirty days, and then evaluate. In the beginning, we have found it helpful to put the exercise on a cassette tape and play it while you are in a relaxed position. After several times, you probably will not need the tape. In recording, read the instructions slowly, giving yourself ample time to follow them.

Grounding is a technique that can be used to keep your centeredness. It is better done when standing but can be done sitting. Get in a comfortable position and imagine that you are a tree with roots going deep into the earth below your feet. You can imagine your arms as branches of the tree that are solidly connected to the earth, as is the tree. You can then imagine the energy flowing from the tips of your branches down to your roots in the earth. You can do this whenever you wish to feel solid and connected. Sometimes in meetings, we lose our concentration and our trend of thought. When we do this, we have lost our grounding. Quickly changing to an upright sitting position with feet flat on the floor and imagining that we are connected to the earth will help us regain our grounding, concentration, and thought processes in the here and now. The more often you do this, the faster you will be able to accomplish it in meetings or other places. Another grounding technique is imagining a rope coming from the center of the earth, up through your feet and legs, into your body, with the energy from the center of the earth flowing up through the rope and into your body. This is a way of replenishing energy when you are tired or sluggish.

AFFIRMATIONS

The word *affirm* means "make firm." An affirmation is a strong, positive statement that something is already so, making firm what you are imagining (Gawain, 1978). When you experience a relaxation exercise or meditation, you become aware of the activity of your thoughts. Sometimes it is fun to let these thoughts just pass through and count them. Unfortunately, these thought forms are often negative and will color what you do. It has been said that you are what you think. If you think the worst, that is usually what will happen. We can conclude from this that we have good skills in talking to ourselves and programming ourselves to carry out our thoughts. The use of affirmations, or declarations, as they are sometimes called, allows you to replace these negative or less helpful thoughts with positive ideas that will lead you to your goals or the conditions that you want in your work and your life. It is a powerful technique that will in a short time transform your attitudes and expectations about life and thereby change what you create for yourself.

Spice (1982) teaches the use of affirmations under the title "Up Your Thinking." She advises replacing negative thoughts with positive ones: "I can't" is replaced with "I did," "that's impossible" with "that wasn't so hard," and "nothing will work" with "I can." One method of replacing thoughts is to identify existing thoughts and replace the ones that will not support performance goals with those that will. When people are fuzzy about what they want to do, have them recite out loud, "I know exactly what I want to do." For improving time management, we suggest that you think "I have all the time in the world to do what I need or want to do." With conscious selection of more useful thoughts supporting what you want to do in your professional and personal life, you become your own reinforcer. Spice comments, "Our context is 'merely' that the thoughts we have affect the reality we experience, and that we must seek harmony between stated performance goals and previously unarticulated self-perceptions. The one formula is a simple one: knowledge plus congruent beliefs equals action. Knowledge plus negating beliefs equals good intentions and often guilt" (Spice, 1982, p. 57).

Writing Affirmations. Use the present tense, not the past or the future. For example, "I organize my time each day," not "I will organize" or "I plan to organize." Be positive. Affirm the attitude you wish to have. For example, "I am relaxed at work," instead of "I don't lose my temper." Be personal. Use "I" and follow it with your name. For example, "I, Jane Doe, am solving problems creatively."

Use terms of accomplishment. State that your goal has already been achieved. For example, "My work is well organized each day," not "I am getting better organized." Be accurate and realistic. If you desire a certain weight, state that weight, not an approximate weight or one lower than desired. For example, "I weight 155 pounds." Add drama and excitement. "I weight 155 pounds and feel slim and trim," or "I, Joe Dokes, lead an exciting life." Use active verbs, such as "I remember names very easily" rather than "I am able to remember names."

Be positive, without comparison. Rather than "I am getting better in listening," say "I enjoy listening to others." Avoid comparing yourself with others by using words such as *most* or *better than.* Affirm yourself only. Use "I enjoy building positive working relationships with others," rather than "My associates like me."

Using Affirmations. We recommend writing each affirmation twenty times each day for at least ten days. In this way, you are reaching your senses. You see the affirmation, and you hear it when you repeat it silently or — preferably — out loud as you write. You hear the pen scratching the paper, you feel the pen in your hand, and you touch the paper. Typing is faster for some people. It will accomplish the same result.

Each day, as you write the affirmation twenty times, be aware of any negative thoughts or feelings or barriers to achievement. Make note of these negatives and replace them with affirmations. An example of such a switch would be to change "This is boring" to a positive affirmation like "This is fun." This process is described in some detail in *The Only Diet There Is* (Ray, 1981). This delightful book has many useful affirmations and techniques for weight reduction that can be adapted to any goal you may have.

We find that working with affirmations daily, both writing them and repeating them in a relaxed state of mind, will gradually cause them to become totally integrated with your consciousness. You will notice when your mind is responding positively and you are beginning to experience the intended results. Then you can reduce the number of times you write or repeat the specific affirmations. You will find that repeating the affirmation once a day, or whenever you find yourself behaving in an undesired manner, is a good reinforcer. Once you are programmed with the positive thought, the affirmation will serve as an anchor that you can use at any time.

In addition to writing them down on paper, say them to yourself while in a relaxed state. It is easier and more effective to program your unconscious while in this alpha state. The positive statement becomes a part of you, and you will find yourself unconsciously doing what you wish to do. We also recommend that you put your affirmation on cards. Display them in prominent places (bedroom mirror, bathroom, desk at office and home, sun visor of car, wallet, dining room table, and so forth) to constantly remind you. Repeating the affirmation while stopped in traffic is a productive use of this time.

The time that it takes to reprogram yourself will vary according to how deep-seated your old behavior is. A friend of ours required many months to achieve forgiveness through affirmations and visualization. Now a recitation of his forgiveness affirmation will quickly remove hostile thoughts of retribution and blaming from his conscious mind. Visualizing the end result while saying the affirmation strengthens the programming and will speed up the process. Another reinforcement is putting your affirmations on a cassette tape and listening to them each day. The only limit to the number of affirmations that you can work with at the same time is the amount of time you make available for this powerful effort.

Some examples of affirmations that you can use in the area of managing are "I delegate to my subordinates with clarity," "All my projects are profitable," "I identify problems in order to gain successful solutions," "I make good decisions when I have the facts," and "I put others at ease with my sincerity." For increasing self-worth, you might use "My skills and special experience attract special opportunities," "Positive thoughts bring benefits I desire," "I have the right to feel good about myself," "My body is now free of any tension, and I feel good everywhere," "I am whole and complete within myself," or "I deserve to get compliments on my accomplishments." If you wish to achieve greater calmness, you could use affirmations such as "I am completely calm when people disagree with me," "People can reject my ideas without rejecting me," "I no longer resent John Smith and forgive him completely," "I have the right to say no to people without losing their friendship," and "Other people have the right to say no to me without hurting me." And examples of affirmations useful in the area of success are "I am always in the right place at the right time, successfully engaged in the right activity," "I now have enough time, energy, wisdom, and money to accomplish all my desires," "Money flows to me freely and effortlessly," "My ability to complete transactions compliments my skill at finding good deals," and "I deserve the very best in life."

As you can see, there is no limit to how affirmations can be used — in fact, you can use an affirmation to start this process: "Every day, I write my affirmations twenty times." It takes practice and repetition. Do it for thirty days and then evaluate. You will probably be pleasantly surprised with the results.

VISUALIZATION

Visualization is the process by which an individual mentally pictures a desired goal or result, creating his or her own positive models in the mind. In setting objectives, we have found it helpful to visualize the end results before writing the objective. This makes it easier to avoid the activity trap. When we think in terms of the end result, it is easier to see the alternative paths available to accomplish the objective.

Visualization techniques are being used widely in athletics and cancer treatment. *Getting Well Again* (Simonton, Matthews-Simonton, and Creighton, 1978) describes the visualization and imagery work being used with cancer patients with some interesting results. Russell (Russell and Branch, 1979) of the Boston Celtics describes how he found that when he visualized new plays and moves on the back of his eyelids after watching other stars perform, he could execute these moves on the basketball court. Garfield (1982) describes how athletes and business executives use these techniques to improve their performance. In his research with "terminally ill" patients who recovered, he found that they feel they used hidden reserves that they had been unaware of. In his seminars on peak performance, Garfield trains people to visualize themselves performing successfully. "To use this master skill, you have to learn to relax enough to plant images of excellent performance. Whether it's in a sport or on a job, you'll begin to perform that way. You mentally rehearse. Peak performers view their imaginations as internal playing grounds; they have learned to control the images they send to their brains" (Garfield, 1982, p. 6).

Successful visualization relies on this most basic type of learning — the creation and patterning of ourselves after the perfect and rich images we envision. Henry Kaiser conceded that every one of his business accomplishments was realized first in his imagination, long before he achieved it in the real world. Conrad Hilton, too, said that he visualized himself running a hotel many years before he purchased his first one (McKay, Davis, and Fannig, 1981). Emil Coué, a French pharmacist, believed that you can persuade yourself through your imagination to do anything that is physically possible. Belief in success inspires success. Coué argued that our thoughts, good or bad, become concrete reality. He was convinced that physical diseases are generally more easily cured than mental ones (Trubo, 1982).

By forming an image, you can make a clear mental statement of what you want to accomplish. By repeating this image again and again, you come to expect that what you want will occur. In addition to consciously programming change through these positive images, you can use visualization to gain access to your unconscious mind. The potency of imagery can be found in the research of physiologist Edmund Jacobson, who has shown that when an individual visually imagines running, there are small but measurable contractions in the muscles, comparable to the changes that occur during actual running. Similarly, by holding the image of being chased by a vicious mad dog, you can raise your blood pressure, accelerate your pulse rate, and even provoke goosebumps and perspiration. Steve DeVore, an educational psychologist and a specialist in visualization, states that if you can get in touch with the sounds associated with your objectives as well as the tastes and odor, you have taken a great step forward toward achieving your goal. What you are doing is flooding the brain and nervous system with pure, specific, sensory vision of what you desire. Electrochemistry has shown us that the brain incorporates all these details as if they were already accomplished.

Developing Visualization Skills. To use visualization, it is not necessary to "see" an image. Some people are able to see clear, sharp images with their eyes closed; others state that they do not actually see anything but just "think about" it or imagine that they are looking at it. Since you use your imagination regularly, continue with whatever approach you find yourself using. The following exercise, adapted from *Creative Visualization* (Gawain, 1978, pp. 13-14) will help you to understand what it means to visualize:

> Close your eyes and relax deeply (this may require five minutes using an exercise you are comfortable with). Think of a room that is familiar to you. Remember the details of the room, color of the carpet, pieces of furniture, where they are located, windows, pictures, etc. Imagine yourself walking into the room and sitting in one of the chairs.
>
> Now with your eyes still closed, visualize a pleasant experience (situation) you have had in recent weeks. Remember the experience as vividly and in as much detail as possible. Enjoy, again, the pleasurable sensations you had at that time.
>
> Now imagine that you are in a setting from nature—grass, stream, woods, and so on—and put yourself in this scene. It may be a place you have been or a picture you have seen. Think of the details and create it the way you would like it to be.

Practicing an exercise similar to this daily will improve your visualization skills until you can visualize your goals. Visualizing a goal is more important than knowing every detail of how you will reach it. When you set out to climb a mountain, you need a clear image of the top of the hill. You do not need to know every twist or turn of the trail or the functions of your muscles. Gawain (1978) identifies four basic steps for creative visualization: (1) setting your goal; (2) creating a clear idea or picture; (3) focusing on it often; and (4) giving it positive energy with strong affirmations and feelings that the goal is real and possible.

Using Visualization. Visualization and imagery are even more effective when used with affirmation in a relaxed state of mind. There are three elements in you that influence your success—desire, belief, and acceptance. You must have a clear, strong feeling of purpose—something you really want or desire. The more you believe in a chosen goal and the possibility of attaining it, the more likely it is that you will attain it. You must be willing to accept and have what you are seeking! We have found that people often set and work toward goals that they think they should not and do not really want to achieve. Using this visualization technique will make you aware of whether these are the goals you really want in your life. If you discover that these goals are not what you want, it is appropriate for you to use life and career planning to clarify your situation.

MEDITATION

Meditation is a process, not a state. It is a continuous stream of effortless concentration over an extended period of time. LeShan (1974) describes it as being like coming home. A goal of meditation is the fullest use of what it means to be human. The attainment of the meditative state is another way of perceiving and relating to reality while achieving a greater efficiency and enthusiasm for everyday life.

Neurenberger (1981) points out that *meditation* is not a religious word, although it is used in many religions. He calls it a practical, systematic method that allows one (1) to understand oneself at all levels of being, (2) to understand one's environment completely, (3) to eliminate and prevent inner conflicts, and (4) to obtain a tranquil and peaceful mind. It is a personal technique for increasing internal awareness and expanding conscious self-control. It is a tool, not a way of life.

Meditation is practiced extensively in Eastern cultures, and many of the teachers of meditation are Indian yogis and Buddhist monks who meditate long periods each day. These people are noted for their relaxed warmth, openness, and alertness, no matter what the situation. Some highly pressured members of organizations in our busy society resist taking the time to relax. When Benson (1974) wrote an article in the *Harvard Business Review* urging businesses to give employees time for a meditation break, there was a flood of letters protesting that stress and tension were essential to good business management and suggesting that meditation would make zombies of us. It is interesting that Harry Truman and Winston Churchill were but two of many world leaders who used brief rest periods of this sort to sustain their energy and vitality. It has been said that fifteen to twenty minutes of meditation is comparable to two hours of sleep. We have found that if we are tired before starting a trip, the most relaxing thing we can do is to meditate for fifteen minutes with a focus on a safe arrival at the destination. We are then refreshed, with sufficient energy for the trip. The positive payoff, organizationally and individually, will be discussed in the following paragraphs.

Benefits of Meditation. In *The Holistic Way to Health and Happiness*, Bloomfield and Kory (1978, pp. 64-65) presented a list they had compiled from a review of more than 400 published scientific studies on the results of meditation. Their list includes the following beneficial effects:

Effects on physical health:

1. Increased energy.

2. Increased resistance to disease.

3. Increased physical capacity to handle stress.

4. Improved mind-body coordination and physical agility.

5. Reduced incidence of insomnia, tension headaches, and bodily aches and pains.

6. Control of high blood pressure.

7. Relief of psychosomatic conditions such as asthma, neurodermatitis, and gastrointestinal problems.

8. Help in normalizing weight.

Effects on mental and emotional well-being:

9. Reduced anxiety and nervousness.

10. Reduced depression.

11. Reduced neuroticism and inhibitions.

12. Reduced irritability.

13. Improved self-esteem and self-regard.

14. Increased ego strength.

15. Improved problem-solving ability.

16. Improved organization of thinking.

17. Increased creativity.

18. Increased productivity.

Effects on spiritual well-being:

19. Promotion of self-actualization.

20. Fostering of trust, capacity for intimate contact.

21. Enhanced ability to love and express affection.

22. Development of inner wholeness.

23. Increased autonomy and self-reliance.

24. Increased satisfaction at home and at work.

25. Reduced feelings of alienation and meaninglessness.

26. Strengthening of religious affiliations.

Our experience with meditation substantiates many of these findings. At the office, when we are feeling low on energy in midafternoon or have many things to do and feel fragmented, fifteen minutes of relaxation and meditation gives us sufficient energy to complete the tasks before us, as well as a sense of direction. At home, meditation after morning exercise gives us energy, calmness, and guidance for the day and helps us to feel more enthusiastic and positive about what the day has to offer. An evening meditation, before sleep or before dinner, also is helpful in achieving calmness and direction. The before-dinner meditation usually results in a decreased desire for alcohol and food, supporting our weight goal. The before-sleep meditation results in more restful sleep and pleasant dreams.

Meditative Techniques. There are many theories on the proper way to meditate. We think that the best way is the one that is most comfortable and effective for you. This may be a combination of several techniques. However, there are some basic factors to be considered. Muktananda (1980) describes four factors in meditation. The first is dealing with the mind. We cannot subdue our mind forcibly and should avoid focusing on any one thought. It is advisable to let your thoughts pass through and let the mind wander wherever it likes. Gradually, your mind will become calm; that is meditation. The second factor is using a mantra, which is a Sanskrit term for a word or phrase that is repeated continuously. This repeated recitation is an effective technique of disengaging the mind. Muktananda's mantra is "Om Namah Shivaya" ("I bow to the Lord"). Other simple mantras are "I am" and "Let go." The third factor is the posture that you take when meditating. This may be sitting in a chair, sitting on the floor in a "lotus" position (legs folded one over the other), or lying with your back flat on the floor. It is important that the spine be straight. The position you use should be one that you can stay in comfortably, without moving, for the duration of your meditation, although some individuals say that such activities as walking, running, music, prayer, and looking at a mandala can also be used as a form of meditation. In other words, any activity you invest with prolonged and focused attention can be a form of meditation. The fourth factor described by Muktananda is the breathing process. Breathing should be natural and spontaneous. We should not disturb the natural rhythm of the breath, which works in conjunction with the mind. Focusing on your breathing may be all that you need to get into a meditative state. If a mantra is used, it should be synchronized with your breathing.

In preparation for meditation, it is well to select a quiet place where you will not be disturbed. It is desirable to use the same place each day if possible. It is also recommended that you meditate at the same time each day for a minimum of fifteen minutes each time. Three times a day is optimum. We find that when we meditate for three fifteen-minute periods a day, we achieve many of the effects described earlier. When not meditating, we are not as effective in our work and other activities.

To develop your own meditative style, we recommend reading some of the books on meditation, taking training from an experienced meditator, or getting some tapes for guided meditations. You may wish to make your own tapes to help you get started. A support group is also helpful here. The important consideration is to do it and have patience. Do not punish yourself if your thoughts drift off or you doze. Gently bring yourself back to your breathing or mantra. There will be dry periods and plateaus where you think nothing is happening. Keep on meditating and remember that there is no one right way.

Relaxation, affirmations, visualization, and meditation can be integrated and used together for positive results. When you are in the relaxed meditative state (alpha state), it is much easier to program your unconscious to accomplish the goals you want and manage the stress in your life. These powerful tools will help you achieve a positive attitude and a positive environment of hope and achievement.

REFERENCES

Benson, H. "Your Innate Asset for Combating Stress." *Harvard Business Review*, 1974, *52* (4), 49-60.

Benson, H. *The Relaxation Response*. New York: Avon, 1975.

Bloomfield, H. H., and Kory, R. B. *The Holistic Way to Health and Happiness*. New York: Simon & Schuster, 1978.

Garfield, C. A. "How to Be a Peak Performer." *Bank American World*, 1982, *10* (1), 5-7.

Gawain, S. *Creative Visualization*. New York: Bantam Books, 1978.

Hendricks, G., and Roberts, T. B. *The Second Centering Book*. Englewood Cliffs, N.J.: Prentice-Hall, 1977.

Hendricks, G., and Wills, R. *The Centering Book*. Englewood Cliffs, N.J.: Prentice-Hall, 1975.

LeShan, L. *How to Meditate*. Boston: Little, Brown, 1974.

McKay, M., Davis, M., and Fannig, P. *Thoughts and Feelings*. Richmond, Calif.: New Harbinger Publications, 1981.

Muktananda, S. *Meditate*. Albany: State University of New York Press, 1980.

Neurenberger, P. *Freedom from Stress*. Honesdale, Pa.: Himalayan International Institute of Yoga, Science and Philosophy, 1981.

Ray, S. *The Only Diet There Is*. Millbrae, Calif.: Celestial Arts, 1981.

Russell, W. F., and Branch, T. *Second Wind*. New York: Random House, 1979.

Simonton, O. C., Matthews-Simonton, S., and Creighton, J. *Getting Well Again*. Los Angeles: Tarcher, 1978.

Spice, M. B. "The Thought Selection Process: A Tool Worth Exploring." *Training and Development Journal*, 1982, *36* (5), 54-59.

Trubo, R. "How to Tap Your Brain's Success Circuits." *Success*, Mar. 1982.

CHAPTER 12

Interpersonal Communication Skills

Association of Research Libraries,
Office of Management Studies

Being an effective communicator seems to be based on certain interpersonal components such as: an adequate self concept, the ability to be a good listener, the skill of expressing one's thoughts and ideas clearly, being able to cope with one's emotions, particularly angry feelings, and expressing them in a constructive way, and the willingness to disclose oneself to others truthfully and freely. The skills described in this handout are intended to improve both human relationships and the communication process. Attempts to improve communication must stem from a desire to improve interpersonal relationships and to achieve mutual understanding. The skills are neither new nor unique and many people sometimes use them spontaneously when interacting with others. By themselves the skills do not assure increased clarity of communication. In fact, if they are used inappropriately they can arouse antagonism in the other person and obstruct communication. If, however, interpersonal interaction is based upon a genuine desire to understand the other as a person these communication skills provide ways of overcoming many of the problems inherent in the communication process.

ACTIVE LISTENING

Active listening is most noticeable in its absence. When group members carry on more than one conversation at a time, interrupt one another, and jump from one subject to another you can be sure people are not listening to one another. The consequences of the failure, particularly in the work situation, are that vital information is lost and ideas are not properly explored, leading to hasty and poor selection of alternatives. The failure of people to listen to one another is also very time consuming because we tend to repeat ourselves until we feel we've been heard.

Listening as a skill is something we do most poorly. Studies at Florida State University, Michigan State University and the University of Minnesota demonstrate that the average person remembers only 50% of what he/she has heard immediately after hearing it. Two months later, only 25% is remembered. The difficulty of effective listening stems from the fact that we think far faster than we speak. The average rate of speech for most Americans is 125 words per minute while the brain can process the language of our thoughts at a much higher speed. Consequently, since the words we listen to arrive slowly, our brain has surplus time for other things. These other things include thinking of an argument to the

Reprinted with permission from Association of Research Libraries, 1527 New Hampshire Ave., N.W., Washington, D.C. 20036 speaker's position, constructing a question that can't be answered, looking for hidden motives, evaluating the speaker, or generally paying attention to something other than what the speaker is saying.

Active listening is an attempt to understand the speaker from the speaker's point of view. In doing this the listener is required to pick up and remember much more of what is being said. In addition, the speaker has little or no need to defend or protect, and will in turn be more likely to listen.

Four activities contribute to active listening: (1) anticipating where the conversation is leading, (2) objectively weighing the evidence being presented, (3) periodically reviewing and summarizing what is being said, and (4) paying attention to non-verbal behavior as well as the verbal. A key factor in poor communication is that tendency to critically judge and evaluate the speaker and his/her expressions. As a result the listener indulges in selective listening and is likely to force the speaker to justify, rationalize, defend or protect his/her position. Active listening requires that we assume the other person has useful ideas, information, or points of view and we listen carefully and attempt to understand adequately what the person's point of view is.

PARAPHRASING

Paraphrasing is a way of checking with the other person to be sure that you understand their idea or suggestion as it was intended. Any means of revealing your understanding of the other person's comment constitutes a paraphrase. The objective is to provide information to the other person so he/she can determine whether you understand the message as intended. You can have another person clarify what he/she means by asking what was meant or by saying "I don't understand." However, when you paraphrase you show what your present understanding is and thus enable the person to address clarification to the specificity and understanding you have revealed. Before you agree or disagree with a remark you should make sure that the remark you are responding to is really the message the other is sending.

An additional benefit of paraphrasing is that it lets the other person know that you are interested in him/her. It is evident that you want to understand what is meant if you can satisfy the other that you really do understand the point. The other person will probably be more willing to attempt to understand your views too. Paraphrasing increases the accuracy of communication and thus the degree of mutual or shared understanding. The act of paraphrasing itself conveys feeling—your interest in the other, your concern to see how he/she views things.

To develop your skill in understanding others, try different ways of conveying your interests in understanding what they mean and revealing what their statements mean to you. Find out what kind of reponses are helpful ways of paraphrasing for you.

PERCEPTION CHECKING

Another basic skill for understanding another person is checking with them to make sure you understand their feelings. This skill complements paraphrasing in that it focuses on the emotive aspects of a message rather than ideas. To check your perception of the other's feelings, you describe what you perceive to be their feelings. This description should tentatively identify the other's feelings without expressing approval or disapproval of the feelings and without attempting to interpret or explain the causes of the feelings. Checking the feelings of another conveys a message of how I understand your feelings. Am I accurate?

Your perception of another person's feelings often results from what you are feeling or are afraid of or are wishing for rather than from the other person's words, tones, gestures, facial expressions, etc. Our inferences about other people's feelings can be and often are inaccurate. Thus, it is important to check them out. Perception checking responses convey that you want to understand the other as a person, and that means understanding feelings.

Note that a perception check identifies the other's feeling in some way—disappointed, pushed out of line, etc.—and does not express disapproval or approval of the feelings; it merely conveys that this is how you understand his/her feelings and raises the question of whether or not your interpretation is accurate.

DESCRIBING OWN FEELINGS

Describing your own feelings helps the other person understand how you feel so that he/she/they can respond to you with greater efficacy. Although feelings are expressed in many different ways, usually people make no attempt to describe or identify directly the feelings themselves. When you express your feelings, the other person must try to infer your emotional state from a variety of cues. Since these cues are often ambiguous or even contradictory the likelihood of misperception is great. When you directly describe your own feelings, however, the chances of misinterpretation and resultant action based on false assumptions are decreased.

In describing your own feelings you should make clear what feelings you are experiencing by naming or identifying them. The statement should refer to I, me, or my and specify some kind of feeling by name, simile, or figure of speech. The aim in describing your own feelings is to provide the other with accurate information about your emotional state, not an effort to coerce the other into changing annoying actions so that you will not feel as you do.

Although we usually try to describe our ideas clearly and accurately we often do not try to describe our feelings clearly. The aim in describing your own feelings is to start a dialogue that will improve your relationship with the other. After all, others need to know how you feel if they are to take your feelings into account. Negative feelings are signals that something may be going wrong in a relationship. After discussing how each of you sees the situation or your relationship you may discover that your feelings resulted from false perceptions of the situation's and the other's motives.

In short, describing your feelings should not be an effort to coerce the other into changing so that you won't feel as you do. Rather you report your inner state as just one more piece of information that is necessary if the two of you are to understand and improve your relationship.

DESCRIBING BEHAVIOR

In a behavior description you should report specific observable behaviors of the other without evaluating them. As you develop skills in describing behavior you become a better observer of the behavior of others. You may find that there is sometimes little observable evidence to support your conclusions about the other.

Your aim is to let others know what behavior you are responding to by describing it clearly enough, specifically enough that they know what you observed. To do this you describe evidence that can be seen, behavior that is open to anybody's observation. You avoid stating unfavorable motives or intentions or character traits to others and restrict yourself to describing specifically what they did. To develop skill in describing behavior you must sharpen your observation of what actually did occur. As you do you may find that many of your conclusions are based less on observable evidence than on your own feelings of irritation, insecurity or fear. Thus accusations are usually expressions of feeling. If you and another person want to communicate clearly and improve your relationship the behavior description can be a valuable skill. Each of you will become more aware of your impact on the other and you will both achieve a clear picture of your own actions.

Behavior description means reporting specific observable actions of others without placing a value on them as right or wrong, bad or good, or making accusation or generalizations about the other's motives, attitudes, or personality traits.

GIVING AND RECEIVING FEEDBACK

Feedback when it is given or received can be carried out most effectively by using the communication skills described above. Feedback should be given with the following guidelines in mind:

1. It is descriptive rather than evaluative (feedback should involve a clear report of the facts rather than the reasons why things happened as they did).

2. It is specific rather than general.

3. It takes the needs of the people into account (feedback should be given after a careful assessment has been made of the feelings of the recipient. This does not mean that you should avoid showing anger to the other. It means that the other should be ready to deal productively with it).

4. It focuses on modifiable behavior (feedback should be given about behavior that can be changed and should be given so it does not demand the recipient change his/her behavior).

5. It is solicited rather than imposed.

6. It is well timed (feedback should be given as close to the time of the events causing the reaction).

7. It is validated with the receiver.

8. It is validated with others.

REFERENCES

Human Synergistics. *The Project Planning Problem: Synergistic Decision Making.* Plymouth, Mich.: Experimental Learning Methods, 1974.

"Interpersonal Communication Inventories," *The 1974 Annual Handbook for Group Facilitators.* Palo Alto, Calif.: University Associates, 1974.

Pfeiffer, J. William and John E. Jones. "Openness, Collusion and Feedback" in *The 1972 Annual Handbook for Group Facilitators*. Palo Alto, Calif.: University Associates, 1972.

Schmuck, Richard A. and Philip J. Runhel. *Handbook of Organization Development*. Palo Alto, Calif.: 1972 Chapter Three, "Clarifying Communications." pp. 31-97.

CHAPTER 13

Stress in the Library

Charles Bunge

"Librarians have low-stress jobs." So might have read the headline for articles based on a 1986 wire service story about a research study done in England that found that librarians have a stress level of 2.0, compared with miners at 8.3 and construction workers at 7.5. Librarians who read such articles in the popular library press or in *Parade* magazine[1] might have wondered, "Why, then, do *I* feel so stressed? Am I just an oddball?" You might even have felt vaguely guilty for being such a wimp in what others seem to think is an easy job—a feeling that might actually add to your stress.

From reading the library literature and talking with hundreds of librarians, I am convinced that library work can be very stressful and that library staff members need not add feelings of isolation or guilt to their very real feelings of stress and lack of fulfillment in their jobs.

Some four years ago, *LJ* carried one of the early articles on stress and burnout among librarians.[2] In the intervening years this topic has been treated from a number of perspectives in library publications,[3] and the literature on the subject outside of librarianship has grown apace.[4] This literature, in addition to my own experience and reflection,[5] has formed the basis for a workshop on stress management for library staff members that I have presented some 20 times. During these workshop sessions, over 800 library staff members from all types of libraries have reported and discussed aspects of library work that they find stressful. These discussions illustrate and confirm some important points of consensus in the literature.

Categories & Examples	% of Total	Categories & Examples	% of Total
1. **Patrons** "Meeting interesting people" "Meeting with new people" "Working with the public"	8.7	10. **Being of service** "Sharing myself with others" "Making a positive difference" "Giving service"	4.0
2. **Colleagues** "Working with my colleagues" "Supportive colleagues" "The people I work with"	7.6	11. **Students and children** "Students keep me young" "Watching kids develop"	4.0
3. **Variety** "Variety of tasks" "Never the same question" "Diversity of people and tasks"	7.2	12. **Positive feedback** "Appreciation from patrons" "Hearing 'Thank you'" "Recognition from supervisor"	3.6
4. **Flexibility and autonomy** "Flexibility in duties" "Working on my own" "Flexibility in hours"	7.2	13. **Using technology** "Learning new technology" "High-tech atmosphere"	3.3
5. **Problem solving** "Challenge of the problem" "Detective work" "Helping solve a puzzle"	6.2	14. **Quiet**	2.9
		15. **Getting new books first**	2.9
		16. **Getting paid**	2.5
6. **Learning** "Learn every day" "Learning new things"	5.4	17. **Using my own training** **and skills**	2.2 1.8
7. **Accomplishment** "Being proud of what I do" "Completing a job on time" "Feeling that I can help"	5.4	18. **Physical environment**	1.8
		19. **Selecting materials**	1.8
		20. **Providing access through** **cataloging**	1.8
8. **Finding answers** "Finding the right info" "Help people find what they want"	5.1	21. **Supportive administration** **and supervisors**	1.1
		22. **Opportunities to teach**	1.1
9. **Being around books** "The wealth of info" "Working with knowledge" "I like books"	5.1	23. **Security of guidelines**	1.1
		24. **Spending money**	1.1
		25. **Misc. (less than 1% each)**	6.5

Fig. 1. Sources of satisfaction—All Participants.

STRESS MANAGEMENT WORKSHOPS

From the fall of 1983 to the summer of 1986, I conducted somewhat different versions of my workshop on stress management for library staff in 21 locations in Illinois, Minnesota, New York, Tennessee, Texas, and Wisconsin. Some 850 staff members participated, in groups as small as 15 and as large as 70. In some of the workshops all the participants were reference librarians at various types of libraries. In others, there were participants with positions of different types in a variety of libraries. Several sessions were for staff in a single library, and several were for support staff members.

Categories & Examples	% of Total
1. **Patrons**	15.0
"Questions at closing time"	
"People who won't help themselves"	
"Problem patrons"	
"Discipline"	
"Babies at storyhour"	
2. **Workload**	13.4
"More work than I can get done"	
"Not enough staff"	
"Everything is a priority"	
"Lots of deadlines"	
3. **Supervisors and management**	10.5
"Not knowing where my supervisor is"	
"Inconsistent supervisor"	
"Being left out of decisions where I have expertise"	
"Responsibility without authority"	
4. **Schedule and workday**	7.2
"Too many different kinds of tasks"	
"Unscheduled class visits"	
"Can't predict questions"	
"Rigid work schedule"	
"I can't set my priorities"	
5. **Lack of positive feedback**	6.9
"Lack of recognition for a job well done"	
"Getting no positive feedback"	
"The public's perception of my job"	
"Not being seen as a professional"	
"My low salary"	
6. **Other staff members**	6.9
"Sloppy work by others"	
"Lack of teamwork and cooperation"	
"Crabby co-workers"	
7. **Lack of info and training**	6.7
"Having to wing it all the time"	
"Not having enough information to do my job well"	
"A supervisor who won't train me or answer questions"	
"Poor communication from management"	

Categories & Examples	% of Total
8. **Feeling pulled and tugged**	4.1
"Conflicting demands between work and personal life"	
"Differing expectations from different people"	
"Coping with situations beyond my control"	
"Always having to be nice"	
9. **Technology and equipment**	4.1
"Technological breakdowns"	
"Downtime"	
"Slow response time"	
10. **Physical facilities**	4.1
"Cramped, overcrowded office"	
"Having no privacy"	
"Noisy work area"	
11. **Bureaucracy and red tape**	3.6
"Bureaucracy instead of common sense"	
"Rules for the sake of rules"	
"Hierarchy, titles, & status"	
"Elitism"	
12. **Unchallenging work**	3.3
"Boring, routine tasks"	
"Lack of intellectual challenge"	
"My job is a dead end"	
"Doing statistics"	
13. **Failure and uncertainty**	3.3
"Not being sure patron's needs are met"	
"Making mistakes"	
14. **Change**	2.6
"Constant change"	
"Always changing policies and procedures"	
"Changing plans in the middle of a project"	
15. **Lack of budget and resources**	1.9
16. **Misc. (less than 1% each)**	6.4

Fig. 2. Sources of Stress— All Participants.

One of the purposes of the workshops was to have the participants gain insights from sharing feelings and experiences with each other. At one point in each session I divided the participants into two groups. Members of one group were asked to name things about their jobs that gave them satisfaction, joy, and fulfillment. Members of the other group were asked to name things about their jobs that are stressful or frustrating and that seem to block their fulfillment. If the total number of participants was large the reporting groups would also be segmented by type of library and type of position.

The reported items were recorded on large newsprint sheets and displayed for discussion by the participants. Each workshop session would normally produce about one-third as many positive statements as there were participants and about one-half as many negative statements as the number of participants.[6] Afterward, each distinctive statement from each workshop was recorded on a card so that the statements could be grouped in various ways for analysis.

Categories & Examples	% of Total
1. **Patrons**	41.4
"Rude patrons"	
"Patrons breathing down my neck"	
"Patrons expect miracles"	
"Disturbed patrons"	
"Parents doing kids' homework"	
"Mutilated materials"	
2. **The Workload**	12.5
"The hectic pace"	
"Not enough time to be thorough"	
"Line of people & the phone rings"	
"Not enough staff"	
3. **Feelings of inadequacy**	6.6
"Not being able to serve a patron's needs"	
"Finding an answer too late"	
"Not knowing resources"	
4. **Lack of positive feedback**	6.6
"Family and friends don't understand my job"	
"Lack of understanding of library's role and value"	
"Not hearing 'Thank you' "	
5. **Nonreference duties**	5.9
"Supervisory duties interfere with reference work"	
"Photocopier maintenance"	
"Statistics and reports"	

Categories & Examples	% of Total
6. **Fragmentation**	4.6
"Constant interruptions"	
"Fragmentation of my duties"	
"Too many off-desk tasks"	
7. **Physical environment**	3.3
"The reference bull pen"	
"Can't get away from patrons"	
"Overcrowded office"	
8. **Scheduling**	3.3
"Night and weekend work"	
"No unscheduled time"	
9. **Equipment problems**	3.3
10. **Lack of resources**	2.6
"Lack of answering sources"	
"Can't afford the tools we need"	
11. **Having to be diplomatic**	2.0
12. **Repetitive or trivial questions**	1.3
13. **Poor communications**	1.3
14. **Misc. (less than 1% each)**	5.3

Fig. 3. Sources of Stress—Public Services Librarians.

SOURCES OF SATISFACTION AND STRESS

Examination of the statements made by the workshop participants show that they could be grouped into categories that were quite common from session to session. Figure 1 shows the breakdown of positive statements for all participants, and Figure 2 shows the negative statements. Under each category, example statements in the participants' own words are provided, and the percentage of the statements accounted for by each category is shown. (In attempting to interpret these figures, keep in mind that around two-thirds of all the participants are in public services positions.)

One aspect of the two lists in Figures 1 and 2 (i.e., the "raw" lists, without the categorizations done here) that always impresses workshop participants is how similar to each other they are. Other people, both patrons and colleagues, are a chief source of satisfaction, but they can also be important sources of stress. We take joy in the variety that our work offers, but the accompanying fragmentation and lack of predictability can be frustrating. Learning all the time from challenging responsibilities can be very fulfilling; but sometimes it seems that the more we know the more we should know, and at times the challenge seems overwhelming.

Some sessions of the workshop were attended only by reference librarians, and in others records were kept regarding whether statements were made by staff members with public-contact or with non-public contact positions (for convenience, called "public services" and "technical services" here). In all such sessions, the participants held positions at the professional level. This allows separating for examination statements known to have come from persons in each type of position.

Even after one takes out patrons as a source of stress for public services librarians, some interesting differences between the two lists show up. For example, the lack of positive feedback and evaluation is in different positions on the two lists. Within that category there are differences as well. Public services librarians are much more likely to report stress from a

Categories & Examples	% of Total	Categories & Examples	% of Total
1. Workload "Never being done" "Never being caught up" "More special projects, but must get regular work out"	21.7	**4. Physical environment** "Clutter" "No windows"	8.7
2. Lack of positive feedback "Not being appreciated by the rest of the library" "I never see the end results of my work" "I get only complaints"	17.4	**5. Unchallenging work** "Doing the same thing over and over" "Unchallenging, boring work"	8.7
		6. Technology and change "Computer downtime" "Systems change too fast"	8.7
3. Fragmentation My work is all problems, no pattern" "Too many kinds of tasks" "Trying to balance duties"	17.4	**7. Lack of budget and resources**	8.7
		8. Having no input to decisions	4.3
		9. Misc. (less than 1% each)	4.4

Fig. 4. Sources of Stress—Technical Services Librarians

lack of understanding or appreciation on the campus or in the community, while technical services librarians are more likely to feel stressed by lack of appreciation *within* the library (especially from public services staff).

For example, catalogers feel that they never get compliments for good work, only complaints about unhelpful subject headings or slow processing. Technical services librarians also find stressful never seeing the results of their work, such as a fruitful search in the catalog or a book that they selected being used.

The workload is another important source of stress for both public services and technical services librarians. Both groups report being frustrated by what seems like an ever-increasing number of special projects, without any decrease in the volume of "regular" work. However, here too, the statements and discussion of them at workshops reveal some differences. Reference librarians most frequently report being stressed by the sheer volume and hectic pace of reference questions. Technical services librarians seem more frustrated by

Categories & Examples	% of Total
1. **Supervisors and management**	18.4
"Supervisors who won't stand up for our department"	
"No resolutions or closure on problems"	
"Boss with double standard"	
"Supervisor always at meetings"	
2. **Other staff members**	13.2
"People not carrying their weight"	
"Doing other people's work"	
"Incompetent co-workers"	
"Backstabbing"	
"Too much competition"	
3. **Workload**	9.2
"Too much work expected"	
"Quantity over quality"	
"Short (unnecessarily so) deadlines"	
4. **Lack of positive feedback**	7.9
"Evaluation is not timely"	
"Evaluation is not effective"	
"Lack of respect and recognition"	
5. **Physical facilities**	6.6
"Inadequate space"	
"No windows"	
"Fluorescent lights"	
6. **Feeling pulled and tugged**	6.6
"Being in the middle between patrons and library rules"	
"Responsibility without authority"	
"Feeling vulnerable and powerless"	

Categories & Examples	% of Total
7. **Inadequate Training, knowledge**	5.3
"Not having enough training to do my job"	
"Incomplete training"	
"Having to ask too many questions"	
8. **Bureaucracy and procedures**	5.3
"Time-consuming procedures that seem unnecessary"	
"The pecking order"	
"Too many chiefs, too few Indians"	
9. **Poor communication**	
"Nothing in writing"	
"Management doesn't tell us anything"	
10. **Having no input into decisions**	3.9
11. **Equipment and technology**	3.9
"Downtime on OCLC"	
"Not being able to get a terminal or printer"	
12. **Frustrations on the job**	3.9
"I fear making mistakes"	
"When work goes slowly"	
13. **Fragmentation and schedule**	3.9
"No flextime"	
"Can't structure my time"	
"Working in two sections"	
14. **Boredom and tedium**	2.6
"Unchallenging, dead end job"	
15. **Change and uncertainty**	2.6
16. **Misc. (less than 1% each)**	2.6

Fig. 5. Sources of Stress—Support Staff Members

the feeling of never being finished or of having just as much work to do at the end of the day as there is at the beginning, and they seem to envy the sense of closure that reference librarians can get from leaving the reference desk at the end of a shift.

Technical services librarians more frequently report being stressed by unchallenging duties, while some reference librarians report that the necessity of working nights and weekends causes stress. The feelings of inadequacy and frustration at being unable to find answers to reference questions (or at findings answers after the patrons have left the library) are stressful to reference librarians in a way that seems not to have a counterpart among reports from technical services librarians.

SUPPORT STAFF STRESS

The positions held by support staff members range from junior clerical positions to high-level paraprofessional jobs, mainly in public and academic libraries in technical services positions. There are some striking differences between the statements from support staff members and those from the other groups. The categories and percentages in Figure 5 are more similar to reports that would come from support staff in institutions other than libraries than they are to reports from professional staff members in libraries.

In general, as workshop participants discussed their statements, the greatest overall source of stress for support staff members seems to come from their perception of being held accountable for a high volume of high-quality work without the support of good supervision, sufficient training, adequate communication from the organization, or effective feedback and evaluation. Feeling pulled and tugged or enmeshed in a bureaucracy without control, power, or autonomy, is a source of stress commonly reported in the literature, and it is one that shows up prominently in the statements from support staff here (note categories 6, 8, 10, and 13 in Figure 5).

DIFFERENT TYPE, SAME STRESS

Another potential source of variation among reported sources of stress is type of library. It is possible to separate statements known to be from staff members in public, academic, and special libraries (especially in health science and scientific research environments). Examination of statements separated and grouped by type of library fails to reveal important differences in categories or proportions. Special librarians did offer somewhat more statements concerning stress from "high status" patrons who fail to recognize or respect their expertise and skill. Academic librarians report that they are frustrated at being treated like second-class citizens on their campuses, while public librarians report stress from not being respected at City Hall or by being thought to get paid for reading books. The specific nature of "problem" patrons varied from type to type of library, but the proportion of reports of stress from this source are only slightly higher in public libraries than in other types.

YOUR OWN BRAND OF STRESS

What insights can be drawn from these statements and the various breakdowns presented here? Three characteristics of these lists nicely illustrate and confirm important concepts from the literature of stress and stress management: 1) the wide variety of sources of stress reported; 2) the similarity between the list of sources of joy and the list of sources of stress; and 3) the variation in the lists by type and level of library position. Perhaps the most important insight to be drawn from these three characteristics is that stress and its sources are very unique to each of us and to the situation in which we find ourselves. One of the faults of treatments of stress by the popular media is their tendency to treat stress as some global force out there waiting to burn us out.

The fact that the sources of joy and fulfillment and those of frustration and stress are so similar points out that different people (and the same person under different circumstances) can find a particular phenomenon challenging (pleasantly stressful) or frustrating (painfully stressful). The fact that the same items show up on both lists also demonstrates that many or most aspects of library jobs are not inherently stressful (at least not painfully so). Rather, whether or not they produce stress depends on the situation or other factors.

Underlying these observations is a particular definition or concept of stress as a phenomenon or process in our lives. The definition of stress on which there is the most consensus in the literature is that stress is a person's physiological and psychological reaction to a challenge or demand that is placed upon him or her. The demand or challenge (or its source) is commonly called a "stressor."

For most people most of the time, our reactions to challenges and demands are part of the joy and verve of our lives. If they are painful, they are only temporarily or mildly so. To the extent that our reactions to challenges and demands are continually or severely painful, we can say that we have "distress," "strain," or stress as it is commonly understood.

Sometimes, for some people, the strategies that they use to cope with or lessen painful stress seem to contribute to the problem in a vicious-circle way, rather than to be true solutions. To the extent that this is generally true for a person and the vicious circles are out of control, the person might be said to be burning out or to be burned out.

What we all need to keep our reactions to demands from being painful are resources — physical health and stamina, positive attitudes toward ourselves, support and encouragement from those around us, and effective strategies and skills for restoring physiological and psychological balance when confronted with things that are particular stressors for us. Just as each person is unique with regard to the particular things that are stressors for him or her, so each person is unique with regard to the type and mix of resources he or she needs to cope happily and with joy.

One of the most important general stress-management strategies is the continual development of one's awareness regarding these two aspects of one's self, because controlling and avoiding painful stress is largely a matter of maintaining a balance between the challenges and demands we are under and the resources we have to cope and thrive.

LESSONS TO BE LEARNED

Using this way of looking at stress and stress management can allow one to draw confirming examples and insights from the five figures. For example, both public services and technical services librarians need to find ways to deal with workload as a stressor. However, the particular strategy for coping with the hectic situation of a line of patrons at the desk and the ringing telephone should be different from that of coping with the frustration of never seeing the pile of work to be done diminish (because someone is always replacing completed work with new work).

In the latter situation, a potentially helpful technique would be to keep one's eye on the "work completed" pile or shelf and to set targets and keep track of how much work is really completed in a day or week, so that the challenge of the ever-full "in basket" can be balanced with a feeling of accomplishment and pride in the work turned out. In the reference desk situation, perhaps developing skills at concentration on the patron at hand, using self-calming techniques, and using technology to reduce the disruptiveness of the telephone would be effective strategies. (For both, developing skills at assertively asking for more realistic workloads might be important, as well!)

Certainly, persons with supervisory and management responsibilities can take some lessons from Figure 5. Even if a supervisor believes that perceptions such as those expressed about supervisors do not reflect reality, the perceptions and the stress reactions to them are realities and may well be reducing the productivity (surely the happiness) of the staff members holding them.

The supervisor's absence from the department was a frequently mentioned stressor. Being aware of this for one's own staff (and sensitively trying to sort out whether the stress is due to frustration at the supervisor's lack of availability for consultation and direction, the fact that the supervisor's absence leaves the department shorthanded, or envy of the variety of the supervisor's day), the supervisor can work with affected staff members to keep the stress related to such absences at a reasonable level.

Effectively and happily managing stress in our lives starts with awareness and understanding of ourselves as unique, complex human beings: awareness of what uniquely makes me happy, gives me joy, and can serve as resources for meeting challenges and demands; continual awareness and monitoring of what is stressing me, in what situations, and how I am reacting; and sensitivity to messages of pain and hurting that my mind and body are trying to give me regarding imbalances between the challenges I am under and the resources I have available to cope.

With such self-knowledge, we are in a good position to identify the unique mix of resources and skills that each of us should continually be developing, in order to avoid or manage the specific stressors that are problems for us, be they skills at reaching out to others for support, skills at asking for our rights assertively, relaxation skills, better nutrition habits, or a clearer sense of our values and priorities.

Surely, with the current and projected economic situation and the increasing complexity of the library and information world, sources of stress are not going to decrease for library staff. And surely, some of us at some times will not cope with our stress effectively. Turning the situation around and restoring the balance will not always (or even usually) be easy, but the happiness and joy that can come from library work are certainly worth the effort.

NOTES

[1] *Parade*, August 17, 1986, p. 9.

[2] Blood, Rudolph, "Librarian Burnout," *LJ*, Nov. 1, 1982, p. 2048-51.

[3]For a useful listing of such treatments see: Hack, Mary, John W. Jones, and Tina Roose, "Occupational Burnout Among Librarians," *Drexel Library Quarterly*, Spring 1984, p. 46-72.

[4]This literature is vast. Among the books that have usefully synthesized the findings of research and clinical practice for a lay audience are: Cherniss, Cary. *Staff Burnout: Job Stress in the Human Services*, Sage, 1980; Freudenberger, Herbert J. and Geraldine Richelson. *Burn-Out: the High Cost of High Achievement*. Anchor: Doubleday, 1980; Maslach, Christina. *Burnout: the Cost of Caring*. Prentice-Hall, 1982; and Shaffer, Martin. *Life After Stress*. Plenum, 1982.

[5]Some of these experiences and reflections are reported in: Bunge, Charles A., "Potential and Reality at the Reference Desk: Reflections on a 'Return to the Field,'" *Journal of Academic Librarianship*, July 1984, p. 128-132.

[6]No particular conclusions should be drawn from this disparity in numbers. Participants tend to be more general in statements about sources of satisfaction and more detailed about sources of stress. Also, the nature of the workshop topics and the time allocations encouraged fuller reporting of sources of stress.

CHAPTER 14

Time Management and the Woman Library Manager

Helen M. Gothberg

You've got your first big break in library management, but after a few months on the job are beginning to wonder if you really can cut it. There never seems to be enough time to get everything done that's expected of you. Your husband's complaining about your long work hours, and the children are getting into trouble at school and constantly fighting among themselves. Or, maybe you are in a position where you feel you could and would like to move into a management role but are wondering if you will be faced with some of these problems.

THE DUAL ENVIRONMENT

Does this mean women should stay out of management? Definitely not! But new women managers or women seeking management positions need to recognize the value of ETM — efficient time management — in their dual environments of career and home. Even before a woman takes a paying job, whether she is single or married, has a family or not, she is in most cases a home manager. While everyone, male or female, who moves into management for the first time will find ETM an important job skill, the woman manager soon learns that if she is not going to join the ranks of the harried, overworked executive, she will need ETM not only at work, but also at home.

The Women's Movement has brought about increased opportunities for women to move into positions of greater responsibility with better pay. Men are more open to sharing the workload at home, thus enabling women to take advantage of these opportunities. Yet, the primary responsibility for household management continues, for the most part, to belong to women. For today's woman manager, the slogan "work smarter not harder" is not just a maxim but a survival necessity.

Time, or its lack, according to some writers, is one of management's most pressing problems. An American Management Association study indicated that most presidents and vice-presidents of U.S. companies work 62 hours a week or more. That's an alarmingly high number of "workaholics." If time is indeed the "stuff life is made of," as Benjamin Franklin suggested, then it appears that managers are paying a very high price for their careers. Perhaps it is not time that needs to be managed—but ourselves.

Experts on time management recommend that in order to develop ETM, you need to gain an accurate picture of how you are currently spending your time. Block out a grid with either 15-minute or half-hour intervals and write down what you have accomplished within each time frame. Chart your activities for a week, rating each one as A, B, or C in terms of priorities.

If your work varies considerably, you will find it useful to pick three or four weeks out of the year to keep a time chart. If you don't have time to keep such a record, have your secretary or other person keep it at work. You are probably on your own for keeping track of those hours away from work, but you could be lucky and talk a family member or friend into keeping it for you. Once you have an accurate record of how you spend your time, you can identify where you are wasting it and then begin to make changes to improve your ETM.

PHONE CALL MANAGEMENT

Many time wasters can be turned into time savers or can be effectively dealt with to one extent or another; take telephone calls for example. Few people could survive the busy and demanding life of a manager without a phone, but it is always at the top of the list in studies intended to identify the worst time wasters. The telephone can be a time saver if it takes the place of a meeting or helps to improve communication.

Train your secretary or other staff members to screen calls. Be sure to leave a list of exceptions such as the mayor, president of the library board or city manager, and the child care center director. Not everyone will like it when they can't get through to you, and you will need to weight how serious this problem is against the need for ETM. If too many phone calls are a serious problem, take and return calls only at specific times of the day. When calling an individual who is loquacious, phone just before lunch or closing time.

THE MEETING GAME

Meetings can either be time wasting or productive. Examine the need for frequent meetings to determine their necessity, and be sure to go in with a written and well-planned agenda. Keep the group on track by not permitting individuals to wander off onto topics not on the agenda.

When the meeting is over, make two lists. One should note everything that you did right, and the second, what you could have done better. File the two lists and review them before your next assembly. Holding a meeting to determine how meetings could be shortened, made more productive, or just plain abolished might be a good idea. Remember, you will never be more effective in bringing about change than in your first six months to a year on the job.

Nine Steps to ETM

1. List your goals. Note both long- and short-term goals. Include family as well as career goals, such as taking a vacation or sending a child to computer camp or to college.

2. Next, rank your goals as A—most important, B—second in importance, and C—least important. Reexamine your B goals and turn them into either A or C goals. Once you have established your A goals, discard the others.

3. Set priorities in terms of what you need to do to reach your A goals. We all know what those priorities are, but sometimes we get bogged down in doing tasks that lead nowhere.

4. Make a daily "To Do" list. If applicable, the woman manager will want to keep in mind her dual roles as library and home manager. It may even be useful to maintain two lists, one under each heading. Make each list at the same time of the day.

5. Prioritize your list. Not everything on the list is an A. File the Cs and start with the As remembering that the As are those tasks which are going to help you to reach the priorities that you have set in terms of both long- and short-term goals.

6. Continually ask yourself, "What is the best use of my time right now?" If you know that you are going to have a 15- or 20-minute wait at the dentist's office, take along that professional journal article that you haven't had time to read, or put together the agenda for the next staff meeting. It may also be time to sit and be quiet for a few minutes if that's the best thing for you to be doing at the moment.

7. Handle each piece of paper only once. This recommendation is probably one of the most difficult for library managers. Librarians are awash in paper. In spite of computers and automation, paper remains much of what our work is about.

8. Delegate an appropriate amount of the workload. As a manager it is up to you to set parameters and guide others in the operation of the library.

9. *Do it now!* If you have earned a position as a library manager, you are probably not given to procrastination to any serious degree. However, there are always those jobs that few managers enjoy doing, such as performance evaluations. One way to make the job easier is to use the Swiss cheese approach—take one small bite of a large project at a time until it is completed.

Time Wasters

There are many ways of wasting time, and you will be able to come up with a few of your own. Some of the most frequently noted time wasters from the literature on time management are listed below. They are divided between "external" or those time wasters that are essentially environmental, and "internal" or those which are closely related to our personalities and habits.

External Time Wasters

1. Telephone calls.

2. Meetings (both planned and unplanned).

3. Drop-in visitors.

4. A lack of objectives, policies, and procedures.

5. Handling emergencies.

6. Dealing with the personal problems of employees and patrons at work.

7. Confused responsibility and lines of authority.

Internal Time Wasters

1. Unclear communication with others.

2. Indecision and procrastination.

3. Attemping to do too much at once and estimating time unrealistically.

4. Inability to say no.

5. Personal disorganization, such as cluttered desk and/or inadequate filing systems.

6. Lack of self discipline.

7. Failure to delegate responsibility appropriately.

HOW ACCESSIBLE SHOULD YOU BE?

Many managers like to maintain an open-door policy for both library staff and the public. It's certain to be good for staff morale and public relations, but every person in a position of responsibility needs blocks of time to work and to think. Here again, a well-trained secretary can be a great help in screening people.

Consider limiting the open-door policy to certain hours and days of the week, which can be flexible. One successful department head, without a secretary, had three signals using the door to her office to indicate her availability. A closed door meant that she was not to be disturbed unless it was an emergency; partly open indicated that she was working but could be disturbed for something important; and wide-open was an invitation to visitors. Her reference staff was quick to check the door before showing patrons to her office, and regulars soon learned to interpret the signals for themselves.

Another factor that affects time is visitors. Understanding nonverbal communication can be useful; stand when a drop-in visitor comes to your office and do not ask the person to sit down. This action will keep the meeting short. Office arrangement affects the number of people who drop by. If your desk faces the door, you invite more people to walk in than if your back or profile is toward the door.

PREPARING YOUR STAFF

Every new manager should take time to discover whether a mission statement, along with recent goals and objectives, has been written for the library and major departments. Mission, goals, and objectives statements form the basis for the development of policies and procedures—all of which should be in writing. If such statements do not exist or have not been revised within the last three to five years, they should be developed with staff input, as soon as possible.

Although much time is involved in such planning activities, they help ease the burden of confused responsibility and lines of authority, and help clarify communication. Every staff member should be familiar with the statements and be able to interpret them to the public with a conviction born out of understanding, because he or she has had a hand in shaping them.

Emergencies are difficult to anticipate. One time saver is to keep a list of emergency numbers at the reference and/or public service desks. A once-a-year briefing on disaster plans is a good idea, as is CPR training and a briefing from the local psychologist on how to cope with difficult or emotionally disturbed patrons. Other less catastrophic events also arise, and achievement-oriented people plan well ahead so they are not constantly putting out fires and missing deadlines. Setting up artificial deadlines that are earlier than the real ones and keeping clocks ahead of time are two ways to maintain ETM—even when a crisis does arise.

PEOPLE AND THEIR PROBLEMS

The people you manage may come to you with personal problems. A wise woman manager will listen carefully and make notes for the individual's personnel file, but will be cautious about falling needlessly into the "nurturing mother" role. Listening with understanding and empathy to staff's problems is important to their morale, but it should never become an excuse for poor job performance—not for more than a very short period of time. Nor should a manager attempt to counsel staff members about their personal lives. If problems persist and job performance is a serious problem, insist that the individual seek professional help.

The chronic complainer is another story. One way to deal with this individual is to immediately turn the conversation to the subject of his or her work. Ask how a certain project is moving along or what does the person think about a given problem in the library. This communication tells the person that you are interested in their work and their ideas, but you are not willing to spend time in a personal gripe session.

ORGANIZED AT WORK

If you are seriously interested in ETM, the internal time wasters are a good place to start because they are the ones over which you have the most control. Stephanie Winston, an expert on managing time and paperwork, believes that disorganization is a universal problem, and that the root of it is psychological. When disorganization becomes chronic, the cause may go back to a parent who was too controlling. Old childhood habits of resistance can continue into the adult years without our even being aware of it.

Clutter is one of the handmaidens of disorganization. Begin with keeping your desk well organized but also check out your handbag and briefcase, Winston recommends. Do you really need all that stuff you carry around?

Be certain that you are not doing excessive office record keeping. This practice is a symptom of insecurity. Comprehensive files are useful, but are they worth the time and money to keep up? What is the worst thing that could happen if you got rid of some files or part of their contents? Is there another source where you could locate the same information? One rule of thumb is that if you haven't used it in a year, it probably should be filed in the wastebasket. Office filing systems should be a librarian's forte, but, all the same, remember not to overspecify the subjects on file folders. Regard a file that lacks bulk with suspicion; perhaps it could be combined with others.

Paperwork can be one of a manager's biggest headaches. Some ETM tips in this area include using speed-letter forms with carbons already inserted with space for a reply. If possible, use a dictating machine or a microprocessor. A well-trained secretary can answer many letters with only a few notations on the original for guidance. Letter forms are also useful and can be personalized by changing a word here and there.

Deal with correspondence and other paperwork during one period of the day, keeping in mind the maxim to handle paper only once. It is becoming an acceptable practice to answer some kinds of letters on the bottom of the original. Robert Townsend suggests that in order to speed up this process, correspondence should be answered on the top of the copy machine. Keep responses short and to the point; don't perpetuate polysyllabic obfuscation.

ORGANIZED AT HOME

Getting organized at home is often as important for the woman library manager as it is at work. Stock your car with the essentials you need to keep it operating—a compressor for flat tires, extra belts, water in a hot climate, and traction grids in a cold one. Keep extra gloves, an umbrella, change, stamps, a city map, and other useful objects in the car. Organize shopping trips and errands so that you only need to make one trip instead of several. Better yet, consider whether you can afford to hire a service such as "Rent a Wife/Husband" to do it for you.

Take care of yourself. Don't try to do too many things simultaneously. Finish one large project before starting another. Bear in mind that there is a difference between excellence and perfection. The first is striving for that which is attainable and gratifying; the second, not attainable and neurotic. It is not necessary to be perfect all the time and at everything you do.

Nor does ETM mean scheduling every minute of the day and then killing yourself to accomplish unrealistic goals and objectives. ETM does mean working smarter, not harder, and building flexibility into your schedule. For example, don't apologize for leaving early a meeting that has gone on too long. Jean Fitzpatrick advises that the working woman flaunt her efficiency and make it known what she's accomplished during a day—talking up her time-management efficiency.

It may be a dichotomy, but managers need time out for relaxation and exercise to be more efficient. If you are too busy to exercise or spend time enjoying the company of friends and/or family, *you are too busy* for your own good. Pay attention to your eating habits as well. Large meals and alcohol are not a good idea for lunch; they make most people sluggish in the afternoon.

You might find it helpful to postpone lunch until 1 p.m. so you can use the noon hour for work when you are less apt to be interrupted. Restaurant rush hour is over by that time, and you will get quicker service. Ross Webber, well-known management expert, reported that medical research supports skipping the working lunch in favor of eating alone because talking while eating is stressful.

YOU CAN'T DO EVERYTHING

Delegating work is crucial to ETM—recognize that it is not a matter of dumping unpleasant work on subordinates. Giving more responsibility is one of the keys to better management and improved job performance as long as people have the skills or are given the training to carry out the work to both their and your satisfaction.

One example of a failure to delegate is the library director being a member of every library committee. If a committee cannot function without her, then the manager should be the chair; otherwise, meet with commitee heads in *one* meeting instead of many. Brief written reports of committee activities are appropriate to supplement such meetings. In making judgments about whether to delegate or not, consider these three guidelines:

1. Maintain control over those activities or projects where as a library manager you have considerably more expertise and information than your staff.

2. Maintain control over those activities where change in current practice is involved.

3. Delegate those activities or projects that are routine and maintain stability and work flow.

Give thought and consideration to how in-service training or other educational opportunities could be used to broaden the responsibilities of professional and other library staff. A common example is training library assistants to answer ready-reference questions, especially in a library where a telephone reference service has been established. This leaves the professional reference librarian free to answer more difficult questions and assume greater management responsibility.

A word of caution is in order here. When you take away lesser job responsibilities and give them to a person in a lower-ranked position, let the person whose duties you are going to change know that you feel he or she is good on the job and capable of doing more sophisticated work.

Don't permit others to make too many demands on your time, including staff who want to delegate their problems upward. Expect achievement, keep organizational structure as uncomplicated as possible, and encourage staff competence with the zest of a football coach. Learn to say no. Although our society is changing, many women are products of an earlier environment where they were expected to always provide support and nurturing. Don't be afraid to say no to a superior if the demand is unrealistic or the deadline impossible.

Webber reported on one study which indicated that managers who ignored demands that interfered with their own job performance were given higher ratings by their supervisors than those who conformed. If you are new to the community or state, or are a new library director, every library professional organization and local community service organization is going to want a piece of your time. Give yourself a few months on the job before accepting outside obligations. Suggest that one of your staff would be suitable, thereby giving others an opportunity to grow and yourself time to find out which organizations will be helpful in achieving your priorities.

Effective time management takes self-discipline and effort. In some initial cases you must spend time to gain it later on. Keep in mind the words of an anonymous philosopher:

Yesterday is a cancelled check.
Tomorrow is a promissory note.
Today is ready cash. Use it!

REFERENCES

Askenas, Ronald N. and Robert M. Schafer, "Time Managers Can Avoid Wasting It," *Working Woman*, January 1984, p. 38-43.

Bliss, Edwin C. *Getting Things Done: the ABC's of Time Management*. Scribner, 1976.

Braid, Robert W., "Learning To Say No," *Supervisory Management*, July 1983, p. 9-14.

Davenport, Rita. *Making Time, Making Money: A Step-by-Step Program for Setting Your Goals and Achieving Success*. St. Martin's, 1982.

Fitzpatrick, Jean Grasso, "Time: Stop Working Late," *Working Woman*, October 1983, p. 7, 72.

Heyel, Carl. *Getting Results with Time Management*. 2d ed. rev. by David V. Lewis. Education for Management, 1987.

Lakein, Alan. *How To Get Control of Your Time and Your Life*. Peter H. Wyden, Inc., 1973.
Mackenzie, R. Alec. *The Time Trap*. AMACOM: American Management Assn., 1972.

LeBoeuf, Michael, "Managing Time Means Managing Yourself," *Business Horizons*, February 1980, p. 41-46.

Roe, Jessica, "The Top 20 Time-Wasters," *Working Woman*, October 1982, p. 74.

Steffen, R. James, "How To Stop Wasting Time," *Supervisory Management,* May 1982, p. 22-25.

Townsend, Robert. *Up the Organization*. Knopf, 1970. rev. 1984 under the title *Further Up the Organization*.

Webber, Ross A., "Finding More Time," *Working Woman*, October 1982, p. 113-116.

Winston, Stephanie, "How To Get Organized at Work and Home," *U.S. News & World Report*, May 7, 1979, p. 76-81.

CHAPTER 15

Ethics and Values in the Workplace

Thomas W. Shaughnessy

This brief essay is divided into three parts: the librarian's responsibility to library users (actual and potential); his or responsibility to the organization, including co-workers; and finally, the librarian's responsibility to himself or herself. "Well," you might say, "when is he going to talk about ethics?" To the extent that responsibilities are based upon a perception of one's duty, and because duty is one of the foundations of ethical theory, this chapter is also about ethics.

John Kultgen, in *Ethics and Professionalism*, defines ethics as encompassing three concepts: ideals, aspirations, and rules of conduct.[1] He goes on to say that ideals are comprehensive norms that generate specific objectives and even modes of being for the professional.

To the extent that our ideals and aspirations can be seen as the basis for ethical conduct, it is useful to ponder the question, Where does the librarian get his or her ideals? Certainly many, perhaps most, people entering the library field come with an appropriate set of values, a service orientation, and a predisposition to intellectual freedom. While these ideals are not initially fully developed, the process of professionalization builds on the new recruit's predispositions, and this process typically occurs in library school. I believe it was a Supreme Court justice who once described law schools as places where students learn to "think like lawyers." Similarly, library schools might be viewed as places where new recruits learn to think like librarians, that is, to learn the attitudes and ethics of their profession. Contributing to the professionalization process are role models and mentors. In fact, these may be more important to the student's development than formal coursework.

Because of the importance of this process in terms of value formation and professionalization, I am an advocate of full-time attendance (at least for one semester) in library school. There is no substitute, in my view, for this experience or for the attitudinal changes which it can engender.

The value system which an individual brings with him or her to a profession, combined with those values cultivated and nurtured during one's professional education, become the bases on which the new professional dispatches his or her ethical responsibilities.

RESPONSIBILITY TO USERS

The first responsibility of any professional is to the client. This is true of individual librarians (regardless of their position in the workplace) and of the library organization. Users should expect nothing less than excellent service. Their encounters with the library and its staff should be characterized by all of the elements which are indicative of quality: reliability and consistency, timeliness, competence, approachability, courtesy, effective communication, credibility, confidentiality, and an understanding of client needs. Our own code of ethics puts the matter this way: "Librarians must provide the highest level of service through appropriate and usefully organized collections, fair and equitable circulation and service policies, and skillful, accurate, unbiased and courteous responses to all requests for assistance."

If this is truly the ethic that guides our profession, then I would suggest that we are suffering from an ethics gap. Several of the services which we offer are not of the highest level: according to several studies of reference service, we provide correct answers roughly half the time. Similarly, book availability studies conducted in academic libraries reveal a patron success rate of only about 60 percent. Statistics such as these indicate that for some patrons, library staff are not adding much value to the patrons' encounters with the library. Yet we know that all contacts with an organization are a critical part of one's perceptions and judgments about that organization. But the quality of the people contacts are often the firmest and longest lasting.

Why do such service breakdowns occur? Is there a certain inevitability of malpractice in our profession as well? I don't think so. Virtually every librarian I know has read Thomas J. Peters's *In Search of Excellence*, along with similar works. We know what outstanding performance is, we know that we are ethically bound to do the best we can for our users, but oftentimes we seem to apply lower standards and rationalize the situation by citing library policy, pressures of one kind or another, or other reasons. Yet as consumers of various professional services, each of us knows that the minimalist approach to meeting client needs is rarely satisfactory. Minimalism tends to produce over a period of time professionals who are too grudging, too calculating, too lacking in spontaneity, too quickly exhausted to go the extra mile. It weakens our commitment and dulls our perception of our ethical responsibilities.

RESPONSIBILITY TO THE ORGANIZATION

While the user has first claim on the library professional's time, all librarians also bear certain responsibilities to the organization of which they are a part. If an organization is defined as a group of people coming together to achieve common goals, the relationships between and among the individuals who comprise the organization are critical. Many, if not most, of these relationships should be guided by ethical principles.

Barbara Toffler reports in *Tough Choices: Managers Talk Ethics* on interviews conducted with thirty-three managers in a variety of U.S. corporations.[2] She found that ethical concerns are part of the routine practices of managers. Of the fifty-nine cases described in her study, two-thirds focus on personnel issues and interpersonal relationships.

But it shouldn't be just managers who are concerned about workplace ethics. This should be of concern to all staff, regardless of level. I know of one library where, because of the tension and conflicts within a particular division, several staff members began keeping bottles of antacid in their desk drawers! How can any work be done in such an environment? More important, how will staff be able to treat users with courtesy, respect, and care if they don't act properly toward each other? The norms which should guide our actions vis-à-vis user groups must necessarily influence our behavior toward each other. Consultants to the health care industry report that it is very difficult to get hospital nurses, technicians, and attendants to be warm and caring toward their patients if doctors treat them disrespectfully. In other words, the way we treat each other has to affect the treatment our patrons receive. This is an essential point because librarianship is not practiced autonomously, except perhaps in a freelance mode. Library services are typically provided in organizational settings and are heavily dependent on teamwork. The success of service transactions at the reference desk, the circulation desk, the children's room, or on the bookmobile depends on many other people—in acquisitions, cataloging, shelving, etc., having done their job.

But being a member of a team should not lead to a lessening in one's sense of duty, to the rationalizing of performance failures, or to a sense of anonymity. On the contrary, professionals must be conscious of their obligation to set an example, to serve as role models and even mentors for less experienced staff. Most teams have at least a few star players and it is these individuals who often give the team (or organization) its spirit or character. And to the extent that a great deal of ethical behavior is based upon perceptions of what one's duty is as well as role modeling, it is important that librarians, particularly senior staff, appreciate their responsibilities in this regard. Not only do they hold formal, organizational power over subordinates, but they also can exert considerable moral influence.

Quite often, ethical issues are raised over the use of power within the organization. People are sometimes placed in situations which leave them morally uneasy, uncomfortable, or unhappy with themselves. From the individual's point of view, these feelings are signs that one's conscience is alive and well, and that one's ethical sensibilities have not been dulled. But it should not be surprising that not everyone has such gifts. Some have to develop an appreciation of what is and what is not ethical behavior, and this may be difficult in a bureaucratic environment. A study conducted several years ago by the social scientist, Stanley Milgram, illustrates this problem.[3] Milgram selected several individuals at random and asked them to participate in a learning experiment. The individuals selected were to be the "teachers," while others in the experiment were the "students." Unknown to the teachers, the student participants were hired for their parts. The teachers were told to apply electric shocks when the students gave incorrect answers to certain questions. Repeated wrong answers resulted in much stronger shocks. The screams of the students got to a few of the teachers, and they protested to Dr. Milgram. He assured them, however, that what they were doing was right and told them to continue with the experiment. Two-thirds of the teachers did continue, despite agonizing screams from the students.

Among the several lessons to be learned from this study are an appreciation of the enormous influence (or power) which managers hold over their subordinates, and their obligation to exercise such influence very judiciously.

RESPONSIBILITY TO ONESELF

Librarians also have certain ethical responsibilities to themselves. They are, for example, obliged to maintain their skills and competencies regardless of whether their employers provide release time or funds with which to attend workshops and conferences. A true professional doesn't blame his or her employer for becoming stale or out of touch with current developments in the field. And although librarians work in organizational settings, they cannot allow themselves to be overcome by group-think, or by a culture which may be oriented more to mediocrity than to excellence. While all librarians have the responsibility to participate in decision making, to become involved in organizational processes, they continue to be responsible for taking control of their own professional lives, to become "masters of their own universes" (to use Tom Wolfe's phrase). To the extent that C. Wright Mills's description of bureaucracies as vast systems of organized irresponsibility describes the libraries in which we work, each of us is ethically bound to change that image, to assume greater personal responsibility for the actions or lack thereof of the communities in which we work, and to maintain our collective and individual integrity.

How might the typical librarian become more sensitive and responsive to these more or less abstract concerns? The first step is to make them real rather than abstract, and this can only be done through reflection and self-assessment. We need to become more critical of our own individual performance, and perhaps become less judgmental of the performance of our colleagues. "But who has time for reflection?" you may ask. Well, all of us make time, every day, for those matters which are truly important to us. A brief review of our relationships with the library's users, our co-workers, and our personal standards of behavior would seem to be a matter of some importance. As we reflect upon and assess for ourselves each day's interactions, it should be possible to get back in touch with the values and ideals that led us into this field and to identify new sources of personal energy.

NOTES

[1]John H. Kultgen. *Ethics and Professionalism* (Philadelphia: University of Pennsylvania Press, 1988).

[2]Barbara Ley Toffler. *Tough Choices: Managers Talk Ethics* (New York: Wiley, 1986).

[3]Stanley Milgram. *The Individual in a Social World: Essays and Experiments* (Reading, Mass.: Addison-Wesley, 1977).

Professional Growth and Development
Enhancing Individual Effectiveness

Introduction

Leadership seems to be the marshalling of skills possessed by a majority but used by a minority. But it's something that can be used by anyone, taught to anyone, denied to no one.
— Warren Bennis and Bert Nanus,
Leaders: The Strategies for Taking Charge

Just as effective leadership depends on the leader's understanding of certain principles of human relations and application of sound management practices, professional growth depends first and foremost on one's personal growth and maturation. While there are numerous accounts of successful executives who claim to have sacrificed their personal lives for their professional lives, it appears that in a number of such cases, the distinction between personal and professional becomes moot. Regardless of how one resolves this issue — whether to maintain some separation between one's professional and personal life or to allow the distinction to become quite blurred — it is important that the individual come to terms with this dilemma in as constructive a manner as possible.

There are many parallels between professional and personal growth. While the latter typically requires a great deal of nurturing on the part of parents and on supportive relationships with significant others, professional growth is usually dependent on relationships with mentors or role models, on the moral support offered by peers and professional colleagues, and on one's level of commitment to one's chosen profession.

Other important players in professional development are professional schools, associations, and the organizations in which professionals work. Graduate library schools are too often narrowly viewed as being the gatekeepers for the field: they are the avenues through which new recruits are academically prepared and socialized into the profession. But all professionals should realize that graduation from library school represents the beginning, not the end, of one's development and growth as a professional. The speed with which technology is changing the nature of librarianship, the growth of subspecialties within the discipline, and the expanding range of issues with which the professional must deal — all serve to underscore the essential importance of continuing education and the responsibility of library schools to provide such education.

As the effective librarian establishes and maintains an ongoing relationship with agencies offering professional educational opportunities, he or she will also become actively involved in those professional associations and scholarly societies which are most relevant to his or her own career goals. While attendance at professional meetings is important for the information that is presented, it also provides the opportunity to make contact with other professionals and to build networks of professional relationships.

Participation on association committees or discussion groups can provide excellent opportunities for the aspiring librarian to practice leadership skills, to observe group dynamics, and to come to a better understanding of the nature of teamwork. At the same time, one should be careful not to pervert the purpose of committee assignments. Because the goal of various committees is to advance the work of professional associations, they should not be used as forums for advancing personal agendas or for personal aggrandizement. Librarianship continues to be a field which is so tightly knit that it is most unlikely that leadership ability and professional contributions would go unrecognized. Accolades from colleagues are all the more significant when they arise spontaneously and freely.

A third player in the growth of the professional librarian is the library employer. Employers must provide an environment which is conducive to staff development. Providing opportunities for professional growth should be a prominent goal of the organization. Similarly, the presence or absence of this goal should become an important criterion by which the professional evaluates prospective employers. Both employers and employees need to appreciate the difference between, say, five years of experience which is progressive and developmental in nature, and five years of experience which is nothing more than the first year repeated for four more years.

A commitment to *professional* growth involves more than the mere accumulation of continuing education courses, workshops, and similar events; it involves more than attainment of progressively more responsible positions; it involves more than a series of committee assignments. While all professionals build their careers on such opportunities and experiences, the most effective development occurs when the professional consciously evaluates his or her progress over a period of time, tries to understand what lessons might be derived from particularly challenging experiences or critical incidents, and evaluates as objectively as possible the extent to which he or she is service-oriented, is cognizant of the responsibilities of the profession, and is observant of ethical principles. In the last analysis, the real professional is devoted not only to maintaining competence based on the acquisition of new knowledge and skills, but also to serving constituent groups while maintaining high ethical standards, and to sharing his or her knowledge with colleagues.

Although the question of self-assessment is treated elsewhere in this book, it is obviously the basis for both personal *and* professional growth. In the professional arena, self-evaluation would include an examination of one's work habits, attitudes, and behaviors. It is particularly obligatory for professionals to avoid "group-think," to take risks when they are warranted, and to set high standards of professional performance. While there are countless ways of testing one's self in these areas, some of the more salient include seizing opportunities to make presentations, publish articles, chair association committees, or be of service to one's community. All of these endeavors require a certain degree of professional exposure, which is useful in building confidence and self-esteem and in enhancing leadership skills. Similarly, job interviews can often have the same effect. The exposure one receives in an interview along with the rigorous questioning that typically occurs can also contribute to the librarian's professional growth.

While most librarians are organized in various staff groupings, not all groups are teams. This is an important concept because successful organizations—profit-oriented as well as nonprofit—are characterized by teamwork and group cohesiveness, or "we-ness." The feelings, values, attitudes, and sentiments of the group are the glue that keeps it intact. Other important attributes include a set of common purposes; opportunities for interaction; and customs, norms, and rituals—factors that combine to determine the culture of the group.

Despite the forces that work to keep groups together, it is inevitable that conflicts within a group or between the group (the so-called loyal opposition) and the organization's management team. Virtually all organizations have procedures for dealing with *individual* employee conflicts, but not all managers have developed an effective methodology for dealing with group conflict. It must be recognized, however, that not all conflicts are dysfunctional. Some are indicative of healthy interpersonal or intergroup competition. They are dysfunctional when they drain members' energy, decrease the group's attention span, or reduce the group's effectiveness.

The departments, divisions, and relationships represented on organization charts indicate a library's formal structure. However, this structure is often supplemented and strengthened by committees and task forces. Most committees operate in a consultative or advisory capacity, but some are charged with the accomplishment of certain projects. For example, a collection development committee might advise on serial additions or cancellations, a task force might be charged with planning a preservation program for the library, or an exhibits committee might be responsible for both planning and mounting library exhibits. Occasionally, committees and task forces are used as boundary-spanning mechanisms. They have been effective in numerous instances in addressing problems which cut across the organization and in reducing the insularity which sometimes affects departments within a library. In large libraries, it is particularly important that there be a variety of boundary-spanning mechanisms to facilitate coordination among units and to enhance organizational performance.

The chapters in this section focus on professional growth and development. Keith Cottam's article, "Professional Identity and 'Intrapreneurial' Behavior," which begins by providing some background on entrepreneurial behavior in organizations, quickly proceeds to discuss the degree to which such behavior characterizes "exceptionally successful" librarians. The author's survey results indicate that librarians who are entrepreneurs exhibit a strong identity with their profession, are highly motivated and self-reliant, are risk-takers, and possess superior conceptual ability. It is interesting to note how the concepts presented in the last two chapters in part III find application, inadvertent though it may be, in Cottam's article.

While some of the chapters in previous sections have identified the key elements underlying professional growth and development, articles by Daniel Levinson and Judith Bardwick discuss important changes—physical, psychological, emotional—in the lives of maturing men and women. Levinson's study is based on an analysis of the lives of forty men. It traces the evolution of the male personality from the "novice stage," in which one's dreams of success are poorly articulated, to the formation of mentoring relationships and occupational goals, and finally the transition from middle-age. The importance of each individual's "dream" is stressed along with the relationship between career goals and the formation of intimate relationships. "Dream" in this context refers to the vision or an imagined possibility that generates excitement and vitality. Although the discussion focuses on personal growth and development, there is an obvious relationship between the stages of one's personal life and the stages of one's career and professional growth.

Judith Bardwick examines the stages of a woman's life. She characterizes some of the issues and conflicts that confront women at various stages in their lives, discusses typical responses to these challenges, and then presents some insights and strategies for effectively resolving them. This article is excellent for the many insights it offers, particularly with respect to women in organizations, role conflict, and family relationships. It is highly relevant to the ascendancy of women to leadership positions in the field of library and information science, and like the Levinson article, provides a framework within which professional development can take place.

Although it is clear that professional growth depends on personal development, it also is fairly dependent on career planning. "The Career Planning Process" presents several factors which help to define career success and then goes on to describe the importance of career planning: setting a direction, establishing time frames for achievement, dealing with transitions and change, and defining outcomes. The second part of this chapter addresses the role of the organization in participating in or facilitating career planning, and the danger of promising continued upward mobility to all of the organization's members.

The chapter reprinted from *American Libraries* on plateauing obviously relates to career planning. It reports on a survey of some 1,400 ALA members, the findings of which indicate that about one-third of the respondents believe that they will advance and achieve career goals, while 41 percent believe the exact opposite. The chapter concludes that senior library managers must find new ways to motivate staff who do not have access to traditional reward systems.

The last reading in this section is Marsha Burruss-Ballard's "Mentoring for Leadership." Burruss-Ballard states that a mentor is a seasoned professional who takes an active interest in the career development of a younger or less experienced professional. She then proceeds to discuss the many benefits of mentoring, the characteristics of mentors and protégés, the importance of developing interpersonal skills, and organizational support for mentoring programs. She concludes by emphasizing the importance of mentoring in the library field and its relevance to leadership development.

Because professional growth is so closely allied with personal well-being, one exercise, "Quality-of-Life Index," is included in appendix I. It enables the reader to evaluate himself or herself using a five-point scale on physical well-being, on the psychological, spiritual, and social care that one takes of one's self, and on lifestyle. In effect, the exercise or inventory provides the professional with a means for self-assessment of his or her regimen for well-being. An exercise that is useful in resolving conflict situations is included as appendix J. The exercise attempts to enable an individual to gain some understanding of his or her attitudes toward conflict. The second part of the exercise provides a series of steps which lead to resolving the conflict.

The information contained in the readings and exercises selected for this section will provide an introduction to some of the more salient issues affecting professional growth.

ADDITIONAL READINGS

Albritton, Rosie L. "Leadership Development." *College & Research Libraries News* 48 (November 1987): 618-23.

Bardwick, Judith M. *The Plateauing Trap.* New York: AMACOM, 1986.

Bartunek, J. N. "What to Do When Your Employees Plateau." *Supervisory Management* 29 (July 1984): 23-26.

"Capitalizing on Group Resources: Do You Have a Crowd or a Team?" In *Leadership: Strategies for Organizational Effectiveness*, by James J. Cribben, 156-72. New York: AMACOM, 1981.

Geddie, C. and B. Strickland. "From Plateau to Progress: A Model for Career Development." *Training* 21 (June 1984): 56-61.

Goddard, Robert W. "The Psychological Contract." *Management World* 13 (August 1984): 12-14, 35.

"Group Decision-Making: Lost at Sea." In *The 1975 Annual Handbook for Group Facilitators*, edited by J. E. Jones and J. W. Pfeiffer. San Diego, Calif.: University Associates, 1975.

"The Groupthink Syndrome." In *Groupthink: Psychological Studies of Policy Decisions and Fiascoes*, by Irving L. Janis. Boston: Houghton-Mifflin, 1983.

Martell, Charles, and John Tyson. "QWL Strategies: Quality Circles." *The Journal of Academic Librarianship* 9 (November 1983): 285-87.

"Mentoring: The Tool for Integrating Management." In *The Human Side of Management*, by George S. Odiorne, 185-201. Lexington, Mass.: D.C. Heath, 1987.

Niehouse, O. L. "Measuring Your Burnout Potential." *Supervisory Management* 29 (July 1984): 27-33.

Ross, Austin. "The Mentor's Role in Developing New Leaders." *Hospital and Health Services Administration* 29 (September/October 1984): 21-29.

Shaughnessy, Thomas W. "Organizational Culture in Libraries: Some Management Perspectives." *Journal of Library Administration* 9, no. 3 (1988): 5-10.

CHAPTER 16

Professional Identity and "Intrapreneurial" Behavior

Keith M. Cottam

Since John Naisbitt predicted an "entrepreneurial explosion" and concluded that "we are shifting from a managerial society to an entrepreneurial society," a spate of writers have given the subject attention.[1] A few librarians were looking at the possibilities as early as the mid-70s, probably due largely to the depressed job market at the time, but nevertheless with a good deal of determination and success. In 1979 some 50 case studies were published in *What Else You Can Do With a Library Degree*, showing how librarians had stepped out on their own as entrepreneurs.[2] The cases featured seemed to score high on individuality, determination, persistence, vision for new ideas and opportunities, flexibility and a willingness to take calculated risks. In a more recent survey, Helena Strauch describes the history of entrepreneurship in the information industry and gives some how-to advice on starting and managing an information business.[3]

Even before Naisbitt's predictions, an entrepreneurial movement had begun 15-20 years earlier and many people were thinking about its significance; others were already practicing the concept. Organizations were also looking at entrepreneurial principles. In a 1976 *Economist* article, for example, Norman Macrae described "the coming entrepreneurial revolution" and suggested ways that business, industry and other organizations might take advantage of the opportunities and "devolve into becoming 'confederations of entrepreneurs.'"[4]

At first glance the idea of people working in organizations as "entrepreneurs" seems a contradiction. After all, Webster's modern definition of an entrepreneur is "one who organizes, manages, and assumes the risks of a business or enterprise," usually independently and through good old fashioned self-reliance, hard work and a boost from venture capital or seed money. But why should not an entrepreneurial climate and the behaviors and practical skills of entrepreneurship thrive in a hierarchical organization? Why should not people with courage and original thought and willing to take risks be encouraged and supported to achieve within organizations? Why should not the same kind of creative and stimulating librarians distinguished in the Sellen book populate libraries and be identified, cultivated, supported and encouraged?

The primary stumbling blocks are semantics and real or imagined organizational constraints. Two initial responses to the survey for this article characterize these problems: "I do not understand how I can be an entrepreneur working in a library," and "I really do not think

Reprinted with permission from the *Journal of Library Administration*, Vol. 8(1), Spring 1987. Copyright 1987 by the Haworth Press, Inc., New York.

I am an entrepreneur in the traditional sense of the term." People in organizations do not see themselves as entrepreneurs within an acceptable connotation of the term. Organizations do not quite know how to deal with those who want to behave as entrepreneurs.

What is needed is a concept to facilitate an organization's ability to "devolve," to bridge the gap between the denotation constraints and to encourage a way of thinking to achieve creative innovation and success within an organization. How can the concept of entrepreneur be applied in an organization? In 1985 Gifford Pinchot III published the best-selling *Intrapreneuring*,[5] a book with an idea that was highlighted three years earlier by Macrae in another *Economist* article on "Intrapreneurial Now."[6]

Pinochot develops the thesis that an "intrapreneur" is

> any of the "dreamers who do." Those who take hands-on responsibility for creating innovation of any kind within an organization. The intrapreneur may be the creator or inventor but is always the dreamer who figures out how to turn an idea into a profitable reality.[7]

The heart of the volume is how-to discourse, replete with profiles of successful intrapreneurs, on becoming an organizational dreamer, innovator and achiever, and on how to nurture an intrapreneurial environment. Throughout the remainder of this article the "intrapreneurial" concept will be used.

In addition to Pinchot's definition, intrapreneurs also take certain risks. They assume a willingness to risk their dreams and ideas, even their job security for the opportunity to figure out ways to achieve—not for goals themselves but for what it takes to get there. On the other hand, the risks are usually calculated. Intrapreneurs anticipate obstacles to reduce the risks. They plan and avoid high risk situations. They eschew uncontrollable circumstances and work to minimize the risks within a defined area of endeavor. In the balance, careful risk has its compensation.[8]

Librarians, moreover, are not known generally as risk takers. While the librarian stereotype is not necessarily negative, it is sometimes perceived unfavorably and sets up librarians for personal and professional behavior, such as risk avoidance, which projects a less than favorable self-concept.[9]

In *Pathfinders*, Gail Sheehy concludes that a willingness to take risks is an outgrowth of a positive self-concept reflecting a person's ability to trust others, to be confident in assuming responsibilities and to direct initiative toward changing the self and the environment. She further explains that a sense of right timing is an outcome of a positive self-concept, reflecting a person's ability to anticipate present needs as well as to prepare for the future.[10]

So how do librarians in organizational life become "intrapreneurs"? From where does the courage come to step beyond a job and into the realm of ideas, innovation and achievement? How are they able to facilitate an institutional climate and environment which is supportive, not only with resources but also politically? How can they be motivated to assume personal responsibility and accountability?

Every individual has certain personal assumptions, expectations, beliefs and values which play a major part in their substance and style, decisions and behaviors. For librarians there is also a professional identity framework from which development may occur and it is this framework which served as part of the foundation for this inquiry.

The author assumes that (1) librarianship is a profession and uses the methods of a profession to achieve its goals; (2) there is a relationship between professional identity and characteristics and intrapreneurial skills and behaviors; and (3) intrapreneurial behavior will be apparent in the professional and organizational lives of exceptionally successful librarians.

To explore these assumptions and further define the field of thought, letters were sent to 75 librarians who might be expected to have a strong professional identity and who have possibly demonstrated intrapreneurial skills and behavior. They were asked to respond by telephone or free-form letter and describe themselves as entrepreneurs — intrapreneurs in an organizational context — against a backdrop of:

1. a definition of an entrepreneur — one who is willing to take risks in organizing, managing and directing an enterprise.

2. a list of the attributes[11] common to a profession —
   - possesses a distinctive and systematic body of theoretical and practical knowledge;
   - recognizes the need to extend the body of knowledge through critical thinking, scholarly inquiry and communication;
   - benefits from an established system of specialized educational programs (particularly those accredited by the American Library Association in the case of librarianship);
   - functions under the control of codes of ethics;
   - identifies with one or more professional organizations (such as the American Library Association);
   - manifests an altruistic service attitude;
   - commands recognition and respect because of the knowledge, skills and abilities of its members;
   - promotes the autonomy of its members to make independent judgments.

3. a brief inventory of personal professional qualities —
   - self-assured
   - self-reliant
   - clear professional identity
   - trust in one's colleagues
   - autonomy or ability to stand on one's own in meeting role responsibilities
   - aptitude for initiative
   - imagination
   - critical thinking ability
   - visionary
   - industrious
   - clarity of purpose in one's role
   - willingness to commit to collaborative relationships
   - productive
   - honest (integrity)
   - accountable

The letter was sent to selected participants from the Council on Library Resources/University of California, Los Angeles (CLR/UCLA) Senior Fellows Program, the Association of Research Libraries Office of Management Studies (ARL/OMS) Consultant Training Program, and others with whom the author is personally acquainted and who appear to have demonstrated intrapreneurial behavior in their performance.[12] While it is recognized that this approach is self-selecting and not scientific, it set the stage and helped illuminate and generally confirm a profile for librarian intrapreneurs.

Fifteen written responses were received, as well as four by telephone. Eleven other respondents either telephoned or wrote indicating that for various reasons they were too busy striving for higher levels of achievement to take the time to respond. Several respondents acknowledged that they had never thought of themselves as either independent or organizational entrepreneurs; however, on closer examination they realized they might be and the characteristic skills and abilities are worth cultivating. Others were intrigued by the self-analysis exercise and the personal insight gained. Yet others saw the concept being explored as a way to define how to widen circles of accomplishment and thrive in the dynamic political climate of a complex library environment.

Drawing a clear relationship between the professional identity issue and intrapreneurial behavior is at best a tentative exercise without instruments for some kind of formal measurements, although some assumptions may be drawn from casual observation. There are several examples. Theoretical and practical knowledge appears to drive certain behaviors. A professionally oriented person frequently feels an urgency to pursue critical thinking and inquiry and risk peer review in communicating the results. Professional ethics appear to shape a librarian's risk taking behavior in the political arena. The extent of an educational background seems to support such qualities as self-confidence, conceptual ability, reasoning and interpersonal skills. Generally, though, these observations only suggest that professional identity and qualifications are directly linked with intrapreneurial behavior. One cannot conclude from a survey of this type that they are exclusive determining factors, and the professional model relationship for the survey, then, has served primarily as a springboard into the inquiry on the intrapreneurial behavior of librarians.

In fact, several survey respondents expressed the sentiment stated by Anne Woodsworth, Associate Provost and Director of University Libraries at the University of Pittsburgh:

> My personality and personal traits would lead me to make choices and decisions in the same way whether I were president of a widget manufacturing company or a library director. The formula for an entrepreneurial approach to life and career is based on clarity of thinking combined with vision, a dash of drive, a measure of self-confidence, a dose of charisma and a sprinkling of a "what the hell" attitude. People with this mix of characteristics transcend and supersede any professional affiliations they may or may not have.

Librarians as a group, if they are intrapreneurial, appear to share some common characteristics described in other studies and which serve as a model for this analysis.[13] The profiles which follow characterize librarian intrapreneurial behavior from the lives of successful professionals.

ENERGY AND HEALTH

Librarian intrapreneurs report possessing high levels of energy and in most cases seem to be impervious to time constraints or illness which extract heavy tolls from others. The key seems to be found in an attitude that staying on top of one's physical well-being is paramount to staying on top of professional and organizational life. One respondent noted that exercise is a critical key to "staying on top" of everything.

Exercise is an important factor for most librarian intrapreneurs: biking, running, walking, swimming, dancing, sailing, weight lifting. Sometimes, though, librarian intrapreneurs report neglecting exercise with debilitating consequences that contradict the energy and health characteristics. The author has learned from experience that when the mind and emotions are spent, go out and exercise the body.

The clock and fatigue frequently seem irrelevant. One respondent reported, "My staff seems impressed that I am usually the first one in the office, I stay a little later, and I seldom take a sick day." Others report getting headaches and coming down with the common cold like everyone else, but they seem to ignore both and continue to function.

Several report a personal work style characterized by a relentless drive and a restless dissatisfaction with the status quo—their's or the organization's. Vacations often come as changes in a weekly schedule or a few days away attending professional meetings rather than a week off. On the other hand, librarian intrapreneurs seem to "work at" their vacations with as much enthusiasm as they work at their jobs. "Workload," "working hard" and "playing hard" are more common and acceptable concepts than are the ideas of a 40-hour week or "a few days off."

AUTONOMY, RESPONSIBILITY, AND ACCOUNTABILITY

Even though librarians in organizations may have little control over many of the daily functions of their jobs, librarian intrapreneurs report that their professional identity is probably enhanced because they strive for a high level of autonomy and exercise professional responsibility and personal accountability. They demonstrate creative, critical and independent thinking; they apply specialized knowledge and technical competence; they are given freedom to take calculated risks within the context of assigned responsibilities; they assume responsibility and accountability for their own actions; they are, to as large an extent possible, self-determined and self-regulated.

Herb White, Dean of the School of Library and Information Science at Indiana University, said, in his response, "What a profession does is stake out what it ought to do—and then never lose sight of those premises." Librarian intrapreneurs appear to understand that concept well—to "control their 'turf,'" as Herb noted, but with full awareness of the need for responsible and accountable behavior in achieving results.

SELF-CONFIDENCE

Librarian intrapreneurs are notably self-confident. A typical response came from Louella Wetherbee, Executive Director of AMIGOS: "I have always believed I could accomplish whatever task I really set my mind to. I don't see many barriers as insurmountable." Such innate self-confidence is matched by others who have learned to be self-confident through education, special training and practice.

Respondents generally said they approach problems carefully, but they do not procrastinate so long as they are in control. Control, of course, is sometimes illusive, and librarian intrapreneurs will not hesitate to delay or even abandon an initiative in favor of a better day for action. They report calculating the potential for mistakes or even failures, but they seem not to worry about either; when one or the other occurs, they assess the damage, learn from the experience, and move on.

Perhaps the ultimate mark of self-confidence was illuminated by Dale Cluff, Director of Libraries at Texas Tech University: "I work on the assumption that I don't have all the answers and, as painful as it may be, admit that there are many in our organization smarter than I in many areas. I am willing to admit mistakes and to change my mind."

ACHIEVEMENT MOTIVE

Librarian intrapreneurs are busy people, with their library organizations as well as their professional and personal lives. Some describe themselves as hard driving, "fast-track" personalities—perhaps even impatient at times but usually able to control the trait. They seem compelled to be active, productive and achieving, and the attitude often translates into expectations for others. "I expect employees to perform at their maximum most of the time," said Dale Cluff. Another respondent said his office is described as "charged with energy" and it is sometimes difficult for his staff to keep up with his ideas and activities. For people in an organization who may be marching to a different drummer, though, the motivation for higher and higher achievement may become threatening, and intrapreneurs report they must find ways to temper the drive.

As individuals their desire to be active and accomplishing something—making things better—is characterized by Joan Worley, Director of the Library at Maryville College in Tennessee: "I think there are always improvements to be made. I recognize that I am motivated by a service ideal that looks a lot like crusading zeal. So be it ... I hold the strong conviction that one person can change events and outcomes significantly."

Joanne Harrar, Director of Libraries at The University of Maryland, observed:

> ...chief behaviors and qualities (of intrapreneurs in her library) have to do with an excitement and involvement in the project or projects which they are pursuing. That excitement extends not only to the accomplishment of the task at hand, but also to the just plain tedious hard work which goes into its realization. There is a vision, a sense of purpose, almost a kind of religious mission which seems to carry such individuals forward. The fear of failure is far outweighed by the emphasis on the possible gains, be they personal or institutional, to be realized by success.

David Weber, Director of Libraries at Stanford, made a related observation:

> I would suspect that there is a great deal of risk taking by those who are quite young and new to the field—but their endeavors may not be as practical as those who are in mid career and this may have a stultifying affect. Those who are the senior librarians in a college or university have more opportunity to act on their own, to be entrepreneurs, and it therefore seems probable that the taking of risks may actually increase when one moves from a subordinate to a higher position in an organization.

COMPREHENSIVE AWARENESS

Referring to his views on the necessity for cost analysis in libraries, Malcolm Getz, Director of the Library at Vanderbilt, said in his response, "Managers rise to statesmen when they look beyond the present position and plot a course to a new location. The strategic thinking required for statesmanship will have a greater chance for success when based on analysis."

Librarian intrapreneurs seem acutely aware of the need to understand the entire environment in which they work, to see not only the details on top of their desks but also that which is out in the organization and that which is impacting the organization from the outside. They invest in the problems and opportunities at hand; they also develop and maintain a vision and understanding of the library's role in the life of the institution.

Dale Cluff said he works "very hard at keeping the global view in mind and not having (his) thinking clouded by a warped or lopsided perspective." The view is common among library intrapreneurs, and the complementary point of view is expressed by Louella Wetherbee: "I am analytical and pragmatic. I like to look for the logical way to do things."

REALITY

Intrapreneurial behavior is frequently tempered and even blocked by the reality of organizational contstraints. For example, David Weber observed, "The environmental circumstances ... can markedly alter the feasibility of taking risk." He further observed that institutions are "pretty chary of providing developmental funds, private resources through friends' groups are very limited, and foundations and government agencies provide very modest funds to education that are directed to libraries; thus, the total picture is pretty restrictive."

So while librarians in organizations may wish to lean toward intrapreneurial behavior, they often find obstacles in their way. One can be a fountain of intrapreneurial ideas, but without institutional support there is small hope for achievement. One respondent noted, however, that with timely facts in hand and self-assurance of her ability to exert influence over potential events, she tends "to forge ahead despite known and possible adverse consequences." Another sentiment was expressed by Louella Wetherbee: "I have a high tolerance for ambiguity. I believe that is the single most important factor in willingness to take risks. I accept the fact that there are going to be no clear answers or solutions to many problems. I see my job as picking the best of any number of available paths."

The key issue here was expressed by Ken Peterson, Dean of Library Affairs at Southern Illinois University, Carbondale: "Be realistic and honest in the process — with yourself and your organization." From this attitude springs the critical quality of integrity, essential for continuing and uncompromised success and achievement.

SUPERIOR CONCEPTUAL ABILITY

Closely related to the characteristics of "comprehensive awareness" and "reality" is the ability to synthesize the reality of the environment, to put things and functions into perspective, to draw relationships and conceptualize solutions, plans and actions. Librarian intrapreneurs report that obstacles are typically overcome because of this ability.

The capacity to sort a situation and conceptualize an appropriate response is enhanced by "collaboration," said George Soete, Assistant University Librarian for Collections at the University of California, San Diego, "which is not a mode that seems to come naturally to most librarians." Librarian intrapreneurs, on the other hand, seem to thrive on drawing inspiration from their colleagues. The author is convinced of this and believes that intrapreneurial success is nurtured through an exchange of formal and informal communication; and on the basis of valuable, continued, and close interaction with particular individuals. Dale Cluff says he gets his "greatest satisfaction from sitting with colleagues in problem solving sessions."

Flowing from this, respondents report the need to delegate effectively in order to allow them to direct their attention to new ideas, problems and opportunities.

STATUS

With a few exceptions respondents seem to place small emphasis on status. They appear to be more occupied with process and results and less conscious of personal status symbols, authority, and how they appear personally to others. They would rather be doing something than receiving praise for what they have done.

Tom Shaughnessy, Director of Libraries at the University of Missouri-Columbia, expresses an interesting point of view in citing library intrapreneurs as "gifted marketers," or people focused on selling their library enterprises rather than themselves. He said in his letter, "They never miss an opportunity to promote the library or to inject its presence into arenas to which it had either not been invited, or more typically had simply been ignored."

In spite of how much they accomplish, the egos of most librarian intrapreneurs seem rather mellow. Several respondents acknowledged some embarrassment at being singled out by the survey, and George Soete may have summed it up for others: "I believe it is important to take yourself and others — especially their problems — seriously, but not to be deadly about it."

INTERPERSONAL SKILLS

Librarian intrapreneurs invest in people as well as institutions. This is a different attitude than that typically described in the literature for independent entrepreneurs who build enterprises with only secondary thought for strong organizational relationships and sound interpersonal behavior.

A librarian intrapreneur may or may not choose to build close interpersonal relationships within an organization, but they all report being sensitive to organizational climate and personal feelings. On the other hand, several respondents reported a feeling that relationships, whatever they may be, must sometimes be severed in order to progress toward certain goals.

Assuming, then, that interpersonal skills are important, Dale Cluff cites several factors which enhance his intrapreneurial behavior: (1) have faith in one's fellow beings, (2) cultivate trust, (3) give credit to deserving staff, praising in public when appropriate and correcting in private, (4) assume that people want to be heard; and (5) expect, encourage and support professionalism.

EMOTIONAL STABILITY

Related to self-confidence appears to be a librarian intrapreneur's ability to exercise self-control. Respondents noted that with the achievement motive pulling them along, they often require a strong ability to handle pressure and stress and to remain calm and unemotional in the face of difficult situations or criticism. Ken Peterson observes that an intrapreneur cannot avoid or ignore criticism and problems, but when confronted, a successful intrapreneur cannot be thrown.

CHALLENGES, NOT RISKS

The concept of risk has been addressed, but respondents emphasized the point in several ways. All suggested that risk is highly situational, that interesting situations should not be allowed to become overwhelming circumstances, and that calculating and influencing the odds is essential. A number of professional attributes were cited as very supportive in removing or lessening risk: specialized knowledge and skills, critical thinking, codes of ethics, collegial relationships and professional autonomy.

While most librarian intrapreneurs would rather do something than write about it, David Walch, Interim Associate Provost for Information Systems at California Polytechnic State University, describes his careful research and writing as one form of calculated risk.

> I wouldn't consider this as being too risky; however, it does cause one to put his thoughts in print and open them up for scrutiny and criticism. In a sense one's reputation is at stake. I suppose the "safe" course would be to avoid writing at all....

As with other areas of endeavor, librarian intrapreneurs who decide to write cannot put off the high need for freedom to act and to achieve.

CONCLUSIONS

Research into the concept and practice of intrapreneurial behavior in libraries should continue. The conclusions from this survey are exploratory and tentative. Further inquiry should discover more precisely the relationships between professional characteristics and attitudes and intrapreneurial behavior, particularly how to influence both in a library organizational context. How can librarians in complex organizations learn intrapreneurial behavior? How can organizations be encouraged to support the behavior? With answers and guidance, more librarians might envison and cultivate an intrapreneurial self-concept and spirit, thus raising opportunities for more successful professional performance. For those willing to pay the price, the rewards may be significant. Additional study will probably clarify and demonstrate substantial differences between those who dare to dream and strive for achievement and those who are satisfied to seek a level of acceptable performance within the constraints of an eight-hour day.

NOTES

[1]Naisbitt, John. *Megatrends: Ten new directions transforming our lives*. New York: Warner Books, 1982, pp. 145-149. Other writers on the subject of entrepreneurship include Philip Holland, *The entrepreneur's guide*. New York: G. P. Putnam's Sons, 1984; James R. Cook, *The start-up entrepreneur*. New York: Truman Talley Books/E. P. Dutton, 1986; Donald L.

Sexton and Raymond W. Smilor, *The art and science of entrepreneurship*. Cambridge, MA: Ballinger Publishing Co., 1986; Calvin A. Kent, *The environment for entrepreneurship*. Lexington, MA: Lexington Books, 1984; and Victor Kiam, *Going for it! How to succeed as an entrepreneur*. New York: William Morrow and Co., 1986.

[2]Sellen, Betty-Carol (ed). *What else you can do with a library degree*. New York: Gaylord Professional Publications in association with Neal-Schuman Publishers, 1979.

[3]Strauch, Helena M. "Entrepreneurship in the information industry." In Jane F. Spivack, *Careers in Information*. White Plains, New York: Knowledge Industry Publications, 1982, pp. 73-101.

[4]Macrae, Norman. "The coming entrepreneurial revolution: A survey." *The Economist*, 261, December 25, 1976, pp. 41-65.

[5]Pinchot III, Gifford. *Intrapreneuring: Why you don't have to leave the corporation to become an entrepreneur*. New York: Harper & Row, 1985.

[6]Macrae, Norman. "Intrapreneurial now." *The Economist*, 283, April 17, 1982, pp. 67-72.

[7]Idem. *Intrapreneuring*. New York: Harper & Row, 1985, p. ix.

[8]Risk-taking was the theme of a program during the 1983 Los Angeles ALA Annual Conference. "Best Bets: Middle Managers as Risk-Takers" was sponsored by the LAMA Middle Management Discussion Group and included papers subsequently published in the LAMA *Newsletter* by Ronald Leach, "Risk-taking: Don't ask yourself why; ask why not!" January 1984, vol. 10, no. 1. pp. 6, 11-12; Sheila Merrell, "Risk taking in middle management," March 1984, vol. 10, no. 2,, pp. 19-20; Patricia K. Swanson, "Eliminating a special library service for art history faculty: A case study," June 1984, vol. 10, no.3, pp. 47-49.

[9]Wilson, Pauline. *Stereotype and status: Librarians in the United States*. Westport, Greenwood, 1982.

[10]Sheehy, Gail. *Pathfinders*. New York: William Morrow and Co., 1981, pp. 76-139.

[11]These are drawn primarily from the literature of sociology. A seminal piece is Talcott Parson's "Professions" in the *International encyclopedia of the social sciences*, vol. 12, The Macmillan Company and The Free Press, 1968, pp. 537-546. An interrogatory discussion of these attributes as related to librarians is in "The MLS: For the public good or for our good?" by Keith M. Cottam, *Library Journal* 111, January 15, 1986, pp. 111-114.

[12]The successful career and achievement oriented characteristics of CLR/UCLA Senior Fellows have been studied by Dorothy J. Anderson, "Comparative career profiles of academic librarians: Are leaders different?" *The Journal of Academic Librarianship*, 10, January 1985, pp. 326-332. The ARL/OMS Consultant Training Program is discussed in a symposium edited by Joanne R. Euster, "ARL/OMS consultant training program," *The Journal of Academic Librarianship*, 8, September 1982, pp. 200-210.

[13]See John A. Welsh, "Entrepreneurial characteristics: The driving force" in Raymond W. Smilor and Robert Lawrence Kuhn, eds., *Corporate creativity: Robust companies and the entrepreneurial spirit*. New York: Praeger, 1984, pp. 53-63.

CHAPTER 17

Growing Up with the Dream

Daniel J. Levinson

In everyday language, we speak of someone "succeeding beyond his wildest dreams" or "dreaming of a world he could never attain." We use the word "dream" here in a special sense; it refers neither to what we do during sleep nor to casual daydreams. From our study of the lives of 40 men — biologists, novelists, executives, working men — we have concluded that many young men have a Dream (we will use the capital to emphasize our specific use of the word) of the kind of life they want to lead as adults. The Dream in its primordial form is a vague sense of self-in-the-adult-world. It has the quality of a vision, an imagined possibility that generates excitement and vitality. The meaning is the one Delmore Schwartz intended with the title of his book of poetry *In Dreams Begin Responsibilities*.

The fate of the Dream has fundamental consequences for a man's life. A few men by their early 40s have achieved all or most of what they had set out to do; they feel that they have truly succeeded and are assured of a happy future. Others find themselves seriously disappointed and unable to avoid the conclusion that the satisfactions and peace of mind they thought success would bring were an illusion. Those who have fallen short of their Dreams, on the other hand, may come to believe that they have failed in a profound sense, that they have been found wanting and without value not only in their work but also as persons.

Whatever the nature of his Dream, a young man has the task of giving it greater definition and finding ways to live it out. The process of entering adulthood is more lengthy and complex than has usually been imagined. It begins around age 17 and continues until 33 (plus or minus two years at either end). A young man needs about 15 years to emerge from adolescence, find his place in adult society, and commit himself to a more stable life. This time is an intrinsic part of adulthood and not, even in its most chaotic or immature form, a "delayed adolescence."

So important is this developmental sequence that we have given it a special name: the novice phase. It is composed of three distinct periods: the Early-Adult Transition, which usually lasts from age 17 to 22 (with a variation of two or three years at the beginning or end); Entering the Adult World, roughly from 22 to 28; and the Age-30 Transition, from about 28-33.

Reprinted with permission from *Psychology Today*, January 1978.

During the novice phase, a young man is exploring the adult world, developing adult interests and values, and making important choices with regard to work, marriage, and family. There are other tasks common to this period: for instance, he must learn to relate to authorities and to gain greater authority himself; form peer relations with men and women; relate as an adult to people of different ages; form mature attitudes toward religion, politics, community. In reviewing the lives of our men, however, we found that four developmental tasks were most important and merited special attention: forming a Dream and giving it a place in the life structure; forming mentor relationships; forming an occupation; and forming love relationships, including marriage and family.

FORMING THE DREAM

At the start of the novice phase, the Dream is poorly articulated and only tenuously connected to reality. It may contain concrete images, such as winning the Nobel Prize or making the all-star team in some sport. Or it may take a dramatic form, as in the myth of the hero: the great artist, business tycoon, athlete, or intellectual performing magnificent feats and receiving special honors. It may also take mundane forms that are yet inspiring and sustaining: the excellent craftsman, the husband-father in a certain kind of family, the highly respected member of his community.

A young man's growth depends a good deal on whether his early life structure is consonant with, and infused by, the Dream—or is opposed to it. If the Dream remains unconnected to his life, it may simply die, and with it will die his sense of aliveness and purpose.

Many young men develop a conflict between a life direction expressing the Dream and another that is quite different. A man may be pushed away from the Dream by his parents, by lack of money or opportunity, and by various aspects of his own personality, such as guilt, submission, competitiveness, or special talents. He may thus succeed in an occupation that holds no interest for him. The conflict may extend over years, evolving through various forms. Those who betray the Dream in their 20s will have to deal later with the consequences. Those who build a life structure around it in early adulthood have a better chance for personal fulfillment, though years of struggle may be required to maintain the commitment and to work toward realizing it.

For about half of the biologists we studied, entry into their field was the realization of a powerful, exciting Dream. Their interests in nature and science began in childhood. They thought seriously about biology as an occupation in high school and then made the decision to pursue it in college.

Yet even when the choice reflected the Dream, there were often inner conflicts and external difficulties. In some cases, the father strongly wanted his son to enter another occupation, such as business or law. The father sensed, often correctly, that the son's choice was based partly upon a rejection of the father's values and personal qualities; often, he would express this view to the young man. The son, who also loved his father and was vulnerable to such criticisms, got caught up in the conflict and could not devote himself wholeheartedly to his work. One of these men became more creative and free in his research only in his early 30s, after his father's death.

For several biologists, the Dream was ambiguous or poorly formed. After considering various options near the end of college, they decided on biology because it was interesting and their professors were encouraging—but they had no sense of its special rightness for them. Their lack of excitement and their limited investment of self led to continuing career problems.

Several novelists had a youthful Dream of becoming a writer, and for them, too, the Dream had different fates. Four of them began writing in high school or earlier, decided in college to make writing their vocation, and spent the novice phase becoming accomplished in their craft. Three had established themselves as serious, promising young novelists at the end of the novice phase. The fourth, after writing several novels and some documentary nonfiction, decided at this point to give up novels. He decided instead on a career writing nonfiction, which was better suited to his talents and character. In making this choice, he turned partially away from the original Dream, but he continued to use creativity in becoming a first-rate nonfiction author.

For some novelists, the Dream remained stunted. One of those we studied formed some literary interests in college but assumed that he would take over his father's business and become an executive. But disagreements between him and his father were so severe that he soon left the business, determined to become a writer. Though he published two novels during his 20s, he remained very divided in his commitment to writing. He was in tremendous conflict with his father, to whom the idea of novel-writing as an occupation was simply absurd. Under the circumstances, the Dream could not grow. It was not until his early 30s, after he had made some progress in resolving his inner conflicts and had married a loving woman, that he could devote himself more single-mindedly to writing. By this time, however, it was rather late to develop his talents. Perhaps the wonder is the Dream survived at all, that the undernourished seedling became even a small tree.

In contrast to the biologists and novelists, only a few of the 10 executives we studied had been driven by a youthful Dream of occupational success. One of the few was Frank Radovich, who, during his college years, had formed the Dream of leaving his lower-middle-class origins and becoming the head of a major corporation. By age 32, Radovich (all names have been changed) had become vice-president of a great company and had amassed a personal fortune of over $1 million. But this was merely the end of his novice phase: he was now preparing to make his mark in a new world. As the Age-30 Transition ended, he founded his own small corporation. He resolved to make his firm the giant of its industry and to become an international figure himself.

The development of the Dream during the novice phase was especially difficult for the workers in our sample. Only one of them, Ralph Ochs, went through the relatively simple sequence of forming a stable occupation, getting married, and starting a family. At the end of high school, he became an apprentice plumber, under his father, in a manufacturing firm. Over the next 15 years, Ochs became a master plumber, no longer subject to his father's authority, took an active part in establishing a union, and started a family.

All the workers went through a more complex sequence, with recurrent difficulties, during the novice phase. Most of them had a Dream relating to occupation, but they could not live it out. In two cases, the Dream was to be a professional athlete. Alby Russell was a star athlete in high school and wanted to play professional ball. After high school, he was in the military for almost 20 years. He devoted himself mainly to starring on service teams in football, baseball, and basketball. It was only in the Age-30 Transition that he gave up the Dream of becoming—and perhaps the illusion of actually being—a major-league athlete.

He had married at 19 and started a family soon afterward. In his early 30s, he was seriously involved with his family life. He became a Little League coach and a teacher-mentor to young servicemen. Meanwhile, in his abundant leisure time, he followed several teams in different sports, watching them on TV, reading about them avidly, and imagining what he would do if he were the owner, scout, or manager. His erudition in sports was amazing. The expertise enriched his private life and his relationships with his sons, youth groups, and friends (though it often tested his wife's patience). He thus continued to live out the Dream in a special way, as a virtually full-time avocation; but he could not make a true occupation of it.

Alby Russell was fortunate. For most workers, the Dream remains inchoate. Perhaps the largest number begin the Early-Adult Transition with fantasies about exciting kinds of work and accomplishment, but they have not yet started to articulate or explore the incipient Dream. It is gradually forgotten as they are forced to cope with the more immediate problems of survival.

FORMING A MENTOR RELATIONSHIP

The most crucial developmental function of a mentor is to support and facilitate the realization of the Dream. The "true mentor" fosters the young adult's development by believing in him, sharing the youthful Dream and giving it his blessing, helping to define the newly emerging self in its newly discovered world, and also creating a space in which the young man is able to form a reasonably satisfactory life structure that contains the Dream.

The mentor is usually several years older, a person of greater experience and seniority in the world the young man is entering. I can think of no word to describe adequately the essence of this relationship. Words such as "counselor" or "guru" suggest the more subtle meanings, but they have other connotations that would be misleading. The term "mentor" is generally used in a much narrower sense, to mean teacher, adviser, or sponsor. As we use this term, it means all these things, and more.

The mentoring relationship often develops in a work setting, where the functions of mentor are assumed by a teacher, boss, editor, or senior colleague. It may also evolve informally, when the mentor is a friend, neighbor, or relative. "Mentoring" is defined not in terms of formal roles but in terms of the character of the relationship and the functions it serves. A student may receive very little mentoring from his teacher-adviser, and very important mentoring from an older friend or relative. We have to examine a relationship closely to discover the amount and kind of mentoring it provides.

I shall speak of mentors in the male gender, since the men in our study had male mentors almost exclusively. (Indeed, except for wives or lovers, they rarely had women as close friends.) This is further evidence of the gap between the sexes in our society. In principle, however, a mentor may be of either gender.

The mentor may act as a teacher to enhance the young man's skills and intellectual development. As a sponsor, he may use his influence to promote the young man's entry and advancement. He may be a host and guide, welcoming the initiate into a new occupational and social world and acquainting him with its values, customs, resources, and characters. Through his own virtues, achievements, and way of life, the mentor may be an exemplar that the younger man can admire and emulate. He may provide counsel and moral support in times of stress.

The mentor's primary function, however, is to be a transitional figure, one who fosters the young man's development from child-in-relation-to-parental-adults to adult-in-peer-relation-with-other-adults. The mentor is a mixture of parent and peer. If he is too much a peer, he cannot represent the advanced level toward which the younger man is striving. If he is too parental, it is difficult for both of them to overcome the generational difference and move toward the peer relationship that is the ultimate (though never fully realized) goal. The actual parents can serve certain mentoring functions, but are too closely tied to their son's preadult development, in both his mind and theirs, to be primary mentor figures.

In the usual course of the mentor relationship, the young man first experiences himself as an apprentice to a more advanced and expert adult. As the relationship evolves, he gains a fuller sense of his own authority and capability for autonomous, responsible action. The balance of giving and receiving becomes more equal, and the personal relationship becomes more mutual. This shift serves a crucial developmental function: it is part of the process by which the young man transcends the father-son, man-boy division of his childhood. Although he is officially defined as an adult at 18 or 21, and desperately wants to be one, it takes many years to overcome the sense of being a son or a boy in relation to "real" adults.

A relationship may be remarkably beneficial to the younger person and yet be seriously flawed. For example, a teacher or boss cares for and sponsors a protégé, and yet is so afraid of being eclipsed that he behaves destructively at crucial moments. A relationship may be very limited and yet have great value in certain respects. Some men have a purely symbolic mentor whom they never meet. Thus, an aspiring young novelist may admire an older writer, devour his books, learn a great deal about his life, and create an idealized internal figure with whom he has a complex relationship.

Mentoring is best understood as a love relationship. It is difficult to terminate in a reasonable manner, for it has some of the same intensity as the feelings between parents and growing children, or between husbands and wives.

The mentoring relationship lasts perhaps two or three years on the average, eight to 10 years at most. It may end when one man moves, changes jobs, or dies. Sometimes it comes to a natural end, and, after a cooling-off period, the pair retain a warm but modest friendship. It may end totally, with a gradual loss of involvement.

Most often, however, an intense mentor relationship ends with strong conflict and bad feeling. The young man may have feelings of bitterness, grief, and abandonment, along with a positive sense of liberation and rejuvenation. He now experiences the mentor as critical and demanding, or as seeking to remake him in the mentor's own image rather than fostering his individuality. The mentor, for his part, finds the young man touchy, unreceptive to even the best counsel, rebellious, and ungrateful. By the time they are through, there is generally some validity in each man's criticism of the other.

And so it ends. After the separation, the younger man may adopt many of the qualities of the mentor. His personality is enriched as he makes the mentor a more intrinsic part of himself. The internalization of models is a major source of development in adulthood.

FORMING AN OCCUPATION

It is often assumed that by his early 20s, a man has made a firm occupational choice and is launched on a well-defined career. This assumption stems from the widespread but erroneous belief that development is normally complete by the end of adolescence. We have found that the sequence of occupational development is longer and more difficult. The notion of *choosing* an occupation is too narrow and superficial. It is far more useful to speak of *forming* an occupation, a complex, social-psychological process that extends over the entire novice phase and often beyond.

A young man usually makes an initial serious choice sometime between 17 and 29, during the periods of Early Adult Transition or Entering the Adult World. Even when the first choice seems very definite, it usually turns out to be a preliminary definition of interests and values. The transformation of interests into occupation is rarely a simple or direct process. A young man may struggle for several years to sort out his interests, to discover what occupations might enable him to live them out, and to commit himself to one of them.

Once his initial choice is made, a man must acquire occupational skills, values, and credentials. He must develop a more differentiated occupational identity and establish himself within his chosen world. Along the way, he may fail or drop out, to begin again on a new path. He may stay narrowly within a single track, or try several directions before settling firmly on one. The sequence lasts several years.

Some men, but not many, set a course and maintain their momentum within it until they are fully "in" the occupation and ready to settle down. A relatively stable one-track sequence is well illustrated by several of the biologists in our study. In college, they made the decision to become academic biologists, a choice that was consistent with earlier interests in the outdoors and nature, in hiking, tinkering, or experimenting in the basement with a chemistry set. A few considered other occupational choices, such as medicine or engineering, but set them aside at the end of college—perhaps to take them up again in a later period. After four or five years in graduate school, they often did a year or two of postdoctoral study, and then took a position as an assistant professor.

But not all men form an occupation in this steady, single-minded way. Indeed, this sequence was not the norm in any of our occupational groups. One of the most creative biologists, Barry Morgan, left high school at 16, against his parents' wishes. He spent three years in the military, then returned home and completed college at 24. Not yet ready to go out on his own, he remained for two years of graduate study and did excellent independent research. He could then make the shift to graduate work in a first-rank biology department, where he completed his doctoral degree at 31.

Morgan's choice of biology was made in college, during the Early-Adult Transition. It was consonant with his early interests and his Dream of adult life. Still, he had recurrent doubts about this choice, and went through a three-year "crisis of commitment" in graduate school before finishing the Ph.D. degree. It was only at 33, after a postdoctoral fellowship and a year's teaching at an elite university, that he completed the novice phase and embarked upon a more responsible, autonomous career. About this time he was also able to get married.

The novelists went through other complications during this formative phase. Most of them had strong preadult interests in writing. By the Early-Adult Transition, they had formed the Dream of becoming a writer and were actively writing. The vicissitudes of that Dream over the next 15 years differed widely from one writer to another. In no case was the course simple or monotonic.

Much the same was true, surprisingly, of the working-class men. The life course of the worker in early adulthood is usually assumed to be simple and static: they complete all or most of high school, get a job, marry and start a family, and by the mid-20s are on a path that will continue with minimal change—barring surprises of fortune or misfortune—for many years. Our findings contradict this view. Working men go through the same developmental periods as men in other classes and occupations, though they have their own class-related problems of entering the adult world and establishing a place for themselves in it. Eight of the 10 workers in our sample experienced great difficulty forming a satisfactory occupation in Entering the Adult World and had a moderate or severe crisis in the Age-30 Transition.

For all occupations, our general finding was that the task of forming an occupation extends over the novice phase of early adulthood. Even for those who make an early, intense commitment to an occupation, the process goes on. For they may still have inner conflicts and inhibitions to overcome, they also may be subject to opposing external pressures, and they must struggle as apprentices in a complex occupational world. The process is even more complicated for those who remain undecided, and for those who make major occupational shifts during their 20s. At the end of the Age-30 Transition, the more open, formative phase is concluded. A man must now make more enduring choices and build on the groundwork established by his experience and training.

FORMING A MARRIAGE AND FAMILY

While the wedding ceremony and the birth of the first child are important marker events in the history of the family, the process of forming a marriage and family starts well before the marker events and continues long afterward. As with a man's occupation, his marriage and family life go through a highly formative process.

The process starts in a man's Early-Adult Transition and continues in the succeeding periods. It takes time for a young man to learn about his inner resources and vulnerabilities in relation to women, and about the characteristics of women who attract or repel him, and what it is about him that women find appealing or objectionable. His preadult development prepares him partially to undertake this developmental work. But it also leaves him with a legacy of guilt, anxiety, and mystification. This legacy complicates his efforts to know women, to take them seriously, and to join with one woman in the long-term enterprise of building a marriage and family. In the light of these difficulties, it is small wonder that a man remains a novice at this task until the early 30s, and that relating to the feminine in others and in himself should be a lifelong developmental task.

And yet, ready or not, young men in all cultures, for countless generations, have been marrying and starting families in the novice phase. There has probably never been a society in which the average age at first marriage for the general population was greater than 25 years. (China, through rigorous government policy, may be a modern exception, but this remains to be seen.) There are, of course, individuals and sub-groups who marry later or not at all. But powerful forces in society and in the biological and psychological makeup of the individual impel us toward some form of marriage and family. The question is not *whether* to have the family as a social institution, but *what form* of family institution is best suited to the development of children and parents.

A man in early adulthood needs to accept the responsibilities and pleasures of parenthood and to live out, in some measure, both the masculine and the feminine aspects of the self. Under reasonably favorable conditions, being a husband and father contributes to his development. It is, in part, a developmental failure when a young man is unable to function adequately in the family. When this occurs on a large scale, it is also a failure of society and might very well have destructive consequences for that society.

If a man marries during his Early-Adult transition, as about half of our sample did, he has had little experience in forming peer relationships with adult women. For him, courtship and marital choice are likely to be bound up with the tasks of the Early-Adult Transition, and especially with efforts to separate from his parents. He wants to be very grown-up, and, at the same time, to maintain his preadult ties to parents and others. He is hardly a step beyond adolescence, when sex is often a frightening mystery or an exploitative act.

In the Early-Adult Transition, a young man's efforts to establish an intimate marital relationship are complicated by his continuing sense of himself as a little boy in relation to a powerful maternal figure. He is engaged in a struggle both to express and to control his various fantasies of this figure as devouring witch, feeding breast, sexual seducer, humiliating rejecter, willing servant, and demanding master. His wife attracts him, in part, because she seems to lack the qualities he fears and resents in his image of his mother. Yet their relationship often contains many aspects of the mother-son interaction (for instance, the mother's tendency to admire or indulge her son) that will, in time, become more problematic.

About 30 percent of the men in our study got married during the period of Entering the Adult World (roughly ages 22 to 28). Couples who marry in this period have frequently known each other since the Early-Adult Transition or before. These early relationships may prove less suitable for subsequent periods. Romances in the teens usually break up after years of seeming inseparability. If the couple does marry, it is frequently with serious misgivings in one or both partners—misgivings that are suppressed out of a sense of obligation to the partner or the family and social network.

If a man is still a bachelor in his late 20s, he is likely to get more serious about marrying during his Age-30 Transition. He is encouraged or pressed to marry by parents, friends, and colleagues, as well as his own inner urgings. His years as a bachelor may have provided an opportunity to explore, to be sexually promiscuous, to have a few serious (but flawed) love affairs, while remaining emotionally distant from women. During his Age-30 Transition, however, being unmarried is usually experienced as a gap in his life or a problem. The man who begins married life during this period, as 20 percent of our sample did, possibly knows more about himself and his relationships with women, and may have resolved more fully some of the conflicts from the past. But he also may be marrying under pressure; this may be his last chance. He may decide to marry in an effort to "normalize" his life more than for love.

A couple is never fully prepared for marriage, whatever the period in which it occurs, and no matter how long or well the partners have known each other. Some couples may find that a very limited relationship is sufficient for a while, but, in time, one or the other spouse will grow discontented, conflict will erupt, or the marriage will stagnate unless both partners continue the developmental work that is necessary in successive stages of life.

THE SPECIAL WOMAN

A man's love relationships with women can take many forms and serve many functions. One of the most interesting people in a man's life is what we call the special woman. The special woman is like the true mentor: she helps to animate the part of the young man's self that contains the Dream. (The woman, too, may experience the young man as special.) This is a unique relationship that ordinarily includes sexual, romantic, and loving feelings. But a woman is special because she facilitates his entry into the adult world and helps him shape and live out the Dream.

She does this partly through her own actual efforts as teacher and guide, host, critic, sponsor. At a deeper psychological level, she enables him to project onto her his own internal figure—the "anima," as Jung has depicted it—who generates and supports his heroic strivings. The special woman shares in the Dream, believes in him as its hero, gives it her blessing, and creates a "boundary space" within which the young man's aspirations can be imagined and his hopes nourished.

Like the mentor, the special woman is a transitional figure. During early adulthood, a man is struggling to outgrow the little boy in himself and to become an autonomous adult. The special woman can foster his adult aspirations while accepting his dependency, his incompleteness, and his need to make her into something more than (and less than) she actually is. Later, in the Mid-life Transition, he will have to become a more individual person. With further development, he will be more complete and have less need of the special woman.

A couple can form a lasting relationship that furthers his development only if it also furthers hers. If his sense of her as the special woman stems mainly from his wishful projections and not from her own desires and efforts, sooner or later the bubble will burst and both will feel cheated. If in supporting his Dream she loses her own, then her development will suffer and both will later pay the price. Disparities of this kind often surface in transitional periods such as the Age-30 Transition and the Midlife Transition.

A man's wife may be his special woman. Alternatively, they may have a relationship that is loving and supporting but that has little connection to his Dream. The wife may, in crucial respects, be antithetical to his Dream. What she loves in him and wants to build into their life may hinder or preclude the pursuit of the Dream. His decision to marry her may have been, in effect, a decision to head in a direction away from the Dream. If her Dream is different from his, or antagonistic to it, their marriage starts with a contradiction that will have to be dealt with in time. A disparity of this kind may emerge only after years of marriage, often to become a source of bitter discontent and conflict.

SETTLING DOWN AFTER THE NOVICE PHASE

By the end of the novice phase, a qualitatively new life structure is emerging. It always contains some elements from the past, but their meanings have changed within the context of a new life. In the Early-Adult Transition, starting at about age 17, a man's life is still strongly rooted in the family of origin and the preadult world; the process of separation is just getting underway. He has a Dream, inchoate or differentiated, along with diverse hopes, fears, fantasies, and plans for the future.

Fifteen years later, in the early 30s, his adolescence seems part of the distant past, far removed from the current world. By this time he almost certainly has a wife and family—perhaps he has even been divorced and remarried. His sense of what it means to be a husband and father has altered dramatically. So, too, has the meaning of being a son: one or both parents may have died; if they are alive, he may be losing contact with them, or, as the balance shifts, becoming a parent to them. The character of his occupational life is taking a new shape. Even if his present occupation is the one he had hoped for, it contains possibilities and limitations he did not imagine in the Early-Adult Transition. In most cases, the occupation is different in crucial ways from his earlier expectations.

As the Age-30 Transition ends, a man moves toward major new choices or rededicates himself to past choices. A great deal depends on how he chooses at this time. If he chooses poorly and the new structure is flawed, his life in the Settling Down period will become increasingly painful and his attempts to create a more satisfactory structure more difficult and costly. If he chooses well—from the viewpoint of his Dream, values, talents, possibilities—he will have built the foundation for a satisfactory life structure.

After the Age-30 Transition, a man has completed the time for exploring and getting established in the adult world. It is time to enter the Settling Down period (roughly age 33 to 40), when a man works to fulfill his Dream, pursue his ambitions, and become the hero in the scenario of his youth. At the start, he has the sense of being on the low rung of a ladder and preparing to make his way to the top. The ladder may have many rungs or few. His ambitions may be vast and burning, or modestly pragmatic. The ladder may lead toward the realization of the Dream or in another direction. But, one way or the other, at the close of Settling Down, men enter what we call the Midlife Transition—roughly age 40-45—when they must reappraise their lives and work on new developmental tasks.

Now it becomes important to ask, What have I done with my life? What do I really get from, and give to, my wife, children, friends, work, community—and self? What are my central values and how are they reflected in my life? What are my greatest talents and how am I using, or wasting them? What have I done with my early Dream and what do I want with it now?

For the great majority of men — about 80 percent of our subjects — the Midlife Transition is a time of moderate to severe crisis. It evokes tumultuous struggles within the self, and between the self and the external world. Every aspect of a man's life comes into question, and he is horrified by much that is revealed. He experiences more fully his own mortality and the actual or impending death of others. At the same time, he has a strong desire to be more creative; to create products that have value for himself and others, to join in enterprises that advance human welfare, to contribute more fully to coming generations. In middle adulthood, a man comes to know that powerful forces of destructiveness and creativity coexist in the human soul and he strives to integrate them in new ways.

FORTY LIVES: HOW THE
YALE STUDY WAS DONE

The most conspicuous missing persons in Daniel Levinson's study of "adult development" are women. Levinson believes that women go through the same developmental periods as men, but "in partially different ways that reflect differences in biology and social circumstances." The differences are sufficiently great, he thinks, that "they would have to become a major focus of analysis," which would have broadened the scope of his study considerably. (He is now beginning to study women.) But Levinson in his book admits to a personal reason for concentrating on men: "I chose men partly because I wanted so deeply to understand my own adult development."

The 40 men in the study were chosen by occupation because Levinson and his colleagues believe a man's work is "the primary base for his life in society ... a vehicle for the fulfillment or negation of central aspects of the self." To choose the 40, the researchers immersed themselves, like anthropologists on a field trip, in the working environments of four occupational groups.

Ten business executives and 10 working men on hourly wages were chosen from two companies within 50 miles of New Haven — a division of a major national corporation making a small number of products, from recreational equipment to munitions, and a young but rapidly growing electronic-communications firm. The sample was drawn about equally from Company A and Company B, as Levinson calls them, Chinese-menu style, to maximize diversity in age, rank, specialization (engineering, sales, finance, and so on), line and staff positions.

To represent professionals — and within that group a subgroup of scientists — Levinson's team picked 10 biologists from two major universities in the New York-Boston corridor. Why biologists only, and not a variety of scientists? For one thing, selecting only a few occupations would permit comparisons of development among individuals who share a common working environment. More important, Levinson believes each occupation "has its own particular character that exercises a strong socializing influence on the individual." He selected only a few occupations because he wanted to examine in detail the socialization process and how it affects the individual development. Again in the case of the biologists, the men were selected to assure some spread in age, specialty, department, and academic rank.

To represent artists, the researchers chose 10 novelists from a list of 100 men living in the New York-Boston region and culled from various sources. Some were considered highly gifted, serious writers, others were less well known but regarded as promising, and still others were popular but less talented writers who nonetheless worked hard at their craft.

In choosing the 40 men, Levinson's team tried to achieve diversity in social class, religion, racial and ethnic background. About 15 percent were from poor urban and rural backgrounds, 42 percent from working or lower-middle classes, 32 percent from the middle class, and 10 percent from the wealthiest class. There were five blacks, including three novelists and two workers; no black biologists or executives were in the organizations sampled by the study team.

Levinson refers to his main study technique as "biographical interviewing." He describes it as combining qualities of a research interview, a clinical interview, and a conversation between friends. "What is involved," he adds, "is not simply an interviewing technique or procedure, but a relationship of some intimacy, intensity, and duration." Levinson admits there are risks to such an approach: "At its best, this method yields a valuable biography and enables the subject to review his life. At its worst, it yields a distorted life story and is hurtful to the man who tries to tell it. It needs to be used with discretion."

CHAPTER 18

The Seasons of
a Woman's Life

Judith M. Bardwick

Because psychoanalysis dominated the social sciences for half a century, focusing on development in the earliest years, there has been a widespread assumption that the critical tasks of psychological maturation were completed during childhood and adolescence. As a result, there have been very few studies of the changes which normally occur through the adult years.*

A detailed and useful model of adult maturation is that of Daniel Levinson and his colleagues, who found that at the level of specifics everyone's life is obviously unique, but at another level of analysis every life is consistent.[1] Throughout the adult years there is an ebb and flow, a regular alternation of stable phases lasting about seven to ten years, with intervening periods of evaluation-transition lasting some four to five years.

The magnitude and the profundity of the psychological and reality tasks during these periods are demonstrated by the sheer length of time that they take. During stable periods we attempt to arrive at our most important objectives. While we can experience these periods as difficult if the goals are hard to achieve, they are, in a sense, psychodynamically easy in that we know what we are pursuing. During evaluation-transition phases we assess how far we have traveled and whether or not we are on the right road. After living within a life-style which has specific responsibilities and objectives for seven to ten years, we are propelled, by psychological forces entwined with the facts of our reality, to assess what we are doing with our lives. We ask ourselves what we have gained and what we have lost as a result of the decisions made and the objectives sought during the preceding stable period. While it is impossible to begin this process with relative dispassion, most persons will experience great emotion, simply because one comes to realize that each time one chose to pursue some things, one gave up others.

The evaluation of what our lives are like can become the preparation for deciding actively on future goals of what one wishes to do or become. Underlying the possibility of

---

*The few which have been published recently have studied men. Without comparable longitudinal data about women we can only surmise, speculating about the ways in which the developmental tasks and processes of the sexes might be alike and different.

Reprinted with permission of the author. From *Women's Lives—New Theory, Research and Policy*, edited by Dorothy G. Mcguigan, University of Michigan, Center for Continuing Education of Women, 1980.

change is a dynamic tension between the desire for generativity-change and for stagnation-security. While people can be characterized as tending more easily toward change and risk-taking or toward risk-avoidance and not changing, this push-pull tension also exists within any individual. In the period of evaluation each is faced with the existential collision between staying within the life which exists and is therefore known, and altering that life, thereby taking as one's future that which cannot be known.

There is a great range in people's willingness to experience the evaluation consciously because it is scary to question the core of one's life and of one's Self. But despite the fear most people will acknowledge, at least for a certain period of time, that something is wrong. The most salient point of awareness is in one's major role and one may feel plateaued either at work or within the home. When the promotion is gained and there is no higher place to go, when the youngest child is in school all day, when economic security is banked, then one can most easily realize how habits derived from old responsibilities persist and unnecessarily govern and limit how we live.

With this awareness we try to move toward new fulfillments, but there is always pain. Whenever one questions objectives, values and commitments, one's very fluidity creates anxiety. This anxiety in itself generates a powerful need to achieve closure, to settle some things, to make some decisions. But despite a passionate longing to set one's course, the profundity of what is involved requires years for resolution.

The period of assessment and change is completed when the imperative need to ask questions and to make choices is moderated. Then, with less intense emotions, one feels able to accept all or some of one's previous commitments and values, or else one begins to construct new ones. Sometimes people recommit themselves to prior goals but in a different way, as their emergent awareness guides them toward altering, perhaps enriching, those involvements. Even when people appear unchanged because their behaviors remain consistent, they are altered to the extent of their self-knowledge.

During a stable stage we try to achieve goals of psychological maturation, of establishment or extension of interpersonal commitments, and of occupational accomplisments. As social expectations differ at different ages, particular accomplishments feel more crucial at different ages. Our concept of ourselves and our self-confidence — and thus our ability or willingness to alter our lives — will derive, in part, from our past successes or failures in terms of these specific goals.

Some people will not change their lives because they feel and believe that external constraints cannot be overcome. Others will not alter their lives because they are made passive by their fears of the unfamiliar, the anticipation of guilt, or their profound self-doubts. We can expect those who cannot transform the future in some way differently to be grateful if they can accept the compromised life which is their reality; some will exist in self-disparaging despair.

This is a model of human development based on the idea that psychological growth and change are intertwined and never cease. It assumes that human beings desire the sense of actualization which accompanies and requires psychological and realistic change in controllable measure. At this abstract level we can agree that this model applies to both sexes, because it is essentially a description of what happens when we perceive that we are aging, of how people feel when they realize that they have accomplished or failed to accomplish what they set out to do, or how people seek a future in which they will attain or experience or become what they have not, and how sometimes change is blocked.

GENDER DIFFERENCES
IN ADULT DEVELOPMENT

Levinson believes that women go through the same developmental periods that men do and in the sense just described, that is true. But in other, more specific ways, there are important gender differences. One difference is that a larger number of women compared to men will evade an evaluation of their lives, because any assessment heightens their perception that they do not determine their life-style but, relatively powerless, are limited to responding to the directives and initiatives of others. For a certain kind of woman, selfless to the extreme, even asking questions, "Who am *I*? What do *I* want to do?" is decimating; it forces the realization that she is a Self reflected and relational — existing only as long as there is a relationship in which someone responds and assures her that she does exist.

Another major difference between the two sexes is that for women certain important value changes evolved during the 1970s that resulted in basically different attitudes among women of any one generation as well as differences between generations of women. In terms of the major involvements of work and family, some women's lives have changed dramatically whereas most men's lives have not. We would, therefore, find much greater cohort differences among women. A wider range of styles and objectives exists among women today, because since the changes in society are so recent, women can have values, a self-perception, and a life-style either deriving from or combining both traditional and modern patterns.*

THE CRUCIAL MENTAL
GENDER DIFFERENCE

Levinson describes late adolescence and early adulthood as enormously important because the four developmental tasks of that period provide a foundation for the rest of adulthood. During that time men construct their dream, that is, their image of themselves as

---

*As women are living longer and having fewer children, the period of child rearing is short; most women are in their thirties when their youngest child enters school, and the departure of children comes earlier. While that may be the single most important change, the complex of differences becomes clear when we compare women who are presently entering old age, those entering middle age, and women who will be middle-aged by the end of the 1980s.

The oldest group had the least education, grew up in large familes in which their parents were often immigrants; since they became adults during the depression, they delayed marriage and had few children. The second group had more education but relatively few finished college; they grew up in small families and, as they became adults during a period of economic expansion, they tended to marry early and have many children. The youngest group had more education; 25 percent of them are in professional or technical jobs; they plan to have small families and as they are expected to live into their eighties, they will have many years which are child-free.

Compared with their grandmothers and their mothers, the lives of those in the youngest group will involve more education, higher levels of work, new combinations of family and work, more divorce, more single-parent households, and a high probability that they will take care of their aged parents.

Today, in households in which there are both a wife and husband, in fewer than 50 percent is the wife a homemaker and the husband the only wage earner. While the majority of young American women have always been employed, today that is equally true of those aged 45 to 54, over half of whom are in the labor force.[2]

they will be in the world of adults. In addition to constructing the dream, they form their occupational aspiration, they find and relate to a mentor, and they create a relationship of love. Three of these four developmental tasks involve work.

To the extent that men *are* their work—they identify with it, their sense of identity is endangered when they are unemployed, and their work is a major determinant of their position in society—then, if you want "to know about men," you study men in different occupational groups. That, of course, is what Levinson did.

But if you were to study women, what kinds of groups would you select? While we would consider the type of work women either did or were trained to do, we would include women who were employed or not, married or not, divorced or not, rearing children or not.

Those are still the fundamental bifurcations; they remain the role distinctions which determine women's experiences and exemplify and influence their values. For only a minor percentage of women is occupation the major involvement in which they fulfill or frustrate core aspects of themselves. For the majority, at least in early adulthood, the traditional roles remain the locus of identity. Like work, women's traditional role defines many obligations; unlike work, it cuts across class lines. More importantly, despite the prominence of feminist values, the occupational commitments of the sexes in young adulthood are based on very different psychological stances.

In a recent study, Rosalind Barnett and Grace Baruch asked 60 women, aged 35 to 55, if the four psychological tasks which Levinson cites as crucial in young adulthood had been important to them.[3] Only one, that of creating a relationship involving love, had been significant when they were young adults. While they had assumed that they would work, it wasn't really important because they expected to marry and to be supported. Only women whose fathers had been absent and whose mothers had earned their living had considered work in a serious way. Even those who had been poor thought of their future in terms of a man they would meet and not in terms of a career upon which they had decided. The future was imagined interpersonally and not egocentrically.

A very major difference between the sexes is the extent to which young women still prepare for adulthood by romantically anticipating whom they will marry. Although many will be college educated and employed, their major psychological tasks derive from constructing relationships and not from accomplishing self-determined, egocentric goals. In that respect women are basically different from men who, even within relationships, relate and evaluate from the egocentric core of their dream.

THE DREAM OF WOMEN

Women's dream is relational and either because the partner is not yet known or because its specific form is so enmeshed with the priorities of someone else, their dream is always, to some extent, tentative and unformed. *There is a basic difference, perhaps a fundamental tension, between an interdependent and an egocentric sense of self, between a formulated and a fluid set of objectives. It is important that we do not assume that identical behaviors, especially in school and work, are based upon identical mental postures. The major gender difference is not that of role participation. Rather, psychological egocentricity or psychological dependence or interdependence is the basic sex difference.*

Adult development, as Levinson describes it, is archetypically American, stressing doing rather than being, focussing on individuality rather than on connecting. Assessments of life involve questions of, "Who am I? Who am I as differentiated from anyone else? Who am I as a result of what I have accomplished? Am I worthy of esteem in terms of being near or far from my goals? What shall I do next?"

These egocentric questions begin from the assumption that the Self is the center. Accomplishments are thought of primarily in terms of achievements and those relate primarily to work. Maturation is described as the process of individuation, of becoming an individual, of "becoming one's own man" in the largest sense. That too is very American and very male. Other cultures, including the traditional one of American women, have conceptualized adulthood as meeting responsibilities within relationships.*

WOMEN AND THE
MULTIPLE ROLE MODEL

Another gender difference is that we can talk in terms of a single model of male maturation, because there is only one major concept or role participation and maturity for men. But there are at least two major concepts about what adult women should be like and they are the opposite of each other. For many women — in some age groups it will be the majority — the psychological tasks are not so much to model the Self upon one or the other ideal, but to combine them in a way which is workable to the Self, and to the Self within relationships. How to achieve this combination of roles and ideal Selves, especially when women are changing more quickly and more profoundly than their male partners are, is not clear. While some women will seem more like men, asking similar questions and having similar ambitions, the great majority retain some self-concepts, priorities and objectives from the traditional model, even when their lives do not appear to reflect that.

We can describe the goals and values of different groups of women over the age span and think of those as the objectives of the stable periods. Their experiences will gratify or frustrate with considerable variance between the groups, as the expectations and desires of women reflect their age and cultural values. The evaluation phases may be very emotionally volatile, and therefore the transitions to new values and life-styles are likely to be more extreme than in previous generations. We know that there have been major changes in the self-concepts, goals and behaviors of many women; we want to know the life stage patterns among women and the extent to which sex differences remain or are dissolved. While everyone experiences periods of growth and stagnation, striving and assessing, the issues in terms of sex differences can be summarized in two questions: 1) what percentage of women develop a complex psyche or an egocentric mental stance after young adulthood? 2) what percent of women younger than 27 now have a more egocentric stance than was typical of traditional women?

Since we do not have longitudinal studies of women, we can only guess. But if we were to graph the population of women, constructing a portrait of what women are like in 1980, dividing them by age and psychological stance, we might have something like Figure 1.**

Actually, there is an illusion of autonomy here, because as male identity and self-esteem remain dependent upon success in work, then egocentricity has been confused with autonomy. Truly autonomous people have developed an inner sense of Self which is retained even when roles and responsibilities are lost. The vulnerabilities of the sexes are not greater or lesser, only different.

**Figure 1 is a static and not a developmental model. It is an estimate of what the generations are like *now* and is *not* a statement of the psychological changes that would be experienced over the lifetime of anyone. The latter is implied but cannot be stated with certainty, because socio-cultural values are a major influence and it is difficult to predict such values for the future.

Age	Egocentric	Interdependent Complex	Dependent
Childhood*	5	10	85
Adolescence	15	10	75
20s	15	35	50
30s	25	40	35
40s	15	55	30
50s	10	40	50
60s & older	5	30	65

Fig. 1. The Mental Stance of a College Educated Population of Women**

The analysis in Figure 1 focuses on mental stance or psychological core, conceptualized as a continuous variable, ranging from dependent to interdependent to egocentric. While the psychological sense of self can evolve from or can be maintained within any life-style, there are plausible relations between them.

A dependent sense of Self, which is basically relational, is more likely to be associated with a traditional life-style and with a heterosexual relationship in which there is both psychological and economic dependence. If the woman is employed, she is likely to earn significantly less than her husband, but more importantly, is likely to think of her earnings as an additional contribution to the family.

The interdependent mental stance is one in which a sense of Self and a keen awareness of being a contributing and receiving member of an affectional relationship exist simultaneously. This mixture of qualities is most easily developed in a complex reality which includes both familial and non-familial involvements.†

A permanent egocentric stance in women is rare because socialization pressures and the concept of femininity tend toward an interdependent or dependent sense of Self. In most

---

*Children are literal, conformist and conservative.

**A non-college educated population would be more traditional.

†"Familial" includes cohabitation and other forms of stable, committed, relationships in addition to marriages.

women egocentricism is probably a relatively short-term response to embittered rage or grief following on the destruction of an affective relationship and/or the realization that their lives are essentially frustrated. This stance can be the mainspring, the energizer, especially if it involves anger, which enables them to make major changes in their lives. Once real changes are achieved which construct opportunities for achieving the missing gratifications, and once rage is abated, the egocentric stance is likely to alter, usually toward the complex or interdependent mentality.

In order to organize ideas I am proceeding chronologically, and in order to reduce repetition, events have been assigned to a specific age — marriage in the twenties, for example, the departure of the children in the forties. In addition to noting that the same event can obviously occur at different ages, it is appropriate to underline Levinson's point that the same event at a different age is in many ways not the same task because we are psychologically so changed. Lastly, without data comparable to Levinson's, this can only be a sketch, tentative and lacking the rich pigments of intensive, long-term studies of real individuals.

AGE 17 TO 18: EARLY
ADULT TRANSITION FOR WOMEN

The first task of becoming an adult is to assess the values of your adolescent world and to begin to evolve those you will hold as an adult. One constructs goals, especially in education and work; one develops relationships with peers, particularly those involving sex, love and commitment; and, most crucially, one accelerates the process of separating from parents.

While most American children do not in the long run sustain values very different from those of their parents, during adolescence, when individuation is a major issue, differences in values can evolve which are greater than they will ever be again. As more young women leave home and are exposed to radicalized values, increasing percentages of them may behave non-traditionally, especially sexually, and hold radicalized values significantly different from those of their parents concerning politics, homosexuality, sex, abortion, marriage, maternity and careers.

These new values are not necessarily the result of increased autonomy but may well represent conformity to the values of a self-selected group of peers. Especially influential on the young person whose sense of self is fluid, who is embarked on a conscious search for new directions, are friends, older students or co-workers who seem to have achieved clear values and direction. Professors are likely to be especially influential. A considerable amount of behavior or attitudes may be based as much on negating perceived parental directives as on structuring independence. The emergence of increasingly liberal or radical values and behaviors in young women will not mean a basic change in psychological stance if underneath overt egocentricism the core continues to be dependent and the behavior conforming — only conforming to a different set of authority and reference figures. Levinson describes the early adult phase as one in which there is a major conflict between making commitments, including the fundamental ones associated with adulthood — occupation, marriage, paternity — and not making commitments in order to keep one's options open. Pressure to make the commitments is great if most of one's peers are doing that. Besides, one wants to seem to others — but mostly to the Self — as adult, and adulthood is most easily achieved by moving into these roles.

During adolescence one of the crucial tasks is to internalize a sense of gender and to develop a sense of one's body, specifically one's sexuality. Women traditionally focused on marriage, since this was the conclusion of the evolution of heterosexual intimacy and sexuality, as well as being the crucial achievement of becoming an adult woman.

Insofar as young women continue to place priority on and to find their core identity within relationships, they can evolve some sense of themselves which is egocentric and formed, but basically maintain considerable psychological fluidity, their essential core usually dependent or infrequently interdependent.* Males are developing similarly, but the proportions are reversed so that their fluidity and interpersonal dependence are much less than their egocentricity.

Despite the marked increase in young women's awareness that they ought to decide actively upon career goals because they know they will be employed, I think there has been relatively little change in regard to the priority of a committed relationship and a sense of self and adulthood developed within relationships. For young women that area can now be one of additional conflict. In addition to the conflicts Levinson describes, the issues are usually in terms of realistic problems: how does a couple find two jobs in the same locale? How can one combine rearing children with a demanding career? While those are real problems, the conflict itself is based on a fear that realization of one's own ambitions may cost one a relationship. At the core is the conflict between fulfillment of egocentric or interpersonal/dependent priorities and the different sense of oneself which stems from those different psychological stances.**

Women who are now in their twenties have grown up with both traditional and feminist values. Probably they have been taken more seriously than their mothers were as individuals and as workers, and most have experienced the negative and positive aspects of work, marriage, maternity—and sometimes divorce. At this age most will have children, and the desirability or functional quality of the egocentric mentality in young women is most problematic in regard to maternity. Whether child care is gratifying or frustrating depends not only on reality considerations, such as the availability of money or the health of the child, it is very much influenced by the over-riding egocentricity of the child, which demands non-egocentricity in the caretakers. If the mother is the primary caretaker, it is therefore functional if she has not evolved an egocentric psychic structure. But if she has not, she may experience the demands of the child, especially if they are joined by the egocentric needs of the husband, as engulfing her. Then she can feel that she has no Self.†

---

*Since middle aged women often become markedly assertive, initiating and autonomous, it would be more accurate to say that young women delay forming egocentric attitudes, values and goals. That is, while internal maturation is occurring, it is greatly influenced, over many years, by how a young woman experiences herself in the significant relationships she has with men, in terms of what qualities in her she thinks they esteem.

**Ambivalence is likely to be high if there have been divorces within one's circle of friends or relatives. Marriage rates in this age group are extremely high but the divorce rates are soaring. it is currently estimated that about 40 percent of first marriages of those who are now 25 to 35 will end in divorce. That statistic leads, appropriately, to a mistrust of marriage or to conflict about having children as the difficulties of being a single parent become evident. The population statistics alone should increase young women's seriousness about their careers, since the most significant demographic trend is that of households headed by women.[4]

†Alarmingly, almost all studies find that couples report their satisfaction with marriage declining after the birth of a first child.[5]

Because the percentages of women who are seriously involved in their education, in their careers and in relationships is increasing within this age group and there is widespread articulation of the need for women to have their own independent goals, perhaps 35 percent are evolving from a dependent to an interdependent stance.

We can estimate that 15 percent are egocentric, either because, very atypically, they begin formulating a future in terms of self-control and self-objectives in late adolescence, or because, as young as they are, they are old enough to have been bitterly hurt within a traditional life-style. Among those in their twenties, who divorce, the majority probably do not basically change but simply remarry. While the percentage who will undergo fundamental change after divorce will be greater among older women, a group more likely to be both more confident and more angry, some in the younger group will become egocentric, unwilling ever again to give someone else so much power over how they regard themselves.

AGE 28 TO 39: THE AGE 30 TRANSITION AND THE SETTLING DOWN PERIOD OF THE SECOND ADULT LIFE STRUCTURE

Levinson found that a major transition phase begins between the ages of 28 to 30. At that point one has to give up the self-image of being young, the feeling that one's involvements are tentative and one's options are still open. The majority who made major commitments at the usual ages have now been married, have been parents, have been working, for about 5 years—long enough to assess those choices and their consequences. Those who have not made the commitments are forced by the same awareness of age *per se*, to wonder why they have not; their task is either to make the commitments at this point or to readjust to their absence.

Levinson says that after the transition phase and until the age of 40, a man tries to achieve the goals he developed as a youth and invests even more strongly in work, family, friendship, leisure, community—whatever feels like the most important components of his life. He has a sense of being on a timetable, of climbing a ladder, of needing to advance upward. He wants to experience himself and be affirmed by others as a man who has become a senior member of his world.

Around 36 to 40 occurs a phase for men which is so special that Levinson has given it a specific name: *Becoming One's Own Man.* In these years a man has to give up his mentor, give up even more of his internal little boy self, and speak with his own voice based on his sense of autonomous authority. To the extent that he identifies with his work, and, successful in that activity, has access to promotions and increased responsibilities, to others asking for his advice and leadership, then the feeling of being senior to some, of being accepted as a peer by those perceived as senior, will follow. *The external structure of work thus facilitates the internal task of experiencing oneself as an independent, adult man.*

Very few women will have the same experiences or the same psychological outcomes. While the sense of being adult may be gained by women successful in their work, few would *Become One's Own Woman*, reassured by occupational success as to the normalcy of their adult status as women. On the contrary, those who are achieving significantly may feel especially anxious about their femininity unless they are in significant heterosexual relationships. *The factors which can generate the sense of independence in men may have the paradoxical effect of highlighting dependent needs in women.*

Independence as a crucial characteristic of adulthood is much clearer or more salient for men than women. As the focus is on masculinity earned by achievements, rather than masculinity earned within relationships, then men focus on achieving that status by becoming independent at work.

Femininity with its suggestion of warmth, nurturance, supportiveness of others, is a quality generated within relationships. Even if women had mentors—which few do—they might not consider it important, as men do, to separate from them. Interdependence and not egocentricity or autonomy is the feminine ideal.

Women who are now in their thirties are likely to experience a more profound and prolonged transition period than men of the same age.*

In this group most will have begun their adult life with essentially traditional values; most will also have changed toward more feminist or more egalitarian life patterns as their experiences forced them to evaluate and then to reject what their life was like, especially as the new values became the majority position. While a substantial number may have begun their thirties with feminist values and may live according to them—especially with regard to responsibilities and rights within marriage, parenting and careers—the responses of others and their own psychological tendencies will make them aware that older values and ideas about appropriate behaviors and qualities remain powerful.

The great majority of women in their thirties will be married, the mothers of school age children, employed but not on a career path, or unemployed and out of school for about ten years. The first task of becoming an adult woman was accomplished by marriage and maternity; the children are now old enough to need less and less mothering, while the husband's career is launched and he is increasingly involved in it; as the years 35 to 40 approach, there is a good chance that a woman will change her life. Frequently women return to work or work more ambitiously; some return to school, and some have love affairs.**

Perhaps inevitably family members, especially husbands find that, even though they agree in principle to changes in the lives of the wives, as those changes impact upon their own

---

*The thirties produce pressure on everyone, because at that age the level of one's abilities is tested, one's probable occupational future becomes clearer; the age of 35 is roughly half-way through a life. Probably women's confrontation with life's basic issues occurs nearer to 35 to 40 because of their biological clock. If they have not conceived by then, they may fear that their reproductive capacities are declining. If they did have 2 or 3 children beginning around the statistically normal age of 25, then at 35 the youngest child is in school all day. To the extent that women depend upon appearance for self-esteem, aging can be frightening: 35 is no longer young. When Rubin asked women to describe themselves in such a way that she could get a good sense of who and what they were, almost all began with a physical description.[6] The aging of the body may be more stressful for women but paradoxically, studies find that women's sexual responsiveness often increases in middle age. That may be pleasant or unpleasant depending upon the interest expressed by their partners—or by whether or not a woman has a partner. In any event, the task is not only to accept one's own aging body but that of your partner; that is not only an issue of attractiveness but of age since your partner's aging body is a continuous reminder of your own.

**While premarital and extra-marital sexual activity are not the same, it is nonetheless interesting that in a national study of attitudes concerning premarital sexual behavior, the greatest change—and in the direction of liberalization—had taken place among women aged 30 to 39.[7]

lives, they feel confused and resentful. There is a convergence of stress for both husband and wife, while hers characteristically arises out of changes within the family, his originates outside the family.

In complex organizations the pyramid begins to narrow dramatically as a person nears middle management and the number of promotion possibilities diminishes sharply. This means that at the time when the man's psychological task is to perceive himself as an independent and successful adult, he begins to run the risks of being plateaued or fired. If his sense of masculinity is endangered, it can be harder for him to cope with a wife who is less deferent and less dependent.*

I think the value changes of the 1970s have been experienced more severely by those now in their thirties than by any other age group. Those who are 35 in 1980, were 25 in 1970. The feminist movement began in the late 1960s and by 1974 had been accepted by the majority of Americans.[9] This group therefore grew up when values were traditional; they became young adults however, when they were supposed to make choices and not passively to accept tradition. Those now in their thirties have less sense of certainty about what the real rules are than do those who are older or younger, because the other groups had more consistent experiences.

Because they had both the reality and the illusion of choice, I think that there is more stress and confusion and a greater chance for anger among women in their thirties than in any other group. Those who followed ambition may have to come to terms with loneliness and a despair bred out of the feeling that it may be too late. Those striving to juggle all roles are doing that without consensual rules of what is all right to do or not to do within relationships.

Those who do respond with anger will for some time be egocentric. If that enables them to formulate fulfilling and obtainable objectives, and they create a more complex life cycle, most will become psychologically interdependent. Because women's traditional roles involve economic, social and psychological dependence, most who move from a dependent to an interdependent stance will achieve that because they increased their involvements outside the home. That choice becomes feasible as their childcare responsibilities have declined.

Thus, I would guess that while there is a large percentage who are psychologically dependent, perhaps 35 percent, that is substantially less than the 50 percent among those now in their twenties. Since I think there is considerable frustration and anger, as many as 25 percent could be egocentric, but for most women that is a transition phase. The largest group, about 40 percent, are likely to be developing new rules of responsibility and obligation within relationships, and they will be interdependent.

AGE 40 TO 50: THE MID-LIFE TRANSITION AND MIDDLE ADULTHOOD

As men approach the symbolically powerful age of 40, Levinson found that they question what they receive and what they give to work, wife, children, friends, community.

---

*There are data demonstrating that a substantial number of men in their thirties and older tend to become less assertive and dominant, while their wives reverse that direction, diminishing their passivity and their willingness to be limited to home and family. If the husband is in a psychological decline, especially if his occupational future is pessimistic, the wife and children tend to maintain the forms of dependence, which are intended to sustain the husband's declining self-esteem. They protect him so that he can continue to function and thereby allow them the development of their autonomy and interests. For all concerned, the idea that he is a strong husband and father is comforting.[8]

Since 40 is associated with aging and aging is frightening for us, probably the few who do not assess their lives at this time are especially frightened and feel powerless, unable to change their lives.

The basic stress is that this age in itself signifies that the future is shortening; if you will ever experience and become what you have not, you must do it now. This period can be more emotionally intense than any which preceded it because, while there is still a substantial future, death is in the wings. One's own mortality becomes harder to deny as some develop chronic diseases, some have friends die, many will have their parents die, and before this decade ends, some will have their spouses die.

Levinson tells us that the great majority experience the mid-life transition as a significant struggle within themselves and with the Self in the world. While the final outcome may well be positive, the evaluation-transition period is painful; one acknowledges, for example, that the past 20 years in an occupation has realistically foreclosed work options and the work future is an extension of what one is doing now. Similarly, the 15-year-old marriage is comfortable but not exhilarating; ending it however, means losing crucial roots and injuring a spouse whose only sin was being around too long.

While some men decline in this period, Levinson found that many experience middle adulthood as their fullest and most creative period. He describes those men as less tyrannized by the passions, ambitions, and illusions of youth. Most of them achieved a new level of autonomy in their late thirties that enabled them to be both more aware of and more centered in the Self, and more responsive and sensitive to others. This is the optimal evolution of the egocentric stance and it is the development of the interpersonal mentality in men.

The sexes begin adulthood at opposite ends of the psychodynamic continuum; as men are enabled by success in achievement to give up their egocentric preoccupation, and as women succeed within relationships and become more autonomous, both become interdependent. This implies that men will become more involved with their internal psychological needs and states and be more sensitive to their dependence upon affirmation within relationships. Women will be better able to engage the world, experiencing themselves as initiators, having gratifications as individuals.

Realistically and psychodynamically less confined, people in their forties are freer to construct richer relationships with their spouses, grown children, friends and colleagues. But today the criteria of satisfaction in relationships, especially in marriage, are changing toward more egocentric and hedonistic gratifications. Women and men are assessing what they gain and what they lose in all commitments: since there are costs in all commitments, and since awareness of aging is likely to precipitate feelings of desperation, then the chances of major upheavals in long-term relationships are increased.

Divorce has increased markedly among those now in their forties. While those in their thirties were most affected by the illusion of free options, I think those now in their forties were most affected by the visibility of egocentric hedonism.[10] They are old enough to feel cheated if they followed the rules and led a duty-filled life, but they are young enough to have a future of sufficient extent to make change worth while. Especially if one is plateaued or otherwise trapped in one's work, then the marital relationship can come to feel like the only commitment large enough to be blamed for one's losses, whereas a new relationship can feel important enough to be capable of reconstructing the feelings and pleasures of youth.

While we are focussing on change in middle age, the oppressive fact is that for most people this is a relatively eventless period which has far fewer significant events than does youth.[11]

Women who are now 40 and older became adults when there were essentially no choices, and their traditional obligations dictated that the great majority were never seriously involved occupationally. While the costs of that are obvious, it also offers the specifics of major change. While an unemployed or under-employed housewife can be fearful, becoming really involved is an obvious opportunity to create beginnings. The easiest changes are external, and those whose lives have included all of the major role engagements don't have an obvious new activity to pursue. In that sense middle-aged women have an easier resolution than do men, who have normally been employed, married, a parent and active in the community. Now, especially if life in general is set and no more significant accomplishments seem available in the external world, then they may be forced to accomplish an extraordinary transition by generating new values internally, in regard to what they *are* rather than in terms of what they *do*. That same task confronts unmarried career women who are an especially vulnerable group, given the chance that their careers have plateaued and they have neither the haven of a supportive marriage nor much chance that they will find a partner.

During their forties the probability of women experiencing loneliness increases greatly because of the children leaving home, widowhood, and divorce. In this age group the remarriage rate for men is much higher than for women. In 1977 over 3,000,000 women aged 40 to 64 were widowed and 2,200,000 were divorced.[13]

While many have described the empty nest period as depressed, national data do not support that view. Adjustments have to be made; for some it may be a crisis, for the majority, whether employed or not, it is sad and joyful and generally benign. But, if when your children leave, your spouse leaves too, and for the first time you are not centrally important in anyone's life, depression is inevitable and a major life transition is crucial. That will be especially difficult for those whose lives were not complex and who were basically dependent.*

I think that despite the significant divorce rate, if we compare women in their forties with those now in their thirties, fewer will be angry because they are less likely to feel that, as a generation, society lied to them. When they were young, there were no alternatives. One married and had children and while in middle age one might now regret what one did, there isn't the self-blame that comes from having made the wrong choices. Therefore, the percentage who would be egocentric would be smaller, perhaps 15 percent. The majority have probably made a reality transition, as evidenced simply by their very high employment rate. Having expanded their activities, being mature and often self-confident, the largest number are likely to have become interdependent. *The percentage of complex women in this group may be larger than in any other cohort because social permission to engage in work was given to them at exactly the time when their traditional responsibilities declined.* Believing that the traditional roles were important and were therefore a route to self-esteem, if they fulfilled those obligations well, relatively unambivalently compared to women in their thirties, they could use the traditional roles as the route to affirm themselves as successful adults. Since so many are likely to have constructed complex lives and a sense of interdependence, the percent who are dependent is probably smaller than among those in their thirties estimated at 30 percent.

I am hypothesizing that the majority of women in their forties will have had the experience of realizing that a very major life phase ended during this decade, and they had to come

---

*For some, the problems are less psychological than economic. Increasing numbers of midlife former homemakers (40-65), who have no history of paid employment, find that when they are divorced they have no health insurance or retirement benefits and while they are too young for Social Security, they are considered too old for jobs.[14] The changes which are required of these people are stupendous, ranging from learning job skills, learning to think of themselves as competent; able to organize and decide, and most basically, transducing depression into anger, learning to think of themselves egocentrically.[15]

to terms with that and with the end of responsibilities most had just automatically accepted. Equally difficult, they had to decide what they would do next. But, free from responsibilities, grown up and capable, with the world more and more accepting of their venturing out into it, the possibility is very good that most successfully develop a sense of Self, and a new level of autonomy. Beginning the phase depressed and scared, the majority are likely to have made the transition so that they regard themselves differently, with some autonomy and considerable self-esteem.

AGE 50 AND OLDER

Levinson's study ended when the men were in their forties. He believes, but did not directly observe, a transition phase existing from 50 to 55. From 55 to 60 he believes there is a stable period in which those who are able to rejuvenate themselves are able to achieve significant fulfillments and enrich their lives. From 60 to 65 he hypothesizes a late adult transition phase, which is significant as it marks the end of middle age and creates the basis for old age. The single most important task in this phase is preparing for death. Symbolic forms of dying occur as one enters or is in old age—for women, the menopause and especially for men, retirement.

Children who are in their fifties usually have parents who are 70 and older. Aging parents often become increasingly dependent upon their children, psychologically as well as economically. While most old people want to remain independent as long as possible, and the actual frequency of contact between aged parents and middle aged children is low, the parents do expect that their children will aid them when they can no longer manage and that is normally the case. Women in late middle age are increasingly becoming the caretakers of their parents. In 1970, for every aged person in an institution, three were living with one of their children, usually a daughter.[16]

That can serve as a mechanism by which women who are homemakers can perpetuate that life-style. For example, I know a woman who is in her early fifties and for the past four years has had her 87-year-old father living with her. An RN, she taught nursing before her two daughters were born. The wife of a successful physician, she has not worked since the first birth. Her older daughter has graduated from college and the other leaves for school in several months. It is impossible for her to evade the realization that her role as a mother is ending; for the past several years she has been saying that she "ought to do something," and she means that she should get a job. "But," she will then complain, "I have to take care of my father!" The truth is that his presence has given her a plausible excuse to avoid really thinking about her Self, and she will postpone this evaluation at least until he dies.

Women now in their fifties and older were at least 40 when new options for participating in the world opened up. Many, probably the majority, felt that it was too late for them to change the way they lived. Partly a matter of feeling old, partly because few of their friends were employed, partly because of the conservatism of husbands, and largely because most were psychodynamically dependent. The great majority, I think, continued to live within the homemaker role. When you cannot achieve goals, one response is to reject the goal or the values upon which that goal is based. In contrast with those in their forties, who appear to have entered the work force in very large numbers, the employment rate of this group is much lower. I would not be surprised if some of this group responded to not being able to live according to the new values of the majority by intensifying their traditionalism in lifestyle and values.

Now that we are studying adults we are learning that psychological development never ends unless someone indraws psychologically or withdraws from engaging reality. Increasingly it seems that the mental deterioration which has customarily been attributed to aging is, instead, a response to an invariant world of no challenge or stimulation. When your world is too repetitive and simple, then you lose the feeling that you can cope with change. Those least able to risk something new are probably aging housewives who are psychologically dependent and not significantly involved in much of anything.*

But that may imply an overly pessimistic view. It is plausible that while the majority of older women may be psychologically dependent, those whose traditional life was in accord with their values and was a source of fulfillment, and who are likely to have led complex lives whether or not they were employed, would have become interdependent. I have described a larger percentage of women in their fifties as interdependent than those who are 60 and older, because it is possible that more of the younger group were enabled to participate in more outside activities as the world opened up for women in the second half of the 1970s. That hypothesis may be wrong if those who were older when values changed were less affected by them, less likely to question the value of how they had spent their lives, better able to maintain the sense that they had done what they were supposed to do, and done it well. While most would be depressed, some will be angry and I have assumed that small percentages of older women are egocentric because they have become widows and especially divorced, displaced homemakers.

CONCLUSION

When we are young we imagine that when we are grown we will really know what we want and things will be settled. It is disconcerting and yet hopeful to learn that nothing is ever settled "forever." In 1980 there are many women who have taken hold of their lives, and there are many others who feel resentful because they have lost the sense of comfort from knowing what is expected of them.

Neither the traditional homemaker role nor the career role nor the combination of them is without stress. A very major change in this past decade is the increased number of employed women, especially married mothers. While those who lead complex lives, combining responsibilities of worker, wife, mother, and community member may feel rushed and continuously pressured, Baruch and Barnett found that employed women who were also wives and mothers were no more stressed than those who were not in the labor force.[17] They found that the lives of those who were at home and those who left to go to work, could all be hectic. But chances are that work contributes more rewards to life than it generates additional pressures, especially if the family cooperates, because work can simplify life and provide objective criteria of adequate achievement. Work can be a buffer; women who are not employed have no protection from endless family demands and a childcare norm which generates guilt, anxiety and endless responsibility because one strives to be a perfect mother in order to have perfect children.

Overall, with as much confusion as value change generates, most of the changes seem to have been constructive. Having choices can create cultural ambiguity and personal uncertainty, but having no choices must ultimately frustrate a significant part of the population. In 1971 and 1978 in major national studies Campbell compared a large group of homemakers and employed wives.[18] One difference was that many more women were employed in

---

*Men are especially at risk when they retire and their mortality rate makes that clear.

1978 than had been in 1971. The most important finding was that the sense of satisfaction and the level of happiness with their lives did not differ between the two groups. While many have moved into the labor force, those who were full-time housewives were as satisfied with their lives and their sense of Self as were those who were employed. As values changed so did opportunities, and while there are always some people who feel frustrated, apparently the majority are now able to live as they prefer.

If one has the sense that one's life is plateaued, then that feeling can provoke efforts to make changes. While an opportunity to alter your life can clearly be positive, the experience will be negative if you cannot make changes in your world or within yourself. At their worst the evaluation phases can be experienced as crises; they can lead to depression or rage, to withdrawing, or to clinging to commitments and values which are inappropriate but familiar. Or, a sense of panic can result in extreme change, characterized primarily by a total reversal of everything in the past. Maturing is not only change. It also involves coping with what one has to do, accepting compromises and one's ambivalence in every commitment. Optimistically, one hopes that most people will experience their changing lives as a series of developments in which, as life phases end, they can then construct and engage their futures, generating the sense that they are alive, and that they have value.

In a way, life is a dialectic process of continuously separating and attaching, connecting and individuating. The ultimate separation is from life, and part of the process of living, is preparing to die. In that, the sexes are identical.

NOTES

[1]Levinson, Daniel J., Darrow, Charlotte, N., Klein, Edward B., Levinson, Maria H., and McKee, Braxton. *The Seasons of a Man's Life*. New York: Ballantine Books, 1978.

[2]Neugarten, B. L. and Brown-Rezanka, L. "Midlife Women in the 1980s. Women in Midlife—Security and Fulfillment (Part I)." A compendium of papers submitted to the Select Committee on Aging, and the Subcommittee on Retirement Income and Employment, U.S. House of Representatives, 95th Congress, Dec. 1978, Comm. Pub. 95-170, U.S. Government Printing Office, Washington, D.C., 1978, 23-28.

[3]Barnett, R. and Baruch, G. "On Being an Economic Provider: Women's Involvement in Multiple Roles." See pp. 69-82, of *Women's Lives* (as cited on p. 162 of this volume).

[4]Neugarten and Brown-Rezanka. "Midlife Women in the 1980s," 23-28.

[5]Schram, Rosalyn W. "Marital Satisfaction over the Family Life Cycle: A Critique and Proposal." *Journal of Marriage and the Family*, 41(1)(1979): 7-12.

[6]Rubin, L. *Women of a Certain Age: the Midlife Search for Self*. New York: Harper & Row, 1979.

[7]Mahoney, E. R. "Age Differences in attitude change toward pre-marital coitus." *Archives of Sexual Behavior* 7(5)(1978): 493-501.

[8]Rosenberg, S. D. and Farrell, M. P. "Changes in Life Course at Midlife: A Pattern of Psychosocial Decline." Unpublished paper presented at annual meeting of American Soc. Assoc., San Francisco, Calif., Aug. 26, 1975.

[9]Mason, Karen, Czajka, J. L., Arber S. "Change in U. S. Women's Sex-role Attitudes, 1964-1974." *American Sociological Review*, 41 (4): 573-596.

[10]Bardwick, J. M. *In Transition*. New York: Holt, Rinehart & Winston, 1979.

[11]Duncan, G. and Morgan, J. N. "The Incidence and Some Consequences of Major Life Events." See p. 147 of *Women's Lives* (as cited on p. 162 here).

[12]Bardwick, J. M. "Middle Age and a Sense of Future." *Merrill-Palmer Quarterly* 24(2): 128-138.

[13]Butler, N. R. "Prospects for Middle-Aged Women." (same as note 2), 323-333.

[14]Sommers, T. and Shields, L. "Problems of the displaced homemaker." (same as note 2), 86-106.

[15]Tatro, C. and Boles, J. "Developing New Careers and Financial Independence." (same as note 2), 190-201.

[16]Neugarten and Brown-Rezanka. "Midlife Women in the 1980s," 23-38.

[17]Barnett and Baruch. "On Being an Economic Provider," 69-82.

[18]Campbell, Angus. "Changes in Psychological Well-being During the 1970s: Homemakers and Employed Wives." See p. 291 of *Women's Lives* (as cited on p. 162 in this work).

CHAPTER 19

The Career Planning Process

John J. Leach

Seemingly, career planning as a *process* has received much less attention than the description of career planning tools, techniques and programs. Many personnel departments unwittingly insert career planning modules in the firm's overall program mix without first thinking through their connections with other personnel policies and practices.

This article discusses the notion of "career success" and the four underlying factors which are fundamental to any career planning program. The article concludes with several implications for the personnel function regarding career planning programs or career management systems.

DEFINING CAREER SUCCESS

The person preparing a career plan has career success as the major objective of his or her career. And the major criterion of a career plan is the attainment of career success. But what is "career success"? Career success is highly subjective, having as many meanings and definitions as there are people planning careers. There are four elements of the work experience that invariably generate the feeling and perception of personal career success:

Belonging. All individuals pursuing a career have a need to belong and a need for identification. In fact, a major cause of anxiety is the fear of exclusion from one or more perceived primary groups. As a process, sound career planning should provide the individual with the feeling that he or she "belongs" and can identify with a company, a profession, a department, a team or a project.

Growth. A career plan or career path that demonstrably helps a person to "stretch" and to extend his or her abilities and overall competence leads to a feeling of career success. Our careers represent competitive arenas. The challenge of one's work has the potential to satisfy this basic human development or growth need.

Self-Esteem. People have a basic need to "feel good" about themselves. This need is responsible for our ultimate levels of motivation. Regardless of our immediate career objectives, everything we do is to achieve a sense of adequacy, well-being and self-worth. A key ingredient of career success, then, is a job or career path where one's efforts are perceived to be useful and worthwhile.

Reprinted with the permission of *Personnel Journal*, Costa Mesa, California; copyright April 1981; all rights reserved.

Personal Significance. The last element of career success, which in a sense encompasses the first three elements, relates to whether one's work serves to give meaning and purpose to life. In this context, we can define career success as the ongoing search for personal significance. In the final analysis, all comparisons are social comparisions. Everyone is looking for that piece of turf that is theirs and no one else's. Everybody wants to be a "somebody." Fortunately, because people are different, everyone's definition of a "somebody" is relatively different. And because the world of work provides many different options, most people have choices regarding the meaning they will bring to and receive from their work.

Thus, a person is a success in his or her career to the extent that a career path provides a feeling that one belongs; ongoing challenge and growth; a feeling that one is useful and contributing; and perceived personal significance.

It is critically important to remember what is not included in the above definitions, namely, "getting ahead." Getting ahead is not always moving forward. Psychologically, career success can take place in one's existing job or assignment. To the extent this working definition of career success is exhibited in large numbers of employees within the firm — even within a firm with only modest career opportunities — that firm has a dedicated, committed and productive workforce.

The career planning process therefore, is not to be taken lightly. Career planning programs invariably alter, then elevate human expectations. By its very nature, once employees are asked to plan careers, the definition of career success discussed above rises to the conscious level, and the organization must be prepared to accommodate aspirations of employees.

THE CAREER PLANNING PROCESS

Career planning involves four fundamental elements which, when taken together, represent the career planning process:

Direction. This involves the career goals one sets and the Company's ability to act favorably upon these goals, especially in light of business objectives and realities.

Career Time. This relates to distance and velocity factors: how far one wants to go in an organization or on the career path and how fast the person expects to get there.

Transitions. This is the resistance one encounters while moving toward career goals. Transitions relate to the changes expected, say, in knowledge, skill and attitude enroute to a career goal.

Outcomes. This relates to the probabilities that one's investments and sacrifices for career progress will pay off.

DIRECTION OR GOAL SETTING

Goal setting has "push" and "pull" characteristics. The push feature relates to the employee's unique set of abilities, interests and values. The best career goal is that career path that totally taps into the employee's mix of what he or she does well, is of interest, and has intrinsic value. This is the first moment of truth in career planning.

The next moment of truth relates to whether the company can accommodate the employee's objectives or the pull characteristic of goal setting. The pull characteristic is sometimes quite difficult to assess. For example, most companies are not entirely sure what they will need in the way of human resources three, five or ten years from now. And even if a plan is in force, it is rarely communicated to the workforce. Yet, making an assessment of the pull characteristic is imperative.

The remaining combinations of push and pull are less desirable. For example, the high push/low pull combination suggests that the employee will hit his or her head against a brick wall. In this situation, either the company has many, many candidates for the opening the person seeks, hence the competition is fierce, or there is simply very little demand for the skill. In the low push/high pull combination, there are numerous company opportunities but if the employee pursues the option, there will be little, if any, genuine satisfaction because the activities of the work run counter to the person's real mix of skills, interests and values. The low push/low pull combination, of course, represents the dismal case. Here, even if the employee could develop high levels of skill and interests, the activity itself is not important to the company.

Sound goal-setting must attend to both sides of the equation: what the employee *really wants to do* versus what the company *really needs to have done*. Learning about one's push characteristics represents self-assessment. Learning about the pull characteristics represents company-assessment. Most employees are better prepared to perform the former analysis than the latter. Realistic and objective assessment of career goals, however, involves both analyses.

CAREER TIME

A simple physics formula for time is distance divided by velocity. In a sense, we all have career clocks and think of career progress in terms of career time: the distance we travel (typically upward) and the speed or velocity of advancement. Employees have built-in career clocks that tell them to reach a certain point in the organization, one should do this or that by say, age 34 or 45. In this case, employees are gauging their progress in terms of being "on schedule," "ahead of schedule" or "behind schedule." The key issue here is who are they comparing themselves to? It is wise for a person to keep his or her own schedule book. Usually, mature people tend to set realistic distance and velocity goals and realistic career time schedules. They recognize they are different from others (in terms of skills, interests and values) and keep a perspective regarding "getting ahead." They compete with themselves, not others.

Of all the career planning elements in this process, career time seems to give people the most trouble. What is a realistic schedule? What is rational or irrational? Are these career goals impulsive, insatiable, compulsive, too low or too high? While difficult to answer, the career planner must wrestle with the question. No plan, including a career plan, is worthy of the name without some targets or milestones to shoot for with respect to time. The career planning process is best served, however, with the employee calculates distance estimates (aspiration level) and velocity objectives (speed toward the goal) that are realistic and truly represent his or her own unique set of growth needs.

TRANSITIONS

Transitions are resistance factors that employees must overcome in order to make good their career plans. When employees want to advance in their careers, they frequently forget that they will have to make significant changes in their behavior relating to new knowledge, skills or approaches. It is a psychological fact-of-life that as people plan a career move, they tend to focus immediately on advancement (the reward) and not on the changes necessary to prepare them to play new and more responsible roles within the company. For example, many employees want to become supervisors or managers because of the status. But they fail to recognize the changes needed to cope with the more complex responsibilities. It is at this point in the career planning process that the notion of investment is introduced. In most career plans, there are numerous sacrifices involved. If one is expected to be prepared for more responsibility, one may have to expend more energy, more time, and perhaps even money in order to be ready.

Therefore, one major career planning process issue relates to precisely what price the employee is prepared to pay in order to change. Moreover, assuming the transition gap can be bridged, is the employee absolutely certain that he or she will be happy and satisfied in the new assignment? For example, there are people who ultimately learn to be managers, but if they are absolutely honest with themselves, they don't enjoy the role of management.

Transitions involve the most thinking and planning. It is a gap problem in terms of what it will take to leap to a different time and situation. Setting goals and a timetable only initiates the career planning process. The transition factors must be considered and analyzed in detail. Because it is very difficult to be absolutely objective, the person needs both information and feedback from others in order to calculate the transitions involved.

OUTCOMES

The last element of the career planning process relates to predicted and actual outcomes of the career plan. Predicted outcomes flow, at least indirectly, from an analysis of the transitions the person sees needing to take place to achieve a career objective. When considering predicted outcomes, the person must also calculate the *risks* attached to various actions in the career plan. Risk is the potential loss of something the person values: comfortable habits, confidence level, present knowledge, skill levels, and, of course, the probabilities of success or failure. When attempting to predict outcomes, the employee is well advised to seek out feedback from others who know the employee and from those people who have a fuller understanding of the company, what it really needs, and how it actually operates.

When there are high risks and high investments associated with a given career plan, it becomes immediately clear that the person is entering into a high stakes game, and the employee must be realistic and ascertain whether he or she is really prepared to play that game. At the other extreme, the low risk/low investment combination probably will produce a quick victory, but what has the person won? Will the employee really be challenged, and once the career goal is achieved, will the employee really feel a sense of satisfaction? If research is any guide, a career goal with a 50/50 chance of achievement is the most motivating. It is not so outlandish that, if achieved, it can be chalked up to "gambler's luck" and not so easy that anyone could make it. In other words, the career goals predicted to involve medium risk and medium investment represent better goals to select.

The actual outcomes are self-evident. These represent the facts of life. They will be sufficiently obvious to tell the employee whether he or she has set realistic goals and time-targets and whether the employee has judged correctly (or miscalculated) the various transitions involved. Over an extended career, even negative outcomes represent worthwhile information since most employees presumably learn from their mistakes.

IMPLICATIONS FOR
PERSONNEL MANAGERS

This article has attempted to direct the attention of personnel practitioners to the logic of career development. This logic needs to be considered in terms of the subjective notions of career success and the underlying dimensions of the career planning process. Is it possible that many personnel managers prematurely enter into career planning programs without first thinking through the implications? If so, this would account for the many career planning activities that meet with relative disappointment and, sometimes, out-and-out failure. Several illustrative traps that personnel managers fall into are noted below:

All problems of the firm are not career development problems. While research findings are sparse, it is very likely that less than one-third of any employee population is disgruntled solely because of career problems. Often, the career complaints of employees are simply thinly-disguised frustrations related to other aspects of the firm's policies and practices.

Many employee career complaints also relate to psychological culture and climate features of the firm. Introducing career planning programs into these situations represents a poor investment of time, money and energy. Organization development programs, on the other hand, may be an excellent investment because root causes—such as dysfunctional operating philosophies, inappropriate leadership styles, malfunctioning norms, rituals and rules—not symptoms, are being addressed.

The higher employees advance within the hierarchy, the more candidates there are for fewer and fewer position openings. Career planning programs that even implicitly promise continued and unending upward mobility simply cannot live up to that promise. Most firms, however, can attend to and improve those areas related to career success by providing work and programs that allow employees the feeling of belonging and identification, the opportunity for growth, heightened levels of self-esteem, and some sense of personal significance. A great deal of career development can take place in existing jobs if these subjective dimensions of career success are attended to by personnel and the line organization.

Many personnel departments introduce career planning programs without first anticipating the new roles that supervision will have to play. For example, as large numbers of employees within a firm begin to participate in career planning, the probabilities increase that these people will look to their bosses to critique their career plans. This is a new role for the supervisor because he or she must now act as a "career coach." Clearly, the personnel function should prepare supervisors for this role or run the risk that the career planning efforts of individual employees will fail.

IMPLEMENTATION

When it is relevant to invest in career planning programs, it is well advised to include the career planning dimensions discussed in this article. For example, programs that focus solely on the "push" characteristics of the direction or goal-setting component are insufficient. There is more to career planning than the "who am I?" question. Similarly, job clarification instruments represent only the beginnings of a program. All four dimensions of the career planning process must be included in a career planning program: direction, career time, transitions and outcome analyses.

The firm entering into career planning programs for the first time must have in place personnel support activities that assist employees to analyze "pull" characteristics of their career plans. For example, the firm should have a human resources planning data base (short and longer term); high-grade career information related to actual requirements of jobs; career pathing and job-family data (what leads to what); and open-posting. Without these "pull" or demand inputs, employees may prepare the most insightful career plans, but they may be at variance with the goals and intentions of the organization.

In many firms, there is an intact apparatus to deal with the career time, transition and outcome dimensions of the career planning process, if only the personnel function would direct corporate attention to it and assist in coordinating and consolidating the data. These existing programs include MBO programs, performance appraisals, assessment center findings and attitude survey data. Too frequently these programs operate in isolation from each other and make little contribution toward improving career planning within the firm. One quick example relates to assessment center data. If a relatively large number of employees going through an assessment center are collectively assessed marginal in terms of needed job skills, there is a company-wide training need. These data, however, also shed light on a company-wide career planning needs related to transition projections, and need to be analyzed as potential self-development needs.

CHAPTER 20

Plateau

Ellen Bernstein and John Leach

A survey of more than 1,400 ALA members on needs for career development has concluded that career satisfaction for substantial numbers of librarians in the 1980s will have to take place in existing jobs. Although some one-third of the respondents feel they will move satisfactorily toward their goals, many librarians believe they will have to wrestle with limited opportunities for career advancement. In career development literature, this phenomenon is called a "plateaued condition."

CAREER DEVELOPMENT AND TRAINING

Career obstacles. Thirty percent of survey respondents cited lack of available jobs as a major concern in this area. Relocation concerns ranked second (22%). A cluster of concerns ranked third and were related to achieving financial security (13%), internal (office) politics (10%), and difficulty gaining needed experience (10%). Approximately one-fifth of the total sample expressed no concerns about career obstacles. This last group was largely made up of librarians with over 20 years of experience, males, and senior management subgroups.

Respondents from the different library settings included in the sample (public, school, academic, and special) all ranked lack of available jobs as their primary concern. Special librarians appeared to be slightly more concerned than other types of librarians with achieving financial security and with "politics." Public librarians appeared to be more concerned than other librarians with difficulty gaining needed experience. Eighty percent of all types of librarians feel there are not good career opportunities where they work.

Achievement of career goals. Respondents assessed the probability that they would achieve their career goals. Fifty-one percent of all respondents predicted their career would take the direction they wished it to. Specifically, 32% felt they would make a move in a desired direction (to a larger library, management, etc.); 16% felt that they would remain in present jobs and wished to do so; and 3% would retire and wished to do so.

Conversely, 41% predicted they would not achieve their desired career goals. Of these, approximately one-third (32%) indicated they would remain on their present jobs, but did not wish to; 7% would change jobs, but the change would not be to a desired position or organization; and 2% would retire but did not wish to retire. Eight percent of the total sample predicted they would "leave librarianship." This 8% figure was consistent across all sub-groups analyzed.

Job satisfaction. One section of the survey dealt with motivation in the work setting. The majority of the sample (82%) selected challenging/varied work as the most important factor in job satisfaction. Opportunities for growth/advancement and independence/autonomy were ranked second and third in importance respectively (45% and 38%). High salary was ranked second to last by the total sample (20%). Least important to respondents was authority/influence over others (3%). Clearly "salary" and "power" are not significant factors in job satisfaction. These patterns were similar for all librarians responding, regardless of type of library, years of experience, and management or nonmanagement positions sampled.

Why people become librarians. The reasons most often cited by the total sample regarding attraction to the profession were: "Love of books/reading," "Worked in a library and liked it," "Education/academic environment," and "Desire to work with/serve others." The second group of reasons included "An alternative to teaching," "Influence of a librarian," and "Interest in research."

Training needs. Regarding adequacy of library school training, slightly under half of all respondents agreed that the training they received was very good preparation for work they are doing. New librarians and school librarians were the most favorably disposed to their academic training. Least satisfied was the senior management group (in terms of preparation for their current management jobs.)

Computer and technology training and management development training (59% and 50% respectively) were most frequently mentioned as areas in which professional development is needed. The need for interpersonal skill training and for subject training (science, business, language, etc.) was noted by 20% of the total sample. Fourteen percent cited career planning as a professional need. (Because respondents could select two content areas, the percentages above total over 100%.)

The need for interpersonal skill training increased in importance with each succeeding seniority group (under 3, 3-10, 11-20 and over 20 years of service). The need for career planning programs decreased in importance with each succeeding seniority group.

For professional development, librarians would most likely participate in workshops and seminars (71% of the total sample). Professional association activities and reading professional journals ranked second (38% and 35% respectively). Regular university courses were noted by 24% of the sample; home study programs and computerized, programmed instruction were selected by 10% and 8%, respectively.

IMPLICATIONS FOR LIBRARIES

As noted above, librarians are most motivated by challenging and varied work. High salary and the need to have authority or power over others fall at the bottom of their list of motivators. Advancement was ranked second as a motivator, although this option was listed on the questionnaire as the "opportunity for growth/advancement." Would "growth" without "advancement" be equally motivating? Perhaps this question should be explored further because it relates to how librarians feel about being "plateaued" in their careers.

Independence, autonomy, the opportunity to serve, job security, the opportunity to innovate, and pleasant coworkers were factors checked by 25% or more of the respondents as motivators. We conclude that, with the exception of advancement and job security, these motivators are controllable and are, in large measure, under the control of senior management in library organizations.

Senior management librarians, therefore, are challenged — perhaps as never before — to find new ways to motivate staff who do not have access to traditional rewards such as promotions. These new approaches (e.g., quality circles, job enrichment, opportunity to innovate, team building, etc.) will most likely require acquisition of new knowledge and skills by all levels of managers in library organizations. This is a distinctive and pressing need in management development training.

Perhaps one of the most surprising findings in the study as that a large number of respondents want feedback regarding job-related strengths and weaknesses. The conclusion here is that many libraries need to re-examine and improve their performance appraisal and performance feedback systems.

IMPLICATIONS FOR ALA

While librarians, regardless of sub-group analyzed, are remarkably alike in several respects (why they are attracted to the profession; what they seek most in their work, etc), in other respects they are quite different from one another. For example, the data suggest that entry-level libarians, the 3-10 year seniority group, nonmanagement people, and public and school librarians are more frequently troubled by career concerns and obstacles. These librarians need more help in career development areas than the over-20-year seniority group, senior management, or academic and special librarians.

ALA might also assist senior management in acquiring the skills necessary to motivate their staffs in the areas discussed above.

There appear to be numerous opportunities for ALA to exercise leadership in creating programs and services in areas of management development and career development for specific segments of its membership.

Note: As a result of the consultants' recommendations, the OLPR Advisory Committee has established a task force to explore these findings more fully and to develop additional career development activities. A copy of the survey report may be requested from OLPR, ALA, 50 E. Huron St., Chicago, IL 60611 for $2 prepaid.

WHY THIS STUDY?

The Chicago Consulting Center was asked to conduct a survey of American Library Association members[1] regarding career development needs, problems, and plans. The study was prepared for the ALA Office for Library Personnel Resources (OLPR). The survey results are intended to assist OLPR in planning future career development services and programs for ALA members and others in the profession.

---

[1]ALA has approximately 40,000 members. In selecting the sample for this survey, student members, foreign librarians, other special categories, and retirees were eliminated from the membership list, reducing the size of the list to approximately 25,200. A random sample of 10 percent was drawn from this list. A total of 2,519 questionnaires were mailed and 1,402 or 56 percent were completed and returned.

The study was designed to answer: 1) why people are attracted to library careers; 2) what librarians seek most in their careers 3) what career plans librarians have; 4) what they perceive as obstacles to attainment of career goals; and 5) what they think about general career issues, e.g., adequacy of academic preparation, career progress, relocation, continuing education, etc.

Major OLPR planning issues guiding the study included: 1) how heterogeneous is the ALA membership regarding career development needs and what are the implications for ALA programs and initiatives? and 2) when there are negative career development factors surrounding librarianship, which are within ALA's capabilities to address and remedy?

CHAPTER 21

Mentoring for Leadership

Marsha A. Burruss-Ballard

> *Mentors take risks with people. They bet initially on talent they perceive in younger people. Mentors also risk emotional involvement in working closely with their juniors. The risks do not always pay off, but the willingness to take them appears crucial in developing leaders.* (Zaleznik, 76)

A mentor is a seasoned professional who takes an active interest in the career development of a younger or less experienced professional. The mentor, by turns, serves as a teacher, sponsor, protector, promoter, coach, counselor, and role model. In my own career, someone took the risk of becoming my mentor, and it has been one of the most valuable and important factors in the development of my professional and leadership abilities. I am no longer a novice to the library profession, and my mentor and I have parted. However, I have retained a lasting appreciation for this individual and a great support for and interest in the process of mentoring. The library field is full of talented professionals and leaders, and mentoring is one avenue for sharing and developing this talent in other members of the profession.

What are the benefits to the mentor, the protégé, and the library organization that make the mentor/protégé function worth developing? What besides the ability to take risks does it take to be a mentor? What does the protégé need to bring to the relationship? What specific communication skills can facilitate the mentoring process? How does the quality of communication within the organization affect the success of the mentor/protégé relationship? What steps can librarians take to insure more mentoring within the profession? This chapter is an exploration of the answers to these questions.

BENEFITS OF MENTORING

Mentoring can be a mutually enhancing relationship for both individuals involved. Having a protégé can assist in the mentor's job performance. The protégé can help with projects and work assignments, provide fresh ideas and feedback, and free up time for the mentor to fulfill other responsibilities (Zey 80). The mentor may also find that mentoring develops his or her own reputation as a leader and speeds advancement within the organization:

> When [protégés] perform well, [they] reflect favorably upon [their] mentors. This serves to validate [the] mentors' worth and good judgment—not only to themselves, but in the eyes of their bosses. (Phillips-Jones 55)

Organizations value managers who can attract and develop bright, hard-working individuals. Furthermore, having someone who knows how to do the mentor's job provides that individual with the possibility of moving to higher levels of responsibility without leaving a hole within the organization.

The rewards for the mentor are not all in terms of career support and advancement. There are also psychic rewards. Mentors develop greater self-esteem and competence by sharing their knowledge and skills with someone who admires and values their advice and counsel (Kram 7). In addition, the challenge and stimulation of assisting in another's career can provide increased job satisfaction for the mentor:

> The mentor is doing something for himself. He is making productive use of his own knowledge and skills in middle age. He is learning in ways not otherwise thought possible. He is maintaining his connection with the forces of youthful energy in the world and in himself. He needs the recipient of mentoring as much as the recipient needs him. (Levinson 253)

While being mentored, the protégé will work hard, but will also find that mentoring provides an education and opportunities for growth unavailable in the typical graduate school of library science. My own experience as a protégé is typical of the benefits available. Mentors provide advice and support for career goals. My mentor and I evaluated my professional strengths and weaknesses. She then helped me map out strategies to enhance my technical and people skills. She provided me with opportunities and challenging work assignments. She allowed me access to information and resources and treated me as a peer. She gave me the freedom to fail, but also the help and advice to keep me from making the same mistakes again. She supported my progress and growth as a professional and encouraged me to attempt tasks I might have otherwise thought myself incapable of accomplishing. She introduced me to her network of contacts within the library profession. She invited me to attend professional meetings with her and occasionally allowed me to attend in her place. She increased my exposure and visibility within the organization and taught me about its structure, politics, and people. This information was often crucial to my job performance and would have taken a great deal of time to assimilate on my own. She critiqued, counseled, and corrected. Her character, integrity, and friendship provided me with a role model professionally and personally.

Because mentoring can have such influence on the lives and careers of the mentor and the protégé, it also affects and benefits the organization. In *The Mentor Connection*, Michael Zey identifies a number of ways in which mentoring helps the organization:

> through mentoring the goals, moral precepts, cultural tastes, and prescriptions of the organization become more acceptable to the young manager. He feels that he is being introduced to these concepts and values, not impersonally, but by a "friend." (Zey 95)

By integrating the individual and recognizing his or her potential, frustration is lessened and turnover is reduced. The protégé also serves as a communications link between levels of the organization. The protégé operates on one level while at the same time having access to information and viewpoints taking place at the mentor's level. In this way, communication can flow up and down between organizational levels. Another organizational benefit of mentoring is that it enables the transfer of skills from the senior to the junior member.

This in turn facilitates managerial succession. Finally, mentoring benefits the organization in terms of productivity. It helps create an environment in which ideas can be "developed, nurtured, experimented with, and successfully introduced." (Zey 106)

CHARACTERISTICS OF MENTORS AND PROTÉGÉS

Nancy W. Collins, in *Professional Women and Their Mentors*, identifies five characteristics as necessary for an individual to function as a mentor. First, the mentor must be higher up the organizational ladder than the protégé. Second, the mentor must possess greater experience and knowledge of the profession than the protégé. Often this means that the mentor is older, but it is greater experience and not necessarily age which is the factor. Third, the mentor must have influence and "be close to the lines of authority and power" (Collins 7). The degree of influence and power may vary within the levels of the organization. Fourth, the mentor must be sincerely interested in the growth and development of the protégé. The mentor is recognizing the protégé's potential, and he or she should like and respect this person. Fifth, the mentor must be willing to commit time and emotion to the relationship. "There is mutual trust and caring, confidentiality, and a willingness to develop and foster the relationship" (Collins 7-8). In addition to these five factors, one other element must be present: access. The mentor and protégé must have opportunities for frequent interaction.

Even with these factors present the individual contemplating mentoring for the first time should examine his or her motives and goals before initiating a mentor/protégé relationship. The prospective mentor should identify why he or she wants to be a mentor and what his or her expectations are in terms of his or her own career needs. "The person who can command respect through performance, professional stature or interpersonal abilities is perceived as a good mentor candidate" (Zey 169). Each individual should review what he or she can contribute in terms of skills and experience, and honestly assess both strengths and weaknesses.

Answering the following questions can assist in this review:

1. Are you good at what you do?

2. Are you able to teach and share your knowledge with others?

3. Are you able to encourage and motivate others?

4. Are you able to recognize talent?

5. Are you able to be demanding?

6. Are you able to be supportive?

7. Do you set high performance standards?

8. Are you willing to share credit with another individual?

9. Are you able to publicize a protégé's achievements?

10. Are you able to let go when the time comes? (Phillips-Jones 188; Missirian 91)

If after completing this self-review, the prospective mentor is ready to go forward, the next step is to develop a set of criteria identifying desired characteristics in a protégé. These criteria will, of course, vary from individual to individual. Some mentors seek protégés similar to themselves; others seek protégés whose talents complement their own. Once these criteria are established, the mentor should measure the qualifications of prospective protégés against them.

How does the librarian who wants to become a protégé get the recognition of a mentor? Most protégés are "not sitting patiently at their desks waiting to be 'discovered' " (Missirian 97). They are hard at work within their organizations developing their professional skills. The following are some of the characteristics identified as attracting a mentor to a protégé:

1. Intelligence

2. Enthusiasm

3. Ambition

4. Loyalty

5. Dedication

6. Integrity

7. Professional competence

8. A desire to learn

9. Commitment to the organization

10. Ability to accept responsibility

11. Ability to take initiative

12. Ability to work with others

13. Ability to listen

14. Ability to ask for guidance

15. Willingness to speak up and at times to disagree (Zey 175, 182; Missirian 98; Phillips-Jones 98-99)

One of the most important things prospective protégés can do is to recognize they want to be developed:

> You must know you need special coaching or grooming and be willing to learn for this kind of relationship to develop. Be willing to admit you don't know everything about certain areas. It is also important not to get caught up in a mentor's style that is not your own. It is necessary to be yourself. You can observe someone else's pattern, but you need to be comfortable in developing your own style against their framework (Collins 36).

INTERPERSONAL COMMUNICATION AND MENTORING

"Mentoring ... is an interpersonal exchange requiring one-to-one communication skills ... With such a personal approach, communication must be open and trusting, objective, and frank as well as helpful" (Conroy and Jones 40-41). The functions of mentoring are limited or enhanced to the extent that the individuals in the mentor/protégé relationship have mastered communication skills such as active listening, giving and receiving feedback, counseling, coaching, and managing conflict and disagreement (Kram 41).

Listening involves the attempt to understand and interpret what others are saying from their point of view. We must ascertain both the literal meaning and the intention of the message. People spend more time on listening than on any other aspect of communication, but few people have any real training in how to listen. As a result "research shows that most people listen at twenty-five percent efficiency. That doesn't mean they actually heard twenty-five percent of what was said; that means of what they heard, they got twenty-five percent of it right" (Conroy and Jones 114). Listening is not a passive activity, and one way of improving our ability is to practice active listening.

Active listening involves listening to a speaker with the intention of understanding the message from the speaker's point of view. Often instead of listening to the speaker, the listener begins to evaluate and think about the speaker's motive or to think about how to respond. These dilemmas can be avoided by practicing the strategies of active listening. First, anticipate where the conversation is leading. Second, objectively consider the statements being made. Third, mentally review and summarize what is being said. Fourth, be attentive to nonverbal as well as verbal messages. Fifth, use techniques such as paraphrasing, probing, and perception checking to test whether the message has been received accurately.

Paraphrasing involves restating back to the speaker what you believe has been said. For example, "What I hear you saying is ..." It is not merely parroting back to the individual the words just spoken. The purpose is to show the other person how well you understand the message, not whether you agree or disagree with it. Therefore, paraphrasing should be descriptive rather than evaluative. In addition to clarifying meaning, paraphrasing also helps the other individual know the listener is interested.

Probing is the use of clarifying questions by the listener to verify the speaker's message. Questions such as, "Do I understand you to mean ...?" are clarifying. They allow the listener to paraphrase the speaker and give the speaker the opportunity to correct any misconceptions. This process also communicates to the speaker that you are indeed listening and are interested in understanding, rather than just hearing, what is being said.

Perception checking relates to the feelings which are being communicated by the message. It is a measure of the emotional content rather than the ideas being stated. Instead of describing what the speaker has said, the listener attempts to describe what he or she believes the speaker is feeling. The purpose is to identify the speaker's feelings, not to judge, evaluate, or interpret them. Often feelings are incorrectly identified by the listener; therefore, it is important to check these perceptions.

Feedback is the response which the receiver of the message gives back to the sender. It indicates that the listener has received the message and allows him or her to clarify the message's meaning. Feedback can be utilized most effectively if the following guidelines are considered:

1. Feedback should be timely. Feedback given too late can be ineffective. Feedback is most effective when given as soon as possible after the message is received. It should also be given at a time when the individual receiving it is attentive and listening.

2. Feedback should be descriptive rather than evaluative. It should involve a clear report of the facts, not an analysis of them. Evaluate only if asked to do so and when it is appropriate.

3. Feedback should be offered not imposed. Does the other individual want feedback?

4. Feedback should take into account the needs of the receiver.

5. Feedback should be specific rather than general.

6. Feedback should be focused on things which can be changed.

7. Feedback should be given to be helpful.

If you are the individual desiring feedback, you can assist the other individual by clearly stating exactly what it is you would like feedback about. Once the feedback has been given, clarify that you have heard the message accurately. Share your responses to the feedback. Let the other individual know what was helpful and how it was helpful.

In counseling:

> the individual finds a forum in which to talk openly about anxieties, fears, and ambivalence that detract from productive work. The more experienced senior colleague provides a sounding board for this self-exploration, offers personal experience as an alternative perspective, and helps resolve problems through feedback and active listening (Kram 36).

When acting as a counselor, the role of the mentor is to listen, observe, and clarify. It is not to evaluate nor to give advice. The counselor's goal is to help the protégé realize he or she can develop solutions for dealing with problems.

Coaching is another communication role sometimes assumed by the mentor. Coaching implies working with someone to help that person perform at higher levels. The mentor offers specific feedback about how the protégé can improve. It can involve sharing knowledge about how to improve a presentation, whom to contact for information, or how to handle increased job responsibilities. The mentor is showing the protégé how to do something better.

The ability to manage conflict and disagreement is one of the most vital skills of leadership.

> Conflict is a completely natural activity. It is a healthy activity that promotes creativity and forces people to defend their positions and to strive for what will most benefit them and perhaps in the long run, the organization. Conflict should be avoided only when it is nonproductive. (Bogard 115)

In *Improving Communication in the Library*, Conroy and Jones state that "Communication is very often what gets us into conflict in the first place, and it can also be what keeps the conflict going or resolves it" (Conroy and Jones 101). They offer these methods for using communication to help end conflict:

1. Examine the language individuals use to describe the conflict. Then try to get them to change their perception of the conflict by re-labeling it. Disasters, battles, and stand-offs can also be referred to as challenges, opportunities for change, or just problems.

2. Put active listening to use. Be clear about exactly what is being said and what is not being said. Charged emotions often distort the ability to listen perceptively.

3. Check your perceptions with the other individual. Attempt to clarify and amplify your understanding of him. This can begin to identify where the conflict lies.

4. State the other side's position as articulately as you can and demonstrate the ability to listen accurately and be objective.

5. State your position in terms of "I" messages rather then "You" messages. Claim ownership for your feelings rather than placing the responsibility for them on others.

6. Describe your own feelings to help others understand your nonverbal messages.

7. Clarify the goals and purposes of each side in the disagreement. Establish criteria for evaluating proposed solutions in terms of these goals and purposes.

8. Try to identify and emphasize areas of agreement.

9. Break large conflicts into sub-issues and address these smaller issues one at a time rather than trying to resolve everything at once. (Conroy and Jones 101-103)

These skills in active listening, giving and receiving feedback, counseling, coaching, and managing conflict and disagreement are bases for establishing relationships which can lead to mentoring:

> The lack of self-awareness and interpersonal skills limits the availability of mentor relationships ... If individuals do not understand what they need for relationships and developmental opportunities, they will be unable to actively manage their careers. (Kram 199)

COMMUNICATION WITHIN THE ORGANIZATION

The nature of the organization can either encourage or discourage the development of mentor relationships. Kathy Kram identifies certain conditions which must exist before the benefits of mentoring can be realized:

1. There need to be opportunities for frequent and open interaction between managers at different career stages and hierarchical levels.

2. Individuals must have the interpersonal skills to create and sustain helpful relationships. They must also have an interest in and desire to do this.

3. The "organization's reward system, culture and norms must value and encourage relationship building activities." (Kram 160)

Obstacles occur when the organization does not value the development of human resources, and the design of work can also influence how relationships develop. Work which is highly individualized makes it difficult to initiate relationships. In contrast, collaborative projects or team work can help to foster the development of supportive relationships:

> Equally important are the culture's values about the kinds of communication, the degree to which individuals can trust each other (particularly at different hierarchical levels), and the extent to which openness and trust are valued. When the culture perpetuates closed and superficial communication, and when a lack of trust for those in authority prevails, it is difficult to provide mentoring functions. Meaningful coaching, counseling, friendship, and role modeling are almost impossible in a situation characterized by low trust and minimal communication (Kram 164).

The final obstacle to mentoring is the failure to communicate and to create an awareness of its potential.

ROLE OF LIBRARIANS

It is unrealistic to expect that all newcomers to the library profession will have mentors, but those of us who are interested in and value mentoring can take steps to see that more of it takes place. I support the statement that "the mentor relationship can perhaps be facilitated but not legislated" (Shapiro 56). I do not believe that the answer to more and better mentoring lies in formal programs in which mentors and protégés are assigned to one another. I believe that the answer lies in the preparations we make, our ability to risk initiating relationships, and our desire to help one another become better at what we do. We can encourage the development of better interpersonal and communication skills through education and practice. We can examine or organizational structures to see if they promote collaboration and teamwork, and we can encourage organizational climates which value and reward the development of human resources. In these ways we can promote leadership through mentoring.

REFERENCES

Bogard, Morris R. *The Manager's Handbook: Communication Skills to Improve Your Performance*. Englewood Cliffs, N.J.: Prentice-Hall, 1979.

Collins, Nancy W. *Professional Women and Their Mentors*. Englewood Cliffs, N.J.: Prentice-Hall, 1983.

Conroy, Barbara, and Barbara Schindler Jones. *Improving Communication in the Library*. Phoenix, Ariz.: Oryx Press, 1986.

Kram, Kathy E. *Mentoring at Work: Developmental Relationships in Organizational Life.* Glenview, Ill.: Scott, Foresman and Company, 1985.

Levinson, D. et al. *Season's of a Man's Life.* New York: Knopf, 1978.

Missirian, Agnes K. *The Corporate Connection: Why Executive Women Need Mentors to Reach the Top.* Englewood Cliffs, N.J.: Prentice-Hall, 1982.

Phillips-Jones, Linda. *Mentors and Proteges.* New York: Arbor House, 1982.

Shapiro, Ellen, Florence Haseltine, and Mary P. Rowe. "Moving Up: Role Models, Mentors, and the 'Patron System'," *Sloan Management Review* (Spring 1978): 51-58.

Zaleznik, Abraham. "Managers and Leaders: Are They Different?" *Harvard Business Review* (May/June 1977): 55, 67-78.

Zey, Michael G. *The Mentor Connection.* Homewood, Ill.: Dow Jones-Irwin, 1984.

Libraries, Technology, and Change
The Leadership Challenge

Introduction

*All service institutions are threatened by the tendencies to cling to yester-
day rather than slough it off, and to put their best and ablest people on
defending what no longer makes sense or serves a purpose.*
     —Peter F. Drucker
     Management: Tasks, Responsibilities, Practices

One can assess the library and information science profession from an indefinite number of perspectives. One could argue, probably successfully, that this is truly the best of times for the field. Extraordinary strides have been taken in the application of new technologies to library programs and services, in resource sharing and networking, and in the integration of print and nonprint formats. At least one writer has stated that the new technology has changed not only *how* libraries do things, but even *what* they do. Conversely, one might argue with equal force and validity that we are in the midst of the worst of times. Because of the forces of inflation and dollar devaluation, library acquisition rates are declining, competition from other information providers is significantly increasing, and attempts to censor and to erect barriers to information access seem to be rising precipitously. However, no one would argue that these are not very turbulent times.

The forces of change—technological developments, political and social pressures, monetary trends, and other factors—are felt in libraries on a daily basis. At the same time, new demands and responsibilities are added to the shoulders of library managers as their organizations are asked to do more, without corresponding increases in support. In some cases, it has been suggested that libraries attempt to redefine themselves or modify their missions so as to provide what are alleged to be greater benefits to the communities that they serve.

One director of a research library recently described these trends as having a "decentering" effect on the library. That is to say that libraries may no longer be viewed as central to the mission of higher education and research, or if they are, they share the center, of which they might once have had singular possession, with other entities. Some administrators believe that they need to focus resources on those programs which provide more immediate and tangible returns on investment. It is difficult for them to take the long view, particularly when the tenure of top administrators is relatively brief (five to seven years). Furthermore, there are few programs that require as much investment and careful development over an extended period as do research library collections. Those who want to see results tomorrow will focus resources on other programs.

Not too many years ago it was commonplace for public, academic, and school libraries to benefit from end-of-fiscal year funding windfalls. Some college and university library directors were so confident of getting leftover dollars that they used to build these monies into their budgets. For the most part, such events are now a thing of the past, not because of the absence of such funding, but because of the intense competition for these funds.

In retrospect, it seems that two or three decades ago librarianship was a less ambiguous profession. There seemed to be clearer answers to our questions, a firmer notion of the role which libraries should play in society, and greater unity of purpose within the field. Some would argue that that was a period of great professional leadership, a period in which senior statesmen and women articulated a vision of librarianship which invited participation and provided individual professionals with a sense of both mission and pride.

Each of us has our own honor roll of heroes and heroines, but most would probably include the likes of Ralph Shaw, Lowell Martin, Fred Kilgour, Mary Gaver, Robert Downs, and Allie Beth Martin. It seems much more difficult to name librarians of equal caliber today. Of course, the passage of time causes one to emphasize a leader's strong points and minimize his or her deficiencies. One need only consider the rehabilitation of Richard Nixon to appreciate this.

Is the library and information science profession experiencing a leadership gap? Richard Dougherty suggests in an editorial on library leadership that it is. But regardless of one's position on this question, all would agree that it is not possible to have a surfeit of leadership. Consequently, it is essential that strong efforts be taken first, to nurture and develop whatever leadership currently exists in the library profession, and second, to attract persons with leadership potential into the field.

Elsewhere in this book the point is made that while certain personal traits tend to be associated with leaders, the key element in leadership development is an environment or context in which personal and professional growth is stimulated and developed. For example, it is said that risk-taking behavior is a characteristic of strong leaders. Obviously, no one is going to take risks in an organization which prizes perfect harmony and group-think.

Due to the increased pace of change, libraries cannot afford to wait until new leaders are recruited into the profession. Of course, recruitment is important; the quality of professional staff is the key not only to libraries' present success, but to their future success as well. However, most library managers must try to do the best they can with the staff presently available. Lou Holtz is quoted as saying that every coach must try to win with the team that's on the field. This is perhaps the most compelling case that can be made for implementing innovative staff development programs. Keys to success include creativity in realizing staff potential, the ability to uncover latent talents, and providing an array of opportunities for personal and professional growth.

The readings included in this section were selected because they offer various perspectives on the leadership challenge facing libraries. Robin Downes presents a case for the library as an entrepreneurial organization. He begins by arguing that innovation in any organization is most often the product of the culture of that organization. If staff can be convinced that they can determine the destiny of the organization; if they hold the requisite values; if they are committed to quality, service, and innovation, the library organization will most likely be successful.

One "test" discussed by Downes to demonstrate the organization's readiness for change and the ability of management and staff to respond to new technologies and innovation was the introduction of an integrated library system (ILS) into the library. The author states that an ILS touches almost every library program, and the decision to acquire an ILS is the first of a series of steps which, if the opportunity is taken, will teach staff more about the economics and organization of libraries than most will have previously known. In this environment, "programs would not be funded because they were sure bets, but because they were interesting and showed promise of improved service or reduced costs."

In effect, Downes is calling for a new model of library service, one that requires that we take greater control of the environments in which we operate. He suggests that through entrepreneurial behavior, successful libraries will capitalize on new technologies and use them as a basis for improved user services and heightened productivity.

While Robin Downes sets forth some important concepts relative to the management of innovation in libraries, Patricia Battin describes a highly service-intensive library of the future in "The Electronic Library — A Vision for the Future." Like Downes, she begins by stressing the importance of not simply exploring the role of computers on the campus, but of integrating information technology into the organization's infrastructure in a way that "preserves the linkages to the existing knowledge base, encourages and stimulates the productive use of new technologies, and provides coordinated gateway access to the universe of knowledge in a manner convenient and invisible to the end user." Battin emphasizes that one of the important characteristics of libraries has been freedom of choice for the user: the control of the system has been principally in the hands of the user. It is important that in whatever new systems emerge, the needs of the individual scholar be recognized. Battin then describes three generations of library computing, each of which has built or will build upon the preceding application. The first of these was the application of computing and telecommunication technologies to library processing. The second was the development of integrated local systems, and the third will focus on the scholar's workstation, to enable the selective downloading and interactive manipulation of information by the end user. However, the pace of innovation in this area has already outstripped efforts to control it, and consequently both the library profession and scholars generally are faced with proliferating databases, incompatible hardware and software systems, continual expansion of printed publications (often on poor-quality paper), uncoordinated indexing systems, and "the unacceptable intrusion into the academic enterprise of economic discrimination governing access to scholarly information." To address these and related problems, the author proposed the creation of a Scholarly Information Center merging the campus libraries with the computing center. This article is extremely provocative, and challenges us to take a fresh look at the information systems of which libraries are an essential part.

Many of the points argued in "Leadership Versus Management in Technical Services" apply with equal validity to all library services, and this is why this reading was included in this volume. Riggs has a thorough grasp of management literature and combines this knowledge with the ability to apply it to library settings.

He succeeds in taking some fairly abstract concepts — for example, transformational leadership, power, and vision — and providing concrete applications or examples to which most librarians will easily relate. He stresses the need for all managers to engage in strategic planning, and suggests that effective planning is the key to both entrepreneurial behavior and effective staff development. He concludes the article by presenting a very personal view of leadership (what it is and what it is not), and then proceeds to identify a few key traits that all true leaders have in common: a positive self-regard, compassion, and the ability to motivate and inspire. Most library managers and leaders (actual and potential) will benefit from Riggs's many insights and learn from his special ability to relate theory to practice.

In 1979 Miriam Drake published a very provocative and prescient article on the changes that are affecting libraries. "Managing Innovation in Academic Libraries," hit a number of chords similar to those struck by Robin Downes. Her thesis is that fundamental changes in the economics and technology of academic libraries have stimulated librarians to seek ways of introducing and implementing innovation in libraries. She begins by examining the sometimes wide gap that is found between a library's aspirations and user expectations on the one hand, and actual performance on the other. The lack of congruence between objectives and performance could call for a number of remedies, but the author argues that innovation strategies should be given priority consideration. Innovation in this context is not a device or a scheme. Rather, it represents a change in human behavior. This change may be the adoption of a new technology or it may be a new managerial or social process. In either case, it relies heavily on human perceptions of a better future.

There are, of course, numerous obstacles to innovation and change, the more salient of which are discussed by Drake. These include psychological and organizational factors, economic constraints, and political issues that must be resolved. Yet libraries must change, and those which aspire to be most successful will inevitably become innovative organizations. The responsibility for creating the climate for change rests with management. However, management should not be viewed as having a monopoly on innovation. "Ideally, innovative ideas should originate at both ends of an organizational hierarchy."

Although this discussion first appeared several years ago, it continues to be relevant to the turbulent period in which we currently find ourselves. Certainly some of the applications have changed, and were the article to be written today, different examples would be cited. Nevertheless, the basic message would remain the same, and for this reason, it was included.

While it is important to understand the theories underlying organizational behavior and leadership, it is even more important to have concrete examples of how such theories might be implemented in the day-to-day operation of a library. Two authors – Judy Labovitz and Meryl Swanigan – have made a special contribution to the literature of librarianship in their highly personal accounts ("Managing a Special Library," Parts I and II) of their leadership experiences and operating styles. Labovitz emphasizes the importance of having a bias towards action, a genuine concern for people accompanied by a commitment to staff development, and extraordinary commitment to the user. Specific examples are presented which illustrate how these values are introduced into the library organization. Two other points which the author highlights are the need to measure results (measurement is important in establishing the manager's credibility), and the importance of thinking in terms of options (for example, what if one's favorite plan is scratched?).

Meryl Swanigan picks up on several of the points made by Labovitz and elaborates upon them. Her main thesis is that libraries are prime targets for excellence. She claims that with leadership and commitment to certain values, librarians can become masters of their own fate and develop their organizations as true centers of excellence. She cites many of the principles espoused by Thomas J. Peters and Robert H. Waterman in *In Search of Excellence* (New York: Harper & Row, 1982), and expounds upon them. Because of the very personal manner in which Swanigan presents her ideas, the reader is left with feelings of encouragement and the motivation to become more productive and innovative, and to make the library more essential to its parent organization.

ADDITIONAL READINGS

Bundy, Mary Lee. "Automation as Innovation." *Drexel Library Quarterly* 4 (October 1968): 317-28.

Dionne, Richard J. "Science Libraries at a Crossroads." *American Scientist* 76 (May/June 1988): 268-72.

Dougherty, Richard M. "Libraries and Computing Centers: A Blueprint for Collaboration." *College & Research Libraries* 48 (July 1987): 289-96.

Fine, Sara F. "Technological Innovation, Diffusion and Resistance: An Historical Perspective." *Journal of Library Administration* 7 (Spring 1986): 83-108.

Jones, C. Lee. "Academic Libraries and Computing: A Time for Change." *Educom Bulletin* 20 (Spring 1985): 9-12.

Moran, Barbara B. *Academic Libraries: The Changing Knowledge Centers of Colleges and Universities*. Washington, D.C.: Association for the Study of Higher Education, 1984.

Mowry, Barbara. "Managing Change in a Rapid Growth Environment." *Business Insights* 4 (Spring 1988): 17-18.

Shaughnessy, Thomas W. "Technology and the Structure of Libraries." *Libri* 32, no. 2 (1982): 149-55.

Shaw, Edward E. "The Courage to Fail." In *Library Leadership: Visualizing the Future*, edited by Donald Riggs, 53-65. Phoenix: Oryx, 1982.

Watson, Tom G. "The Librarian as Change Agent." In *Advances in Library Administration and Organization*, vol. 2, 85-97. Greenwich, Conn.: JAI Press, 1983.

CHAPTER 22

Library Leadership

Richard M. Dougherty

Judging by several job announcements appearing in the *Chronicle of Higher Education* for Library Director, some universities have decided that neither the MLS nor experience as a library administrator is a necessary requirement for the position of director. While I don't feel the profession is faced with a leadership crisis, I get concerned when prestigious universities decide to broaden their applicant pools to include "qualified" administrators or scholars who don't possess prior library experience. I believe that there are several factors that, while not unique to librarianship, have inhibited the development of leaders in our profession in rather significant ways: We don't fully value those who rock the boat; we seem to have a low tolerance for dissonance in organizations; we are often hypercritical of each other; and we tend to personalize disagreements on professional issues. Let me explain more fully my concerns.

I lay a large share of the blame for whatever leadership gap exists on the governance structure of organizations such as ALA, ARL, and CRL. Decision making within those organizations places a high premium on group participation; every proposal of substance must endure a thorough scrutiny. By the time agreement is achieved, what is significant or innovative about the proposal, may have been compromised during the consensus-building process.

I have participated in more than one discussion when a decision was reported later as if it were a consensus when in fact no consensus existed. Those who held contrary views opted for silence; the absence of open discussion was misinterpreted to be a signal of general agreement. This failure to bring to the surface and examine minority views happens all too often in our professional organizations. When minority viewpoints are ignored or dismissed the diversity of options and visions is reduced and we all lose out. In the context of leadership development, our potential leaders are denied the opportunity to listen to or participate in informed, constructive discussion and to hone their own debating skills. And isn't that ironic, since our leaders of the future are preparing themselves for campus environments which are known for debate, even when consensus is an unlikely expectation.

A decision-making process which is reliant on consensus building can also inhibit leadership development in another way. Our organizations, replete with their customary complement of committees, task forces, councils, and boards are not always receptive to individualists who march to the beat of their own drummer. Protected by a group environment, it is very easy to dismiss an individualist. I've heard explanations such as s/he's nothing more than a curmudgeon, a nay-sayer, or a crank to be tolerated, as reasons for ignoring an outspoken person. But it is this person—who sees the future differently—who is often the rare visionary among us. The importance of vision is underscored in a recent study of leadership authored by Bennis and Nanus.[1] These investigators found that one leadership quality common among the sixty contemporary leders they interviewed was the ability to project a vision and to convince colleagues that their vision was worthy of transformation into reality.

Our profession has enjoyed its share of visionaries. It is interesting to speculate how the ideas of Ralph Shaw, Jesse Shera, or Fred Kilgour would have fared had they had to endure the bureaucratic committee review processes of ALA, ARL, or CRL. Our organizations should be structured to encourage open discussion, debate, and the identification of visionaries. We ought to be able to survive a little verbal jousting now and then. It is in this potential environment that our future leaders will gain the experience and exposure which is the mark of a mature leader.

Sam Rothstein provides us with some plausible explanations as to why it is difficult to exert leadership in our profession. In his insightful essay, "Why People Really Hate Library Schools," Rothstein suggests we are loners who harbor serious doubts about ourselves, and we tend, consequently, to be critical of our institutions and colleagues. He also advises us to "give up being so critical of our fellow librarians and ourselves."[2]

It is my feeling also that we tend to be hypercritical of each other; we seem reluctant to permit others to lead, particularly if a person is outspoken. I've overheard colleagues admonishing others for espousing views not held by the majority. There seems to be a fear that by expressing contrary views a climate of divisiveness will prevail. Why are we reluctant to embrace debate, to use such opportunities to air fully the issues that confront our organizations? Is it because we have allowed issues to become too personalized? We forget that tomorrow will bring a new issue with a different cast of allies and opponents. Let's borrow a leaf from the behavior pattern of lawyers who after arguing all day as courtroom adversaries, go out for drinks after court adjourns and talk about last Saturday's golf match.

If arguments are confined to issues and do not focus on personalities, and if we learn to use existing governance structures more efficiently, then we will ensure that important issues are thoroughly discussed. The atmosphere should become more conducive to the exercise of leadership. Considering the number and complexity of issues facing us today, the need for professional leadership has rarely been more pressing.

I know of many capable librarians who possess leadership potential, but the challenge is to see that this potential is realized. It is in our best interest to see that the finest among our profession represent us in positions of leadership. I look forward to the day when the most serious problem facing a university search committee seeking a library director is its struggle to narrow the field of qualified librarian candidates.

NOTES

[1]Warren Bennis and Burt Nanus, *Leaders: The Strategies for Taking Charge* (New York: Harper & Row, 1985).

[2]Samuel Rothstein, "Why People Really Hate Library Schools," *Library Journal*, (April 1985): 47.

CHAPTER 23

Managing for Innovation in the Age of Information Technology

Robin N. Downes

INTRODUCTION

Librarians are rarely entrepreneurs as individuals, but libraries as organizations can and do act like entrepreneurs. The initiative for creating such an organizational climate in a library must come from the administration, but can only be implemented with the understanding and support of key elements of the staff. What must be "understood and supported" is nothing less than a philosophy of creative organizational behavior. This paper examines some of the elements of such an organizational philosophy, and places this philosophy in a hypothetical library setting in which a management style and organizational culture contribute to innovation and entrepreneurship resulting in the successful installation of a new generation of information technology. The management techniques used in the installation are presented as complementary to the desired organizational culture, and as both supporting and merging with it. The installation process is seen as an opportunity to introduce a creative and entrepreneurial environment, and to prepare the staff for the next stage of information technology.

INNOVATION AS A PRODUCT OF AN ORGANIZATIONAL CULTURE

Many of us have become familiar with the popularized theories of organizational behavior expressed, for example, in Peters and Waterman's book, *In Search of Excellence*. The authors devote major attention to organizational climates which encourage innovation and creativity. The theories of Peters and Waterman are easily adapted to a university library setting. Some of their most important arguments, rephrased for this purpose, would include the following: (1) establishing the very highest standards of quality—service to faculty and students, strong book and journal collections, state-of-the-art technology, attractive study facilities—and assuming they are the *minimum* values of the organization; (2) staying in touch with the people served by the organization; (3) not just encouraging, but *requiring* members of the organization at all levels to be innovative; (4) providing the financial support and the freedom and flexibility needed for entrepreneurs to flourish; (5) not just *allowing*

Reprinted with permission from the *Journal of Library Administration*, Vol. 8(1), Spring 1987. Copyright 1987, The Haworth Press, Inc., New York.

every member of the organization the right to a point of view, but *requiring* them to have one and expecting them to express it; (6) being action oriented—when in doubt, do something; (7) depending on intensely held core values to provide centralized control, while giving maximum autonomy to the real source of creativity in the organization—its people; and (8) assuming that individual creativity is common and that it is the responsibility of organizations to be receptive to it.

Management scientists other than Peters and Waterman have found an additional quality in the most innovative organizations. They also describe this quality in terms of values, and find these values most often when members of organizations see themselves as keystones in creating fundamental changes in the way their organizations work. The people in organizations with these values often make an unusual investment of energy and creativity. They become convinced that they can reshape the destiny of the organization, and that given the autonomy they need, they will be successful. If this is true, what are the fundamental changes to which the people of libraries must commit themselves? The most pervasive theme in the 1980s is the introduction of successive stages of computer-based information technology. The paper examines in the following sections the links between management techniques, the installation of information technology, and the development of an entrepreneurial environment.

INNOVATION, TECHNOLOGY, AND MANAGEMENT—THE CONTROL OF A CHANGING ENVIRONMENT

As the 1980s began, it was clear that every university would need to replace during the decade its conventional technology for handling bibliographic data, financial data, and transaction data with a new generation of computerized systems. Typically, the new technology has been defined as an "integrated library system" (ILS). Aside from the technology issues, a change from a personnel-intensive to a hardware-intensive environment also carries implications for budget, organizational structure, service programs, and job content. It also offers the potential for a fresh look at the organizational culture of the library—that is, the way people work.

An ILS touches almost every library program in some way. A decision to acquire an ILS is therefore the first in a series of steps which, if the opportunity is taken, will teach librarians more about the economics and organization of the work of libraries than most of them previously knew. Librarians can come out of the process with a sophisticated understanding of organization and management.

An ILS installation forces librarians to look analytically at each library program affected by the technology. Program planning and budgeting is a standard method of collecting analytical management information, and offers a classic justification for its use. It can be argued that institutions such as libraries have limited use for the amount of information thus collected, when basic elements of cost in library programs are stable. But library programs and costs are not stable in an ILS environment, and as the installation progresses the lack of analytical data may lead to errors in program changes, to insufficient reallocation of funds among programs, or—the worst case—no decisions on program changes or budget reallocations. A systematic analytical approach to the impact of an ILS on existing library programs and budgets is thus of equal importance to planning for acquiring the system. Success in this "management" aspect of the project is as crucial as success in the technology phase.

Taking the program management approach a step further, it is possible to merge the "program" approach with the "team" concept, in which individual professionals work on a project basis. The commonplace committee or team of library staff is given moderate independence, but with major constraints on moving from data collection and analysis to actual program management. The philosophy offered in this paper is to give the program team unusual independence. In this environment, most short or long-term tasks would be defined as programs and given a budget to support them, with management autonomy within broad policies, so long as goals are met. To add flexibility to budgeting and to encourage new ideas, a significant percentage of the library budget should be set aside each year for onetime investment in 1-3 year projects, with dollars to be awarded to proposals which promise to improve service or reduce costs. It is helpful if a personnel system exists or is developed which defines the librarians in the university as a self-governing professional group, as distinct in its role as faculty are in theirs. Appointments, promotions, and retention decisions should be peer responsibilities, and advancement in rank and salary should not be tied to rank in the management structure.

Most tasks would be assigned to these program groups, whose assignments and members may cross many traditional functional and hierarchical lines. The lifespan of a program would range from 6 weeks to semi-permanent status. In many cases, if a task couldn't be done in 6 weeks, it would be assumed that the charge probably was badly written. In this task-oriented organization, goals would be defined not in repetitive incremental day-to-day terms but as targets of opportunity requiring changing points of view, a constantly changing cast of characters, and flexible funding.

In this environment, programs would not be funded because they were sure bets, but because they were interesting and showed promise of improved service or reduced costs. Entrepreneurs would be encouraged, failure expected as often as success, and the prevailing philosophy would be "when in doubt, do something."

It would be helpful, further, if except for personnel matters, the organization had no secrets. Everything should be open—budget documents, planning documents, progress reports, status reports, productivity statistics, and program plans. Internal and external newsletters should flourish. The library should be mentioned often in university publications and in the local newspapers. An extensive system of achievement awards should be established, but positive reinforcement for staff accomplishments would continue to operate best on the informal level. A plaque awarded by the library is fine, but recognition given by colleagues is even better.

The librarians would thus work in an environment that satisfies personal and professional needs for meaning. They would operate in a setting which encouraged them to take control of their work. They would set ambitious goals, and probably win more often than not. And they would demonstrate that the success of an organization cannot be predicted, but it can—in a looser sense—almost be prophesized, by combining the innovative use of information technology with a creative philosophy of organizational behavior.

FUNDAMENTAL CHANGES IN VALUES— THE POTENTIAL AND LIMITATIONS OF TECHNOLOGY

As described in the preceding section, academic libraries began in the 1980s to reap the reward of two decades of research and development in the application of computing to library operations. The "Integrated Library System" for the first time became available in the marketplace as a realistic option to the paper files on which libraries had relied since the 1890s for bibliographic, transaction, and financial data. In the preceding section, this paper examined the organizational and management implications of an ILS, and concluded with a successful ILS installation operating in an open and creative environment. Is this enough to aim for? Or, is it possible that a new set of expectations by users must be faced?

The best-known feature of the ILS is the computerized catalog, which can be made accessible through hundreds of dedicated terminals in campus libraries, in offices and in homes through a personal computer with a modem, and through links to a campus local area network to any terminal on the network.

The computerized catalog brings important increases in speed and efficiency in retrieving information, and adds new and powerful search strategies. Beyond these invaluable qualities, it raises the first glimmer of a philosophical change in the definition of a library. A library is "where the information is." In the new environment, a key component in finding the information in a library can be searched on a terminal located anywhere in a community in which the library is located. The "availability status" of a book or journal issue can be displayed on the terminal screen and "holds" placed at the terminal so that books can be reserved and picked up later. What is the potential impact on the definition of a "library," if remote access to a library's holdings is combined with electronic mail and — for an academic library — a campus delivery service? What is the "location" of the library?

This advanced library technology on the local level parallels technological and organizational innovations by libraries on a national scale over the last 20 years. All of the major university research libraries and thousands of smaller academic and public libraries in North America are linked into national on-line computerized networks, connected by the public-switched telephone network. The largest such network is OCLC, whose central computer files hold 12 million records for over 200 million copies of books and journals, and hold records identifying which libraries own copies of these books and journals. Any of these 12 million records can be identified in seconds on computer terminals in thousands of libraries. A library which owns the book can be selected, and an electronic subsystem can be used to transmit a request for the book to an identical terminal in another library. The same philosophical question arises — if the library is "where the information is" does this technology require that we recast our definition of the "library"?

Unfortunately, the answer in almost every university library is "not yet." One possible definition of the problem can be found in the incomplete conception held by most libraries of what constitutes a complete transaction between a user and the library. Many surveys have found that users experience approximately a 50 percent success rate when they seek information from the collections and services of a university library. If, for example, 3,000 faculty and students per day enter a library on a medium-sized university campus, and are successful in finding the information they need only one-half of the time, what conclusions should be drawn? Is this success rate dictated by unreasonable expectations by users? By inadequate instructional programs offered at the library? By insufficient resources or the lack of cooperative interlibrary resource sharing programs?

To broaden the discussion of these issues, it can be pointed out that in the conventional university library, much of the economic burden of acquiring a desired unit of information is borne by the user. The library has traditionally been viewed as a self-service system, with units of space and information being organized with this concept in mind. Indeed, some leaders in the application of computing to campus environments have used the "self-service" concept of the library as a model for the design of such environments. A computing model with these characteristics, it is suggested, would be organized for use with minimal instruction, and its complex internal organization would only be known to, and be of concern to, the management and technical staff of the computing center.

There is reason to believe that this model of the library—once viable—is now incomplete and outdated. It can be argued, in fact, that the vastly increased number of information sources have thrust librarians into the role—if only, at this stage, by default—of information brokers. If this line of reasoning is accurate, it may be time to do more than enhance the self-service model through such devices as user education programs and cooperative interagency agreements, invaluable and necessary as they may be. For the purpose of this paper, it is suggested that librarians should, in fact, intervene more actively in the "information transaction."

Arguing against a global application of this interventionist model is the possibility that removing the user's economic contribution from the information transaction would push costs out of reach. Granting this limitation does not, however, rule out a philosophy of controlled intervention. Viewed in this way, the inefficiency—that is, the 50 percent failure rate—of university libraries can be addressed by matching the failure states—in an individual and organizational sense of the term—with interventionist programs which are explicit to the user and the staff, but which control costs by limiting intervention only to the most significant "failure states" and by designing intervention systems which are not personnel intensive.

At this stage of the argument, the opportunity arises for creativity and innovation in designing intervention programs, and in organizing them into service units. A first step, and a key one is defining what is a completed transaction. The user clearly will consider it complete when (1) he has found the specific item or the sample of a class of information, or (2) he has used all of the systems offered by the library to find the item of information, whether it is held by the library or by an external source. These "systems" are basic concerns in themselves, but the argument made here deals primarily with who is accountable for each stage of a "transaction."

It may be assumed that a significant number of users are not aware of all the systems by which a library can provide a completed transaction, and that those who are aware of them often find the systems cumbersome and time-consuming. In designing its intervention programs, a library may decide to bring together in one program those services which are the source of a completed transaction. It may define them, in terms of staff training, job content, and library instruction programs, as an integrated series of steps. As a result of these measures, all staff members in all service programs would view their responsibilities in terms of a global strategy for satisfying a user's information needs. Service policies would be based on a holistic "mirrored" view of the user's expectation for a complete information-seeking transaction.

These assumptions regarding the economic and programmatic implications of what constitutes "successful" service to library users would thus represent the first stage of a hypothetical follow-up cycle of innovation after the successful installation of an ILS. They would represent the essential first stage in a questioning of the new, post-ILS status quo, and the conceptualizing of a fresh approach, which would precede any period of creativity. These ideas would next be tested in the entrepreneurial environment described in this paper, in which innovation is both strongly encouraged and rigorously tested.

The cycle of innovation which begins with the installation of new information technology will be carried out in an organizational culture which encourages independent entrepreneurial activity in all stages of implementation. The need for a high level of analytical management information leads to a program-based collection and analysis of such information. Acting opportunistically, the librarians adopt the "program" as a planning and management unit, with the program unit serving as a flexible overlay upon the traditional library organization. And because the librarians become accustomed to a continual critical evaluation of their role, they quickly absorb and move beyond the immediate values of a new generation of information technology to an examination of the broader philosophical implications of this technology.

CONCLUSION

The effect of information technology on the organization and management of a library can thus be somewhat opportunistic on the part of management, and partly dictated by necessity. Program planning and budgeting can be adapted to the team approach, and can be used to supplement or replace the traditional departmental organization of a university library. Staffing, planning and budgeting can take place in flexible task oriented programs, which together can make up the overall information service program of the library. In this task-oriented organization, goals can be defined as moving targets, requiring changing points of view, flexible planning and budgeting, and a high level of timely management information. The traditional library organization can be like the card catalog—to be left unchanged for the present, but with a better system of organization gradually replacing it.

Innovation in technology can in this way lead to an organizational culture in which creativity is encouraged, and in which the organization itself is flexible and adaptive to the changes which entrepreneurial librarians will propose. From the librarian's point of view, the organization will be seen as encouraging a role of manager and entrepreneur, utilizing technology to increase productivity and efficiency, and marketing information skills and services as well as a collection of books and journals. From the administrator's point of view, improvements in service to faculty and students and productivity increases will be basic, but equally important will be the synergistic effects of technology on the organization, management, creativity, and productivity of libraries and their staff.

CHAPTER 24

The Electronic Library
A Vision for the Future
Patricia Battin

It is ironic that the disciplines of engineering and computer science, which are essentially leading the information technology revolution and the development of academic information systems, are the two disciplines in the university that have been traditionally the least dependent upon library services and support. In contrast, and because of a decade of intensive automation activity in libraries, librarians probably know far more about computing than computer specialists know about libraries. Our respective images of each other continue to keep us apart. The sensible and successful introduction of information technology into the university demands that we draw on the strengths of both disciplines.

With this in mind, in the rest of this paper, I will cover: 1) the nature of scholarship as we have known it and the characteristics of the traditional relationship between scholars and their information sources; 2) a brief summary of three generations of library computing; 3) organizational issues surrounding the advent of the wired scholar; and 4) a glimpse of the future.

The word "information" is a troublesome one, and I would like to make a distinction here that I think is critical. Academic librarians have always distinguished between "information" and "knowledge," and our basic philosophies and objectives have arisen from a commitment to the organization of knowledge and the support of continuing scholarship. Contemporary "information managers" and computer specialists tend to treat all information as data and have been typically more concerned with the technical aspects of hardware and systems than with the substantive content of "data" and its influence on systems of organization, storage, access, and retrieval. I use the term "scholarly information" to define that subset of the information society vital to the university, and the term "librarian" to describe professionals historically concerned with scholarly information support services.

What is the role of the institution's traditional academic information system—the library—in the new high-tech environment? Will it be, as any number of technical gurus and disaffected academics predict, an irrelevant, obsolete museum of the book? Or will it be, as grumpily forecast by many humanists and historians, who fear the replacement of the book by the computer, an empty shell ineptly managed by library technocrats for their own obscure purpose?

In my view, if either of these predictions proves accurate, we will have failed to realize the promise and potential of technology for the productive expansion of scholarship and the advancement of knowledge. My vision reflects the following logic: the library in its role as the knowledge center of the academic enterprise represents the meat in the electronic sandwich and that role must be enhanced and expanded to meet the needs of the electronic scholar.

Reprinted with permission. First published in the *EDUCOM Bulletin* 19 (Summer 1984): 12-17, 34.

I want to emphasize as strongly as I can that in my view the personal computer does not mean an end to books—I think the printed word will be with us for a very long time. There are many kinds of communication that lend themselves to the printed page—reflective, contemplative works, for example, or information that changes relatively infrequently and requires portability. There are also many research and learning activities that are best supported by printed formats.

What the personal computer does mean is the end of the printed page as the sole means of scholarly communication and information storage and retrieval. There will be, in the future, a mix of formats as well as a mix of hardware. If the new, expanded information systems are to be successful, we will need to create a new information infrastructure to provide the electronic scholar with the same kind of universal gateway across to recorded knowledge as the traditional library provided for printed materials.

The challenge for universities is not simply to explore the role of computers on campus —as so many institutions have interpreted the issue—but also to integrate information technology into the existing information system in a way that preserves the linkages to the existing knowledge base, encourages and stimulates the productive use of new technologies, and provides coordinated gateway access to the universe of knowledge in a manner convenient and invisible to the end user. That is the dream. I believe it is essential that we maintain a clear distinction between end and means—between tools and substance.

It is only fair that I state my bias early in this paper. I am not in agreement with the current trend to "wire" the university from outside the scholarly process—to build the system from the imperative of the technological capacities rather than from the perspective and requirements of the scholar and the student. The paradox of our situation is that the achievement of our goal, because of the character and cost of computer and communications technologies, will require a substantial level of initial cooperation and centralization that runs counter to the strongly autonomous nature of scholarly inquiry. The very diversity of scholarly inquiry and information needs requires in the electronic age an unprecedented degree of centralized, coordinated linkages and compatibilities to serve that diversity and permit the autonomy necessary for productive and creative scholarship. It is essential that we do it well and that scholars from all disciplines actively participate, instead of letting it happen to them. I am convinced that the way universities integrate and use the new technologies will have an enormously significant influence on the strength and vitality of higher education, and on society as well.

I emphasize the traditional relationship between the library and the scholar because important lessons are to be learned from the past as we move to construct a new kind of technical architecture and electronic systems to facilitate the transfer of knowledge from one mind to another. It may come as a surprise to you to learn that most people cannot tell you how they use information and what their specific needs are. I can tell you, after twenty years in the research library profession, that it is sheer arrogance unencumbered by the facts to assume that one's own information needs can serve as a model for anyone else in academia. A principle characteristic of libraries has been the provision of freedom of choice—the control of the system has been in the hands of the user. The role of the University has been, and should be, as noted by Roger Bagnall, "not one of prescribing uses but of making resources available to all of its members who need them. Past decisions about the use of traditional information sources have come from individual faculty members and students, and we see no reason to believe this situation will change."[1]

Librarians have been at the center of the research process in our universities for the past century, and it is essential to recognize that the whole structure of research activity in the United States, as we know it, is based upon knowledge access structures conceived and built over the years by the library profession. It is my conviction that the personal computer—no matter how ingeniously networked around the campus—will remain an interesting toy unless it provides to the owner true gateway access to the entire range of information required for his/her particular scholarly concerns.

The pursuit of knowledge has always been driven by the creativity of the individual scholar. Bill Ward, President of the American Council for Learned Societies, recently defined for librarians the ideal in library service from the scholarly perspective: Scholars want what they want when they want it whether or not they know what it is they want. In the past the university has sought to serve this fundamental need by maintaining bibliographically controlled archival collections of the printed record. Since scholarly needs are not well defined in advance, a particularly essential contribution has been the development of bibliographic control systems with logical hierarchical linkages, standards, and compatibilities to insure open-ended access to the universe of knowledge. In contrast, scholarly applications of technology to date generally have focused on highly specific disciplinary concerns, and tended to emphasize the capacities of the technology for a discrete avenue of research or the processing of unique data rather than the broader requirements of the scholarly community at large. Frequently, the products of such applications have been compilations of data inaccessible to all but the creators (and sometimes even to them), incompatible systems, and lack of universal standards.

One of the library profession's best kept secrets is the system of national bibliographic control, which can now lead you to a specific item among the 251,210,388 volumes—at last count—housed in our nation's research libraries. The complex control systems underlying card catalogs provide the information retrieval capacity long taken for granted by the higher education community for access to monographic literature, and it is the transformation of that capacity into machine-readable format that has occupied the library profession during the past decade. In addition, abstracting and indexing services, employing techniques ranging from keywords to controlled thesauri, will lead you to individual articles published in journal titles numbering in the tens of thousands. The wired scholar now requires an additional dimension—access to information no longer packaged in neat bibliographic bundles. Nina Matheson, who has been active in the development of new strategies for organizing information delivery to the health sciences sector, has noted that "We need to keep in mind that information is not a property of documents, nor of bibliographic records, but the relationship between the data and the recipient. Increasingly, the burden and the responsibility of libraries in the INFORMATION AGE is to deal with that relationship."[2]

THREE GENERATIONS OF LIBRARY COMPUTING

In the library profession today, we speak of three generations of computing—not to be confused with the five generations of computer design.[3] The first generation—which has essentially occupied us for the past fifteen years—has been the application of computer and communications technologies to library processing activities. We used the computer to print catalog cards and the telecommunications capacities to share the by-product of machine-readable information. We essentially revolutionized the way we run our internal operations. The resulting information is not generally available to the public, except through mediated terminals at reference desks. The technical environment is homogeneous—a large central computer linked by long communications lines to terminals across the country. The era is generally referred to as "library automation," and it is basically over.

During this period, much of the work that will make the workstation useful to scholars was accomplished. I will summarize as succinctly as I can the historical activities significant for the wired scholar.

The needs of scholars have always transcended local barriers. The American National Library is a decentralized system composed of the Library of Congress, the National Library of Medicine, the National Library of Agriculture, and approximately one hundred private and public research libraries across the nation.

The Library of Congress (LC) provides via its MARC tape service the records of its catalog in machine-readable form. The MARC format is a machine-readable format accepted across the nation as the standardized method for recording bibliographic data elements describing scholarly publications. To date, we have MARC formats for books, journals, scores, maps, sound recordings, films, and microfilms. Recently, agreement was reached on the new format for machine-readable data files, which means we can now begin to organize bibliographic access to what appears to be the Nightmare of the Nineties.

The LC Name Authority File is also available on line as are the bibliographic records from the Government Printing Office and the National Library of Medicine. There are three bibliographic utilities that distribute these machine-readable records to libraries across the country. At present, transfer to the utilities from LC is by means of magnetic tapes. In turn, the participating libraries, connected to the utilities' computers, contribute bibliographic records with location symbols prepared for materials not yet recorded in the data base. The phenomenal growth of these data bases has resulted in a vastly increased capacity to share cataloging responsibilities and thus reduce local institutional expenses. The existence of these large data resources has revolutionized interlibrary loan capacities and made possible the potential for developing a coordinated national collection through new means of access to decentralized collections.

The two major bibliographic networks—OCLC and RLIN—provide information currently on a combined total of 24 million unique records for books, maps, manuscripts, periodicals, audiovisual materials, sound recordings, and music scores, with the numbers increasing daily at a rapid pace.

At the present time, the utilities are not linked, thus creating serious access problems for scholars since institutional participation is usually limited to one utility. The Council on Library Resources, a privately funded foundation, launched some years ago a Bibliographic Services Development Program to help bring into existence a comprehensive, logically consistent, non-redundant data base of bibliographic records. To insure comprehensiveness, the data base must be built by a set of standards. Non-redundancy requires the use of an authority file to record the entities that have been created according to the set of accepted rules. The objective of this program is to create a widely available, cost-effective bibliographic record service that will incorporate the resources of the major shared cataloging services and provide access to a variety of bibliographic data bases in a manner transparent to the end-user—our wired scholar.

For the past three years, the Library of Congress and the two major utilities have worked on a cooperative project funded by the Council on Library Resources to develop a standard network interconnection consisting of a seven-layer communications protocol that will permit computer-to-computer communications. This project will be completed by the end of 1984 and represents an extraordinary example of library leadership in the application of communications technology for academic purposes. This system of linkages provides the basic national architecture for the Electronic Scholar to gain open access to all available machine-readable data from the individual workstation. The first transmissions will be authority records, followed by the capacity for bibliographic searching of citations and ultimately, the transmission of full text.

The Research Libraries Group, of which Columbia is a charter member, represents a focused effort by twenty-six research universities and their libraries to reshape information services for scholars. In contrast to OCLC, which is a mass-market driven enterprise, RLG derives its direction from the program needs of its owner-member research institutions. RLG has four major program areas:

1. the development of the Research Libraries Information Network, specifically designed for the information retrieval requirements of scholars

2. shared resources, driven by an electronic message system for interlibrary loan, which has reduced document delivery time to an average of six days (RLG is now experimenting with facsimile transmission technology on a national scale)

3. a collection development and management program, which has produced an on-line inventory of the disciplinary strengths of the library collections in member institutions and which is now being extended to all research institutions across the nation.

4. a preservation program, which has developed an on-line enhancement to display both the existence of master negatives and queueing status of materials to be filmed.

RLG is still filming deteriorating materials, in a cooperative program, while awaiting the outcome of the Library of Congress' $6 million pilot project to explore the use of optical disk for preservation purposes. We expect the preservation medium of the future to be optical disk, which will then make available in machine-readable form the full text of much historical material now only in printed format. The LC project is specifically focused on the use of optical disk for prospective preservation—that is, storing the information, which may also be published in printed format, on optical disk for archival purposes.

In addition to the standard bibliographic services, RLG maintains on RLIN several special data bases, including the Avery Architecture Index, produced at Columbia; SCIPIO, a data base of arts sales catalogs; and the Eighteenth Century Short Title Catalog. On March 1, the British Library and RLG signed an agreement to extend a communications link from the RLG host computer, located at Stanford University, to the British Library for combined, on-line production of an Eighteenth Century Short Title Catalog. To date, collaboration of the project has been carried out by transatlantic tape-loads. RLIN terminals will be installed in the Reading Room of the British Library as the first step toward a truly international scholar's network.

THE SECOND GENERATION

Enter the Second Generation. Because the market was not perceived to be profitable, and because of the complex, arcane nature of the technical requirements of authority files and cross-referencing systems, all the first-generation development work was carried out in academic libraries, funded primarily by foundation and federal grants. A number of commercial vendors have emerged from the first generation with software and hardware products to support the maintenance of integrated local systems—comprising cataloging, acquisitions, and circulation records—which can be made available to local scholars via terminals connected either to system-specific hardware or mainframes in the institution's computer center. The distributed architecture will eliminate the first-generation communications costs and the technical capacity constraints of a single processing site and bring us one step closer to the workstation. However, the central data resource—the on-line union catalog, is essential for scholarly purposes, so a major challenge for the second generation is to plan an orderly path for the distribution of appropriate software applications to the local scene, to develop a new set of technical and staff capabilities for the central node, and to establish effective financial strategies for sharing the costs of the new services. We expect that by 1990, most major institutions will have fully integrated local systems in operation.

The software for Columbia Libraries Information Online (CLIO), Columbia's online catalog—300,000 lines of programming code—was installed in March, after five years of planning, which should give you some notion of the complexity of the systems with which we are dealing. CLIO will run on an IBM mainframe in the Computer Center and is potentially available from all terminals of the PACX network. The second generation software is user-friendly, in contrast to the first generation, and provides vastly expanded access points to bibliographic information. These access points include personal name, title, keyword, and call-number browsing. In addition, the Boolean logic capability enables the user to frame a variety of logical search strategies, impossible in card or book catalogs.

Initially, the Columbia data base will include the snapshot of Columbia records, spun off from RLIN, supplemented by weekly transaction tapes. When the Standard Network Interconnection link is implemented in early 1985, records will be passed via the link, and we can dispense with tape-loading. If all goes well, as we expect it to, we will stop filing cards in the catalog in 1985 or 86.

The needs of the Electronic Scholar will require a major and costly one-time capital investment in the retrospective conversion of card catalog records into machine-readable form. Using current technology, we estimate at Columbia that it will take us about five years and $8 million to convert the 2½ million records in the card catalog. (Half our volume count are serials.) RLG is working on a national strategy to enable its member libraries to improve efficiency and reduce costs in these efforts. The labor-intensive nature of the keying process accounts for the bulk of the cost. It is also important to find the appropriate balance between quick and dirty strategies—which turn out to be penny wise and pound foolish—and the unrealistic penchant for polished perfection of each record.

We have begun the planning and development efforts for the Third Generation, which will move a set of software applications to the scholar's workstation, enabling the selective downloading and interactive manipulation of this wealth of information by individual users. We assume that all institutions will, by the early nineties, have local area networks to accommodate the workstations, and that these local networks will be linked via gateway software. The local on-line catalog will evolve into a data base server on the local area network, making it available at all workstations. In addition, the RLG union data base will also be available as a server on the network. It will probably arrive weekly at member institutions in the form of an optical disk. There will also be a document storage and retrieval server and a gateway to all other forms of machine-readable information, including, among others, commercial data bases, full-text journals, Library of Congress, OCLC, and the British Library. RLG is currently organizing its research and development effort to achieve these goals in concert with the workstation development at Carnegie-Mellon and Brown Universities.

Despite all these efforts, the nightmare is already upon us in the guise of rapidly proliferating data bases, incompatible hardware and software systems, rapidly evolving technologies, communications systems which provide marvelously efficient but closed loops and links to nowhere, continuing expansion of printed publications characterized by poor quality paper and cheap ephemeral bindings, growing inefficiency of card catalogs and printed indexes, lack of any effective or coordinated indexing of machine-readable data files, a significant and alarming shift from the University's capacity to provide subsidized browsing and use of information through the library to a fee-for-use basis in which the ownership and control of access remains with the publisher in the for-profit sector, substantial incremental costs required to provide adequate information services to the university, and the unacceptable intrusion into the academic enterprise of economic discrimination governing access to scholarly information.

Chemical Abstracts represents a good paradigm of the present organizational chaos and the incremental costs of providing information services. At the present time, the University, through the Libraries, makes the printed copy available to students and faculty at no cost to the individual. *Chem Abstracts* is also available in machine-readable form through the library's institutional access or password. Typically, a reference librarian trained in the specific protocols performs the search for the client who pays the line charges and cpu costs. Now, researchers with personal computers want direct access to the data base from a variety of locations. ACS does not have the capacity to accommodate the uncontrolled multitude of individual users, so in response to this need, ACS now provides for an annual fee of $6,000 one institutional password to be used ad seriatim in the institution during off-peak hours, which are after 2 p.m. EST.

There are several significant points to be noted:

1. For the forseeable future, an institution must provide all three types of access. One is not a substitute for the other:
    — certain kinds of scholarly inquiry require the information capacities provided by the printed format
    — there will always be students, researchers, and faculty who require access to ACS but who are not sufficiently specialized to possess the skills for independent searching of the data base
    — there will be a core of specialists with personal computers who require direct access

2. The costs are not substitutional, but substantially incremental.

3. The fragmentation of access to data bases is inimical to the academic purposes of the institution. Therefore, a centralized infra-structure is required to make sure that access to all available information sources is coordinated and provided on an institution-wide basis to eliminate the costs of redundancy.

4. The traditional procedures for allocation of costs and control of expenditures have undergone a radical transformation.

Another example of the current anarchy is the following treasure hunt: In January, 1984, a graduate student asked Barbara List, Science Division reference librarian, if she could find a table giving the complete protein sequence for *E. coli* RNA polymerase. She knew that the sequence had been completed in the last year and said that the work had been done by many different researchers who published their results in many different journals. She had also heard that the National Library of Medicine had a data base that might contain the answer.

Various books in the Biology Library supplied parts of the sequence, but not the whole sequence. *Chem Abstracts* had many citations but not the actual data. Eventually, via the New York Academy of Medicine, Barbara connected with a lab at the National Biomedical Research Foundation at Georgetown University. They had the sequence in a set of 7 tables, which they would run off and send to Columbia. They also told her that the National Institutes of Health had just acquired the data bases, which would become public sometime in April 1984. Up to that time, an individual had to make special arrangements for access. As it then turned out, after all these efforts, one researcher at the Cancer Research Center, College of Physicians and Surgeons, Columbia University, had such access, but no one else knew it. This example also indicates that far from being extinct in the electronic university, librarians will be in greater demand than in the more serene and organized world of the book.

Another example involved a specialized data base produced by Bell Laboratories. A researcher in the social sciences, wishing to use this particular data base, called Bell Labs to find out how to gain access to the data and was told that it was already available on Columbia's computers for researchers at the Health Sciences.

And to dispel the persistent myth that information needs can be categorized and confined to a given faculty or discipline, a review of our searching logs for the BIOSIS database for the past few months indicates that researchers from geography, psychology, law, anthropology, and Teachers College requested literature searches from BIOSIS.

If we back off and look at the information scene from a global point of view, that is, the perspective of the Electronic Scholar, sitting at his or her microcomputer at home or in the office in 1984, this is what we see:

- A huge stock of books and journals, housed locally and across the world, reasonably accessible—although in slow and inconvenient fashion—through internationally standardized protocols. The overwhelming majority of these access protocols—card catalogs and printed indexes—are not yet available at the workstation. A small percentage of the bibliographic records are available in machine-readable form.

- A well-designed and internationally standardized machine-readable format for the control of bibliographic access to information in a variety of formats.

- The national capacity to link existing bibliographic data bases.

- A growing number of scholar-generated machine-readable data files with no orderly form of access. The invisible network is generally the source for information about these data bases.

- A growing number of commercially available data bases, again with no orderly form of access. Currently, there are 1600 of these data bases, of which 38% require some sort of subscription fee in addition to computer time and communications charges. Columbia provides access to around 350 at the present time. Lists published by the Libraries, either in flyers unevenly distributed around the campus or on computer bulletin boards, are the usual means of communication about these resources.

- Incompatible hardware, software, and communications networks that have developed out of the normal scholarly characteristics of autonomous entrepreneurship in the pursuit of knowledge.

- Inefficient expenditure of individual and institutional funds because of lack of agreement on institutional compatabilities and standards, duplication of resources that could be shared, waste of faculty and student time in identifying information resources and seeking access to them.

- Serious questions involving copyright and the ownership of information, which threaten the traditional unobstructed access to scholarly information.

- Increasing shift of cost of use of information sources to the individual, with the resulting division between information have and have-nots within the academic community.

A SCHOLARLY INFORMATION CENTER

The obvious answer to the Electronics Scholar's plight is the formation of a Scholarly Information Center by merging the Libraries and the Computer Center to provide an information infra-structure to stimulate the continuing autonomous use of information sources. The integration of Libraries and the Computer Center, each with its specific strengths and expertise, will provide one-stop shopping for the University community as well as a stabilizing planning mechanism for effective and flexible response to rapidly changing technologies. The Electronic Scholar will require both the capacity for flexible response to change and the assurance of stability as he/she becomes dependent upon electronic information systems.

Again it is important not to seek a visual image for the vision, since we are dealing with a process, not an entity. My vision of the Scholarly Information Center does not imply a building and rigid hierarchy of chains of command. Rather, it is the development of an organizational structure with responsibility for the information function of the university which will evolve in response to the needs of the clientele and the imperatives of the technology. We have already begun such a process at Columbia. A year ago, the senior officers of both organizations held a planning session to identify the areas of joint concern. The staffs have worked in close collaboration to select and implement on-line catalog software. A new joint Task Force is at work defining the policy issues surrounding bibliographic, technical, and financial implications of access to machine-readable data bases and data files.

You may have noticed that I haven't said anything about money and who will pay. The topic is a paper in itself, but I would just like to mention a few of the more troublesome issues.

1. Traditionally, universities have subsidized the process of scholarly communication through books and journals by supporting library services and have passed on to users the costs of access to computerized information.

2. In the print era, universities provided subsidized browsing by purchasing books and journals and making them freely available to members of the university community.

The costs of publication and dissemination of research have been traditionally borne by the scholar and the publisher, not the university.

Technology has shattered these comfortable simplicities. The vastly expanded potential for expensive services makes it necessary to analyze our information functions, regardless of format, and establish new policies for centrally subsidized services with a series of optional, incremental fee-based services available on request. It is important that faculty participate in the identification of those services to be included in the tuition in order to avoid the unacceptable intrusion of economic discrimination into the academic process.

Publishers are moving as rapidly as possible to a fee-per-use basis for supplying information. I think the scholarly societies have a significant responsibility in this arena to prevent the loss of control over scholarly information in the commercial sector. We need to seek fair and equitable accommodation with academic publishers to permit affordable, subsidized browsing. One suggestion has been the purchase and local maintenance of heavily used data bases, such as *Chem Abstracts*. At the present time, purchase price of *Chem Abstracts* is $18,000 per year. In other words, if Columbia wanted to buy 10 years from 1974-84, the cost would be $180,000 *per year*.

The workstation will provide the capacity for scholar-driven dissemination of machine-readable products of research. Who will pay the overhead and storage costs for scholarly output? These costs represent another set of incremental costs not now included in the University's budget.

And finally, how will we fund the availability of trained subject specialists and technical consultants on the staff of the Scholarly Information Center to provide a wide range of services to a clientele ranging from the freshman to the specialized scholar? We now provide search services to about 350 commercial data bases. Our reference librarians need continuing education to update their skills as protocols change and new specialized resources become available. Both the Computer Center and the Libraries could easily expand their user services staff several times over and still not meet the demand, which shows signs only of increasing as knowledge continues to explode.

If we assume that we are successful in reorganizing our information services to reflect new capacities, and that we miraculously resolve the financial and copyright issues, our Electronic Scholar of the '90s will find the following opportunities at the workstation:

- On-line gateway access to the universe of knowledge

- Bibliographic data for all printed works and machine-readable data bases and files

- Extremely user-friendly access by natural language subject searching, keywords, titles, etc.

- Boolean logic, call-number searching, backward and forward browsing

- Information on on-order and circulation status of documents

In short, the capacity to rummage around in the bibliographic wealth of recorded knowledge, organized in meaningful fashion with logically controlled searches:

- Downloading capacities and local interactive manipulation of all files

- Full text access to data bases, data files and published works also preserved on optical disk

- High resolution graphics

- Capacity to order off-line prints of machine-readable text, facsimile transmissions of journal articles identified through on-line abstracting and indexing services and/or delivery of printed publications

- Links to printed works through on-line indexes of books, tables of contents

- Access to current scholarly output through author-supplied access

- Access to on-line Pre-print Exchange, with papers maintained on-line for six months and then purged unless refereed and preserved in an archival record according to scholarly standards; the refereeing process would be coordinated by a national network of scholarly societies with accepted data sets being maintained at the home institution and entered into the national data resource—either RLIN or OCLC now linked into one national resource.

- On-line access to education, training and consulting services run by the Scholarly Information Center:

  — information on new services and access
  — technical information on hardware, software, etc.
  — tutorials and consulting services on literature structures, protocols for specialists, seminars for beginners
  — literature search services for those who don't want to do their own

According to the traditional cliche, the Library is the heart of the University. I think it is time for a new metaphor — and that metaphor is more appropriately DNA. The new process will be a helix — we provide a basic set of services and technical capacities, users interact and experiment with the new technical dimensions and develop new requirements, which then influence the evolution of a new shape for the infra-structure. As the genetic code of the University, the character and quality of the Scholarly Information Center will determine the character and quality of the institution.

And that is why it is so important that we find a way, as a community of scholars, to counteract the fragmenting forces of traditional fiercely held autonomy, the chaos of market-driven incompatibilities and resistance to change, and seek new ways to collaborate effectively to exploit the power of new technologies in the collective interest of the community. Gerald Holton, in a 1977 essay describing the fruitless contemporary search for a unity of knowledge — a synthesis of sciences and the humanities — concluded that as a result of the lack of such a unity, "the need is greater than ever to recognize how small one's own portion of the world is, to view from one's own narrow platform the search of others with interest and sympathy, and so attempt to reestablish a community of learning on the recognition that what binds us together is perhaps chiefly the integrity of our individual concerns.[4]

If we can do that, we will leave a legacy for scholarship and the Electronic Scholar as invaluable for the life of the mind and the advancement of scholarship as the book collections amassed for us by our predecessors.

NOTES

[1]Bagnall, Roger, in *Columbia University Presidential Task Force on Information Processing. Subcommittee on User Needs*. Unpublished, April 1984, p. 10.

[2]Matheson, Nina. *The Academic Library Nexus*, Yuri Nakata Lecture, University of Illinois at Chicago, 1983. Unpublished, p. 1.

[3]Schroeder, John. *The Third Generation*. Unpublished, 1984.

[4]Holton, Gerald. "Introduction. Discoveries and Interpretations: Studies in Contemporary Scholarship." *Daedalus*, Fall 1977, v. 2, p. 6.

CHAPTER 25

Leadership versus Management in Technical Services

Donald E. Riggs

Technical services have always included some of the most complex activities in libraries. Technology and more sophisticated personnel practices have contributed little toward simplifying technical services. The changing environment in this area of the library poses a challenge for those librarians who are responsible for planning the technical services future and making it happen. The implementation of AACR2 is a good example of a challenge that found many libraries unprepared to handle. Closing the card catalog and automating serials are other examples of projects that caught technical services managers off guard.

Tauber defined technical services as "services involving the operations and techniques for acquiring, recording, and preserving materials."[1] This definition remains applicable to today's composition of technical services. In some settings, collection development responsibilities have been removed from technical services, and circulation functions have been added to technical services. The complexities and challenges remain, notwithstanding the few changes in technical services. "Exactness," "production driven," "task oriented," and "high cerebral" are some adjectives commonly used to describe the work performed in technical services.

Prior to the introduction of modern technology to operations and procedures, only a few library science students expressed an interest in technical services. Reference services tended to be a favorite area for the holder of the freshly-minted MLS. It was not uncommon to hear these entry-level librarians say that they did not want to go into technical services because the work was too demanding, too much "clerical-like," and too boring. In the late 1970s a library would receive three times as many applications for a vacant reference position as it would for a vacant cataloger position. However, there has been a turn in this employment interest to where the applications for reference and cataloging positions are similar in number.

Technology is definitely a determining factor in this renewed interest in technical services. Moreover, a different type of leader providing strategic direction has made technical services work more exciting. This new breed of technical services leader has provided vision, zeal, and fervor. It is very important to keep production levels high, manage the day-to-day operations in an highly efficient manner, and maintain ordely processes, *but* it is more important for the head of technical services to be a leader. Leadership begins where management ends.

DIFFERENT BOUGHS ON SAME TREE

Naturally, technical services require someone who can take charge and be responsible for getting the work done. Increasing and sustaining productivity is a responsibility that cannot be slighted. Excellent management of technical services realizes results, and results get attention. Services throughout the library are enhanced when technical operations, processing, and techniques are performed in the most efficient manner. Management and Leadership belong on the same tree, but they have to be recognized as different boughs. Bennis and Nanus in *Leaders* describe the difference between leadership and management:

> The problem with many organizations, and especially the ones that are failing, is that they tend to be overmanaged and underled. They may excel in the ability to handle the daily routine, yet never question whether the routine should be done at all. There is a profound difference between management and leadership, and both are important. "To manage" means "to bring about, to accomplish, to have charge of or responsibility for, to conduct." "Leading" is "influencing, guiding in direction, course, action, opinion." The distinction is crucial. *Managers are people who do things right* and *leaders are people who do the right thing*. The difference may be summarized as activities of vision and judgment — *effectiveness* versus activities of mastering routines — *efficiency*.[2]

It is believed by some that by simply walking through a library's technical services area, one can detect whether the head of technical services is a leader or a manager. This approach to determining leadership is an oversimplification. An observation of physical arrangement of work areas, installation of modern technology, and the general appearance of technical services is not the way to determine leadership effectiveness. Such an observation may reflect well on management acumen only. The essence of leadership is people. Further, all leadership capacities in technical services are not vested in the head of the technical services division. Department heads (e.g., head of acquisitions) must be recognized as leaders in the division. Leadership over human beings is exercised when motives and purposes mobilize institutional, political, psychological and other resources so as to arouse, engage and satisfy the motives of followers.[3]

TRANSFORMATIVE DIRECTION

Technical services have experienced a major transformation during the past decade. These drastic changes have occurred as a result of both happenstance and design. The implementation of modern technology in technical services has created many changes, and more technological advances can be expected in the future. Managers perform many transactional roles; they are good at seeing that the important day-to-day activities in technical services are completed. Transactional managers take pride in leaving work each day with a clean desk. Every organization needs transactional managers.

A notch above the transactional manager is the transformational leader. This person is creative, possesses "high-octane" energy, and recruits a library staff who reflects an optimum service philosophy. This type of leader enjoys making things happen. A transformative direction is established; changes are made in the way things are done. Professional and support staff in technical services become more confident in their work toward attainment of the division's goals and objectives. The staff's perspective moves from a mechanistic view (direct cause and effect) to an organic view (multiple causes and effects). The transformative direction encourages staff to engage in more innovative levels of technical service activities; there is a movement from task motivation to people-interaction motivation. Targets of opportunity are pounced upon by technical services; new strategies and collective energies are pulled together toward the attainment of agree-upon goals/objectives. These collective aspirations are achieved as a result of the symbiotic relationship between the leaders in technical services and their followers.

PROBLEM FINDERS

One of the most vital things a leader can do for technical services is instilling a new mind state about thinking why processes and techniques need to be completed, why they are performed in the current manner, and why it may be better to do them another way. This type of "critical thinking" places "know-why" ahead of "know how." Managers deal with the "know how" aspects of technical services. Very few managers spend much time thinking about the philosophical basis for having a technical services function in the library. Leaders, on the other hand, fully understand and can articulate why the technical services function is important to the entire fabric of the library and to the library's parent institution. Bennis believes leaders have to look inward as well as forward:

> If a leader is not careful, he will be sucked into spending all his time on the important but stifling and inevitably mundane tasks of organizational maintenance. Leadership is the capacity to infuse new values and goals into the organization, to provide perspective on events and environments which, if unnoticed, can impose constraints on the institutions.... Administration is managing given resources efficiently for a given mission. Leaders question the mission. Once the leader gets sucked into the incredibly strong undertow of routine work, he is no longer leading, he is following, which he is not paid to do.[4]

Managing by Wandering Around (MBWA) is described by Peters and Austin as the technology of the obvious.[5] MBWA gleans for the leader the concerns of the staff at all levels throughout technical services. The basic intent of MBWA is to keep in touch with what is happening across all technical services' fronts. Leaders in technical services should talk with staff outside of the division to see what concerns/perceptions abound about the products and services of the division. Such discussions can occur without circumventing other authorities in the library construct. The feedback from these discussions should benefit the entire library.

Routine problem solving is the responsibility of the manager. Anticipating problems and their solutions is the role of the technical services leader. Thus, it is crucial for the technical services leader to know the heartbeat of the division, to seek out problems, and to critically think through solutions to problems.

POWER

We do not hear the word "power" being discussed by librarians; it is seldom, if ever, carried as a program topic at library conferences, and no one writes about it in the library literature. Why? Perhaps one reason is that library leaders do not want to show any signs of flaunting their power. However, modesty by this group should not curtail discussion and investigation of power in libraries by others interested in the topic. Ironically, we all have a thirst for more outstanding leaders in the profession while concurrently not taking the time to develop a better understanding of the use of power. Librarianship is not alone in its suppression of "power" and "authority." Other professions and the American people at large have turned their backs to the concept of power. However, these same people have a hunger for compelling and creative leadership. It is impossible to have strong leaders who have no power. Is there anything worse than a "powerless" leader? We have failed to recognize that the nucleus of leadership is power. Power is not a process designed to hurt someone, and it should not be perceived as being hostile. Power is not designed to lead to corruption, deceit, cruelty, and insensitivity. To the contrary, power is the essential energy to translate intention into reality. It is merely the ability to make decisions, engage in risk taking, and to make things happen.

Leaders cannot lead without power. This basic energy is necessary for initiating and sustaining action. Technical services leaders cannot make things happen without power. The head librarian has to delegate power to the head of technical services, and in turn the department heads must have appropriate power delegated to them. Ideally, the technical services staff will understand and appreciate the constructive uses of power. Power is the most necessary but most distrusted part of leadership.

VISION

Leadership implies that the holder is visionary, to paraphrase Shelley, to see the present in the past and the future in the present. It in incumbent on the head of technical services to create a vision of success and mobilize the division's employees to align behind that vision. This vision must be reflected in the mission statement for technical services. The head of the division and heads of the departments should collectively create visions of potential opportunities for technical services. Brainstorming in group sessions is an excellent way for identifying windows of opportunities. The "multiple futures" approach will assist participants in projecting what technical services "would like to be," and "is likely to be," and it provides a forum for concentrating on an "extreme contrast" case. Some of the greatest insights may occur from the projection of an extreme contrast of what technical services is likely to be in the future. Formulating alternative futures allows the freewheeling necessary for intellectual glimpses into potential futures. If only a figment of the "real" future of technical services can be envisioned through these exercises, they are worth the effort. Sharing visions of technical services' future will be advantageous and will likely pull the division together as it develops a focused enterprise.

Developing a vision for technical services is not enough. The leaders must also know how to harness the vision and to bring it to fruition. The vision must be realistic, credible, and one that is supported by a consensus within technical services. When the technical services vision of the desired future is established, professional and support staff in the division are able to find their roles not only in the division but also in the library. Staff at all levels in the division will bring greater enthusiasm to their positions when they know that the division has made a commitment to a focused future. People like to participate in designing a future with a purpose and direction, and due to their "buy in" with the endeavor, they will commit energies to bring desired intentions into reality.

PLANNING

Vision precedes planning. Without a vision, planning is nearly impossible. Before planning can actually take place, a vision has to animate, transform, and inspirit purpose into action. Vision deals with emotions, values, aspirations, and other nontangible matters, while planning focuses on more tangible issues; in short, planning is geared more to reality.

Now is an exciting time to engage in planning the future of technical services. However, traditional planning will not suffice. The continual changes being made in technical services demand a planning process that is ongoing and being updated at least annually. Strategic planning is the best planning process for technical services. Strategic planning does not focus principally on daily operations or budgetary issues. It does deal with broad intentions of the library; it serves as a planning process which analyzes future threats and opportunities, and it offers alternative courses of action for the library's consideration.[6] One of the best rewards for engaging in strategic planning is that it enables technical services to critically look at current practices and to ask questions such as:

1.   What is the existing situation of technical services?

2.   What is desired in the future for technical services?

3.   What might inhibit the desired future of technical services?

4.   What actions should be taken to achieve the goals and objectives of technical services?

The concept of strategic planning is powerful. Strategic planning solely for the sake of engaging in this type of planning process is not desirable. The true value of strategic planning is in the thinking it promotes in the technical services' personnel involved in the process and its implementation. Undoubtedly, strategic planning requires more cerebral activity than any other planning technique. Davis describes the "thinking" aspect of strategic planning as follows:

> In the placid world of traditional librarianship, strategic thinking was an unnecessary and indeed alien idea connoting conniving in its worst extreme. The library was meant to be carried wherever the satisfaction of the user needs took it. In the turbulent, resource scarce environment of contemporary librarianship, strategic thinking becomes indispensable. However, most librarians are simply not practiced in strategic thinking, which requires a shift in mind set. A mind which is used to thinking forward from action to consequences, must begin to focus on "backward analysis" from desirable future outcomes to immediate requirements. Capability to think strategically needs to be developed in most managers; unfortunately, it seldom is.[7]

Leaders, rather than managers, prefer strategic planning because the development and implementation of strategies is the backbone of strategic planning. Formation of strategies requires brainstorming and thinking. The strategy-formation activity is never-ending; strategists must keep in tune with new developments impacting technical services and they have to consciously design and regularly assess each strategy.

The strategic plan developed for technical services must be in conformance with the strategic plan for the library. If the library does not have a strategic plan, technical services could develop its own plan. However, it may be a bit awkward to get the support of the head librarian for a localized strategic plan. Assuming that the library has a strategic plan, the first step is to get the technical services strategic plan in sync with the overall library plan. The mission statement for technical services is to support the mission statement for the entire library system. After the mission statement is refined, goals and objectives are established; strategies are formulated for the goals and objectives. Leaders in technical services will find it very prudent to see that individual staff members' annual goals are closely related to the strategic plan's goals/objectives.

Technological advances will continue to have a measurable impact on technical services. The burden is on technical services leaders to put technology in the proper perspective. Technology is not an end; it is a means to an end. Those who operate in the inactive or reactive mode while dealing with new technologies will end up as "strategic failures."

THE ENTREPRENEURIAL LEADER

It is no secret that entrepreneurialism is in vogue. Today, entrepreneurs are hailed as the strength of our country, the hope of the future, the affirmation of our ideals, the cat's meow. Granted, most of the entrepreneurial activities are taking place in the private and corporate world. Nevertheless, the library world most certainly needs an injection of the entrepreneurial spirit.

The entrepreneurial leader in technical services is best described as one who is an innovator, a creative person, and one who dislikes maintaining the status quo. Unquestionably, the entrepreneur wants to see results immediately. It is best to judge the entrepreneur on the attainment of goals/objectives, and not on the process used to achieve the desired output. Very few library managers can be classed as entrepreneurs; this class is reserved for leaders. Managers tend to like things nice and tidy. An entrepreneurial leader in technical services may generate some discomfort among colleagues. An entrepreneur will have the effect of challenging old norms in technical services, something not always looked upon favorably. Some people in technical services may feel threatened by an entrepreneurial leader, mainly because they are most secure in their positions when things are quiet and are made uneasy within a changing environment. The entrepreneurial leader must be sensitive to the discomfort of those who have long resisted any change in technical services' operations and techniques. The change maker should never attack colleagues when challenging a technical services activity; the attack should be upon inflexible objectives, ideas, or procedures. The typical entrepreneur is a tough, competitive risk taker with a firm conviction to succeed. Entrepreneurs may be risk takers, but they are not gamblers. They are calculated risk takers; their risk taking occurs in areas over which they have control, and where their planning and projections can offer some hedge against unpredictable future. Technical services, as other areas of the library, need persons with entrepreneurial attributes. If there is a major reservation about entrepreneurial leaders, it is that they like to do things themselves rather than work through their colleagues. In the corporate world entrepreneurs tend to work independently. Only time will tell how effective an entrepreneurial leader can serve in the library arena.

POSITIVE SELF-REGARD

Leadership is a deeply personal business. The higher one goes in leadership positions, the more interpersonal and human one's work becomes. Executives in Fortune 500 firms spend roughly 90 percent of their time with others. These same executives must pay close attention to managing themselves; the use of their time is vital to their effectiveness. Leaders in technical services are very similar to these high-level executives in many ways. They, too, must first be able to manage themselves before they can manage and lead their colleagues.

In their study of various leaders in all walks of life, Bennis and Nanus found no trace of self-worship or cockiness; they also arrived at the following definition of what positive self-regard is not: "To begin with, it is not a crowing self-importance or egotistic self-centeredness ... Nor is it what's ordinarily meant by a 'narcissistic character.' "[8]

Leaders must have self-respect. They have to believe in their abilities. The self-evoking leaders are those who recognize their strengths and compensate for their weaknesses. It is unwise for any technical services leader to assume universal knowledge of all areas of technical services.

Leaders with positive self-regard interact with others in the following ways:

1. The ability to accept people as they are, not as you would like them to be.

2. The capacity to approach relationships and problems in terms of the present rather than the past.

3. The ability to treat those who are close to you with the same courteous attention that you extend to strangers and casual acquaintances.

4. The ability to trust others, even if the risk seems great.

5. The ability to do without constant approval and recognition from others.[9]

COMPASSION

Effective leaders are compassionate people. They genuinely care about their followers. Technical services leaders will readily see signs of better morale, increased productivity, and more collaborative efforts if colleagues are treated with compassion. Needless to say, the staff is the most precious resource of any library division/department. Library leaders should make an extra effort to formulate goals that will bring out the very best in the staff. Douglas McGregor's Theory Y—the integration of individual and organizational goals—should be in every library leader's repertoire.

Compassion is somewhat like power. Very little is written about it, and it also never appears as a topic on a library conference program. Why? Are library leaders afraid to let their guard down and open admit that they really care about their staffs? The "distance" between the supervisor and subordinate can be maintained in technical services while at the same time treating subordinates in the most humane manner possible. Mutual respect will develop between leaders and followers in such an environment and there will be little or no overfamiliarity issues. The ability to let another working colleague know that the leader of the division/department really cares about the individual and appreciates one's contributions is an important element of effective leadership.

STAFF DEVELOPMENT

Leaders, more than managers, will be more attuned to the imperfections of the technical services staff. Leadership is responsible for developing and refining a more desirable future for followership. With the emphasis on exactness in much of technical services' activities, the comment that "If you haven't ever made a mistake, you haven't been trying hard enough" is appropriate while addressing staff development. A good leader is one who stretches the staff to do more in order to achieve lofty goals. Provision must be made for embracing errors and engaging in calculated risk taking. Leaders have to strive for a fit between the strengths of technical services staff and the established organizational requirements for the division.

Technical services is one of the more dynamic areas in the library. Staffing requirements keep changing to meet the new demands. The online environment has forced modifications in job descriptions. Working with an online public catalog in lieu of the card catalog has necessitated a new approach to catalog maintenance. New technology in serials control has resulted in long-awaited streamlining of procedures. These are only a few changes that have made it necessary for professional and support staff to upgrade their skills or retool for new responsibilities and duties. Leaders in technical services are cognizant of these changes and most are taking the initiative to provide a positive environment for coping with new staff development requirements.

In library circles technical services personnel are held more accountable for sustaining high production levels than personnel in most other library divisions. This expectation has its pros and cons. On the positive side, after a day's work one can reflect proudly on what was accomplished. We all like to see measurable results of our efforts. On the other side, one cannot keep production up at the highest levels if there is an expectation that one should participate in workshops, conferences, and other programs that will update or improve technical services' skills. Understanding leaders will make allowances for participation in these necessary programs. They are aware of the fact that enhancing the skills of staff is a sound investment for the division/department. In addition to making time for program attendance, it is wise for leaders in technical services to allow the professional staff release time per week (e.g., 10 percent) to work on relevant projects. Projects of this nature must have the blessing of the immediate supervisor. Time will reflect that these programs and projects will result in better technical services. Staff will have an improved sense of worth, be more energized, and enjoy a stronger commitment to the division's mission.

MOTIVATE AND INSPIRE

Theory X—motivating by the carrot-and-stick way—no longer works. People want something more meaningful than a few tangible rewards. Improvement in the workplace has always been a high priority for workers in virtually all types of employment. Followers like to know what the intentions of leaders are and appreciate learning about these intentions through direct and concise communication from leaders. Communication is an important responsibility of leaders, and it can be used as a motivating force if the leaders transmit their interpretations and meanings of desired outcomes in such a way that followers feel they are part of the action. Followers must enjoy a true sense of worth in technical services. The leader can motivate and inspire followers by articulating and embodying the ideals toward which technical services are striving. "Striving for excellence" is an appropriate theme for any organization to follow. A theme of this nature inherently develops a "win-win" perspective for all persons associated with the organization. Values shift from a tentative "win-lose" stance to one of a "winner's" feeling. Communicating a clear, attractive, and attainable sense of purpose in technical services is a "must" ingredient in motivating and inspiring staff. Leaders, more than managers, function on the emotional and spiritual resources of the organization, collective values and aspirations are very important aspects to followers. Managers, by contrast, deal with physical resources (e.g., new materials, technology) of the organization.

CONCLUSION

Leaders, not managers, will move technical services into the twenty-first century. Followers of these technical services' leaders want to be shown the way and provided the experiences that convince them that their loyalty to the group is a good thing. Leadership is not a matter of hypnosis or blandishment, nor is it a process of exploiting others for extraneous ends. It is a matter of drawing out from individuals those impulses, motives, and efforts that represent them most truly. Leadership in technical services builds confidence and empowers the staff. It is a matter of directing technical services staff, in associated effort, toward personal improvement, integrated desires, and heightened sensibility. Leadership is known by the personalities it enriches. The proof of leading is in the qualitative growth of those being led in technical services, as individuals and as a group.

NOTES

[1]Maurice F. Tauber, *Technical Services in Libraries* (New York: Columbia University Press, 1954), p. 4.

[2]Warren Bennis and Burt Nanus, *Leaders: The Strategies for Taking Charge* (New York: Harper & Row, 1985), p. 21.

[3]James MacGregor Burns, *Leadership* (New York: Harper & Row, 1978), p. 18.

[4]Warren Bennis, *The Leaning Ivory Tower* (San Francisco: Jossey-Bass Publishers, 1973), pp. 83-84.

[5]Tom Peters and Nancy Austin, *A Passion for Excellence: The Leadership Difference* (New York: Random House, 1985), p. 9.

[6]Russell L. Ackoff, *A Concept of Corporate Planning* (New York: John Wiley & Sons, 1970), p. 2.

[7]Peter Davis, "Libraries at the Turning Point: Issues in Proactive Planning," *Journal of Library Administration* 1 (Summer 1980): 11-24.

[8]Bennis and Nanus, pp. 66-67.

[9]Ibid.

CHAPTER 26

Managing Innovation in Academic Libraries

Miriam A. Drake

Fundamental changes in the economics and technology of academic library operations have stimulated librarians and administrators to seek ways of introducing and implementing innovation in libraries.

Zaltman has observed, "The impetus to innovation arises when organizational decision makers perceive that the organization's present course of action is unsatisfactory. When a discrepancy exists between what the organization is doing and what its decision makers believed it ought to be doing, there is a performance gap."[1]

Many academic library decision makers are feeling the frustration of this "performance gap." Several new ideas and innovations are serving to help close the gap, such as the proposed National Periodicals Center, shared cataloging through RLIN, WLN, and OCLC, and the interlibrary loan system of OCLC.

While these services are contributing to the efficiency of libraries, they are not sufficient, by themselves, to close the gap between current library and information service and the potential for service that could become a reality if existing technology were adapted to user information needs. These services are also not sufficient to close the gaps between user expectations and the library's ability to meet those expectations.

Lancaster has observed, "The profession seems to have its head in the sand. The paperless society is rapidly approaching. Ignoring this fact will not cause it to go away."[2] In a forecast of telecommunications in the year 2000, Martino has stated, "Rather than visiting a library, any individual might be able to search the library files electronically and receive a printout of specific information or a facsimile copy of a desired document."[3]

During the 1980s libraries could be reduced to archival repositories because people will be accessing bibliographic data bases and text through computers in their homes and offices. These predictions while extreme and painful are indicative of trends with which librarians must deal. There is little doubt that technology can make these predictions become a reality; however, they ignore the human service functions fulfilled by libraries.

Adoption of computer and telecommunications technologies to library and information service needs will require capital and innovative thinking in the library profession. How can libraries maintain their function of human service in a machine environment? How can libraries use this technology to provide more responsive service? These questions are only two of the many that need to be addressed.

The purpose of this paper is to present issues related to the managerial aspects of innovation in academic libraries. The specific issues to be covered include performance gaps, incentives to innovate, nature of innovation, barriers and constraints, impact of innovation, and implementation of innovative strategies.

PERFORMANCE GAPS

Library directors, librarians, and support staff appear to agree that something is wrong in the library. In many cases, teaching faculties, students, and institutional administrators agree that the library is not performing as they would like. The performance gaps relate to the differences between services being provided and services that could be provided with the adoption of technology, relationships between library and teaching faculties, library and institutional adminstrations, and library administration and staff.

Perceptions of the service gap cannot be generalized. They vary from library to library and depend on faculty and student awareness of technology, budget situations, and user demands. Several library directors have expressed extreme frustration over the decreasing purchasing power of funds at a time when faculty demands for instant gratification in the form of more books are increasing. Other library directors, dealing with technologically aware faculty, are trying to find capital to provide improved information retrieval services and faster document delivery methods.

These pressures are exacerbated in some institutions by administrators who are trying to compensate for enrollment declines with greater sponsored research activity. More intense competition among faculty members for tenure and promotion causes them to place greater demands on libraries. These demands coupled with budget pressures and other barriers to innovation create a performance gap.

Growing and changing demands will place greater pressure on library administrators to enhance fuzzy mission statements with operational goals and objectives. McClure states, "One must recognize the difference between goals and objectives — they are not the same. Goals provide long-range guidelines (five years or more) for organizational activity; they might never be accomplished, and they are not measured. In contrast, objectives are measurable, short range, and time limited."[4] McAnally and Downs indicated that the libraries have rarely done a good job of planning.[5]

Without purpose, planning is an exercise in futility. Achievement of objectives may require the elimination as well as the addition of services and materials. In order to have operational objectives, the library, teaching faculty, and institutional administration will have to agree on specific services and materials to be provided by the library and adjust their expectations to fit the objectives. This task is particularly difficult in a large university where faculties are often in conflict with one another. Humanities faculties tend to equate good libraries with big libraries, while engineers and management people seek information rather than books. In the setting of goals and objectives, the library and academic administrators become negotiators between the warring factions.

The administration of the college or university will need to acquire a greater understanding and sensitivity to the economics of libraries in terms of costs and benefits as well as inputs and outputs. Since libraries are part of overhead costs and administrators are charged with keeping costs as low as possible, academic administrators are likely to look to the library as a place to cut costs.

Many library budget cuts are not purposeful cuts. The director is told to cut X percent from the budget and may not be given any guidance on what services or materials to cut.

Academic administrators facing severe overhead cost problems engendered by a variety of federal regulations may not realize or be sensitive to the impact of undirected cuts in terms of the library's ability to serve the needs of its clientele.

Staff present a different set of problems to library administrators. McAnally and Downs observed in 1973 that library staff ranked second out of five in the growing pressures on library directors. They further observed, "It may seem strange that the director should be under attack from his own staff, or fail to receive badly needed support in relations with administration and faculty, but it is so in many cases .... They want and expect a share in policy decisions affecting themselves and the library."[6]

Library directors have tried and are trying a variety of schemes to involve staff in the decision-making process. Dickinson has pointed out that "... 'participative management' has been used indiscriminately to mean everything from a situation wherein the library management simply seeks information and/or advice from staff members to one wherein the library is governed by plebiscite."[7]

Despite the best efforts of many library directors to change managerial style, rely more heavily on committees, and generally involve staff in decision-making processes, staff remain dissatisfied. In recent years, staff discontent has been exacerbated by the failure of salaries to keep pace with the cost of living, changing student and faculty demands, and potential changes inherent in computer and telecommunications technologies. Some library staff members may feel that their jobs or work habits are threatened by technological innovation.

INCENTIVES TO INNOVATE

Despite the potential threat to the professional and psychological well-being of some library personnel, library administrators may have no choice but to adopt innovative strategies to meet objectives and goals in a different society. Lancaster and others have raised the question of whether libraries will be needed in an electronic world. He states that the library problem may not be lack of space or financial resources; "rather it is likely to be one of justification for existence and simple survival."[8]

Technology can and will bring information directly into the home and office of the future. The place of the library in society will depend on how rapidly it integrates technology into its operations and how rapidly the engineers and designers of information systems will recognize the library as an important link in the system. While technology appears to be the major driving force for innovation, there are other factors contributing to the need to innovate. As technology has developed more effective and cheaper electronic computing and telecommunications devices, the economics of library operations has changed dramatically.

The rate of increase in the cost of library inputs has been consistently higher than the general inflation rate. Library output costs consisting largely of labor have not risen as rapidly. Because input costs are generally fixed costs in a library, the average cost per unit of output is rising in libraries where output levels have remained relatively constant or decreased.

Labor productivity and user productivity have been declining as collections, catalogs, and files have increased in size. The amount of capital invested in laborsaving equipment and processes is minimal in most libraries. Teaching faculties and librarians may find the term *productivity* offensive as it is usually related to the output of factory workers and farmers. Productivity in a library context relates the value of results obtained by staff or users from a given amount of effort in searching for information or documents.

Changing patterns of demand also provide incentives to innovate. In addition to providing course-related reading material, libraries are being asked to provide substantive information when needed and in a form that is convenient for the user. The potential of technology to provide information when and where needed coupled with the need to reduce the labor intensity of library operations is a prime motivator in innovation.

THE NATURE OF INNOVATION

Innovation is not limited to science and technology. Drucker's broader definition is "... the task of endowing human and material resources with new and greater wealth producing capacity."[9] In Drucker's terms, innovation is economic and social change which does not create new knowledge but creates potential for action and added wealth. Sawyer defines *innovation* as a "usful new combination of resources."[10] Innovation is not a device or a scheme. Rather it is a concept or a change in human activity. The concept is "continually evolving as the uncertainties are made to disappear and the targets turn into outcome."[11] Innovation is a deliberate process rather than a chance happening or discovery. Motivating people to want to change and to implement new plans and ideas is at the heart of innovation.

"Innovation is not R & D, though it begins with research and continues with the entirely different process of development."[12] While research may result in invention and development may refine an invention into a finished, marketable product or process, innovation results in a change in the way people live and accomplish specific tasks. Innovation may be adoption of a technological device or process or it may be a new managerial or social process. Whatever it is, it relies heavily on human perceptions of something better in the future.

This development usually is to achieve a specific purpose and is a directed effort. The development of the MARC record, shared cataloging, electronic message systems, and management by objectives represents innovations that were initiated, developed, and implemented to achieve specific outcomes.

The literature of innovation, for the most part, deals with the concept in profit-making corporations. Discussions of innovation in the public sector point out that service industries and state and local governments are consumers of innovation rather than producers. The federal government is both a consumer and producer of innovation.[13] Innovation in inforamtion retrieval and other areas of human activity was funded initially by the federal government.

BARRIERS TO INNOVATION

There are a wide variety of barriers to innovation in academic institutions and libraries. These barriers relate to psychology, organizational factors, perceptions of the future, and economic factors.

The psychological constraints to innovate stem from fear of change, especially planned change, and the unknown. Library staff and users accustomed to the present-day library are reluctant to give up comfortable habits and established ways of accomplishing tasks. Library staff may feel threatened by systems analysts, computer types, and others who do not speak their language and appear to have little sympathy with their problems. There may be feelings of being manipulated. "People resist being changed by other people...,[14] especially planners and innovators. Their resistance may be based on fear of change, threat of being manipulated, conflicting interests, constrained freedom of choice, or failure to see the value of the innovation. With technological innovation in libraries, users and librarians legitimately fear that the library will be more impersonal and the art of the book will die.

The organizational factors inhibiting change are both internal and external to the library. While most academic administrators believe that a library is essential to an educational institution, for some, the library has retained its "bottomless pit" image. Other administrators see innovation as a way to give the pit a bottom but either don't know how to stimulate and reward innovative thinking or don't want to invest the necessary capital. The lack of understanding and support leaves librarians in an impossible position of being "damned if they do and damned if they don't."

Planning and budgeting in publicly supported colleges and universities are not geared to investment and innovative activity. There is a tendency to allocate the budget on a "use it or lose it" basis rather than a planned basis leading to sufficient funding for academic services that are valuable to the institution. While many universities have obtained funds for the addition of audiovisual equipment and materials and computer-aided instruction, these innovative techniques remain underutilized in many instructional programs. The chalk and blackboard are comfortable and require little new thinking or activity.

Universities also create barriers to innovation because innovation may not be rewarded, especially in the library. Across-the-board salary increases and competitive promotion and tenure situations tend to inhibit rather than stimulate innovation.

The lack of output measures of value in library operations constrains innovation. Academic administrators are more concerned with the cost of input than the value of output. They may be unsympathetic to library innovation because of focus on input and fail to see the contribution to output. Information, knowledge, and reading produce social value that cannot be easily quantified. Measurements of input versus social output or costs versus social benefits are elusive and do not provide needed justification for capital investment.

Economic factors limiting innovation in the library relate to capital, investment, risk, and uncertainty. The "use it or lose it" approach to budgeting does not allow the library to accumulate capital to invest in technology or innovation. Capital appropriations generally are one-shot deals used for new typewriters, buildings, or stacks. The result of this practice is that not only are libraries technologically underdeveloped, they are also starved for capital.

University administrators appear unwilling to invest funds in innovation that will improve library staff and user productivity or make the library more efficient. Payoffs from investments in libraries are difficult to calculate. The value of the librarian is perceived in terms of the salary paid rather than the value produced. There is little consideration given to the value of user time in the library and how that time can be made more productive.

Risk and uncertainty are key factors in the process as well as the economics of innovation. Although innovation is a deliberate process, there is a risk that a particular project will fail or that results will be less than expected. "The most dramatic evidence of the risk involved in ... innovation is the recent experience of Princeton University Library with 3M's automated circulation...."[15] This project ended in failure, the 3M system has been withdrawn from the market, and Princeton has returned to a manual method to charge out books.

This failure, however, is more than balanced by successful projects in many libraries; for example, the Ohio State University circulation system, a high-risk project at its inception, is a success. Implementation of shared cataloging and its by-products, involving hundreds of libraries, is another example of successful change.

Uncertainty is related to project success and failure as well as future conditions and investment. Academic institutions are facing an uncertain future with regard to enrollment, government funding, research activity, and endowment funding. In a highly uncertain economic environment, a natural tendency is to try to conserve what is at hand rather than invest for future gain. Project selection and the process of the individual projects also contain elements of uncertainty. With many projects from which to choose and fuzzy measures of payoff and benefit/cost, management has to live with the idea that the projects chosen may not turn out to have been the best selections. "Uncertainty resides at the level of the individual project, where the 'best' way to proceed seldom is apparent and the individuals involved instead have to be satisfied with finding a promising way."[16]

Until recently, librarians have had the luxury of living in a relatively certain and risk-free environment. An innovative environment calls for new skills in risk assessment, ability to understand uncertainty, and ability to manage increased entrepreneurial activity.

THE IMPACT OF INNOVATION

Innovation has changed and will continue to change everyone's life in dramatic ways. Downs and Mohr have identified three categories of benefits related to innovation: (1) programmatic, (2) prestige, and (3) structural.[17]

Programmatic benefits are greater efficiency or effectiveness in accomplishing organizational goals, such as increased profit or market share in the private sector and production of improved service at the same or lower cost in the public sector.

The prestige benefit is the recognition and approval that are associated with early adoption of a new program or technology.

Structural benefits are related to individuals in the form of greater worker satisfaction or some other internal value.

Innovation in libraries, thus far, has produced both advantages and disadvantages. Shared cataloging systems have resulted in programmatic benefits for libraries but have resulted in some disadvantages for the worker. While some catalogers may feel greater satisfaction at being able to share their knowledge and skill, others may feel that the value of their professional judgment has decreased because they are prisoners of the terminal.

The potential impact of technological and systems innovations on libraries is difficult to forecast. If libraries survive as viable organizations giving useful and valuable service, it is unlikely that their present forms of organization and operation will persist. It is likely that academic libraries will evolve in different ways. The small college library serving primarily instructional programs will not change in the same way as large university libraries serving research as well as instruction. There is not nor should there be uniformity among academic libraries. Each library should be encouraged to recognize the important factors and the unique elements within its own institutional setting. A "me too" approach should be used only when it is compatible with the goals and operations of the library.

As innovation proceeds, library staff and users will need to adapt to new ways of finding information and documents. The library's role in the information process will depend heavily on how quickly it adopts technology to make that process more efficient while retaining personal service.

Information technology is developing rapidly in the private sector. Libraries no longer are the sole sources of information for teaching and research faculties. Many librarians feel that this competition is unfair. In an era of tax revolts and taxpayer demands for spending limitations, competition is probably a fact of life. Competition from the private sector could reduce the importance of libraries in many areas.

IMPLEMENTING INNOVATION

Given the constraints, how can libraries adopt and implement innovative strategies? There is no recipe for transforming libraries into innovative organizations; however, experience in other kinds of organizations has identified some of the characteristics of innovators and innovating organizations.

The first characteristic is a positive attitude about the future and a belief that the future can be modified by decisions made in the present. Drucker has stated, "Innovative organizations spend neither time nor resources defending yesterday."[18] An innovator does not concern himself or herself with the past but focuses on a vision of the future. Within innovative organizations, the climate nurtures creative thinking and change.

The climate does not develop overnight but is built over a period of time. People with new ideas and the ability to develop those ideas are rewarded and recognized in innovative organizations. "Readiness for change gradually becomes a characteristic of certain individuals, groups, organizations and civilizations. They no longer look nostalgically at a golden age in the past but anticipate their utopia in days to come."[19]

The responsibility for creating readiness for change and innovative strategies rests with management. Daft points out that top managers bridge the gap between the organization and technological development. Their status places "... them in a position to introduce change into an organization."[20] They are exposed to new ideas from outside the organization and can stimulate new thinking within the organization. "The individual manager controls in large measure the kind and quality of ideas he will hear, by the questions he asks and the interest he shows in the answers. In that part of the job concerned with innovation, each manager must be reponsible for stimulating the flow of ideas by appropriate questions and interest and by considerate screening of the idea he receives."[21] Most of the ideas received are likely to be rejected; however, acceptance or rejection must be based on standards and appropriateness and be in harmony with organizational goals. Only few ideas will merit further investigation and careful evaluation.

Innovative managers recognize that innovation doesn't just happen. An idea without development remains an idea, good or bad. Innovation is deliberate, purposeful, and, in most cases, a planned process or program. There is an objective or goal to be achieved that requires resources to develop an idea into a program or innovation to be incorporated into library operations. "In ... concentrating effort on the best ideas, the manager takes up the bare essence (which is the idea) and breathes life into it; he gives it form and dimension. He makes the idea his own, not in the sense of taking it from the originator, but in the sense of giving commitment, and adding the weight of his own recommendation to the request for additional development."[22]

Innovation and change require an organizational structure that facilitates the flow of communication up and down. Ideally, innovative ideas should originate at both ends of an organizational hierarchy. Administrative ideas originate at the top and move down while technical innovation originates near the bottom and moves up.[23] A great many words have been written about managerial styles and communication in libraries. McAnally and Downs suggest, "The director has to surrender some of his old authority and becomes more of a leader"[24] in a more participatory environment. The staff dissatisfaction discussed by McAnally and Downs in 1973 has not abated in 1979 despite the good faith efforts of many library directors and programs, such as MRAP.

Dickinson, in his review of participative management, concluded, "Some library managers are unwilling to admit that they want and need control over the operations for which they are accountable ... participative management or power sharing should not — and cannot, if it is to be successful — mean an abdication of responsibility for the library on the part of administrators and managers, in the name of democracy."[25]

Innovation and idea generation rarely occur in groups. Individuals have ideas. Management is the catalyst needed to bring an idea to the point of innovation. The usual library committee structures are not conducive to idea generation or innovative thinking. In using committees in the innovative process, managers should keep the words of L.J. Peter in mind: "No committee could ever come up with anything as revolutionary as a camel — anything as practical and as perfectly designed to perform effectively under such difficult conditions."[26] Committees are useful in studying specific issues and defining problems. A special task force drawn from appropriate departments of the library can be useful in drawing up plans to implement and integrate an innovation into library operations.

In the process of managing innovation, library users can be valuable. People responsible for developing new library programs should be sensitive not only to the user's needs but also to the user's wants. There may be substantial differences between needs and wants. If innovation is to succeed, users will need to be convinced that it is worthwhile.

A manager or library director may work at fine-tuning the climate of the library to produce innovation or new ideas and find that there is no response. He or she may proclaim in a loud voice that upward communications are welcome but find a quiet telephone or empty mailbox. If libraries are to implement significant change and staff is to be part of that change, library administrators will need actively to encourage change.

This encouragement should result in serious review of new ideas and innovation proposals as well as follow-through in development and feedback to the innovator. In addition, it may be necessary to alter the rewards and punishment system substantially so that innovators are recognized and rewarded with salary increases or perquisites.

Lastly, the library director desirous of closing performance gaps and shaping a meaningful rule for the library in the future must present possibilities with enthusiasm, commitment, and confidence. He or she must communicate a sense of excitement and ability to make improvements in the future.

CONCLUSIONS

Innovation is a purposeful economic and social change. If libraries are to continue their important contribution to the instructional and research missions of academic institutions, a climate conducive to change and generation of new ideas must be created. Library administrators must view innovation seriously and provide follow-through to develop ideas into innovations that can be integrated into library operations. Librarianship may be the fastest-changing and most exciting profession today. The potential to improve information service through technology is largely unrealized. Transforming potential into reality will require capital, innovation, perseverance, and leadership.

NOTES

[1]Gerald Zaltman, Robert Duncan, and Jonny Holbek, *Innovations and Organizations* (New York: Wiley, 1973), p. 55.

[2]F. Wilfrid Lancaster, "Whither Libraries? or, Wither Libraries," *College & Research Libraries* 39:357 (Sept. 1978).

[3]Joseph P. Martino, "Telecommunications in the Year 2000," *Futurist* 13:99 (April 1979).

[4]Charles R. McClure, "The Planning Process: Strategies for Action," *College & Research Libraries* 39:459 (Nov. 1978).

[5]Arthur M. McAnally and Robert B. Downs, "The Changing Role of Directors of University Libraries," *College & Research Libraries* 34:112 (March 1973).

[6]Ibid., p. 111.

[7]Dennis W. Dickinson, "Some Reflections on Participative Management in Libraries," *College & Research Libraries* 39:254 (July 1978).

[8]Lancaster, "Whither Libraries?" p. 346.

[9]Peter F. Drucker, *Management: Tasks, Responsibilities, and Practice* (New York: Harper & Row, 1974), p. 67.

[10]George C. Sawyer, "Innovation in Organizations," *Long Range Planning* 11:54 (Dec. 1978).

[11]H. Brian Locke, "Planning Innovation," *Long Range Planning* 11:21 (Dec. 1978).

[12]H. Brian Locke, "Innovation by Design," *Long Range Planning* 9:35 (Aug. 1976).

[13]J. David Roessner, "Incentives to Innovate in Public and Private Organizations," *Administration & Society* 9:341-65 (Nov. 1977).

[14]David E. Ewing, *The Human Side of Planning: Tool or Tyrant?* (London: Macmillan, 1969), p. 44.

[15]Miriam A. Drake and Harold A. Olsen, "The Economics of Library Innovation," *Library Trends* 28:98 (Summer 1979).

[16]Richard R. Nelson and Sidney G. Winter, "In Search of Useful Theory of Innovation," *Research Policy* 6:51 (Jan. 1977).

[17]George W. Downs, Jr., and Lawrence Mohr, "Toward a Theory of Innovation," *Administration & Society* 10:379-408 (Feb. 1979).

[18]Drucker, *Management*, p. 791.

[19]Zaltman, Duncan, and Holbek, *Innovations,* p. 103.

[20]Richard L. Daft, "A Dual-Care Model of Organizational Innovation," *Academy of Management Journal* 21:193 (June 1978).

[21]Sawyer, "Innovation," p. 54.

[22]Ibid., p. 55.

[23]Daft, "A Dual-Care Model," p. 195.

[24]McAnally and Downs, "The Changing Role," p. 120.

[25]Dickinson, "Participative Management," p. 260-61.

[26]Laurence J. Peter, *Peter's Quotations: Ideas for Our Time* (New York: Morrow, 1977), p. 120.

CHAPTER 27

Managing a Special Library
Part I

Judy Labovitz

I have written this talk in my head a dozen times over the last couple of months. As I encountered a situation or read an article or talked to someone, I would think—this is it. This is the main point. This is the essence of excellence in management.

But when I actually sat down to write, I realized it's not just one, or even several major qualities that make for excellence in management. It's all the little things you do day after day. These little day-to-day management techniques transcend the organization you work for.

In an early letter from Bob Bellanti concerning this talk, Bob asked me to compare differences in my management techniques that were associated with the different corporations where I had worked. But, in fact, the techniques I use today I would have used in my past positions, if I had today's knowledge and could start over.

What are these techniques and how do they relate to some of the qualities discussed in the book, *In Search of Excellence*? First, my overall philosophy of management fits in well with the first quality that Peters and Waterman mention—a bias toward action. I am a hands-on, action-oriented, get-it-done-any-way-you-can person, (some people might even say I am rash and aggressive in my approach).

I

If you look around you, you will find there are very few decision-makers in this world. Most people are afraid to take the risk of making a decision. If you want to stand out in a crowd, make a decision. (Or, if appropriate, make someone else make a decision.) How do you accomplish this? Let me give a few ways to proceed to action.

Set time limits for action. "I want you to analyze the situation and have a recommendation by such and such a date." Let your people know that decision-making is something you evaluate them on. What about dealing with your boss or upper management? Try this approach. In writing or verbally, state, "This is what I going to do unless I hear to the contrary from you by such and such a date." If your boss says he will think about an issue and keeps putting it off, don't let him get away with it. Keep reminding him that he owes you an action decision. You may be labelled a pest in the short run, but in the long run your accomplishments will outshine your pest image. You will get a reputation for getting things done.

Reprinted with permission from the *Journal of Library Administration*, Vol. 6(3), Fall 1985. Copyright 1985, The Haworth Press, New York.

One of my secrets of success when dealing with upper management is realizing that they (1) don't like making decisions, (2) do want people to think of them as decision makers, (3) don't have time to read a lot. Using this to best advantage, I always try to present proposals/requests as succinctly as possible. I always give at least three options with an explanation of why the option I want is the one that will work best. I am not implying that upper management is incompetent. It's just that they are usually operating on information overload and have too many demands made on their time. The person that comes in with a clear, concise, and well-thought-out proposal naturally has a better chance of success.

What if you decide on a course of action and you find out you made the wrong decision? That's life. You have to learn to pick yourself off the floor, salvage what you can, and go on to bigger and better mistakes. The real danger is to perpetuate the mistake for fear of letting the world know you are human. Humility once in a while is a good character builder. Needless to say, action over inaction is a necessary element if you are to be a success.

II

Another essential element and perhaps *the one most* important factor is *people*. High productivity, quality products, or services are the result of a highly motivated and well-trained staff. For the manager, creating and maintaining an environment to support the concept of "productivity through people" is a difficult task. Here are some of the ways I try to motivate people:

1. I communicate as honestly as I can about what is going on in the company. I pass down information.

2. I encourage people to speak up and ask for their opinions about their jobs and other issues that affect them.

3. I believe everyone should know what's going on in the library. We have, in fact, a system of back-ups that is two people deep.

4. I encourage people to find better, more efficient ways of working. I give them credit for their ideas and allow them to implement the changes.

5. In addition to training for back-ups, we allow staff to learn something about any function in the library. If enough people are interested, we will hold a general training/information session on the topic.

6. I allow discussion and controversy and challenge people to come up with ideas and solutions. If someone brings up a problem, they will get first crack at a solution.

7. We hold regular staff meetings and to keep them from getting boring, we occasionally ask other departments to speak to us about their departments. Once in a while, I will throw in a psychology test or game.

8. I encourage everyone to give strokes to others when they do a good job. Sometimes it's hard to remember how important this is, especially if we work in a non-stroking institution. I try to keep interactions positive and constructive rather than negative and destructive.

9. I discourage hierarchical job distinctions. All jobs are important to the running of a successful library. In a small library, if any one function is poorly run, it reflects on everyone. Staff are encouraged to chip in and help each other out. This applies to professional staff helping library assistants as well. In other words, I try to build a team.

10. I don't let the institutional environment influence the library group negatively. If morale is low in the company, I ignore it and concentrate on keeping up the morale in the library. If morale is high in the company, I capitalize on it.

It all comes down to a cliché: treat employees the way you would like to be treated. If people know you will go the extra mile for them, they will go the extra mile for you. Actually, my goal has always been to be able to sit in my office drinking champagne and eating bon bons, confident that the library is operating splendidly without me.

III

Another factor found in successful companies, and one that in my opinion is a natural complement to the first two qualities I have talked about, is a hands-on, value-driven approach to management.

I want to thank Peters and Waterman for legitimizing a behavior pattern of mine that I have always been kidded about. I am an MBWA, I Manage by Walking Around. I call it shuffling. It's the best way I know to find out how well your operation is really functioning. It's also the best way I know to stay on top of what's going on in the company—and I don't mean hot gossip. I sit with different people at lunch, I drop by someone's office or chat with them while they are standing in the lunch line. I go to Happy Hours. I stay late to chat with the ones who are hard to catch during the day. The pay-off far outweighs the time I spend.

Although each company I have worked for has had a corporate personality or culture, I find that one really needs to develop a library culture. This library culture should develop naturally out of the service philosophy and energy and personalities of the people that work in the library. If the library works as a team, if they like what they do, if the staff is competent and communication is good, a set of shared values will emerge that will form the basis of a "library personality." The Cetus library personality, for example, has been characterized by our Director of Public Relations as "sensitive to user needs but feisty."

IV

Not only do we managers have to worry about being action-oriented and motivating people to be successful, but most of us have to accomplish this with limited staff. Very few libraries, if any, in private industry are run on an abundance of staff, which in a way is fortunate because (1) this "lean machine" provides many opportunities for creative management and (2) it results in having to follow a successful management principle by necessity rather than design.

We cannot afford layers of management. We are all "working managers." No job is beneath us if the pressure is on. On the other hand, our staff know that what they do today, they may not be doing tomorrow. I always look for flexibility in potential hirees because I know anyone who can't handle constant change will be unhappy working for me.

Time management and simple, easy ways of doing things are a necessity when staff is short and people have to cover for one another periodically. To give staff a feeling of accomplishment, we try to equalize job loads. In addition, time management sessions are held for all new employees. After new employees have been with the library for a while, they are required to fill out a daily half-hour log of their time for two weeks. This is to help people organize their time and their job to best advantage.

V

Now that our libraries are operating efficiently and our staff are eager to provide service, we are ready to turn our attention to our users. User satisfaction, after all, is the ultimate criterion for success in our field. As an aside, I have observed that while most libraries claim to be user-oriented, very few are, in fact, sensitive to user needs. Some of the techniques my staff and I use to achieve user-oriented service are:

1. We never presume to know what users want. We always try to get feedback first.

2. We spend time with people from various user populations trying to understand how they currently obtain and utilize information. Then, we try to fit our services to their patterns of information usage.

3. We try innovative ways of serving users; circulating Tables of Contents, putting our forms on the computer for use in electronic mail, searching UPI daily for hot-off-the-press items of interest to the company.

4. We try to be responsive to the changing information needs of the company. We periodically evaluate current services and make appropriate modifications or drop them if there is little interest (even if it was a service dear to our hearts).

5. We strive for a pro-active approach to library services by trying to anticipate the information implications of the company's long-range or strategic plans.

VI

The last quality from Peters' and Waterman's book that I would like to address today is entrepreneurship. No matter how efficient you are, or how satisfied your users are, you still have to sell the library to those who control the purse strings. Here is where I feel too many librarians fall short. I strongly believe the library world would fare a lot better if more librarians looked at themselves as entrepreneurs. After all, we are a small business competing in the marketplace for a share of the pie.

My situation is no different from yours. I must fight for the money, space, and people. To do this I must sell the value of the library to upper management so that they will be willing to pay for library services. If I don't do this well, then I get less of the pie. Notice I have not blamed upper management for not understanding the intrinsic value of the library. If I get less of the pie, then I have failed to communicate to management in a language they understand, and that is my problem, not theirs.

What I really sell the company is two services that I can provide better than anyone else. These two services are (1) cost-effective provision of information and (2) management of information. Cost-effective provision of information can include:

1. Centralization of information resources to reduce duplicate purchases and increase resource sharing.

2. Centralized purchasing to (a) reduce the number of Purchase Orders processed by the company and (b) to take advantage of bulk discount.

3. Using inter-library loans to review materials before spending the money to purchase.

4. Yearly serial review to evaluate the continuing value of each journal title critically.

The nice thing about these particular techniques is that a dollar figure can be assigned to them to show management out-of-pocket savings. For example, in our monthly statistics, we show a dollar figure for books requested that we didn't buy because we already own a sufficient number of copies or because we could show the requestor we already had several books on the subject that would satisfy his information need.

The second unique service the library can sell to the company is "management of information." Management of information, the way I define it, goes beyond the usual special services such as Selective Dissemination of Information (SDI) and current awareness. Today's executives cannot handle the information deluge. They need an advisor who can assist them in evaluating what is important for them to keep up with and in what format, and then work with them to decide how best to do this. The task is on-going because new material/formats continually appear and executives' information needs periodically change.

VII

There are three additional points that were not specifically discussed in the book that I feel are important to bring up.

The first is to be option-oriented. Thinking in options should be automatic. It will broaden your horizons, keep you from becoming stale, and when the chips are down and you don't get what's been promised or what you are counting on, you don't fall apart. You already have a new plan of action on the back burner.

The second point is measure, measure, measure! Use statistics regularly. Compare what you do and how you do it and how much it costs and how long it takes. In my experience, having this type of data at my fingertips has proved very valuable in getting more money, space, and people. It contributes to my credibility as a good manager.

The last point I want to make relates to a book co-written by tonight's speaker called *The Invisible War*. I have learned over time that politics and self-interest are the name of the current and only game in town. If you want to be successful, you must learn the game.

In Search of Excellence was written as a view from the top for those at the top. However, I believe that successful management techniques apply to any management level, just as they apply to any organization.

Many of the concepts discussed by Peters and Waterman are really quite basic and universal. What happens is that most of us lose sight of them in the day-to-day running of our operations. We need an occasional reminder of what we are working so hard to attain, excellence in libraries.

Part II

Meryl Swanigan

I have the feeling you came here today expecting to hear earthshaking pronouncements on excellence in libraries and librarianship. I fear you will not. What you will hear over and over is very simple fare! That seems to be the magic in the popularity of *In Search of Excellence*. Such simple basic concepts that left me snickering behind my corporate hand. But the simplicity is deceiving; after thinking these issues over, the real challenge is making them work. Judy Labovitz has provided us with some ways to make the principles work.

I

Libraries are prime targets for excellence. We already have many of the "back to basic" traits Peters and Waterman present. So, let's turn our attention to practical application.

Judy has given me a lot to react to. I appreciate her openness and willingness to talk about herself. This openness is one of the favored traits. I will review some points made by Judy and amplify some of them with my own experiences and opinions.

II

Judy's first quality is a bias towards action. I think Judy has shared a couple of ideas worth reemphasizing.

1. How to get prompt action by management. She says, "This is what I'm going to do unless I hear to the contrary...." Not only does that work, but it shows an assertive approach to information management if her planned action is not acceptable, she will hear very quickly from her management.

2. Judy mentions using three management qualities which she turns to her advantage. They are:
    a. Not liking to make decisions;

    b. Wanting to be thought of as decision makers;

    c. And having no time to read.

So she provides succinct proposals and requests to management. She also provides options to management. Later I will talk a bit more about options.

Generally, on the author's bias for action, I think librarians are all action-oriented these days, granted some are more oriented to action than others. It is a survival instinct we are all developing. In other words, I think it is one of the eight basic concepts we have and which we can improve.

Another of Judy's essential elements, perhaps the most important factor, is people. Peters and Waterman call it, "productivity through people." Judy talks about the ten ways she tries to motivate people. I have picked out several items on her list for comment.

1. "I encourage people to speak up and ask for their opinions about their jobs and other issues that affect them." Getting staff to participate actively in their own jobs is essential. If we are assertive about how our job is structured, what our responsibilities are, what changes we want, we begin to take control of our environment. The "we-they" attitudes disappear and team building begins. Everyone becomes a stakeholder in the operations. I am always appalled at how difficult it is to get employees to participate in the development of their own work environment.

2. "Encourage people to find more efficient ways of working and give them credit for the ideas and implementing the changes" is another of Judy's points. I think one of the manager's prime responsibilities is to determine the environment each person needs that will encourage the employee to make changes and take risks. A manager is really a facilitator, a person who provides an environment. Recognition is also very, very important. I give recognition occasionally, not often. But it is earned, genuine, and heart-felt.

3. Judy also discourages hierarchical distinctions. This is part of the nature of special librarians: we are "get it done" people. This fits very neatly with Peters and Waterman's "simple form-lean staff" concept. One of the traits of the excellent companies is a flatter hierarchy. If you are interested in more reading on hierarchies, I suggest you read *The Change Masters: Innovation for Productivity in the American Corporation* by Rosabeth Moss Kanter, published in 1983 by Simon and Schuster.

4. Judy also deals bravely with the institutional environment by not letting it influence the library group negatively. I was so impressed by a recent visitor from an aerospace company who said, "Well, we are down to two people and it's really tough, but we are so excited about doing this project and this other project." With such a positive attitude, that library is bound to be much more than satisfactory. Excellence is not measured by size of staff, or decor, or any of the other institutional trappings that you see.

IV

Judy talks about MBWA: Managing By Walking Around, a concept highly touted by Peters and Waterman. It is the nature of a good information person to MBWA, but I think Judy's greater attribute is carrying MBWA outside her library to the corporation where she develops her alliances and expands her support. She also mentions a library culture, an idea worth pursuing because it fuels a reputation in the parent organization.

Judy mentions the lean machine concept, I have some additional comments. If we forego the "disaster attitude" of staff and space reductions and look at these situations as being an opportunity, we can begin to exercise some of the principles we have been talking about. One of the most interesting ideas the authors promote is the "skunk works." Most special libraries by size definition are skunk works in a larger organization. We can be innovative, quick in decision making, good at brainstorming, and willing to try new ways to provide service. We clearly have all the opportunities to operate in some semblance of a skunk works.

V

Judy next tackles the user issues. Peters and Waterman call it "close to the client." We think we are close to the client; in fact, we pride ourselves on our special library's relationship to our clients. But I doubt we have plumbed the user the way Peters and Waterman suggest in making the customer/client a partner in the development of service. I think much can be done in this area. Judy's techniques regarding users are worth repeating.

1. Never presume to know what the user wants.

2. Spend time with the user population to understand how they obtain and utilize information.

3. Provide innovative service.

4. Respond to changing company needs.

5. Relate library service to the company long-range plans.

VI

Judy addresses entrepreneurship. Peters and Wateman refer to autonomy and entrepreneurship together. In my opinion, there is no better organization than a library or an information center to be an entrepreneurship in a larger organization. We are small and usually independent from the primary objective of our parent company, which may be manufacturing tires, selling computers, or publishing newspapers, obviously not the library business. We operate in a very autonomous environment. Many of our environments are not that of benign neglect, as we sometimes think. But we must think of them as autonomous environments with all the related opportunities.

Judy discusses the two services that her library can provide. They are cost-effective provision of information and management of information. Here, I can share a paradox with you. Peters and Waterman say we must be able to manage ambiguity and paradox. Judy says cost-effective provision of information can include centralizing resources, purchasing, and other services. In a decentralized company, a very popular trend these days, the emphasis is on each division being a profit center. They have complete autonomy to design their divisions in any way they see fit. They decide what kind of information service they want, an entrepreneurial librarian's dream of a skunk works! But it is a paradox when it comes to the economy of scale realized with selected centralization.

VII

Another point from *In Search of Excellence* I would like to mention is "Stick to the knitting." I sincerely doubt that any special library has a problem with sticking to the knitting. More likely, we need to learn to define knitting much more broadly than we do, giving us a chance to exercise a more entrepreneurial mentality.

VIII

I said I would speak more about being options oriented. I cannot overemphasize how important options, or alternative thinking, has been to me or to the Information Research Center at Atlantic Richfield. Very little throws us off track these days because we immediately start to analyze our options. Of course, we spend a good deal of time in developing and nurturing options so that they will be there when we need them. Here are some elements that have fostered options thinking for me:

1. The upper management structure has had all of the following qualities:

    a. They have been open to new ideas.

    b. They have been supportive.

    c. They have chided my mistakes but never used them negatively.

    d. They have given me the freedom to run my own shop.

    e. They have given me few but specific parameters in which to work.

    f. They trust me.

The elements that my staff offer that makes options thinking realistic and makes it work are:

a. Openness to new ideas.

b. Ability to generate new ideas and work on them.

c. The ability to implement change.

d. The ability to work as a team in spite of personal differences.

Two other attributes have helped me with options thinking. One is having developed a trust in my own intuition. And another one is an overall feeling of physical and emotional security which develops an atmosphere in which to think in terms of alternatives.

VI

Exercises and Inventories

Appendix A
Leadership Potential

An effective leader is a valued asset in any enterprise. The deeds of leaders such as Dwight D. Eisenhower, Mao Tse-tung, John F. Kennedy, and Charles de Gaulle easily attest to their importance in shaping the world. The ability to influence makes leaders highly sought after and valued by society. Are you a potential leader?

To gauge your leadership potential, carefully read the following items. After each item, circle whether you would most likely agree or disagree with the item.

LEADERSHIP POTENTIAL

1. Good leaders are born, not made. Agree Disagree

2. I tend to treat my subordinates well so long as they do what I say. Agree Disagree

3. Good leaders depend on their followers as much as they depend on themselves. Agree Disagree

4. As a leader, I would always include the reasons why when asking a subordinate to perform a task. Agree Disagree

5. A good leader will achieve his or her objectives at any costs. Agree Disagree

6. As a group manager, I would never entrust a vital project to anyone but myself, even if that meant working overtime. Agree Disagree

7. A key to good leadership is being consistent in how one leads. Agree Disagree

8. If justified, I would recommend a subordinate for a promotion to a position equal to or even higher than my own position. Agree Disagree

9. Some subordinates can participate in the decision-making process without threatening a leader's position. Agree Disagree

10. If my group failed to achieve an objective because of a group member's failure, I would explain it as such to my superiors. Agree Disagree

11. I consider myself indispensable in my present position. Agree Disagree

Scoring:
To compute your score, add up the points assigned to each item.

1. Agree (0), disagree (1)   7. Agree (0), disagree (1)
2. Agree (0), disagree (1)   8. Agree (1), disagree (0)
3. Agree (1), disagree (0)   9. Agree (1), disagree (0)
4. Agree (1), disagree (0)   10. Agree (0), disagree (1)
5. Agree (0), disagree (1)   11. Agree (0), disagree (1)
6. Agree (0), disagree (1)

What Your Score Means
Bear in mind that this is not a test, but simply an indication of your leadership potential.

    11-9   Excellent potential
    8-6   Good potential
    5-0   Drastic changes needed

Reprinted by permission of publisher, from "How to Measure Your Leadership Potential," by Oliver L. Niehouse. *Supervisory Management* 28 (January 1983), 4. © 1983 American Management Association, New York. All Rights Reserved.

Appendix B
Inventory of Transformational Management Skills

This assessment instrument is divided into four parts and can be used for self-appraisal or for evaluation of another person. On each item, please use the scoring scale of 1 to 5. Consider that a rating of 1 would be the lowest score, indicating that the person never or rarely engages in this behavior; 3 would be average or usually; and 5 would be the highest, meaning excellent or always. Please place your number choice in the right-hand column.

Effective-
ness
rating

Part 1: Leadership Style

This person is:
1. *Open minded*—willing to consider new ideas and approaches, as well as people of different opinions, perspectives, cultures. _____
2. *Flexible*—adaptable to new people, situations, developments, information, or new ways of doing things (processes). _____
3. *Sensitive*—conscious of what is happening to self and others; is person centered and aware of needs and feelings in people; able to respond to others empathetically. _____
4. *Creative*—responds with resourcefulness to new people, situations, and data; exercises initiative, imagination, and innovation. _____

From Philip R. Harris, *Management in Transition*. San Francisco: Jossey-Bass, 1985. Available in quantity with other instruments of Dr. P. R. Harris from: TALICO INC., 2320 S. Third St., Ste. #5, Jacksonville Beach, FL 32250 (904/241-1721).

Effective-
ness
rating

5. *Synergistic*—given to cooperation and collaboration with colleagues; encourages teamwork and group participation. _____

6. *Facilitative*—exercises coaching, counseling, and negotiating skills; exercises knowledge and skill in group process. _____

Subtotal (out of possible 30) _____

Part II: Change Skills

This person demonstrates:

7. *Ultrastability*—perceives relativeness of experiences and does not seek absolutes; can cope with change, ambiguity, and uncertainty. _____

8. *Temporariness*—capacity to establish intense, ad hoc relationships that are meaningful; able to deal with transience and mobility. _____

9. *Resiliancy*—reevaluates his or her image, values, role, goals, and life-style on the basis of new insights and information; is tentative in responses. _____

10. *Analytical thinking*—capable of perceiving and analyzing the driving and resisting forces for and against a change, the change's effects on the organization's future. _____

11. *Balance*—exercises evenhandedness and understanding regarding the rate or pace of change introduced into the organization so that it is neither too radical nor disruptive; plans for change. _____

12. *Strategic ability*—capable of strengthening the driving forces for a change and overcoming the restraining forces; can communicate the case for change and employ a variety of support strategies. _____

Subtotal (out of possible 30) _____

Part III: Communication Skills

This person is:

13. *Self-Confident*—projects a positive image of self and role in body language and appearance, as well as verbally and nonverbally; indicates congruence or comfort with self so as to inspire confidence. _____

14. *Understanding*—demonstrates that he or she listens, is trying to enter into the speaker's frame of reference; is respectful and empathetic. _____

Effective-
ness
rating

15. *Mediawise*—uses as many media as feasible to transmit messages effectively, appealing to multiple senses
and powers in receiver.   _____

16. *Astute*—avoids stereotyping, emotionally loaded
words, and communication barriers; strives to ascertain real meanings behind messages and allows for
clarification.   _____

17. *Authentic*—avoids vagueness and game playing; levels
with others as appropriate; usually tells it like it is. _____

18. *An information professional*—demonstrated by
    a. selection of information sources and contact use;   _____
    b. use of others for information scanning or to sup-
        plement his or her own knowledge;   _____
    c. dissemination of information to organization
        and subordinates appropriately;   _____
    d. balance in terms of information collecting and
        taking actions based on the data;   _____
    e. informedness sufficient for passing judgments,
        making decisions, or giving authorizations;   _____
    f. thoroughness in following up on communications
        to see whether agreements or instructions are
        carried out.   _____
    g. meeting effectiveness in terms of number held
        and quality of group sessions.   _____

    Subtotal (out of possible 60)   _____

Part IV: Managerial Performance

This person practices:
19. *Relationship Building*—is aware of importance of organizational relations and cultivates them both internally and externally; spends appropriate amount of
time linking up with the right persons who affect morale and performance; capable of networking.   _____

20. *Action Planning*—translates mental plans into written
targets, goals, strategies, and actions; maintains long-
term perspectives without neglecting short-term concerns.   _____

21. *Time Management*—maintains systematic scheduling
for appropriate mix of activities to fulfill role; efficient in use of special times of day or week for particular kinds of work; paces self and balances work load
while avoiding fragmentation and excessive interrup-
tions.   _____

Effective-
ness
rating

22. *Stress Management*—blends personal rights and needs with duties and obligation; promotes personal wellness through diet, exercise, and healthy life-style; reflects, studies, and reads appropriately. ⎯⎯⎯⎯

23. *Personal Involvement*—gets around the organization to find out what people are thinking and to observe activity first-hand rather than being remote and detached; encourages same approach with customers. ⎯⎯⎯⎯

24. *Team Management*—functions effectively as a member of a team task force; encourages group participation in problem solving and decision making; shares power. ⎯⎯⎯⎯

25. *Accountability Management*—clarifies systematically roles, relationships, and responsibilities; while ensures that expectations are realized and issues confronted so that problems are solved and services rendered. ⎯⎯⎯⎯

Subtotal (out of possible 35) ⎯⎯⎯⎯

Inventory grand total ⎯⎯⎯⎯

Scoring Note: the ratings on these thirty-one appraisals can be tallied; for effective managers, the total by individual should be in the range of 120 to 150. To compile results from a group evaluation, total all the individual scores and divide by the number of assessors. For example, if 12 persons were evaluating the manager, then a score of 1440 to 1800 on this instrument would indicate a high-performing manager.

What is a Transformational Manager?

Political scientist James MacGregor Burns maintains that a true leader senses and transforms the needs of followers. He envisions subordinates or followers as having different levels of needs; the leader motivates and mobilizes these persons toward higher needs or consciousness. Transformational managers energize themselves and others, arousing hopes, aspirations, and expectations, as well as translating these into constructive actions. Transformational managers provide a behavior model, then inspire others to achieve something beyond the status quo or present activity. Transformational managers sense the capacity in others and then help these persons actualize their potential. Transformational managers sense when it is time for change and then encourage and support others to accomplish the new and different, the unique and exceptional. Transformational managers have vision and share their dreams with others; they assist people in making the transition to the new work culture.

Appendix C
Assertiveness Inventory*

The following questions will be helpful in assessing your assertiveness. Be honest in your responses. All you have to do is draw a circle around the number that describes you best. For some questions the assertive end of the scale is at 0, for others at 4. Key: 0 means *no* or *never*; 1 means *somewhat* or *sometimes*; 2 means *average*; 3 means *usually* or *a good deal*; and 4 means *practically always* or *entirely*.

1. When a person is highly unfair, do you call it to his or her attention?	0	1	2	3	4
2. Do you find it difficult to make decisions?	0	1	2	3	4
3. Are you openly critical of others' ideas, opinions, behavior?	0	1	2	3	4
4. Do you speak out in protest when someone takes your place in line?	0	1	2	3	4
5. Do you often avoid people or situations for fear of embarrassment?	0	1	2	3	4
6. Do you usually have confidence in your own judgment?	0	1	2	3	4
7. Do you insist that your spouse or roommate take on a fair share of household chores?	0	1	2	3	4
8. Are you prone to "fly off the handle"?	0	1	2	3	4
9. When a salesman makes an effort, do you find it hard to say "no" even though the merchandise is not really what you want?	0	1	2	3	4
10. When a latecomer is waited on before you are, do you call attention to the situation?	0	1	2	3	4
11. Are you reluctant to speak up in a discussion or debate?	0	1	2	3	4
12. If a person has borrowed money (or a book, garment, thing of value) and is overdue in returning it, do you mention it?	0	1	2	3	4
13. Do you continue to pursue an argument after the other person has had enough?	0	1	2	3	4
14. Do you generally express what you feel?	0	1	2	3	4
15. Are you disturbed if someone watches you at work?	0	1	2	3	4
16. If someone keeps kicking or bumping your chair in a movie or a lecture, do you ask the person to stop?	0	1	2	3	4
17. Do you find it difficult to keep eye contact when talking to another person?	0	1	2	3	4
18. In a good restaurant, when your meal is improperly prepared or served, do you ask the waiter/waitress to correct the situation?	0	1	2	3	4
19. When you discover merchandise is faulty, do you return it for an adjustment?	0	1	2	3	4
20. Do you show your anger by name calling or obscenities?	0	1	2	3	4

21. Do you try to be a wallflower or a piece of the furniture in social situations?	0	1	2	3	4
22. Do you insist that your landlord (landlady, mechanic, repairman, etc.) make repairs, adjustments, or replacements which are his or her responsibility?	0	1	2	3	4
23. Do you often step in and make decisions for others?	0	1	2	3	4
24. Are you able to express love and affection openly?	0	1	2	3	4
25. Are you able to ask your friends for small favors or help?	0	1	2	3	4
26. Do you think you always have the right answer?	0	1	2	3	4
27. When you differ with a person you respect, are you able to speak up for your own viewpoint?	0	1	2	3	4
28. Are you able to refuse unreasonable requests made by friends?	0	1	2	3	4
29. Do you have difficulty complimenting or praising others?	0	1	2	3	4
30. If you are disturbed by someone smoking near you, can you say so?	0	1	2	3	4
31. Do you shout or use bullying tactics to get others to do as you wish?	0	1	2	3	4
32. Do you finish other people's sentences for them?	0	1	2	3	4
33. Do you get into physical fights with others, especially strangers?	0	1	2	3	4
34. At family meals, do you control the conversation?	0	1	2	3	4
35. When you meet a stranger, are you the first to introduce yourself and begin a conversation?	0	1	2	3	4

The "Assertiveness Inventory" which appeared in *Your Perfect Right: A Guide to Assertive Living* (fifth edition), Impact, 1986, is not a validated psychological instrument. It was devised as a self-help survey utilizing situations common to many persons who have sought assertive behavior training with us. The client, or reader, is typically encouraged to respond to the items as an aid to self-assessment.

Researchers have asked us to provide a scoring key, norms and validity/reliability data. However, we have none, and do not contemplate doing the research necessary to acquire any. Our interest is principally in clinical assessment, for which the "Assertiveness Inventory" items serve merely as anecdotal referents and as a stimulus to the client's further examination of his or her individual life situations relative to assertiveness.

Robert E. Alberti, Ph.D.
Michael L. Emmons, Ph.D.

Appendix D
Assertiveness Checklist

Answer each of the following questions "Yes" or "No." To be more precise, you might use the terms "Always," "Often," "Sometimes," and "Never." Then circle the answers that indicate that you have a difficulty in assertion; try to write a sentence after those circled answers which explains your problems with assertion in your own words.

1. Do you buy things you don't really want because it is difficult to say no to the salesman? _____
2. Do you hesitate to return items to a store even when there is a good reason to do so? _____
3. If someone talks aloud during a movie, play, or concert, can you ask him or her to be quiet? _____
4. Can you begin a conversation with a stranger? _____
5. Do you have trouble maintaining conversations in social situations? _____
6. Do people act as if they find you boring? _____
7. Are you satisfied with your social life? _____
8. When a friend makes an unreasonable request, are you able to refuse? _____
9. Are you able to ask favors and make requests of your friends? _____
10. Can you criticize a friend? _____
11. Can you praise a friend? _____
12. When someone compliments you, do you know what to say? _____
13. Is there someone with whom you can share your intimate feelings? _____
14. Would you rather bottle up your feelings than make a scene? _____
15. Are you satisfied with your work habits? _____
16. Do people tend to exploit you or push you around? _____
17. Can you be open and frank in expressing both tender and angry feelings to men? _____
18. Can you be open and frank in expressing both tender and angry feelings to women? _____
19. Do you find it difficult to make or accept dates? _____
20. Are you spontaneous during sex play and intercourse? _____
21. Are you satisfied with your progress in your career? _____
22. Do you find it difficult to upbraid a subordinate? _____
23. Are you (or would you be) a good model of assertiveness for your own child? _____

Reprinted with permission from *In Managing by Communication* by Michele Tolela Myers and Gail E. Myers, 1982. Copyright 1982, McGraw-Hill.

Appendix E
Interpersonal Communication Inventory

This inventory offers you an opportunity to make an objective study of the degree and patterns of communication in your interpersonal relationships. It will enable you to better understand how you present and use yourself in communicating with persons in your daily contacts and activities. You will find it both interesting and helpful to make this study.

DIRECTIONS

The questions refer to persons other than your family members or relatives.

Please answer each question as quickly as you can according to the way you feel at the moment (not the way you usually feel or felt last week).

Please do not consult anyone while completing this inventory. You may discuss it after you have completed it. Remember that the value of this form will be lost if you change your answer during or after this discussion.

Honest answers are very necessary. Please be as frank as possible, since your answers are confidential.

Use the following examples for practice. Put a check (√) in one of the three blanks on the right to show how the question applies to your situation.

	Yes (Usually)	No (Seldom)	Sometimes
1. Is it easy for you to express your view to others?	_____	_____	_____
2. Do others listen to your point of view?	_____	_____	_____

The Yes column is to be used when the question can be answered as happening most of the time or usually.

The No column is to be used when the question can be answered as seldom or never.

The Sometimes column should be marked when you cannot answer definitely Yes or No. Use this column as little as possible.

Read each question carefully. If you cannot give the exact answer to a question, answer the best you can but be sure to answer each one. There are no right or wrong answers. Answer according to the way you feel at the present time. Remember, do not refer to family members in answering the questions.

	Yes (Usually)	No (Seldom)	Sometimes
1. Do your words come out the way you would like them to in conversation?	_____	_____	_____
2. When you are asked a question that is not clear, do you ask the person to explain?	_____	_____	_____
3. When you are trying to explain something, do other persons have a tendency to put words in your mouth?	_____	_____	_____
4. Do you merely assume the other person knows what you are trying to say without your explaining what you really mean?	_____	_____	_____
5. Do you ever ask another person to tell you how he or she feels about the point you may be trying to make?	_____	_____	_____
6. Is it difficult for you to talk with other people?	_____	_____	_____
7. In conversation, do you talk about things which are of interest to both you and the other person?	_____	_____	_____
8. Do you find it difficult to express your ideas when they differ from those around you?	_____	_____	_____
9. In conversation, do you try to put yourself in the other person's shoes?	_____	_____	_____
10. In conversation, do you have a tendency to do more talking than the other person?	_____	_____	_____

	Yes (Usually)	No (Seldom)	Sometimes
11. Are you aware of how your tone of voice may affect others?	_____	_____	_____
12. Do you refrain from saying something that you know will only hurt others or make matters worse?	_____	_____	_____
13. Is it difficult to accept constructive criticism from others?	_____	_____	_____
14. When someone has hurt your feelings, do you discuss this with him or her?	_____	_____	_____
15. Do you later apologize to someone whose feelings you may have hurt?	_____	_____	_____
16. Does it upset you a great deal when someone disagrees with you?	_____	_____	_____
17. Do you find it difficult to think clearly when you are angry with someone?	_____	_____	_____
18. Do you fail to disagree openly with others because you are afraid they will get angry?	_____	_____	_____
19. When a problem arises between you and another person, can you discuss it without getting angry?	_____	_____	_____
20. Are you satisfied with the way you settle your differences with others?	_____	_____	_____
21. Do you pout and sulk for a long time when someone upsets you?	_____	_____	_____
22. Do you become very uneasy when someone pays you a compliment?	_____	_____	_____
23. Generally, are you able to trust other individuals?	_____	_____	_____
24. Do you find it difficult to compliment and praise others?	_____	_____	_____
25. Do you deliberately try to conceal your faults from others?	_____	_____	_____
26. Do you help others to understand you by saying how you think, feel, and believe?	_____	_____	_____
27. Is it difficult for you to confide in people?	_____	_____	_____
28. Do you have a tendency to change the subject when your feelings enter into a discussion?	_____	_____	_____

	Yes (Usually)	No (Seldom)	Sometimes
29. In conversation, do you let the other person finish talking before reacting to what he or she says?	_____	_____	_____
30. Do you find yourself not paying attention while in conversation with others?	_____	_____	_____
31. Do you ever try to listen for meaning when someone is talking?	_____	_____	_____
32. Do others seem to be listening when you are talking?	_____	_____	_____
33. In a discussion, is it difficult for you to see things from the other person's point of view?	_____	_____	_____
34. Do you pretend you are listening to others when actually you are not?	_____	_____	_____
35. In conversation, can you tell the difference between what a person is saying and what he or she may be feeling?	_____	_____	_____
36. While speaking, are you aware of how others are reacting to what you are saying?	_____	_____	_____
37. Do you feel that other people wish you were a different kind of person?	_____	_____	_____
38. Do other people understand your feelings?	_____	_____	_____
39. Do others remark that you always seem to think you are right?	_____	_____	_____
40. Do you admit that you are wrong when you know that you are wrong about something?	_____	_____	_____

Total Score ☐

**SCORING KEY
AND NORMS**

Instructions

Look at how you responded to each item in the ICI. In front of the item write the appropriate weight from the table on this page. For example, if you answered Yes to item 1, you would find below that you get three points; write the number 3 in front of item 1 in the inventory and proceed to score item 2. When you have finished scoring each of the forty items, add up your total score. Then you may wish to compare your score with the norms listed below.

	Yes	No	Sometimes		Yes	No	Sometimes
1.	3	0	2	21.	0	3	1
2.	3	0	2	22.	0	3	1
3.	0	3	1	23.	3	0	2
4.	0	3	1	24.	0	3	1
5.	3	0	2	25.	0	3	1
6.	0	3	1	26.	3	0	2
7.	3	0	2	27.	0	3	1
8.	0	3	1	28.	0	3	1
9.	3	0	2	29.	3	0	2
10.	0	3	1	30.	0	3	1
11.	3	0	2	31.	3	0	2
12.	3	0	2	32.	3	0	2
13.	0	3	1	33.	0	3	1
14.	3	0	2	34.	0	3	1
15.	3	0	2	35.	3	0	2
16.	0	3	1	36.	3	0	2
17.	0	3	1	37.	0	3	1
18.	0	3	1	38.	3	0	2
19.	3	0	2	39.	0	3	1
20.	3	0	2	40.	3	0	2

MEANS AND STANDARD DEVIATIONS FOR THE ICI

Age Groups	Males	Females
17–21	Mean 81.79 SD 21.56 N 53	Mean 81.48 SD 20.06 N 80
22–25	Mean 86.03 SD 14.74 N 38	Mean 94.46 SD 11.58 N 2ᶠ
26 and up	Mean 90.73 SD 19.50 N 56	Mean 86.93 SD 15.94 N 45
All age groups	Mean 86.39 SD 19.46 N 147	Mean 85.34 SD 18.22 N 151
All age groups; males and females combines		Mean 85.93 SD 19.05 N 298

Appendix F
Testing Your Knowledge of Stress

How much do you know about stress? Take the true and false test that follows, and then check your answers.

TRUE–FALSE TEST

_____ 1. Stress was unknown before the Twentieth Century.

_____ 2. Stress is always bad for us.

_____ 3. Stress can sometimes help us survive.

_____ 4. Stress has links with killer diseases.

_____ 5. When we are under stress, our bodies respond automatically.

_____ 6. Self-assertion usually causes stress.

_____ 7. You always know if you are suffering from high blood pressure.

_____ 8. Stress causes cancer.

_____ 9. Changes in our personal lives can cause stress.

_____10. Success can be stressful.

_____11. Too little stress can make people unable to meet emergencies.

_____12. Stress is an emotional not a physical problem.

_____13. People suffer from hypertension, but they don't die as a result of it.

_____14. Prolonged stress that goes on and on may do more damage than occasional severe stress.

_____15. Children never feel stress.

_____16. There's no way to get away from stress in this day and age.

_____17. Monitoring your blood pressure means a trip to the doctor every six months.

Reprinted with permission from *Strategies for Success: Work/Life Planning*, Bill G. Gooch, Lois A. Carrier, and John Huck. North Scituate, Mass.: Breton, 1983. Copyright © 1983 PWS-Kent Publishing Company.

_____18. Only people with severe mental disorders go to psychologists.

_____19. Exercise is stressful, yet relieves stress.

_____20. How you think and feel about stress has little to do with relieving stress.

Answers

1. False. Even early man suffered stress, just trying to stay alive.
2. False. Lack of stress can make people unable to grow and to strengthen their own resources.
3. True. Stress activates our emergency systems.
4. True. While not the direct cause of these diseases, stress increases the hazard.
5. True. If we would have to think through and plan each move in an emergency situation, we might very well end up dead.
6. True. But, lack of self-assertion can be even more dangerous, because if you don't assert yourself, stress goes underground, where it can't be dealt with very easily.
7. False. Over half the people in the United States who are suffering from high blood pressure don't know it.
8. False. But, prolonged stress breaks down the body's resistance to disease and complicates any illnesses the person may get.
9. True. Studies have shown that even changes for the good cause stress, and people who experience many changes in a short period of time tend to lack stamina and resistance to diseases, temporarily.
10. True. Success is stressful, partly because the successful person usually wants to keep up or to increase the level of success.
11. True. Small successes in coping with small stresses can lead to better management of big stresses.
12. False. Emotional and physical features are too difficult to separate from each other to make this statement a safe one. Stress includes both, generally.
13. False. People do die of hypertension. In addition, other disorders they might have are affected by it.
14. True. Prolonged stress means that the body's emergency system is running almost constantly.
15. False. Think back to your own childhood.
16. False. You probably can't get completely free of stress, but you can eliminate many small stresses through thoughtful planning and evaluation. You can also plan stress-free periods and activities for yourself.
17. False. You can take your own blood pressure at a shopping mall or even at home.

18. False. This idea is left over from the days when "mental" problems were not talked about. Today, many people recognize the interrelatedness of emotional and physical problems, and they use both medical doctors and psychologists to get relief from stress. Going to a psychologist can also be a matter of prevention — a way of attacking a problem before it gets all out of proportion.
19. True. Exercise stresses some parts of your body, but tends to "turn off" worry, insecurity, and small fears.
20. False. Usually, there are several ways you can view a situation. You often have the possibility of choosing the way that best serves to lessen or eliminate the stress involved.

Appendix G
Determining Your Stress Pattern

Not everyone reacts stressfully to the same things. For example, one person doing piece work in a factory gets very nervous trying to do so many pieces per hour. Another finds it exciting to try to beat his own record. He gets tired, but he doesn't feel stress.

What kinds of stressors bother you? If you can be aware of situations that cause you to respond stressfully, you may be able to develop some ideas for avoiding them or lessening the stress associated with them.

IDENTIFYING STRESS

Rate each of the situations listed below on a scale of 1 to 10 to indicate how seriously each affects you. Give a 1 or 2 to the situation that affects you the least. Give a 9 or 10 to the situation that affects you the most. Rate others as they fall in between.

Situation	Rate
▪ Working under pressure on a tight schedule	_____
▪ Not knowing exactly what you are expected to do	_____
▪ Not being invited out to lunch when other people in your office are	_____
▪ Having to work around dangerous chemicals	_____
▪ Having a sick child at home	_____
▪ Having a serious argument with your husband or wife	_____
▪ Making a mistake at work	_____
▪ Learning to use a new machine or a new procedure	_____

Reprinted with permission from *Strategies for Success: Work/Life Planning*, Bill G. Gooch, Lois A. Carrier, and John Huck. North Scituate, Mass.: Breton, 1983. Copyright © 1983 PWS-Kent Publishing Company.

Situation	Rate
■ Feeling that someone has wronged you and that you can't do anything about it	_____
■ Wondering if you can pay your bills with your paycheck	_____
■ Working under a boss who watches you a lot	_____
■ Doing boring work for which you feel overqualified	_____
■ Competing for a promotion	_____
■ Doing a high-risk job, such as certain construction jobs or mining	_____
■ Having a job that involves handling sick or unstable people	_____
■ Getting a C or D in a course that you are taking	_____
■ Feeling that someone is making fun of you or demeaning you	_____
■ Trying to do a job for which you don't feel qualified	_____
■ Getting a traffic ticket	_____
■ Winning the sweepstakes	_____

Next, answer yes or no to the following questions to see whether the things that cause you stress tend to fall into a few broad categories.

1. Do the things that cause you the most stress often have to do with your *ideas of success?* _____

2. Do the things that cause you the most stress tend to involve your *relationships with others?* _____

3. Do the things that cause you the most stress usually involve your *self-image?* That is, do you see stressful situations as times when your abilities, personality, or status are being attacked? _____

4. Do the things that cause you the most stress often involve your *financial and material well-being?* _____

5. Do the things that cause you the most stress have to do with your *social or economic status?* _____

6. Do the things that cause you the most stress have to do with your *health and physical welfare?* _____

In what order would you put the six categories of stressors in relation to your life? Put a 1 next to the most important category and a 6 next to the least important category. Rate the others as they fall between.

Stressors	Rate
▪ Ideas of success	_____
▪ Relationships with others	_____
▪ Self-image	_____
▪ Financial and material well-being	_____
▪ Social or economic status	_____
▪ Health and physical welfare	_____

ONE WAY OF LESSENING STRESS

You can often stop stress from being damaging by looking at the stressful situation from different points of view or by thinking about it in a different way than you usually do. Especially in dealing with the smaller stresses of daily life, you can *choose* to feel differently about them, instead of allowing yourself to get into a self-defeating stress pattern.

Invent a story that describes a situation that would fall into the category of stressors you put on the top of your list. For example, "One day when I took a late lunch, Pete let the boss think I had been gone since noon. When I got back, the boss chewed me out about taking such a long lunch hour. I was so mad I went and told Pete off, but he only laughed. I'll get him back someday."

Your story: _____

_____

_____

_____

_____

Re-read your story. Then list three different ways of looking at the situation.

Alternative 1: _____

_____

Alternative 2: _____

_____

Alternative 3: _____

_____

Appendix H
NASA Exercise

<table>
<tr><td>

Purpose: To compare the results of individual decision making with the results of group decision making.

Class size: Any number of groups of six to eight members.
Time required: 45 minutes to an hour.
Materials needed: A copy of the Individual Worksheet and the Direction Sheet for Scoring for each student; a copy of the Group Worksheet for each group; pencils.
Physical setting: Regular classroom.

</td></tr>
</table>

PROCEDURE

1. The class is divided into groups, and each group is seated in a circle. Each student is given the Individual Worksheet and is instructed to complete it within 8 to 10 minutes.
2. Groups are instructed to discuss and arrive at a group consensus for the rankings. A group recorder is selected to record the group rankings onto the Group Worksheet.

Reprinted with permission from *In Managing by Communication* by Michele Tolela Myers and Gail E. Myers, 1982. Copyright 1982, McGraw-Hill.

  a. Students are not to change answers on their Individual Worksheets as a result of group discussion.
  b. Groups have about 20 minutes to complete the task.
3. Each student is given a Direction Sheet for Scoring and scores his
 or her individual worksheet. The group recorder then computes the
 average of individual scores as well as the score for the group
 resulting from group discussion.
4. The instructor records all data on the board in the following
 manner:

	Group 1	Group 2	Group 3	Group 4
Group Worksheet Score (Consensus Score)	_____	_____	_____	_____
Average of Individual Scores	_____	_____	_____	_____
Range of Individual Scores	_____	_____	_____	_____

NASA EXERCISE INDIVIDUAL WORKSHEET

Instructions

You are a member of a space crew originally scheduled to rendezvous
with a mother ship on the lighted surface of the moon. Due to
mechanical difficulties, however, your ship was forced to land at a
spot some 200 miles from the rendezvous point. During landing, much
of the equipment aboard was damaged, and since survival depends on
reaching the mother ship, the most critical items available must be
chosen for the 200-mile trip. Below are listed the fifteen items left
intact and undamaged after landing. Your task is to rank-order them
in terms of their importance to your crew in reaching the rendezvous
point. Place the number 1 by the most important item, the number 2 by
the second most important, and so on, through number 15, the least
important. You have ten minutes to complete this phase of the
exercise.

_____ Box of matches

_____ Food concentrate

_____ 50 feet of nylon rope

_____ Parachute silk

_____ Portable heating unit

_____ Two .45 caliber pistols

_____ One case dehydrated Pet milk

_____ Two 100-pound tanks of oxygen

_____ Stellar map (of the moon's constellation)

_____ Life raft

_____ Magnetic compass

_____ 5 gallons of water

_____ Signal flares

_____ First-aid kit containing injection needles

_____ Solar-powered FM receiver-transmitter

NASA EXERCISE GROUP WORKSHEET

Instructions

This is an exercise in group decision making. Your group is to employ the method of *group consensus* in reaching its decision. This means that the prediction for each of the fifteen survival items must be agreed upon by each group member before it becomes a part of the group decision. Consensus is difficult to reach. Therefore not every ranking will meet with everyone's complete approval. Try as a group to make each ranking one with which all group members can at least *partially* agree. Here are some guides to use in reaching consensus:

1. Avoid *arguing* for your own individual judgments. Approach the task on the basis of logic.
2. Avoid changing your mind *only* in order to reach agreement and avoid conflict. Support only solutions with which you are able to agree at least somewhat.
3. Avoid "conflict-reducing" techniques such as majority vote and trading.
4. View differences of opinion as helpful rather than as a hindrance in decision making.

_____ Box of matches

_____ Food concentrate

_____ 50 feet of nylon rope

_____ Parachute silk

_____ Portable heating unit

_____ Two .45 caliber pistols

_____ One case dehydrated Pet milk

_____ Two 100-pound tanks of oxygen

_____ Stellar map (of moon's constellation)

_____ Life raft

_____ Magnetic compass

_____ 5 gallons of water

_____ Signal flares

_____ First-aid kit containing injection needles

_____ Solar-powered FM receiver-transmitter

Appendix I
Quality-of-Life Index:
A Manager's Health and Wellness Inventory

Directions: The underlying concept of this index is that staying well gives one greater control over one's life and is less costly than getting well. This instrument provides the manager with a means for self-assessment of his or her regimen for well-being. It can be filled out individually alone or with a team of managers who work together and are concerned about the quality of their life. It can be analyzed in terms of one's own self-health management or in terms of corporate policy to improve the quality of work life. On each item in the six categories, rate yourself on a scale of 1 (lowest) to 5 (highest).

I.   *Physical Self-Care*

1. I have a thorough examination by a physician annually and act on the results for improved health.
    (Note: I get periodic physical check-ups to update both myself and my personal physician as to my conditions/medications.)   ———

2. I seek nourishing food and beverage, trying to control my diet so as to avoid over/underweight conditions.
    (Note: Well-balanced diets are usually low in fat, protein, cholesterol, and calories—that is, containing more fruit and vegetables, fewer animal and dairy products.)   ———

3. I exercise daily with a regular routine and try to maintain balance in my physical fitness regimen.
    (Note: Ideally, this physical activity is built into one's daily schedule and becomes a part of one's life-style.)   ———

From Philip R. Harris, *Management in Transition*. San Francisco: Jossey-Bass, 1985. Available in quantity with other instruments of Dr. P. R. Harris from: TALICO INC., 2320 S. Third St., Ste. #5, Jacksonville Beach, FL 32250 (904/241-1721).

4. I manage to get sufficient and tranquil sleep for maintaining peak performance.
(Note: The number of hours needed for such rest is relative, although six to eight hours a night is recommended, unless supplemented by naps during the day.) ——————

5. I avoid body abuse, whether through overwork, misuse of alcohol or other drugs, cigarettes, or caffeine intake.
(Note: Maintaining body soundness requires positive actions for fitness and avoidance behavior of that which is debilitating.) ——————

6. I project a healthy body image and am able to do what I am capable of doing with energy and intensity.
(Note: This refers to general body appearance from condition of dress and physical cleanliness to body language, as well as physical capacity.) ——————

Part I subtotal (out of six) ——————

II. Psychological Care

7. I strive to keep mentally alert by seeking new and varied input to increase my information/knowledge.
(Note: Mind expansion may occur informally, such as through selected reading, or formally, such as through some means of continuing education.) ——————

8. I try to be creative and open to new ideas.
(Note: This implies an experimental attitude, allowing intuition to be exercised and listening to others.) ——————

9 I cultivate a positive mental attitude and express self-confidence.
(Note: This involves practicing optimism and being comfortable with self versus excess in negativism, depression, or sense of insecurity and inferiority.) ——————

10 I value my independence while not being averse to being interdependent.
(Note: While seeking autonomy of action, one is able to cooperate without becoming overly dependent on people, situations, or substances.) ——————

11. I am able to relax and can "re-create" in diverse ways.
(Note: Leisure is constructively used for both ample and varied activities; one is able to have fun and be interested in many experiences.) ——————

12. I am able to express feeling and experience a full range of human emotions.
(Note: This means one feels and conveys everything from joy to sadness without inhibiting emotions yet can exhibit balance or control in such expressions.) ——————

Part II subtotal (out of six) ——————

III. *Philosophical/Spiritual Care*

13. I have a firm sense of direction and values in my
    life.   _____
    (Note: That is, one strives to achieve goals and sets
    priorities as to what is important.)

14. I can envision my existence in a larger context and
    have purpose to my actions.   _____
    (Note: One is able to relate one's life beyond the ma-
    terial to the spiritual side of the human experience.)

15. I cultivate my talents in some intellectual and cul-
    tural pursuits.   _____
    (Note: This means being a multidimensional person
    who seeks to develop his or her esthetic senses through
    art, music, books, and so on.)

16. I have a zest for life and am enthusiastic for experi-
    encing its variety and richness.   _____
    (Note: This implies the pursuit of life-enhancing rela-
    tionships and activities.)

17. I seek meaning in my life and meaningful associations.   _____
    (Note: Activities are undertaken with purpose, while
    relationships are formed with selectivity; escapism is
    avoided.)

18. I devote time to thinking and contemplating.   _____
    (Note: I develop quiet times to ponder, meditate,
    pray, practice yoga, enjoy nature and its beauties.)

    Part III subtotal (out of six)   _____

IV. *Social Care*

19. I try to stay connected with family, friends, and so-
    cial contacts.   _____
    (Note: I avoid social isolation and reach out to oth-
    ers.)

20. I network with professional and business colleagues.   _____
    (Note: I maintain personal or electronic associations
    for information and knowledge exchanges.)

21. I am capable of meaningful friendships and intimacy.   _____
    (Note: I am able to give and share myself at deeper,
    more personal levels.)

22. I am considerate of others' needs, respect their pri-
    vacy, and am tolerant of their views or foibles.   _____
    (Note: I am able to put myself into the other per-
    son's perspective or life space without prying or im-
    posing.)

23. I am helpful, trusting, and forgiving with others.   _____
    (Note: I can provide appropriate assistance as war-
    ranted and be loyal to those who trust/depend on
    me.)

24. I can confront, negotiate, and handle conflict. _____
(Note: I am able to say no and level with people, to problem solve and compromise, and to channel energies when people disagree.)

Part IV subtotal (out of six) _____

V. *Life-Style*

25. I try to maintain balance in my life and avoid excess. _____
'Note: I am able to regulate or moderate activities so as to avoid addiction to work, hobbies, or substances.)

26. I sense the feedback my body gives me and act to preserve good health. _____
(Note: I am attuned to my biorhythms, symptoms, and signals of fatigue, illness, or potential "burnout," acting to correct the unhealthy or life-threatening situation.)

27. I develop positive and healthy habits/attitudes. _____
(Note: I follow practices that will enhance life quality, such as orderliness, openness, and optimism, as well as nutritional food intake, watching my weight, avoiding salt or smoking, and adequate daily exercise.)

28. I manage stress and tension so that I am not unnerved or overwhelmed. _____
(Note: I have attitudes and practices that counteract hypertension, such as playing, using hot tub/steamroom/sauna, taking a nap or deep breathing exercises, listening to music, practicing dance or gymnastics.)

29. I create a life-style that delimits my personal stressors while enhancing the quality of my existence. _____
(Note: I am aware of stress, exhaustion, or tension symptoms and inaugurate counteractions for better coping/living.)

30. I seek counsel from professionals, colleagues, or friends whom I regard when I am finding it difficult to cope. _____
(Note: I am aware of my limitations and problems and am realistic about obtaining help from others.)

Part V subtotal (out of six) _____

Total Assessment Points _____

Scoring Interpretation

A total score on these thirty inventory items between:

100 - 150 = Excellent quality of life-style
50 - 99 = Average—room for improvement
1 - 49 = Inadequate—remedial action warranted now.

Appendix J
Understanding Conflict

ATTITUDES TOWARD CONFLICT

To get an idea how you feel about conflict situations, read the following pairs of statements, and then check the one in each pair that most closely reflects how you feel. Try not to mark the "right" answers, but rather, the answers that reflect your thoughts about conflict.

_____ A. It is better to remain silent than to state my point of view when it conflicts with that of others.

_____ B. I have the right to state my point of view, even when it conflicts with someone else's.

_____ A. Conflict is unnecessary between mature adults.

_____ B. Conflict can be healthy.

_____ A. Conflict is usually destructive.

_____ B. Conflict can clear the air and can even be creative.

_____ A. Conflict always involves good guys and bad guys.

_____ B. Conflict is a matter of differing points of view.

_____ A. Someone always gets hurt in conflict situations.

_____ B. There are good ways of settling conflicts, such as compromise and arbitration.

_____ A. Conflict is upsetting and depressing.

_____ B. Conflict can be friendly and stimulating.

_____ A. It's hard to forget things people say to me in moments of conflict.

_____ B. When a conflict is settled, it's over. No hard feelings.

If you checked more As than Bs, you need to work on your attitude toward conflict. You may be looking at conflict from too subjective (personal) a point

Reprinted with permission from _Strategies for Success: Work/Life Planning_, Bill G. Gooch, Lois A. Carrier, and John Huck. North Scituate, Mass.: Breton, 1983. Copyright © 1983 PWS-Kent Publishing Company.

of view. If you checked more Bs than As, you have a good start at understanding conflict, and you are ready to begin developing techniques to help you live up to your ideas about conflict. The exercise that follows is designed to show a step-by-step approach to resolving conflict.

STEPS TOWARD CONFLICT RESOLUTION

Think about the following conflict situation, and outline a solution for it as directed below.

Joe and Mary share a secretary — you. You don't enjoy your job because Joe feels that his work is more important and should come first, and Mary feels the same way. Their differing points of view put you in the position of always being hassled and always having to appear to take sides. Your efficiency is lessened by the constant bickering. Go through the following steps to resolve the conflict.

Step 1. State the most important issue in one short sentence. _____

_____

Step 2. Decide whether the issue is important enough to pursue. _____ Yes

_____ No

Step 3. State what you would like the outcome of the conflict to be._____

_____

Step 4. Think of several procedures that you might be able to suggest to lessen the problem. List them in order from most desirable to least desirable.

1. _____

_____

2. _____

_____

3. _____

_____

Step 5. Ask Joe and Mary to sit down with you for a few minutes, at their

convenience. Explain how you feel. _____

_____

Give them your first suggestion. _____

_____

If necessary, follow with your other suggestions.

Step 6. If all three of you can agree on a procedural or scheduling change that would ease the problem, put it into effect as soon as possible. In this case, suppose that they agreed to your first suggestion. What action

would you take the next morning? _____

_____

Step 7. Suppose that they could not agree on a better way of sharing your time. Check the following alternatives that you would seriously consider. Put an X in front of the alternatives that you feel would be immature or unproductive.

_____ Threaten to quit.

_____ Date stamp all work that comes to you from Joe and Mary, and do it in the order in which it comes to you, no matter what either of them says.

_____ Do the best and fastest work for the person who is nicest to you.

_____ Take your problem to their supervisor or to the personnel officer.

_____ Discuss the problem with your co-workers in other offices.

_____ Ask for a transfer to another department.

Now, describe how you think you would feel if you had not taken any of the

steps outlined, and another six months had gone by. _____

_____

_____

Index